The Letters of Conrad Aiken and Malcolm Lowry 1929–1954

Edited and introduced by
Cynthia C. Sugars

ECW PRESS

Copyright ECW PRESS, 1992

CANADIAN CATALOGUING IN PUBLICATION DATA

Aiken, Conrad, 1889–1973
   The letters of Conrad Aiken and Malcolm Lowry, 1929–1954

Includes bibliographical references.
ISBN 1-55022-168-X

1. Aiken, Conrad, 1889–1973 — Correspondence.
2. Lowry, Malcolm, 1909–1957 — Correspondence.
1. Lowry, Malcolm, 1909–1957. II. Sugars, Cynthia Conchita, 1963–   .
III. Title.

PS3501.15Z488 1992   816´.5   C92-095259-3

This book has been published with the assistance of a grant from the
Canadian Federation for the Humanities, using funds provided by the
Social Sciences and Humanities Research Council of Canada. Additional
grants have been provided by the Ontario Arts Council and The Canada
Council.

Design and imaging by ECW Type & Art, Oakville, Ontario.
Printed and bound by Imprimerie Gagné Ltée, Louiseville, Quebec.
Distributed by General Publishing Co. Limited
30 Lesmill Road, Toronto, Ontario M3B 2T6.

Published by ECW PRESS,
1980 Queen Street East, Second Floor, Toronto, Ontario M4L 1J2

For Patrick

"from de rose pink mountains"

TABLE OF CONTENTS

ACKNOWLEDGEMENTS

I wish to thank the copyright holders of the Aiken/Lowry letters: Mrs. Mary Hoover Aiken and the Huntington Library, San Marino, for their permission to reproduce the letters from Conrad Aiken contained in this collection; Charles Schlessiger of Brandt & Brandt Literary Agents for allowing me to reprint seven letters from Yale University Press's 1978 *Selected Letters of Conrad Aiken* (ed. Joseph Killorin); and Peter Matson of Sterling Lord Literistic Agency for permission to reproduce the Lowry letters and poems printed here.

Without the support and guidance of Professor Sherrill Grace at the University of British Columbia, I would never have undertaken this project. Professor Grace supervised this project as my M.A. thesis at the University of British Columbia in 1987-88, and it was while working as her research assistant in 1987 that I was able to undertake a trip to the Huntington Library to view their Aiken/Lowry letters firsthand. Professor Grace's *Sursum Corda: The Collected Letters of Malcolm Lowry*, forthcoming from Jonathan Cape, will contain all of Lowry's extant correspondence. Her sound advice and encouragement has been crucial in my work on Aiken and Lowry. The meticulous and probing comments of all of the members of my thesis committee — Sherrill Grace, Frederick Asals, William New, and Herbert Rosengarten — were enormously helpful in improving the manuscript.

The personal assistance of particular individuals at the two source libraries was also important in aiding my work on these letters. Anne Yandle and George Brandak of the University of British Columbia Special Collections and Sara Hodson of the Huntington Library were especially helpful, untiringly responding to my persistent queries and requests.

I also wish to thank the following people and institutions for their contribution to this edition: the Aid to Scholarly Publications Programme for their grant to publish this book; the University of British Columbia for their two-year graduate fellowship from 1986-88 that provided me with funds to pursue my work; the Social Sciences and Humanities Research Council of Canada for their doctoral fellowship which, as well as supporting my Ph.D. work, has enabled me to get the manuscript ready for publication; Professor Paul Tiessen, the editor of the *Malcolm Lowry Review*, for his detailed reader's report on my manuscript and his unfailing support of my work from the very beginning; Gordon Bowker, Lowry's biographer, for his help in answering my many "searching questions" about Lowry's Cambridge years; Joseph Killorin for responding to my numerous questions regarding his *Selected Letters of Conrad Aiken*; Russell Lowry, Lowry's brother, for writing to me of his recollections of Aiken and Lowry's early friendship; Jenny and Francis Hadfield, the owners of Jeake's House in Rye, for giving me a personal "Conrad Aiken Tour" of the house and its premises when I was there in the summer of 1987 and spring of 1989; Anthony Neville of Neville Books in Rye for introducing me to John (Aiken's son) and Paddy Aiken over a beer at the Ship Inn; Betty Moss for kindly giving me permission, in Margerie Lowry's name, to use Lowry's letters in my thesis; Spectrum Society for Community Living — especially its coordinator Ernie Baatz — for the use of their office space and computer in the hectic early days in 1987–88 when I was working on my thesis; and Paul Davies for his expertise in typesetting a most difficult text. I would also like to acknowledge Chris Ackerley, Stewart Cooke, Sheldon Goldfarb, Stefan Haag, David Markson, Guy Robertson, Kathleen Scherf, Charles Schlessiger, Anthony Slide, and Wayne Templeton for their help with particular details at various stages of this collection.

Finally, I thank Patrick McDonagh for his endless hours of support and for adopting the following guises: "literary colleague," repeatedly discussing minute details of Aiken and Lowry's friendship and writings; "detective," searching with me through bookstores, libraries, archives — even liquor stores — for the most elusive of allusions; "editor," being willing to read through the manuscript critically and discuss such mundane details as Lowry's semicolons; "fellow-traveller," accompanying me on the trail of Aiken and Lowry through Rye, Winchelsea, Cambridge, London, Granada, Boston, Brewster, Vancouver, and Dollarton. Thanks, Patrick — next stop, Cuernavaca!

5 August 1889	Conrad Potter Aiken born the eldest of four children in Savannah, Georgia, to Dr. William Ford Aiken and Anna Potter
27 February 1901	Aiken's father murders his wife and kills himself; Aiken goes to live with his uncle, William Tillinghast, in New Bedford
1907–12	Enters Harvard; writes for the Harvard *Advocate* and becomes friends with T.S. Eliot
1911	Becomes Class Poet at Harvard
25 August 1912	Marries Jessie McDonald, a Radcliffe graduate
10 October 1913	John Kempton Aiken born
4 December 1914	Jane Aiken born
1917	*Nocturne of Remembered Spring* published
1918	*The Charnel Rose, Senlin: A Biography and Other Poems* published
1919	Moves to South Yarmouth from Cambridge
1920	*House of Dust: A Symphony* published
Fall 1921	Moves with family to London
Spring 1922	Rents "Lookout Cottage" in Winchelsea, near Rye
1924	Buys "Jeake's House" in Rye
4 September 1924	Joan Aiken born
1925	*Priapus and the Pool* published
Fall 1926	Returns to Boston alone
November 1926	Meets Clarissa Lorenz ("Jerry"); returns to England
January 1927	Returns to Boston
May 1927	*Blue Voyage* published
September 1927–28	Tutor at Harvard
1929	Divorces Jessie
Summer 1929	Visited by Lowry in Boston
1930	Receives Pulitzer Prize for *Selected Poems*
February 1930	Marries Clarissa Lorenz

---

† N.B. The focus in these chronologies is on the years of Aiken and Lowry's friendship (1929–1954). For a detailed list of their publications, see the bibliography at the end of the volume.

August 1930	Returns to Rye and Jeake's House with Clarissa; put *in loco parentis* of Lowry
1931	*The Coming Forth by Day of Osiris Jones* and *Preludes for Memnon* published
1932	Attempts suicide
1933	*Great Circle* published
Spring 1933	Travels to Spain with Clarissa, Ed Burra, and Lowry
September 1933	Returns to Boston with Clarissa
May 1934	Returns to Rye with Clarissa
August 1936	Goes to New York where he meets Lowry
Winter 1936	Meets Mary Hoover; lives with Mary and Ed Burra in Charlestown
May–July 1937	Visits Lowry in Cuernavaca with Mary and Ed Burra; divorces Clarissa
7 July 1937	Marries Mary Hoover in Cuernavaca
Summer 1937	Returns to Rye with Mary
Summer 1938	Begins summer school in writing and painting at Jeake's House
1939	*A Heart for the Gods of Mexico* published
29 September 1939	Sails to New York and Cape Cod with Mary
October 1939	Re-establishes contact with Lowry
21 May 1940	Buys "Forty-One Doors" in Brewster
1940	*Conversation* and *And in the Human Heart* published
1942	*Brownstone Eclogues* published
1944	*The Soldier* published
November 1945	Returns to Jeake's with Mary
5 August 1946	"Fear No More," play based on "Mr. Arcularis," produced at Lyric Theatre, Hammersmith
June 1947	Returns to Brewster; Mary follows shortly afterwards after selling Jeake's
August 1947	*The Kid* published
1950–52	Poetry Consultant at Library of Congress in Washington; moves to Washington in September 1950 with Mary
1952	*Ushant* and Conrad Aiken issue of *Wake* published
October 1953	*Collected Poems* published
September 1954	Reunited with Lowry in New York
February 1962	Moves to Savannah; spends summers at Forty-One Doors in Brewster
17 August 1973	Dies at age of 84

MALCOLM LOWRY – CHRONOLOGY

28 July 1909	Born the fourth son of Arthur Osborne Lowry and Evelyn Boden in New Brighton, Cheshire
1911	Family moves to new home, "Inglewood," in Caldy, Cheshire
1923–27	Attends The Leys public school, Cambridge
May-September 1927	Works as deck-hand aboard the *Pyrrhus* and travels to China; begins *Ultramarine*
1927 or 1928	Reads Aiken's *Blue Voyage*
1928–29	Attends Jerry Kellett's cramming school in Blackheath, London, to prepare for Cambridge University's entrance exams
Summer 1929	Visits Aiken in Cambridge, Massachusetts
Fall 1929-May 1932	Attends St. Catharine's College, Cambridge University
Summer 1930	Aiken acts *in loco parentis* of Lowry until 1933
September 1930	Introduces Aiken to Cambridge friend, Gerald Noxon
Summer 1931	Travels to Norway aboard the *Fagervik* and meets Nordahl Grieg; begins "In Ballast to the White Sea"
May 1932	Graduates from Cambridge with third-class honours degree in English
1932	Moves to London
Spring 1933	Travels to Spain with Aikens and Ed Burra; meets Jan Gabrial
June 1933	*Ultramarine* published
6 January 1934	Marries Jan Gabrial in Paris
Fall 1934	Follows Jan to New York
1935 or 1936	Treatment for alcoholism in New York's Bellevue Hospital; begins "The Last Address" (*Lunar Caustic*)
August 1936	Visited by Aiken in New York; is separated from Jan
Fall 1936	Leaves with Jan for Los Angeles and visits John Davenport in Hollywood
late 1936	Settles in Cuernavaca with Jan; begins *Under the Volcano*

May–July 1937 Visited by Aiken, Mary Hoover, and Ed Burra in Cuernavaca

December 1937 Jan leaves for Los Angeles; Lowry spends New Year's in jail in Oaxaca

July 1938 Deported from Mexico; goes to Los Angeles

Summer 1939 Meets Margerie Bonner in Hollywood

late July 1939 Taken to Vancouver on pretense of renewing his visa

Fall 1939 Lives with Maurice Carey in Vancouver; joined by Margerie; writes to Aiken for help

15 August 1940 Moves into shack in Dollarton, near Vancouver

1 November 1940 Divorces Jan

2 December 1940 Marries Margerie Bonner

Spring 1941 Buys shack in Dollarton

7 June 1944 Shack burns; loses "In Ballast" and other manuscripts; leaves for Oakville and Niagara-on-the-Lake, Ontario, to stay with Gerald and Betty Noxon

October 1944 Rents house in Niagara

February 1945 Returns to Dollarton; builds new shack

11 February 1945 Father dies

28 November 1945 Travels to Mexico with Margerie; begins notes for *Dark as the Grave*

May 1946 Deported from Mexico; returns to Vancouver

Nov./Dec. 1946 Travels to Haiti via New Orleans

19 February 1947 Arrives in New York; *Under the Volcano* published

March 1947 Visits Noxons in Niagara; returns to Vancouver

7 November 1947 Sails with Margerie to France via the Panama Canal

1948 Stays in Vernon, France, with Joan Black to work on French translation of *Under the Volcano*

January 1949 Returns to Vancouver

6 December 1950 Mother dies

April 1952 Contract with Random House which is ended in January 1954

11 August 1954 Leaves Dollarton for the last time

September 1954 Stays with David Markson in New York; reunited with Aiken for last time

September 1954 Sails to Italy from New York with Margerie

February 1956 Settles in "The White Cottage" in Ripe, Sussex

27 June 1957 Dies in Ripe at age of 47

Aiken and Lowry in the Alhambra gardens, spring 1933

I tell you this young man
So that your outlook may perhaps be broadened.
I who have seen snoring volcanoes
And dismal islands shawled in snow. . . .

Malcolm Lowry
"In Cape Cod with Conrad Aiken"

INTRODUCTION

"We are brothers" . . .
"We are son and father" . . .
"No, we are rivals!"

(*Ushant* 29)

The relationship of Conrad Aiken and Malcolm Lowry has long been a subject of debate among literary scholars. Conrad Aiken was twenty years Lowry's senior: old enough to have been Lowry's father. Aiken had published more than twenty novels and books of poetry before the publication of Lowry's first novel; he was sufficiently experienced, then, to have been Lowry's literary teacher and advisor. Aiken was an American, steeped in the New England writings of Emerson, Thoreau, and Melville, all of which had an aura of exoticism for the young Englishman. Aiken was also a "man of the world," a hard-drinking, womanizing, suicidal man who was so impressively and excitingly apart from the "Wesleyan hush" (letter 27) of Lowry's boyhood home as to have had a marked influence on the young man's attitude toward himself and the world. In all of these guises, Aiken willingly became something of an idol to his young disciple. Yet Lowry's admiration for Aiken steadily grew into repressed rivalry. While admiring his mentor from afar, Lowry secretly coveted for himself the more desirable roles: father, literary master, tragic hero.

The wealth of varying accounts of Aiken and Lowry's relationship has only increased its fascination. On the one hand, there are the biographical accounts: from those of Douglas Day, Muriel Bradbrook, Richard Hauer Costa, and Aiken's second wife, Clarissa Lorenz, to those written by the subjects themselves. Lowry's letter to Seymour Lawrence in the 1952 Aiken issue of *Wake* focuses primarily on his relationship with Aiken, while Aiken frequently commented on their friendship in print and in numerous interviews.

No less valid are the more creative versions of the relationship. As he points out in letter 40 of this collection, Lowry had incorporated much of Aiken into his depiction of the Consul in *Under the Volcano*. Similarly, Aiken included a Lowry character ("Hambo") in *A Heart for the Gods of Mexico*, a novel loosely based on his 1937 visit to Lowry in Cuernavaca.

Later, in 1952, Hambo reappeared in Aiken's fictionalized autobiography, *Ushant*. More recently, in 1984, Michael Mercer wrote a dramatic treatment of Lowry and Aiken's friendship, *Goodnight Disgrace*. Originally conceiving a play solely about Malcolm Lowry, Mercer gradually found himself sympathizing with Aiken's perception of the relationship. In *Goodnight Disgrace* we see a parasitic young Lowry succeeding at his mentor's expense, and an Aiken who is progressively absorbed and usurped by the pupil whom he'd generously guided toward literary success.

Of course the picture is not as simple as this. There are many sides to the Aiken/Lowry story. The present collection of Aiken and Lowry's correspondence provides what is perhaps the most intimate version of their relationship available to date. While select items in the collection have been printed either partially or wholly in the *Selected Letters of Malcolm Lowry* (1965) and *Selected Letters of Conrad Aiken* (1978), three-quarters of these letters have remained unpublished. Here the story is told, both overtly and unconsciously, by the participants themselves within the very relationship itself. It is not, then, an account related after the fact, but, in the context of their letters, an evolving story, beginning in 1929 when Lowry wrote his first letter of introduction to Aiken, and ending, at least where the letters are concerned, with Lowry's ambiguous farewell telegram in 1954.

The resulting picture is very much a multifaceted one. It reveals that no one of the previous accounts was wrong, so much as limited. It reveals also that Aiken and Lowry's relationship contained all of the elements mentioned earlier — elder brother/younger brother, father/son, teacher/pupil, victim/victor — and many more besides.

In late February or early March of 1929, when he was in London preparing for his Cambridge previous examinations, Lowry wrote his first letter to Conrad Aiken, having become enamoured with Aiken's novel, *Blue Voyage*, and the segments of "The House of Dust" published in old *Coterie* magazines. Mistakenly believing Aiken to be living in Rye, Sussex (Aiken was in fact in Cambridge, Massachusetts), Lowry sent his letter there and waited in vain for a reply. In March 1929, he decided to try again, by this time having arranged with his father to have Aiken appointed his tutor and guardian for the summer. In a 1961 interview for George Robertson's CBC "Malcolm Lowry" program, Aiken states that he eventually did receive and respond to Lowry's first two letters. However, since all of his letters to Lowry from this period are missing, we have no record of how the arrangement was finalized. We do know that by 22 July 1929, Aiken was writing to his children of the "young Englishman [who] will be here at the end of the week to be taught how to write novels"

(Killorin 153). Sure enough, at the end of July, Lowry arrived at Aiken's 8 Plympton Street address carrying a ukelele and a battered suitcase containing a rough draft of his first novel, *Ultramarine*, so named in parody after Aiken's own *Blue Voyage* (Aiken, "Malcolm Lowry" 101).

According to Aiken, he and Lowry were "uncannily alike in almost everything" ("Malcolm Lowry" 102). From the very beginning their relationship was more that of an elder and younger brother than of a tutor and his pupil. Writing to his children on 13 August 1929, Aiken says that he and the "young Englishman" "have a good time together" (Huntington Library), and so, indeed, they did. In a *Paris Review* interview Aiken tells of a wrestling match that took place between himself, his brother Robert, and Lowry in celebration of Lowry's arrival in 1929, the prize for which was the porcelain lid of the W.C. tank:

> . . . I suggested we use the lid of the W.C. tank and each take hold of one end of it and wrestle for possession of this thing. . . . I got it away from Malcolm but fell right over backward into the fireplace and went out like a light. . . . It turned out I had a fracture of the skull, and I was in bed for the next two or three weeks. ("Art" 111)

Given this episode, it is perhaps not surprising that in later years Margerie Lowry wrote that Lowry took "a more or less Lawrentian view" of his friendship with Aiken (12 January 1940 letter to Mary Aiken in Appendix 11). In any case, the amount of tutoring done in the first few weeks of Lowry's visit to Boston was probably minimal.

Aiken and Lowry were not separated for long after "that wonderful summer" came to an end (Aiken, "Malcolm Lowry" 101). Less than a year later, by August 1930, Aiken had returned to Rye with his second wife, Clarissa Lorenz. To the latter's despair, it wasn't long before he and Lowry had picked up their carousing where they had left off in Massachusetts. While Lowry was doing his B.A. at Cambridge University, the Aikens' house in Rye, Jeake's House, became his second home. As before, his status was hardly that of an adopted son or diligent pupil. There he and Aiken played raucous ragtime tunes on the piano, Aiken "using almost only the black keys" and Lowry, perhaps accompanying himself on his ukelele, singing the words composed by Aiken: " 'I've got the coffin — and you've got the body' " (John Aiken, *Conrad Aiken Remembered* 31).

The pair were also notorious at this time for their extended and prodigious drinking bouts. Clarissa recalls that their frequent pub crawls to the Ship and Mermaid Inns stirred up gossip in the small town of Rye. She tells of "[o]ne foggy night [when] a couple of muddied, blood-ſtreaked apparitions staggered in, looking sheepish" ("Call It" 60). The two had been having a javelin-launching competition. Aiken, "hurling his javelin in the pitch-dark of a Channel fog . . . in competition with Hambo, had also launched himself into space, and had fallen ten feet down into rich Saltinge mud" (*Ushant* 226). Lowry, none too sober himself, proceeded to fish Aiken out. Lowry's friend and Cambridge tutor, Hugh Sykes Davies, recalls a similar episode in Rye when Lowry proposed they "put Conrad in a wheelbarrow and tip him into the mud at the bottom of the harbour" ("He Was Different" 44). For some reason this plan was never put into action.

Aiken, it seems, simply did not adjuſt well to the father/guardian role. Even with his own children he appears to have preferred the position of companionable buddy over responsible role model. According to his son, John Aiken, Conrad was "an irresponsible and negleĉtful father" (*Conrad Aiken Remembered* 14). And Lowry proved to be a companion who was not only willing to encourage Aiken's every whim, but who was also eager to indulge a few of his own. Viewed in this way, the early encounters with Lowry had perhaps a more damaging effeĉt on the older man than has been realized: a fraĉtured skull, paralyzing hangovers, the disrespeĉt of his Rye neighbours, and a strained marriage. Moreover, their escapades were beginning to hinder Aiken's progress with his work. Writing to G.B. Wilbur from Jeake's House in September 1930, Aiken admitted that Lowry's presence, "much as I like and enjoy him" (Killorin 158), was interfering with his own writing. In Clarissa Lorenz's view, Lowry brought out the worſt in her husband. " 'How much longer will Conrad put up with this madman?' " she wrote in her diary during one of Lowry's frequent visits to Jeake's in the early 1930s ("Call It" 60).

Some, on the other hand, felt that it was Aiken who had had a damaging influence on Lowry. Lowry's brother, Russell, has written that a "less suitable 'tutor' could scarcely have been found" and states that Aiken's "idea of bliss was drinking gin out of a bucket by moonlight" (letter to author). Although Lowry had taken to drinking during his sea voyage in 1927, some time before having met Aiken, Aiken's drinking habits undoubtedly had an influence on his impressionable and romantic protégé, and may have contributed to Lowry's eventual alcoholism. Moreover, Lowry was in awe of Aiken's tragic hiſtory: the child whose father had murdered his mother and then committed suicide; the teenager separated from his siblings and shunted from one relative to another without ever again finding a permanent home; the reſtless poet, torn between America and England, whose writings tried to come to terms with his tragic paſt. In September 1932, despairing at his lack of commercial success as a writer and the loss of his children after his divorce from Jessie McDonald, Aiken even went so far as to attempt suicide. By comparison, Lowry's pampered upper-middle-class background seemed shamefully uninteresting to the aspiring young writer. Competing with Aiken while at the same time trying to win his respect, Lowry took to inventing a tragic past of his own, which included a series of beatings and tortures at the hands of a malicious nanny and a debilitating blindness during his early school years. Encouraged by Aiken's example, Lowry came to view the world and himself with a fatalistic eye, using alcohol as a prop to heighten his tragic aspect. This self-induced fatalism was perhaps a contributing factor to his recurrent depression and paranoia in later years. It was also — and one must not forget this — largely the impetus behind Lowry's 1947 masterpiece, *Under the Volcano*.

Aiken's attitude towards women had a further negative influence on his young protégé. As is clear from many of Lowry's letters to Aiken from the 1930s, Aiken's perpetual womanizing and basic misogyny had rubbed off on the more inexperienced youth. Aiken's was a philosophy of "man with man against woman" (*Ushant* 28–29). As long as Lowry remained single, this presented no problem. Aiken was able to ignore his own wife's grievances and Lowry was more than contented that he should do so. Clarissa Lorenz attests to having gradually "come to feel superfluous at [Aiken's] convivial literary powwows with [his] possessive protégé" (*Lorelei Two* 88). With the appearance of Jan Gabrial, however, soon to become Lowry's first wife, the buddies experienced some discord and rivalry.

This first real rift in Aiken and Lowry's relationship came in the spring of 1933 when Lowry accompanied the Aikens on a trip to Spain. Lowry was his usual self — carefree, dirty, and alcoholic — until "an exotic American girl" (*Lorelei Two* 157), Jan Gabrial, appeared at the Pensión Carmona in Granada where the trio, along with Aiken's artist friend Ed Burra, were staying. Before long, Lowry was roaming the Granada foothills in Jan's company, escorting her to the Alhambra, and relating to her the plot of his new novel, *Ultramarine*. Most people were pleased at the change this new romance brought about in Lowry. Aiken, however, was bitter: " 'All this primping and preening is positively revolting!' " ("Call It" 67).

Aiken's version of the episode appears in *Ushant*. There he implies not only that he had himself previously had an affair with Jan, but that he had "handed her on" to Lowry and proposed that they "share" her: ". . . to hand her on to you, I could thus keep her — at least, at one remove, and with your imagination to magnify it for me" (353). According to Clarissa Lorenz, a version of this conversation took place one night on the patio of the Pensión Carmona. It was accompanied by a tremendous argument between the two men in which Lowry threatened to kill Aiken (*Lorelei Two* 158). Certainly, in some way, Jan had been the cause of a serious rift in their relationship. Yet Lowry's frequent allusions to this event in later letters to Aiken are remarkably tactful. While they do attest to an undercurrent of antagonism running beneath the surface of the letters at this point in their correspondence, they also suggest that Aiken may have embellished his version of the "triangle."†

In his letters Lowry lays the blame entirely on himself. It is as though he is apologising, however ambiguously, for having misjudged Aiken's intentions in the past. Writing from Mexico in 1937, he mentions having "done you dirt once & a half twice but never seriously & always it was with Jealously [sic] — & *love*" (letter 16). In one of his pleading 1939 letters, he acknowledges that Jan "had been the source of a kind of antagonism that had sprung up between us at one time . . . [I] took it out upon you practically to the point of betraying our friendship" (letter 18). Finally, by 9 April 1940, Lowry writes that "much has been resolved between [them]" through Aiken's continued friendship and support (letter 40). Whatever the true circumstances of the dispute, its effect does not not seem to have been as crippling as Aiken's account in *Ushant* would have led one to believe.

However, the trip to Spain did mark the greatest rift in their friendship up to that time. To his brother, Kempton Taylor, Aiken protested that it hadn't been a holiday "by a damned sight — I was in charge of a dipsomaniac, and was paid for it" (Killorin 200), and it was after that summer that Aiken finally stopped accepting payments from Lowry's father.

Ultimately, it would probably be best to say that Aiken and Lowry were each a bad influence on the other. Perhaps it was this in part that contributed to their being "astonishingly *en rapport*" (Aiken, "Malcolm Lowry" 102).

While this brotherly affection and rivalry was a central component of their relationship, Aiken's role as surrogate father to Lowry cannot be ignored. In this guise he performed a crucial service to the young man, who by the time of writing his second letter to Aiken had become "a perpetual source of anxiety to a bewildered parent" (letter 2). In Massachusetts Aiken had acted as an unofficial guardian to Lowry, and on his

---

† Indeed, Jan herself denies ever having met Aiken before her arrival in Granada and attributes his dislike for her, unfairly I think, to her having deprived him of any further income from Lowry's father ("Marriage" 119).

return to Rye in August 1930, he was hired by Lowry's father to act *in loco parentis.* In this capacity he controlled Lowry's finances, provided him with a home during school vacations, and acted as an intermediary, as is implied in letter 7, between Lowry and "the old man." More importantly, Aiken became a sort of "father confessor" or therapist to Lowry, for the younger man was able to confide to him things he would never have dreamed of discussing with his more staunch, upright father: subjects such as his drunken escapades with John Davenport and other Cambridge friends, his obsession with masturbation and venereal disease, and his infatuation with Charlotte Haldane.

From as early as 1929, before actually having met Aiken, Lowry had spoken of his *"filial affection"* for the man "old enough to be [his] father" (letter 2). Wishing above all to avoid a business arrangement, Lowry asked to be accepted, not as Aiken's pupil, but "as a member of [his] household" (letter 2). In 1938, in one of his many pleas for help, he addressed a desperate letter to Aiken with "a mi padre" (letter 16), and in February 1940 reminded Aiken of their bond: "what truer father have I than you" (letter 32). Lowry's actual father, on the other hand, is designated either "the bewildered parent" (letter 2) or, more regularly in later letters, "the O.M." (old man).

Not surprisingly, Aiken gradually came to assume the paternal role more fully. As early as 8 August 1929, from Massachusetts, he complained in a fatherly manner to Maurice Firuski that Lowry was "incredibly dirty and sloppy and helpless" (Killorin 155). In Rye he scolded Lowry on one occasion for having returned home late (letter 6), and worriedly enquired about his progress in the tripos exams at Cambridge (letter 8). In letter 4, Lowry teasingly parodies Aiken's chastisings: "Remember what I've said to you about drink and women. I don't want you to get mixed up in any-er-drinking bouts. . . . And money — please give me a careful account of everything you spend. . . ." In time, Lowry "usurped the succession" of Aiken's own son (*Ushant* 352). He was, after all, the ideal child-substitute for such a man as Aiken, sharing with his mentor a love of words, booze, and literature, and, above all, a yearning to write.

It was fitting, then, that Lowry turned to Aiken during his Vancouver crisis in 1939. Tricked by his father's lawyer, Benjamin Parks, into leaving Los Angeles where he had been living, Lowry entered Canada in July 1939 believing that he had to renew his visa. Instead he was put into the custody of A.B. Carey, a Vancouver businessman and philanthropist, and, without the funds to leave, found himself trapped in Vancouver, "the most hopeless of all cities of the lost" (letter 18). At first Aiken met Lowry's pleas to rescue him from his plight and readopt him with some hesitation.

Although Aiken agreed to watch over Lowry "from a distance" and again act as mediator between Lowry and his father, he was slightly more concerned at the not-so-distant prospect of Lowry coming to live with him and his new wife, Mary Hoover. By this time happily settled in Massachusetts with Mary, whom he'd married in 1937 while visiting the Lowrys in Cuernavaca, Aiken was loath to risk a resurgence of the difficulties he had experienced with Clarissa in the early 1930s. Feeling a responsibility for his wayward son, yet wary lest the "Legend of the Lowry" (letter 28) re-exert itself in its full force, Aiken repeatedly reminded Lowry of his past infringements, hoping thereby to avert any future calamities:

> . . . I hope you'll give me your word before coming that you're really going to . . . *behave well.* . . . No secret drinkings round the corner, eh? No disgracings of us with our friends, no scenes: and above all no continuous argument as to the amount of drink allowed: I'm to be the boss about that, or it's no go. (letter 22)

Aiken also feared a resurrection of the Oedipal rivalry he had experienced in his earlier "pseudo-guardianship" of Lowry (*Ushant* 239). In letter 23 Lowry anticipated his qualms:

> I would beg excusion for the monstrous and ungrateful accusations I made of you in the past on the grounds that they were all in the general Oedipeian [sic] pattern. . . . Such things will not occur again, I assure you. This time a recreated Priam has to deal with an Oedipus in his post-Jocasta period. . . .

By this time, Jan, the main cause of Oedipal unrest between the two men, was out of the picture, as divorce proceedings between her and Lowry were well under way. Now Lowry felt he had to dispel Aiken's doubts about his post-Jocasta partner, Margerie Bonner. Like a son seeking his father's blessing, Lowry repeatedly sings the praises of Margerie, his soon-to-be wife, in the letters of this period. Yet his extended protestations were probably unnecessary. Aiken cared too much for Lowry to let any misgivings of this sort interfere with the welfare of his surrogate son: "I'm doing this, in short, (and there are few I'd do it for) because I've always as you know been damned fond of you and because you've come to me for help at a crisis" (letter 22).

The new arrangement, however, was never put to the test. Although Lowry sincerely yearned to be reunited with Aiken on the East Coast, neither he nor Aiken were able to gather the funds for the journey. Aiken's help had pulled Lowry through the crisis. Now the time had come for the child to break away from the "Benevolent Eye" of the father:

> Your interest and kindness got me over a hell of a difficult period . . .
> as things stand I have been able to reorganize my life to a point where
> I am now really able to cope. . . . (letter 59)

With Margerie, Lowry settled in a squatter's shack on Burrard Inlet near Vancouver. There, with her help, he began in earnest to put the lessons of his master to the test on paper.

The teacher/pupil relationship between the two had, of course, existed from the very beginning when Aiken was hired by Lowry's father to teach Lowry "how to write novels." Although this arrangement was initiated by Lowry, Aiken accepted the role of literary master wholeheartedly and took it upon himself to mould his pupil into a successful writer. During the 1930s, Aiken would spend many an hour engaged in literary discussions with his young pupil. It was, Lowry wrote in letter 21, a conversation with Aiken about poetry that produced his collection of poems, "The Lighthouse Invites the Storm." In fact, Aiken was as much an influence on Lowry's *reading* as on his writing. Lowry's later obsession with such writers as Melville, Hawthorne, Emily Dickinson, Joyce, Eliot, William James, and Henri Bergson — many of whom are mentioned in his letters to Aiken — most likely stems from his early years under Aiken's tutelage. John Aiken recalls their many stimulating conversations about contemporary writing in the Rye house. If they weren't discussing some topical literary subject of the day, such as Olaf Stapledon's *Last and First Men* (*Conrad Aiken Remembered* 17), they were engaged in more abstract debates about "form in art and its possible mathematical basis" (16). John also tells of their discussing *Great Circle* and *Ultramarine* in terms of "musical form and its use in shaping a novel . . ." (35).

In Massachusetts in 1929, and later in Rye, Aiken helped Lowry with his poetry and first novel, "shading, annotating, and connotating the disbursements" of *Ultramarine* (letter 4) to such an extent that Lowry was eventually to call himself a mere "spectre of [Aiken's] discarded ideas" (letter 13). In fact, Aiken was concerned that his influence had hindered Lowry from developing a literary style of his own. Lowry was certainly attracted to Aiken's "subjective aesthetic," particularly to his examination of the evolution of consciousness. After reading a draft of Lowry's "In Ballast to the White Sea," the novel which was irretrievably lost when the Lowrys' shack burned down in 1944, Aiken commented:

My own influence again has been bad. . . . I think it's time you cut yourself adrift from all these here ghostly doppelgangers and projections and identifications and let loose some of your natural joy. . . . (letter 20)

However, if Aiken imposed his ideas and literary tastes too strongly onto Lowry's early writings, Lowry eagerly took what information and guidance he could from his master. Lowry's attempted "absorption" of Aiken and his ideas, by playing "conscious starfish" to his "unconscious oyster," is a key element of *Ushant*, where Hambo (the Lowry character) slyly suggests that it is D.'s (Aiken's) fate "simply to become a better 'you' in me — " (355). Indeed, Lowry was not above passing off Aiken's words as his own; his intended incorporation into *Ultramarine* of the "bone dream" — (appropriately enough, an account of a son devouring his father's skeleton) — from Aiken's *Great Circle* is only the most extreme example (letter 8). In "The Last Address," later to be titled *Lunar Caustic*, Lowry had also originally planned to include passages from *Great Circle* (letter 50). In letter 13, Lowry lists things in *Ultramarine* which may be "hooked out" should Aiken, presumably because he had thought them up first, "want them [him]self." According to Aiken in a 1967 letter to the *TLS*, it had become a lasting joke between him and Lowry that Lowry had incorporated so much of *Blue Voyage* — "style, devices, &c. — in *Ultramarine* and in all the later work as well" (*TLS*; Killorin 324). In fact, Aiken had proposed that Lowry go one step further and call his book "Purple Passage" to echo the title of *Blue Voyage* ("Malcolm Lowry" 102). Clarissa Lorenz confirms these statements in her account of how Aiken spent many an hour in Boston and Rye deleting passages from *Ultramarine* that "read like a parody of *Blue Voyage*" (*Lorelei Two* 73). Similarly, a poem, "In Cape Cod with Conrad Aitken [sic]," ostensibly written by Lowry and published in the March 1930 *Festival Theatre Programme*, is based upon a dream which Aiken himself had had in Cape Cod (Killorin 153) and which Aiken had also "partially translated into a poem" (*Ushant* 167) in part 10 of *Landscape West of Eden*. One of the most striking of Lowry's "liftings" from Aiken's work is revealed in Charlotte Haldane's memoir of Lowry for the 1967 BBC "New Release" program. As evidence of Lowry's gift for poetry, she quotes two of the "jingles" he used to sing at her home in the 1930s — one of which is a segment from Aiken's "The House of Dust" (*Malcolm Lowry Remembered* 56).†

---

† My thanks to Gordon Bowker for calling my attention to this particular instance of Lowry's "absorption" of Aiken's work.

Lowry used phrases from Aiken's letters for similar purposes. Aiken's "indoor marxmanship" pun (letter 20), for instance, appears later both in Lowry's poem, "Where Did That One Go To 'Erbert," and in *Under the Volcano* (8). Aiken's "Every man his own Laocoon" (letter 28) was echoed by Lowry in a 1 July 1949 letter to Frank Taylor (*Selected Letters* 180). Similarly, the prototype of "Oedipuss," the Consul's cat in *Under the Volcano* (89), is Aiken's cat, appearing by name in letter 64. Aiken himself has noted, both in *Ushant* and elsewhere, additional passages in *Under the Volcano* which were likewise inspired by himself. The political discussion between the Consul and Hugh in chapter 10 of *Under the Volcano*, says Aiken, was "a verbatim report of an argument between Malcolm and myself, with the positions reversed: what the Consul says, I said" (*TLS*). In this same letter Aiken claims that he and his wife (Mary Hoover) observed, in Mexico, the scene of the cat catching the insect which the Consul witnesses in chapter 5 of *Under the Volcano*. A similar accusation appears in *Ushant*:

> 'He thinks I'm a bird in a tree' — so D. had observed of the little cat, at his feet, in the garden . . . and Hambo . . . could already be seen in the very act of entering that note, that bird-note, amongst the pile of other notes, in that creative nest of his on the verandah, where the new book was taking shape. (357)

Lowry refers to these episodes in letters 40 and 86, and in the former acknowledges his inclusion of some of Aiken's observations in *Under the Volcano*; ultimately, however, Aiken was not appeased. To Aiken, the most disturbing of Lowry's plagiarisms for *Under the Volcano* was probably his appropriation of Aiken's William Blackstone material, a subject around which Aiken had hoped to focus his grand opus and which he unwittingly shared with Lowry in 1929: ". . .what more natural than that Hambo had at once, and without so much as a by-your-leave, taken over the Blackstone idea as his own" (*Ushant* 294). Aiken later did write his Blackstone book, *The Kid*, published in the same year as *Under the Volcano*, though his dedication of the book to Lowry "as from One Rolling Blackstone to Another" would seem to suggest an acceptance of their literary symbiosis.

Indeed, Aiken's irritation with Lowry's conscious and unconscious plagiarisms did not surface overtly until his own "starfish turn" in *Ushant*. Until that time, he continued to act as Lowry's tutor. Some time after the "bone dream" episode, when visiting Lowry in Mexico in 1937, he gave Lowry a poetry exercise "of writing ten lines of blank verse with the caesura changing one step in each line" ("Art" 99). The result, in letter

14, was sent to Aiken at Lowry's house from a nearby bar. The poems Aiken thought were "very fine, and very funny": "As an example of his attention to vowel sounds, one line still haunts me, 'Airplane or aeroplane, or juſt plain plane.' Couldn't be better" (99). Well into the 1940s Lowry continued to send his roughly hewn poems to his maſter for criticism and correction: "I may be fooling myself about these particular poems and if I am I know you will tell me so . . ." (letter 52). Nor did Aiken hesitate to give an honeſt opinion: "I like the pomes moderate-like. . . . Freedom comes *after* maſtery not before . . ." (letter 55).

The literary relationship, then, had grown into what could be more aptly called a "literary symbiosis," with the "symbiotic sailmakers" (*Ushant* 295) either working together, as they did with *Ultramarine* and at leaſt one poem, "those cokes to newcaſtle blues," in the February 1931 *Feſtival Theatre Review*, or inſtead, working separately, but continually incorporating the thoughts and personality of the other into ever new literary creations.

Their letters show the "symbiotic sailmakers" at work. Phrases originated by one correspondent become refrains in a sort of epiſtolary ping-pong game when repeated by the other. Items such as Aiken's abbreviated Latin phrases — "pro tem," "quam cel," and "d.v." (deo volente) — are littered through Lowry's letters. Likewise Aiken's "knocked oop" reappears in letters 56 and 81 from Lowry, as does his "Poppergetſthebotl" pun in letter 76. Often a reference in one letter is picked up and expanded in the other's reply. In letter 68, Aiken asks Lowry whether "the phoenix [has] clapped its wings" above the burnt remains of his shack. Lowry revives the image in his reply: "Yes, the phoenix clapped its wings all right all right, in fact gave such a bloody great resounding clap that the poor bird nearly broke its neck and had to be immolated all over again" (letter 70). Aiken once said that he and Lowry "spoke the same language" ("Malcolm Lowry" 102); so, too, did they write it, at leaſt to each other.

Perhaps what Aiken thrived on moſt during these years was the intense admiration that Lowry, who considered him "one of the five living greateſt writers" (letter 40), had for his work. From the beginning of their correspondence Lowry praised and quoted Aiken's writings, sometimes, as in letter 6, reproducing entire poems from memory. Aiken's claim that Lowry knew *Blue Voyage* better than he himself did ("Malcolm Lowry" 101) is well subſtantiated by Lowry's frequent allusions to that novel in his letters. As late as 1952 (letter 84) Lowry could still remember and quote passages from *Blue Voyage*, "that work of a satanic and marvelous genius" (letter 45). Aiken's *And in the Human Heart* (1940) Lowry felt to be one of "the higheſt touchſtones of excellence in *all* literature" (letter 57). *The Soldier* (1944) he thought contained some of Aiken's pureſt work and "the fineſt being done to-day" (letter 67). *The Kid* (1947), which Aiken had dedicated to Lowry, prompted Lowry to write a humorous poem in response (letter 77). In many of the later letters Lowry marvels at his good fortune in having been able to study under Aiken:

> How I appreciate now the collossal advantage of having known you and would that I had been better and honeſter and more *conscious* when I did! I sometimes think I am like a man who remembers having known Bill Shakespeare in his youth — but what a pity, he couldn't appreciate anything the fellow said, he was blind and dumb at the time. (letter 51)

Yet with time the teacher/pupil relationship underwent a reversal. By the 1940s Aiken had regularly begun to send Lowry copies of his newly published books in order to hear again the guaranteed and now much needed praise from his old pupil:

> Bless you Malc . . . for all the glowing words and numbers and phine phlattering phrases about my little dead sonnets. . . . I rushed to re-read the ones you liked . . . it's always such fun to read one's own things through somebody else's eyes . . . a kind of twice reflected narcissism. (letter 58)

To Robert Linscott in March 1947, Aiken called Lowry his "beſt critic" (Washington University Library), and in a January 1946 letter to Malcolm Cowley admitted that the only "full-dress consideration" he'd received as a writer was "almoſt wholly private: from my English pupil Malcolm Lowry . . ." (Killorin 268). By this time Aiken had begun to requeſt his pupil's advice. In 1944 he asked Lowry to suggeſt some poems he might include in *Twentieth-Century American Poetry* (letter 65), and, in 1945, wanted advice about the seleſtion for his *Colleſted Poems*: "I value your judgement more highly than any other . . ." (letter 69). In both cases Lowry suggeſted his old favourites, the ones he had often quoted in his early letters to Aiken, seleſtions from "The House of Duſt," "Priapus and the Pool," and even the "Goya" poem from *Blue Voyage*.

With the publication and immediate success of *Under the Volcano*, however, the literary relationship between the two became strained. While Lowry was still thinking of himself as Aiken's "old — & new — pupil" (letter 73), Aiken feared that the pupil might have finally surpassed the maſter. In faſt, Aiken had long been aware of the potential problems the situation could engender. According to Edward Butscher, because Aiken knew "that literary friends [could] be the most dangerous," he limited his friends "to artists and psychiatrists . . . who posed no consistent threat to his own need for center stage" (176). With the success of *Under the Volcano*, Lowry was coming dangerously close to usurping Aiken's place — amongst his own circle of friends at least — in literary centre stage.

Undoubtedly Aiken admired the book; his exalted praise on the Reynal & Hitchcock dust jacket and in letter 74 of this collection makes this quite apparent. And to be fair, Aiken's continued encouragement of Lowry at this point suggests an undeniable affection and generosity of spirit:

> . . . as a piece of literature it is a genuine bona fide first cut off the white whale's hump, godshot, sunshot, bloodshot, spermshot, and altogether the most aiken-satisfying book I've wallowed in for a generation. My god how good to be able to relish the english language again. . . . the elisions and transitions and ellipses and parentheses and asides and time-notations and recapitulations and minatory fingerposts — how infinitely satisfactory to a writer to see all *that* so incomparably well done and understood! . . . O baby, o baby, o baby, it's marvellous Malc. . . . (letter 74)

However, below the surface, other anxieties seethed. Although Lowry had, as early as 1940, intended *Under the Volcano* to be "a gesture on the part of a grateful pupil to his master" (letter 40), and had even thought of dedicating the novel to Aiken (letter 48), Aiken appears to have taken the unexpected success of his formerly drunken and unruly protégé with some bitterness. In an unpublished letter to John Davenport from 1947 (Huntington Library), as well as the published letter in the 1967 *TLS* mentioned earlier, Aiken complained bitterly about the many "liftings" of his own ideas in *Under the Volcano*, despite the fact that Lowry had himself acknowledged these "thefts" seven years before the publication of the novel in letter 40:

> It is the first book of mine that is not in one way or another parasitic on your work. (This time it is parasitic however on some of your wisecracks in Mexico. . . .) If you remember at the time you said you didn't mind about this. . . .

Aiken, however, did mind. Although he made no mention of his feelings to Lowry, he undertook "a starfish turn of his own" (356, 361) with his "haughtybiography" *Ushant*. Aiken told his son John that the writing of *Ushant* constituted not only a "terrific catharsis," but that it was also "an act of revenge" (*Conrad Aiken Remembered* 35). This time it was he who incorporated Lowry's words into a work of fiction.

Lowry remained, perhaps voluntarily, unaware of Aiken's dilemma. Aiken appears to have written *Ushant* partly in an attempt to come to terms with his mixed feelings for Lowry. His paternal and brotherly affection had for some time been at war with an inevitable and steadily increasing perception of literary rivalry between the two, "a greater and deeper rivalry, that of the pride of mind" (*Ushant* 27). In his autobiography he presents both sides of the relationship, if admittedly with excessive emphasis on the latter. Yet, in letter 83, before sending the book to Lowry, Aiken did attempt to explain its purpose: "I pray when you read it you will continually say to yourself, this guy loves me, or he wouldn't be so bloody candid about me."

Lowry, however, responded with the predictable excesses of praise, and with an absence of psychological insight and sympathy:

> A great book, in many ways, technically, a marvel. . . . there are wonders of prose, profound perceptions and apperceptions and complexities expressed in miraculous limpidity. (letter 85)

While he complimented Aiken's writing style, Lowry made no attempt to address the book's content. Before receiving *Ushant*, in letter 84, Lowry expressed hope that Aiken would have "spared [him] some of [his] obscenest failings," yet, he continued, "I would probably plagiarise them anyway." What *Ushant* called for from Lowry was at least an acknowledgement that he understood Aiken's purpose in depicting Hambo as he did. Instead, Lowry stalled in responding to the book, stating that he "ain't really had time" to form a "dispassionate judgement" (letter 85). And when that time came, two years later in 1954, he was still feeling somewhat chastised, though he took care to assure Aiken that he was "honoured," not " 'hurt,' " by the book (letter 86). In a letter to John Davenport dated 17 April 1947, Aiken said that Lowry needed to acknowledge him "as I have acknowledged Eliot; that would release him" (Huntington Library). In this regard Lowry still remained Aiken's pupil, incapable of confronting, let alone criticizing, his former master.

The publication of *Ushant* is supposed by many to have resulted in a "lasting break" between Aiken and Lowry. In truth they had begun to drift apart some years earlier. Both men had changed considerably in the seventeen-year interim since their last meeting. In that time they had both remarried, moved to opposite ends of the continent, embarked on distinct literary careers, and adopted lifestyles that were rather more settled than their earlier carefree and drunken ramblings in Massachusetts, Rye, and Cuernavaca.

Their reunion in 1954 ideally might have stopped the atrophying process. Aiken was overjoyed at the news of the Lowrys' arrival in New York — "Hallileuh" begins his answering telegram (letter 88) — and with some difficulty and little notice made the journey from Brewster to his "cold water flat" in New York. It had been a long wait, but Lowry had finally come East. Although he was anxious to see Aiken after their seventeen-year separation, old behavior patterns resurfaced, and Lowry arrived at their reunion drunk and incoherent:

> . . . Lowry drifted into a kind of rapt silence . . . gazing at nothing; perhaps an hour passed in which he spoke to no one at all, nor did he move from his chair. Then, suddenly, cupping his hands to his mouth, he commenced to make sounds that can only be described as "beeps".
> . . . (Markson 224–25)

While Aiken may have accepted such behavior from his son or pupil in the past, Lowry was now no longer either. Before long, the older man bid a disappointed farewell to his friend: "Good night, disgrace," were his parting words to Lowry (Markson 225). Lucid for the first time that evening and suddenly aware of what he was about to lose, Lowry followed Aiken outside. David Markson gives a touching account of their last encounter:

> In the street, in jest but in sadness, the two began to wrestle as a taxi drew up. Breaking Lowry's hold, Aiken tumbled to the floor as the vehicle took him off.
>   Those next moments, gazing into the empty street where only now a small rain, like a mist, had begun to fall, Lowry could not have appeared more sober. "He is an old man," he said. "And now I will never see him again." (225)

Failing to see Aiken off at the train station the following day, Lowry sent a disguised apology, the farewell telegram printed at the end of this collection (letter 89). To Markson, Lowry still spoke of himself as Aiken's long lost son: " 'After all, he is my father . . .' " ("Malcolm Lowry: A Reminiscence" 225). This time, however, the prodigal son had been finally refused the father's blessing.

Yet I must not allow an introduction to Aiken and Lowry's correspondence to end on as tragic a note as their friendship. Brothers, father and son, literary rivals, their letters reveal them, above all, as vigorous and witty correspondents. That their relationship ended as abruptly as it did is perhaps a testament to the joy and intensity that characterized its beginnings. In their later correspondence one often finds both writers hearkening back to this earlier period of their friendship: the "wonderful summer" of 1929, the Ship and Mermaid Inns in Rye, and their "communistic talk under the banana trees" (letter 27) in Cuernavaca, Aiken's "wedding place" (letter 71). In 1940 Lowry recalls reading "fragments of the House of Dust in old Coteries on Hayes Common twelve years ago" (letter 34), and in the same year remembers how at that time he used to "pray one day I might meet you" (letter 51). In letter 66 Aiken wistfully wonders whether they will "ever again gather by the river" in Rye, and, some years later, poetically recaptures their visits to the Ship Inn:

> Gives one to think. Rye, September 5, 1924, and I am going into the Ship to celebrate the birth of my daughter Joan. . . . And there, only a few bright seconds later, you and I were to appear with an eye out for sausage rolls. (letter 83)

At the end, their correspondence comes full circle. In a 1952 letter to Tom Neeves that Lowry enclosed to Aiken in letter 84, Lowry still marvels at his good fortune in having shared those early years with Aiken:

> . . . these were some of the happiest times of my life; and among the most treasured memories, I am sure, of Mr. Aiken. . . . I have always looked upon him much as a father, besides which he is one of my best friends, and so we have never lost touch. (Huntington Library 2539)

EDITORIAL INTRODUCTION

The two major source libraries for the Aiken/Lowry letters are the Huntington Library in San Marino, which houses the Conrad Aiken Manuscript Collection, and the University of British Columbia Library in Vancouver, containing the Malcolm Lowry Manuscript Collection. While additional libraries and individuals have been contacted, none of these brought to light any letters that were not contained in one of these two collections.

As is usually the case in such collections of correspondence, letters are missing. This is particularly true of the early stages of Lowry and Aiken's correspondence. Section I, spanning the years 1929–1938, contains only letters from Lowry; no doubt Lowry was too much on the move at this time of his life to have saved many of his possessions, let alone his letters. Sections II and III reveal a more balanced correspondence between the two, particularly Section II (1939–1941), which consists of an almost week by week back and forth correspondence over the course of a few months.

In all cases I have attempted to transcribe the letters as faithfully as possible from the handwritten and typed originals (or photocopies of these items when no original was available) located in one of the two source libraries. I have indicated the provenance of the letters in the heading at the top of each, providing a description of the original (holograph or typescript), its location and library call number, the existence of any photocopies of that original in the alternative source library, and, if applicable, the publication reference. I have been unable to locate originals, or photocopies of these, for seven of the letters from Aiken (letters 17, 19, 22, 26, 28, 33, and 74). These items are printed in Joseph Killorin's *Selected Letters of Conrad Aiken* (1978); however, since they are not, as that volume indicates, located in the Huntington Library, I have had to rely solely on Killorin's transcriptions for the texts of these letters. In all other cases, the transcriptions are my own, even where the items have been previously published. This proved to be necessary since, in many cases, the Aiken letters in *Selected Letters of Conrad Aiken* (1978) are printed in incomplete form, while items in *Selected Letters of Malcolm Lowry* (1965) are often riddled with unacknowledged deletions, alterations, and transcriptional errors.

My primary concern in editing Aiken and Lowry's correspondence has been to reproduce the text and appearance of their letters as faithfully as possible, to give an immediate sense of the dramatic unfolding of their relationship as they themselves were constructing it. I have therefore chosen to reproduce all errors or idiosyncrasies in spelling, punctuation, capitalization, etc. For example, I have reproduced Lowry's unpredictable and often faulty use of colons and semicolons, his frequent use of ampersands, his failure to underline book titles, his alternate use of double and single quotation marks, and various spelling inconsistencies and errors. In Aiken's case, I have retained his inconsistent capitalizations, his unusual and often creative spellings, and even his typographical errors (where they do not interfere with the sense of the word or sentence).

Only in cases where punctuation or spelling errors (the latter are usually typographical errors) interfere with the meaning have I altered the text. Where such conflicts occur I have always placed my insertion or alteration within square brackets and shown the change in a textual note, keyed by page and line number at the end of the volume. I have tried to keep such editorial tampering to a minimum; however, in some cases a spelling or typographical error could render a word unintelligible and in these cases I thought it necessary to step in.

Words in the text of the letters that were partially illegible I have transcribed as best I could and placed within square brackets preceded by a question mark; luckily this occurs only once, in letter 70 from Lowry.

Moreover, all deletions, insertions, and other alterations made by the authors themselves are shown in textual notes. Because there came to be such a wealth of textual notes, I chose not to key them with superscript numbers in the text of the letters. Instead they are keyed by page and line number at the end of the volume. These line numbers, of course, do not reflect the precise configuration of lines of the original. The purpose here is to facilitate location of the textual notes in the main text of the letter; the line numbers are therefore intended purely for the reader's convenience.

The deletions, where legible, are shown enclosed within diamond brackets < >, the insertions within wavy brackets { }. Consider, for example, the following:

impossibility in getting\ impossibility <to get> {in getting}

What this fairly simple textual note signifies is that the author (in this case, Lowry in letter 1) has originally written "impossibility to get," and has subsequently deleted the words "to get" and replaced them by "in getting." More complicated notes involve deletions within insertions, deletions within deletions, and so on (see the list of abbreviations and symbols at the end of the editorial introduction):

> break up because — but why go on?\ break up <{& so would I}> because
> <I know she would> { — {{but}} why go on?}

Here, in letter 18, Lowry has inserted "& so would I" between the words "break up" and "because," and has later crossed them out, hence the designation of an insertion within a deletion <{ }>. The words "I know she would" were part of the original sentence but have also been deleted and replaced by "— but why go on?" The latter phrase, as an insertion, originally read "— why go on?" until the word "but" was inserted into it, resulting in my use of the symbol {{ }} to designate an insertion within an insertion.

In some cases the alterations may appear relatively insignificant, yet to avoid as much as possible any oversights due to editorial subjectivity, I have decided to duplicate all of these. The only exceptions are in the letters which exist as typescripts only (these are designated as such in the heading at the top of each letter). In these cases I do not duplicate corrections of typographical errors that were made on the typewriter at the time the letter was being typed. These I considered to be merely slips of the finger which the typist caught immediately as they occurred. Moreover, Margerie Lowry often typed Lowry's letters for him, so these sorts of errors cannot even be considered his own. I do, however, show all alterations made *by hand* in the typescripts, even if these are merely corrections of typographical errors. Accent marks and underlinings introduced by hand into the typescripts are the only exception to this, as these necessarily had to be done by hand. These appear in the main text of the letter, but not in textual notes. In addition, alterations done on the typewriter of anything other than typographical errors (eg., deletions of words, etc.) are reproduced in a textual note and there designated as having been done on the typewriter. Furthermore, entire lines or paragraphs written by hand in a typed letter (or vice versa) are identified as such in a textual note. However, since *all* signatures are handwritten, they have not been noted or designated in any particular way.

Letters from Lowry that appear to exist as drafts only (although even this is debatable since Lowry's letters were often sent in fairly rough form) are identified as such in a textual note at the end of the volume. Appendix 1 contains two variant texts of letters by Lowry: Aiken's typescript transcription of letter 70 and Lowry's handwritten draft of letter 89. In the firſt inſtance, I thought it possible (though unlikely) that Aiken may have received a different version of letter 70 than that contained in the UBC Library; for this reason I decided to reproduce Aiken's transcription of Lowry's letter, incomplete though it appears, in case it should prove of intereſt to the reader. Lowry's draft for the telegram in letter 89 I have reproduced primarily because its text varies from that of the telegram that Aiken a&ually received. These, however, are the only cases where I discovered more than one text for a particular letter. I should also add, at this point, that I do not provide textual notes for the items contained in the appendices; I regarded this as unnecessary, especially for Aiken's transcription of Lowry's letter and the letters (in Appendix II) from Margerie Bonner (Lowry) to Mary Aiken.

All superscript numbers refer the reader to explanatory footnotes. In general, only firſt references have been noted (excepting those that appear only two or three times in the entire volume, or references to John Davenport which, if not noted, could be confused with Aiken's son, John). Such references can be retrieved in the index should the reader wish to find the original note. Proper names are indexed in all forms used by the correspondents. I have not provided explanatory notes for well-known places or personages (Kafka, Melville, Hart Crane, etc.), nor have I fully noted all relevant points of biographical intereſt when these are covered in the introdu&ory pieces at the beginning of the three se&ions. A volume of this sort inevitably assumes an audience with at leaſt a basic knowledge of more well-known literary figures, and it was decided that the reader could, if s/he wished, find detailed information on these persons on his/her own.

Reproducing the overall shape of each letter, particularly the spacing and indentation, proved the moſt difficult matter. Again, I have tried to refle& this as beſt I could, although in many cases it was difficult to tell what the author had himself intended, particularly in holograph originals. In many of the early letters from Lowry, for inſtance, he "indents" his paragraphs from the right rather than the left-hand side. Since it was impossible for me to reproduce these in my typed transcription, I have indented them five spaces from the left-hand margin. All other paragraphs are likewise indented five spaces unless the author had a particular format, as Aiken often did when he indented paragraphs from the end of the salutation. I have likewise attempted to refle& the paragraph and line spacing of the originals. Hence, where Margerie (as Lowry's typiſt) inserted a double space between paragraphs, I have done the same. While this may not refle& Lowry's intention, it does at leaſt duplicate the text of the letter that Aiken received.

The indentation of all salutations and closings I have tried to reflect as closely as possible. Lowry's quotations from Aiken's (and others') works, if indented in the original, are here indented also.

Passages written in the margins I have incorporated into the text of the letters where appropriate (usually they have been keyed to a specific place by the author) and identified in a textual note. The only exception is letter 14 where the marginalia are direct comments on the lines of poetry which they border. In some cases I have introduced dashes within square brackets on either side of the insertion so that these passages could be more clearly incorporated into the text of the letter.

The only place where I have substantially altered the format of the letters is in the address and date of each. While I have always retained the original wording of these, I have not always reproduced their lay-out. Aiken and Lowry were themselves inconsistent in this, although usually the address appears in the top right-hand corner of the letters where I have chosen to put it. Because many readers will be consulting the letters according to the address from which they were written or the date of composition, I thought it best to standardize the location of these for quick and easy reference. Similarly, in order that the two be clearly distinguishable, I have always separated the address and the date by a double space. Again, though, the date itself, and its "wording," is always that of the author.

When no date or address is written by the author, I include my own within square brackets. This information is usually based upon internal evidence within the letters and, where available, postmarks. Where letterhead paper is used, I reproduce its address within square brackets (unless the address is inappropriate for the time the letter was written) and note it in a textual note. Because they are often unreliable and misleading, I have not duplicated librarians' or other people's inscriptions on the letters regarding these matters, except for Conrad Aiken's and, in some cases, Margerie Lowry's, which are then reproduced in a textual note only.

While different philosophies regarding editorial practice render it impossible for an editor to please all of his/her readers, I hope that this volume will satisfy the varying needs of different readers. In any case, I would rather be accused of being too meticulous than not sufficiently so. While I have tried to consider the "readability" of the letters printed here, my primary aim has been to reproduce the original texts as faithfully as possible.

LIST OF ABBREVIATIONS AND SYMBOLS

Following is a list of abbreviations and symbols used in this volume. I have chosen to use "MS" (manuscript) to designate holograph texts to avoid confusion with the designation "H" for Huntington Library:

MS	holograph (manuscript) original
TS	typescript original
MSPC	photocopied holograph (manuscript)
TSPC	photocopied typescript
H	Huntington Library
UBC	University of British Columbia
[illeg.]	illegible
[typo.]	typographical error
< >	deletion
<< >>	deletion within a deletion
{ }	insertion
{{ }}	insertion within an insertion
[ ]	editorial interpolation or alteration
[?]	doubtful reading

1929–1938

I too have heard the sea sound in strange
waters — *sh-sh-sh* like the hush in a conch shell. . . .

— *12 March 1929 letter from Lowry to Aiken*

❦

SOME TIME IN 1927 OR 1928, Lowry found in his possession a copy of Aiken's first novel, *Blue Voyage*, and there began his identification with the American writer. The dedication of *Blue Voyage* — "To C.M.L." — , which was actually intended for Aiken's second wife, Clarissa Lorenz, Lowry thought to be mysteriously meant for himself (Clarence Malcolm Lowry). He was also captivated by Aiken's "The House of Dust," portions of which he had read and memorized in 1928 from old *Coterie* magazines.

At this time, Lowry was concentrating on writing the Cambridge previous examinations, a necessary prelude to gaining entrance to the university. In preparation for the exams, he stayed at 5 Woodville Road in Blackheath, London, at the "cramming school" of the ex-Leys master, Jerry Kellett (Bradbrook, "Literary Friends" 11). In his spare time, Lowry would go to Hayes Common and read Aiken's work, praying one day that he might meet the author (letter 51). It is from his Blackheath address that Lowry wrote his first letter to Aiken at his home in Rye, to which he received no reply. Unbeknownst to Lowry, Aiken was at the time living in Cambridge, Massachusetts, close to Harvard University where he had been tutoring the year before. Lowry wrote another letter a week or two later on 12 March 1929, this time asking Aiken to be his tutor. Lowry's father had agreed to allow his son to spend the summer with Aiken on the condition that he first gain entrance to Cambridge University. By the time of this second letter to Aiken, Lowry had been accepted by St. Catharine's College and, as previously agreed upon, his father was now willing to appoint Aiken a guardian or tutor of his son for the duration of the summer. Aiken, who was both in need of money and impressed by Lowry's extensive familiarity with his writings, agreed to the arrangement, telling Lowry that if he were still interested he would have to make the journey across the Atlantic to Massachusetts (CBC interview 1961). Within a month Lowry had acquired passage as a steerage passenger aboard a cargo ship and travelled to Boston via the West Indies to spend the summer with Aiken.

By October, Lowry had entered Cambridge with the intention of taking an English Tripos. In August of the following year Aiken himself returned to "Jeake's House" in Rye with Clarissa Lorenz, and it was at this time that Arthur O. Lowry put him *in loco parentis* of Malcolm. For the next three years, Lowry was to spend all of his vacations, with intermittent visits to his parents in Cheshire and a trip to Norway in the summer of 1931, with the Aikens in Rye. These vacations included a lengthy break in the summer from July to October, and a month off at both Christmas and Easter. It was during this period, from September 1930 to the summer of 1932, that Lowry and Aiken were closest. Together they discussed their own writings, the literary issues of the day, and their mutual acquaintances in Rye and Cambridge, such as Gerald Noxon, the publisher of *Experiment*, whom Lowry had introduced to Aiken in September 1930, and Lowry's Cambridge friend, John Davenport. It was also at this time that they both contributed to the Cambridge literary magazine, *Experiment*, and together composed a poem for *The Festival Theatre Review* protesting the censorship of literature, "those cokes to newcastle blues."

By June 1932, Lowry had graduated with a third class honours degree in English. After a brief visit to the Aikens, he moved to London where he was to live for the next year, spending most of his time drinking in London's Fitzrovia area and trying to publish his first novel, *Ultramarine*. He was still, as he had been since 1929, discussing the progress of *Ultramarine* with Aiken, feeling it to be "a spectre of [Aiken's] own discarded ideas" (letter 13). In the spring of 1933, a few months before *Ultramarine* was published, he travelled to Granada with the Aikens and their artist friend, Ed Burra, and it was here that he met Jan Gabrial whom he married in Paris in January 1934.

The next existing letter to Aiken is written from Cuernavaca in 1937, although Lowry had seen Aiken in the interim since leaving England in 1934. Jan had left for New York a few months after their wedding, and Lowry followed her there in the Fall. It was in August 1936 that Aiken paid a spontaneous visit to Lowry in New York, as described by Lowry in his letter to Seymour Lawrence which appeared in the Conrad Aiken issue of *Wake* (87–88). Aiken writes of this unexpected meeting with Lowry in a 22 August 1936 letter to Ed Burra (Killorin 208), where he tells how he found Lowry "in very good form," cleaned up and working hard at his short stories and "The Last Address" (*Lunar Caustic*), a novella based on his treatment for alcoholism in New York's Bellevue Hospital earlier in 1935 or 1936. At the time of Aiken's visit, Lowry and Jan were living separately, though by the Fall of 1936 they had moved to Los Angeles together, staying briefly in Hollywood with John Davenport, and then to Acapulco, settling in Cuernavaca some time in December.

In the meantime, Aiken had moved to Boston where he met Mary Augusta Hoover, an artist, with whom he was living, along with Ed Burra, in the winter of 1936. These were probably some of Aiken's happiest times. Ed "painted in the dining room, Mary painted in an upstairs bedroom, and [Conrad] wrote in the 'salon-cellar' " (Killorin 207). The following May, the trio travelled by train to Mexico, a trip that was to become the basis for Aiken's *A Heart for the Gods of Mexico*, and visited the Lowrys in Cuernavaca. In Mexico, Aiken hoped to obtain a "quick" divorce from Clarissa Lorenz and marry Mary Hoover. In the course of this visit, Lowry once again became a sort of pupil under Aiken's tutelage, composing sonnets in Charlie's Bar for Aiken's perusal (letter 14). On July 7th, ten days before leaving to return to England, Conrad and Mary were married in Cuernavaca; Lowry and Jan were present at the wedding. The Lowrys' marriage, however, was deteriorating, and in December 1937, Jan left Lowry and returned to Los Angeles. As the last two letters of this section reveal, Lowry sank into a state of alcoholic despair, somehow got in trouble with the Mexican police, and ended up spending Christmas and New Year's 1937/38 in jail in Oaxaca. It was not until July 1938 that he, too, travelled to Los Angeles, no doubt in the hope of attempting a reconciliation with Jan.

1 : *From* LOWRY *to* AIKEN

MSPC UBC 1–74; BREIT 3

5 Woodville Road,
Blackheath,
London SE 3.

[early 1929]

I have lived only nineteen years and all of them more or less badly. And yet the other day, when I sat in a Lyons (one of those grubby little places which poor Demarest loved, and the grubbier the better, and so do I)[1] I became suddenly and beautifully alive. I read . . . I lay in the warm sweet grass on a blue May morning, my chin in a dandelion, my hands in clover, and drowsed there like a bee . . . blue days behind me stretched like a chain of deep blue pools of magic, enchanted, silent, timeless . . . days before me murmured of blue sea mornings, noons of gold, green evenings streaked with lilac . . .[2]

I sat opposite the Bureau-de-change. The great grey tea urn perspired. But as I read, I became conscious only of a blur of faces: I let the tea that had mysteriously appeared grow clammy and milk starred, the half veal and ham pie remain in its crinkly paper; vaguely, as though she had been speaking upon another continent, I heard the girl opposite me order some more Dundee cake. My pipe went out.

— I lay by the hot white sand-dunes . . .
Small yellow flowers, sapless and squat and spiny,
Stared at the sky. And silently there above us,
Day after day, beyond our dreams and knowledge,
Presences swept, and over us streamed their shadows,
Swift and blue, or dark . . .[3]

---

1 See Aiken's *Blue Voyage* (London: Gerald Howe, 1927): "I remember that you refused to have tea with me, at a Lyons or A.B.C. because they were 'such grubby little places' . . . But as for me, I like them; and the grubbier the better" (342). William Demarest is the protagonist of *Blue Voyage*. A "Lyons" is an English tea-room.
2 See Aiken's "Palimpsest: A Deceitful Portrait," *Coterie* 5 (Autumn 1920): 15. Lowry has quoted correctly from the poem (starting from "I lay in the warm sweet grass") except for having deleted the hyphen in "blue-sea." The poem is reprinted as part IV, sections iii and v of Aiken's *The House of Dust: A Symphony* (Boston: Four Seas, 1920). Cf. letter 34 in which Lowry mentions his reading of "old Coteries."
3 "Palimpsest: A Deceitful Portrait," 16.

I paid the bill and went out. I crossed the Strand and walked down Villiers street to the Embankment. I looked up at the sea gulls, high in sunlight.[1] The sunlight roared above me like a vast invisible sea. The crowd of faces wavered and broke and flowed.[2]

Sometime when you come to London, Conrad Aiken, wilst hog it over the way somewhere with me?[3] You will forgive my presumption, I think, in asking you this.

I am in fact hardly conscious myself of my own presumption. It seems quite fated that I should write this letter just like this on this warm bright day while outside a man shouts Rag-a-bone, Rag-a-bone. My letter may not even interest you; It may not be your intention *ever* to come to London even to chivy up your publishers.

While on the subject of publishers I might as well say that I find a difficulty bordering upon impossibility in getting your Nocturne of Remembered Spring.[4] Have you got a spare copy of this in Rye[5] that you could sell me? If you have, it would be a good excuse for you to write to tell me so. You could also tell me whether, if you are coming to London any time, you would have any time to see me. Charing X is only a quarter of an hour away from here. But perhaps this letter has infuriated you so much that you have not read thus far. te-thrum te-thrum;

te-thrum te-thrum;[6]

Malcolm Lowry.

---

1 See Aiken's "Movements from a Symphony: Sudden Death," *Coterie* 3 (Dec. 1919): "Smiled for a moment at sea-gulls high in sunlight" (56). Reprinted as part II, section x of *The House of Dust*.

2 See Aiken's "Movements from a Symphony: 'Overtones,'" *Coterie* 3 (Dec. 1919): "Sunlight above him / Roars like a vast invisible sea" (53) and "The crowd of faces wavers and breaks and flows" (54). Reprinted as part II, section vii of *The House of Dust*.

3 See *Blue Voyage*: "'Wilst hog it with me over the way?'" (2). The American edition — (New York: Scribner's, 1927) — contains a variant spelling: "'Willst'" (2). Cf. also Aiken's "The Orange Moth," *Bring! Bring! and Other Stories* (New York: Boni & Liveright, 1925): "'. . . where are we going to hog it, tonight?'" (162).

4 Conrad Aiken, *Nocturne of Remembered Spring and Other Poems* (Boston: Four Seas, 1917).

5 In January 1924 Aiken bought "Jeake's House" in Rye, Sussex. At the time of this letter, however, he was living in Cambridge, Massachusetts, where he had been acting as a tutor of English at Harvard University the year before. Lowry has mistakenly assumed that Aiken is still living in England.

6 "te-thrum te-thrum": Refrain running through Aiken's *Blue Voyage* meant to suggest the sound of a ship's engine (222, 223, 224, 359, 360).

2 : *From* LOWRY *to* AIKEN

MS H 2493; MSPC UBC 1–74; BREIT 4

5   5 Woodville Road
Blackheath.

Tuesday night.
[12 March 1929]

10   Sir. (which is a cold but respectful exordium)

It has been said by no less a personage than Chamon Lall once general Editor of a quarterly of which you were an American Editor that — sorry I'm wrong. It has been said by no less a personage than *Russell Green*[1] (and I don't say that it is an original aphorism because one of his others

15   'Sentimentality is a name given to the emotions of others' is sheer Oscar Wilde) that the only criterion of love is the degree of impatience with which you wait for the postman.[2]

Well, I am a boy and you (respectfully again) are a man old enough to be my father, and so I may not talk of love in the way that Russell

20   Green intended, but all the same, I may here substitute love for — shall we say — *filial affection* and, to apply the aphorism, since I wrote to you, my attitude towards postmen has completely changed. Once they were merely bourgeoisie beetles carrying their loads. Now they are divine but hopeless messengers. The mirror opposite the foot of my bed reflects the

25   window set between two mysterious green curtains, to the right of the head of my bed and this window — I cheat myself that this it is good for my health — I keep open all night. In the mirror I can also see the road behind me when it is light. Early yesterday morning, it must have been about Dawn, when I imagined that I could actually *see* in the mirror, I

30   saw a long and never ending procession of postmen labouring along this road. The letters were delivered and among a great pile for other people was one for me from you.

---

1 Russell Green (b. 1893) succeeded Chaman Diwan Lall (b. 1892) as editor of the London little magazine *Coterie, A Quarterly: Art, Prose, and Poetry*. Chaman Lall acted as editor from 1919–20, Russell Green from winter 1920–21, and later, 1925–27, when the journal was continued under the title *New Coterie*. Conrad Aiken was an American editor of *Coterie* from December 1919–Winter 1921 and "appeared to be the agent between the journal and its sizeable number of regular American contributors" (Tollers, *British Literary Magazines* 110). All three editors included their own work in the journal.

2 Both aphorisms are exact quotations from Russell Green's "Aphorisms," *Coterie* 5 (Autumn 1920): 36–37.

I cannot now remember what you said.

You were pleased that I ended off my letter to you with *te-thrum te-thrum*; *te-thrum te-thrum*;[1] but I can't remember anything else except your handwriting. Of course it was, as I realised bitterly when I woke up, merely a rose-festooned illusion.[2] You had no intention of writing me. [—] can't express myself properly here sorry [—] But I'm wandering off the point.

The point is this.

I suppose there are few things you would hate more than to be invested with any academic authority. Well, this I shall say. Next October I am going to Cambridge for three or four years to try and get an English Tripos and a degree.[3] Until October I am more or less of a free lance and a perpetual source of anxiety to a bewildered parent. The bewildered parent in question would be willing to pay you 5 or 6 guineas a week (I should say six personally, but tacitly) if you would tolerate me for any period you like to name between now and then as a member of your household.

Let me hasten to say that I would efface myself and not get in the way of your inspiration when it comes toddling along, that my appetite is flexible and usually entirely satisfied by cheese, that although I can't play chess[4] and know little of the intricacies of gladioli — I too have heard the sea sound in strange waters — *sh-sh-sh* like the hush in a conch shell,[5] and I can wield a fair tennis racket.[6]

All I want to know is why I catch my breath in a sort of agony when I read;

> The lazy sea-waves crumble along the beach
> With a whirring sound like wind in bells

---

1 See letter 1.

2 See Aiken's "Cabaret," *Coterie* 3 (Dec. 1919): "And dance once more in a rose-festooned illusion" (52). This poem was reprinted as part III, section ix of *The House of Dust*.

3 Lowry was accepted at St. Catharine's College, Cambridge, in March 1929 and entered the College in October. In June 1932 he received a third-class honours degree. Triposes are the examinations taken for the honours degree.

4 Chess games figure prominently in *Blue Voyage*.

5 See *Blue Voyage*: "The sound of the sea came softly here, muted, like the hush heard in a conch-shell: *Sh-sh-sh*" (16) and "the softened *sh sh* of the sea" (47).

6 According to Aiken's son, John Aiken, Aiken "had been a notable tennis-player at Harvard," and, during the 1930s in Rye, was "London and tennis correspondent of the *New Yorker* under the pseudonym of Samuel Jeake Jr. . . ." (*Conrad Aiken Remembered* 22).

He lies outstretched on the yellow wind-worn sands
Reaching his lazy hands
Among the golden grains and sea-white shells . . .[1]

5 And I want to be in Rye at twilight and lean *myself* by the wall of the ancient town — *myself*, like ancient wall and dust and sky, and the purple dusk, grown old, grown old in heart.[2] Remember when I write like this, remember that I am not a schoolboy writing a gushing letter to Jeffrey Farnol[3] or somebody.

10 (Remember too that you must respect me a little for having such an intense admiration for your poetry. I know you are a great man in America and that you have your own school of followers, but to me — in the dismal circle in which I move nobody had ever heard of you, my most intellectual moments, such as they are, being spent entirely alone, it was as though I 15 had discovered you and I like to preserve this absurd idea in my childish mind and give myself a great deal of unearned credit for having done so.)[4]

Well, to continue I won't weary you by eulogising what you know yourself to be good (good is quite stupendously the wrong word but I don't want to appear to gush, you understand.)

20 I know almost before you reply — if you do reply — that you are either away or that you would not have the slightest intention of acting for the shortest period of time as my guardian and/or tutor, but at any rate do you mind reading this letter sympathetically because you must have been pretty much the same as me in heart when you were a kid? And 25 I do want to learn from you and to read your earliest and most inaccessible works and perhaps even your contributions to the Dial.[5] I go back home (here is my address — Inglewood, Caldy, Cheshire) next Monday. Nobody reads at home: the only paper we take is The British Weekly;

---

1 Aiken, "Movements from a Symphony: 'Overtones,' " *Coterie* 3 (Dec. 1919): 54. Lowry has omitted the period after "bells"; otherwise the passage is quoted correctly.
2 See Aiken's "Seven Twilights," *Priapus and the Pool and Other Poems* (New York: Boni & Liveright, 1925):
   Now by the wall of the little town I lean
   Myself, like ancient wall and dust and sky,
   And the purple dusk, grown old, grown old in heart. (80)
3 John Jeffrey Farnol (1878–1952), English novelist; author of *The Broad Highway* (1910) and *The Amateur Gentleman* (1913) amongst others.
4 In fact, Russell Lowry, Malcolm's brother, claims that it was *he* who first introduced Malcolm to Aiken's *Blue Voyage* (Bradbrook, *Malcolm Lowry: His Art and Early Life* xiii).
5 Aiken was a contributing editor of *The Dial* from 1917–19 (although his name does not appear on the masthead in 1919) (Joost, *Years of Transition: The Dial 1912–1920* 196).

there are few books in the house more exciting than Religions and Religion by James Hope Moulton[1] (although a careful searcher might find in a somewhat inaccessible region Donne, Chatterton, The Smell of Lebanon,[2] Crabbe's Inebriety and Blue Voyage) and although I have had
5   a certain amount of youthful success as a writer of slow and slippery blues[3] it is as much as my life is worth to play anything in the house — that doesn't worry me so much — but when they see me writing anything serious they don't exactly discourage me but tell me that it should be subordinate to my real work. What my real work is, heaven only knows,
10 as the only other department that I have had any success in, is in writing seriously and that success rarely meant acceptance but quite often sincere encouragement from people whose opinion could hardly be taken to be humble.

But I don't want to worry you with anything I've written and indeed
15 after reading this rackety incoherence you would probably be extremely averse to being worried in that way. Look here you don't hate me already do you? (hate is too dignified a word.)

Now *if* you are in London any time between when you receive this letter and Sunday (inclus) could you let me know, because you see we
20 have put things on somewhat of a business footing?

I could meet you anywhere in London. And anytime. Between now and Montag. If not write to my address in the dismal swamp.

Klio klio.[4]

25   C.M. Lowry.

---

1 James Hope Moulton (1863–1917), classical scholar educated at the Leys School and King's College, Cambridge; author of *Religions and Religion: A Study of the Science of Religion, Pure and Applied* (London: Charles H. Kelly, 1913). His father, Rev. William Fiddian Moulton, was at one time headmaster of the Leys School, Cambridge which Lowry (and his brothers) attended from 1923–Easter 1927.

2 *The Smell of Lebanon: Twenty-four Syrian Folk-songs*, coll. S.H. Stephan, trans. E. Powys Mathers ([Leipzig]: Talybont Dyffryn Merioneth, 1928) [selection reprinted from *Modern Palestinian Parallels to the Song of Songs*, 1923].

3 Lowry had by this time, with Ronald Hill, published two songs: *Three Little Dog-Gone Mice: Just the Latest Charleston Fox-Trot Ever* (London: Worton David, 1927) and *I've Said Good-Bye to Shanghai* (London: B. Feldman, 1927).

4 "Klio klio": A recurring refrain in Aiken's *Blue Voyage* used to suggest the cries of seagulls (304, 305, 307, 309, 310, 312).

3 : *From* LOWRY *to* AIKEN

TS H 2494

5   [Inglewood, Caldy]

[March/April 1929]

Comments about the poems:

10   I have included only the poems which I thought would aid you in getting a better underſtanding of what type of person I am. That does not mean that I'm a raving radical or some maladjuſted fool trying to complain about my fortunes. As a matter of faſt, I am quite carefree and easy to get along with. I have only one word to say in defense for my work
15 and myself; we're both young and could stand a goodly amount of polishing. Mr. Aiken, I plead with you to give me a frank criticism and a word of advice. I need it badly in the right way. And that is: Do you think I have any individual style of my own or am I unconciously imitating someone's work. I have been told by some that I have a tendency to rely
20 upon Whitman. I think not. I feel that my work is going to be and is different both in text and spirit. But do I show it. Please give me your frankeſt opinion.

     In my prelude to the Iron and Steel series,[1] I have placed myself besides Whitman and Sandburg as a singer. I feel that I have a right to.
25 I did not intend the eyes of mortal man to read a word of the iron and steel group until I had eſtablished myself as a singer comparable to both. Perhaps the day will never come, if it didn't I intended to deſtroy every word, because I, only a nineteen year old youngſter, would be called a fool for attempting to even think myself a man comparable in standing to
30 Whitman and Sandburg. As you read the Prelude please remember that I haved lived everyword and that all I need is a better medium of expression for clearer thoughts and words. I hope that I will receive either your honeſt encouragement or your frankeſt discouragement.

35   Please excuse *poor* typing.

---

1   This was presumably an early collеſtion Lowry had made of his poems; no draſt of the series is extant. I am uncertain, since the appended four poems are filed separately from this letter in the Huntington Aiken Colleſtion, whether they belong with this letter. These poems appear in Kathleen Scherf's *The Colleſted Poetry of Malcolm Lowry* (Vancouver: U of British Columbia P, 1992) 40–42.

[*Poems enclosed with letter 3* (TS H 2489)]

Spiderweb

5   The moment hangs from Heaven like a webbed
Bridge to that invisible wherein
Necessity's dimensions sometimes win
Harbors of air, from which the storm has ebbed.

10   But we are spiders. And with waiting eyes
We see sail by, beyond old reach and hope,
Doomed wings of distance, small as periscope,
While dining on a diet of dead flies;

15   The black and gold, the gross and gullible,
We are those spiders who of themselves have spun
Nets of sad time to sway against the sun —
Broken by secrets time can never tell.

20

Alcoholic

I died so many times when drunk
That sober I became
25   Like water where a ship was sunk
That never knew its name.

Old barnacles upon my sides
Ringed round with pitch and toss
30   Were given me by mermaid brides,
Immaculate as moss.

Here now, with neither kin nor quest,
I am so full of sea
35   That whales may make of me a nest
And go to sleep in me.

(Those angels of the upper air
Who sip of the divine
40   May find a haven holier
but less goodbye than mine.)

Dark Path

By no specific dart of gold,
No single singing have I found
5   This path. It travels, dark and cold,
Through dead volcanoes underground.

Here flicker yet the sulphurous
charred ends of fires long since I knew.
10   Long since, I think, and thinking thus,
Ignite, daemonically; anew.

Yet, burning, burning, burning Lord,
Know how this path muſt likewise come
15   Through multitudinous discord
The awful and the long way home.

20   Sonnet

This ruin now, where moonlight walks alone
Uncovering the cobweb and the rose,
I have been here before; loved each dim stone;
25   If there were shadows I was one of those.
There liſtening, as in a shell, I heard
Through some invisible, unlettered whole
One true, if not at all eternal, word
Wrung from the weird mutations of the soul;
30   Palace or hovel, ruin will at laſt
Make peace of what is waſte; take for a time
The hungry future and the bloody paſt
Into her night. Only the moon will climb
Up broken stairs to towerd might have been
35   And reſt a little, like some poor, blind queen.

cheery ain't they? Spirit took the spider, don't
    know why — love l.

40

14

4 : *From* LOWRY *to* AIKEN

MS H 2498

5

[S*t* Catharine's Coll.
Camb.]

[October 1930]

10 My dear Conrad

Many thanks for your letter; and also for shading, annotating, and connotating the disbursements;[1] myself have had quite a smoothly smiling sort of letter from the old man, which presages well for the future. . . I've moved into new rooms (but the same address) and spent yesterday

15 decorating them, and drank a bottle of whiskey in the process. Half my books seem to have been stolen, blast somebody's eyes. But to make it worse I can't remember precisely what I *did* have. My Sir Thomas Browne's gone, anyway, I'm sure of that: and a Thomas Heywood, in the mermaid edition, or did I lend that to somebody?: and 'Dubliners,' —

20 why Dubliners? — —

'Experiment' is out.[2] I'll send you one as soon as I can lay hands on a copy. Everybody thinks the first prelude's swell — but most everybody is mystified by the third.[3] Who is this person who must be disembowelled, and shown in the *marktplatz*?.[4] But I dare say they'll find out, soon

25 enough. There's a large poster of 'Experiment,' with your name in large

---

1 Lowry had been sending chapters of his novel, *Ultramarine*, to Aiken for corrections. *Ultramarine* was published in June 1933 by Jonathan Cape. The manuscript of *Ultramarine* contained in the Huntington Library [Aik 3381] is inscribed by Aiken: "June 4 [1931] 10:30 p.m. Dear Malcolm — I wind my watch for you — but you should be winding my watch for me. ——— C.A."

2 *Experiment*, a Cambridge literary magazine, began in 1928 under the editorship of William Empson. The editors from 1929 to 1931, Jacob Bronowski and Hugh Sykes Davies, changed the editorial policy and decided that the magazine "could represent non-Cambridge writers" (Sawyer, *British Literary Magazines* 177); hence the inclusion of Aiken's poems in the October 1930 issue, no doubt via Lowry who had introduced Aiken to the publishing editor of *Experiment*, Gerald Noxon, in September 1930. Lowry himself had published a short story, "Port Swettenham," in the February 1930 (number five) issue.

3 Conrad Aiken, "Three Preludes," *Experiment* 6 (Oct. 1930): 33–36. These were later published as preludes "i," "x," and "xxxv" in Aiken's *Preludes for Memnon* (New York: Scribner's, 1931).

4 See "xxxv," *Preludes for Memnon*: "God take his bowels out, and break his bones, / And show him in the market as he is . . ." (64).

letters, and all the little suckers in small letters. Damp from the womb!

I played *hockey* for Cambridge town against Fenstanton last Saturday. I've decided on hockey as against rugger, because their team secretary called round (actually!) and said that I was *wanted*, because I hit the ball firmly and hard, and was really quite a person. I'm playing against Peterborough to-morrow, and Trinity Hall college on Saturday, and my own college the week after next sometime which really should be damned good fun. It pleases me immensely playing against my own college. Yet at school I should have hated to play against my own house. . . Still St Caths is different. It looks like a barracks generally. The dining room looks like a mortuary. The college that god forgot! Or a moloch which, sometimes, raises its stone hand to strike — —

Nearly all the other colleges have something cloistral and Canterbury-ian about them, or have produced a Marlowe or a Milton. I'm having dinner to-night in Pembroke in Grays' old room. And both Crashaw & Christopher Smart lived in the same block! . .[1] Canterbury Cathedral.

Christ, that place has ceased to be a fact: I feel it, darkly, in my blood; in the very plasm of my blood, as one might say: transmuted — by some kinship with the insentient as well as the living — into the matrix of my life. The Norman tower. The dark entry. The baptistry garden. Trinity chapel, where lie the canonized bones of St Wilfred and St Odo! St Odo! . .[2] Or am I at Crecy, then, with the Black Prince?[3] I walk gravely beside him. My sword is in its leathern scabbard. My leathern shield is embossed with the lilies of France, the flowers-de-luce. The surcoat is of quilted cotton, faced with velvet, and embroidered with emblems in silk and gold. . .

Well, my boy, I shall write you a long letter, dictated to my typist. Remember what I've said to you about drink and women. I don't want you to get mixed up in any-er-drinking bouts. I never did, and look what I am to-day. There's no need to talk about that other little matter, self-abuse, of course not. I know you don't know anything about that. You won't even be tempted. None of your brothers have been tempted. None

---

1 Milton resided in Christ's College from 1625–32; Marlowe in Corpus Christi from 1581–87; Thomas Gray in Peterhouse from 1734–38 and 1744–56; Richard Crashaw in Pembroke from 1631–34 and Peterhouse 1636–38 (he became a Fellow of Peterhouse in 1637); and Christopher Smart was a Fellow of Pembroke in 1745.

2 Saint Wilfrid, Bishop of York, and Saint Odo, Archbishop of Canterbury, were both at one time supposed to be buried in Canterbury Cathedral.

3 "the Black Prince": Edward, prince of Wales (1330–76); eldest son of Edward III. Commanded the right wing of the English forces in the battle of Crecy (1346). His coat of arms, like his father's, included the French fleur-de-lys. His tomb may still be seen in Canterbury Cathedral.

5

And Then there came a wize man from over the hills . . .

Facsimile reproduction of drawing enclosed with letter 4 (H 2487)

of the Lowry-Lowries of Inglewood-Inglewood have ever drunk, or been tempted in any way whatsoever. And money — please give me a careful account of everything you spend — I think you spend too much money on shooting, and repairing your gun —

As ever
Malcolm

I have a gramophone, with 2 records.

you don't mind waiting a little while for your 'Blue Voyage.'? . . I'd like a game of ping-pong with you, my god! And a visit to Mr Neeves.[1] Or a walk through Gods acre.[2]

---

1 Tom Neeves was the owner of the Ship Inn, Rye, where Lowry and Aiken would drink together. See also Lowry's reference to his letter to Tom Neeves in letter 84.
2 "God's acre": a cemetery. Cf. Aiken's poem, "God's Acre," *Priapus and the Pool*, 28–31.

5 : *From* LOWRY *to* AIKEN

MS H 2496

5

2 Batemanstreet
Cambridge.

[December 1930]

10 My very dear old Conrad:

I am a hell of a god-awful correspondent as you know, but Christmas is coming, and Donner and Blitzen are having their manes combed, and anyway I owe you one. I am working hard here, mostly on the novel.[1] Charlotte Haldane[2] (the wife of J.B.S.) has offered me her body if I finish *15* the revision of it this term. This is all right but I told her that I would masturbate after finishing each chapter in that case with the result that I would run out of semen before *la moment critique*. I think this is very funny. She is very pretty. I don't think I have ever seen anybody so pretty. I read the first chapter, revised and intensified and polished; and she was *20* a bit drunk and fell down on her knees and wept; so I didn't have the heart to tell her that if there was anything good about it it had been copied from you. Christ what a breeze!

Everybody in Cambridge now says Christ what a breeze; and one is not jeered at for an uncritical remark if one says such and such a thing is *25* the 'bees knees' because I tell them you say it.[3] Everybody thought your poems were marvellous, and thinks you are a great man which you are, and a gentle man because you say Christ what a breeze, and bees knees.

I drank a lot of whiskey with Charlotte Haldane last night who is a don's wife and was nearly sick into her mouth when I was kissing her. She *30* says she loves me. This is rather awkward, but very gratifying. She has just published a novel, Chatto and Windus, on monyzygotic twins. It is

---

1 *Ultramarine.*

2 Charlotte (Franken) Haldane (1894–1969), author; married to the British biochemist and geneticist, John Burdon Sanderson Haldane (1892–1964). Charlotte Haldane hosted a literary circle at her "Roebuck House" in Cambridge into which Lowry was introduced by John Davenport in 1929. Among the artists to gather there were William Empson, Michael Redgrave, Hugh Sykes Davies, Martin Case, and Kathleen Raine. Her novel, *I Bring Not Peace* — (London: Chatto & Windus, 1932) — portrays Lowry as "James Dowd."

3 Cf. Aiken's *Great Circle* (London: Wishart, 1933): " 'Christ, what a breeze' " (221, 222), and " 'It was the cat's pajamas. It was the bee's knees' " (315). Cf. also Killorin (169, 174).

good and I have reviewed it favourably in an Oxford paper *Revolt*.[1] It is
not overflowing with sensibility: and the architechtonics are all away to
hell: it is nothing very much, you understand, only very exciting and quite
amusingly bawdy. It is full of bloody awful cock, however, even worse than
Ultramarine in that respect if you can believe it. Its amateurish, but
exciting. She is a first-rate biologist and she wants to meet you. This is
not a very good letter. It is sort of early Portrait of the Artist business,
without cohesion, however, and a sprinkling of bad Hemingway. Never
mind. There is a don's wife in Trinity who has Gonorrhea. Three of my
friends have Gonorrhea and I go with them to Addenbrooks hospital and
see them irrigated. As for me, I wish I had Gonorrhea, because that would
mean I'd had a good fuck which I haven't for the hell of a time. I'm all
inhibited in that direction, and have lost my jumbly girl, and am having
a bad time with masturbation. I think I am glad I have lost my jumbly
girl. Thank god I won't have to buy her horrid little sister a Christmas
present! It's damned good your having a radio: but I like a gramophone
better sometimes, you get such awful programmes from 2LO, &
occasionaly even Königwusterhausen[2] lets you down. I know a man who
makes the noises in broadcast plays from the B.B.C & we went down to
London briefly on one occasion and I saw how it was done. I also know
a man called Redgrave,[3] who reads poetry there. He read The Hollow
men last week, and we all want him to broadcast you and he wants to and
is going to if he can and I have lent him my Priapus and the Pool because
you can't buy it in England. The man who makes the noises is a
homosexual, but quite decent, and I know him because we are taking part
in a film called Bank Holiday,[4] a sort of 'Last Moment' business, next

---

1 Lowry is referring to Haldane's novel *Brother to Bert* (London: Chatto & Windus,
1930); according to Haldane, this novel was inspired by Johannes Lange's *Crime as
Destiny: A Study of Criminal Twins* which she translated in 1931 (*Truth Will Out* 29). I
have been unable to locate Lowry's review.
2 "Königs Wusterhausen": location of Deutschlandsender, a long wave, arts and
education, radio station in Germany.
3 Sir Michael Scudamore Redgrave (1908–85). British stage and film actor, educated
at Clifton College and Magdalene College, Cambridge. Redgrave was one of the
members of Charlotte Haldane's literary set and a joint editor (with John Davenport
and Hugh Sykes) of *Cambridge Poetry, 1930*, Hogarth Living Poets 13 (London:
Hogarth Press, 1930), in which was published Lowry's poem, "For Nordahl Grieg
ship's fireman." In his autobiography, *In My Mind's Eye*, Redgrave speaks of reading
Eliot's "The Waste Land" over the BBC, but not "The Hollow Men" (74). According
to Muriel Bradbrook, the only person other than Conrad Aiken to receive an official
review copy of *Under the Volcano* was Michael Redgrave, " 'the actor, an old and good
college friend of [Lowry's]' " (15).
4 The film *Bank Holiday* (or *Three on a Weekend* in the U.S.A.) was directed by Sir

March. Strange!

I have been elected the Editor of Cambridge Poetry — published by the Hogarth Press every year in Hogarth Livi[n]g Poets series.[1] God — God knows why. Not only my poetic faculty but also my capacity for plagiarism has gone west. But this seems to be an honour. In fact it was the only ambition I had left up here. I must be the first Editor who doesn't know the difference between a trochee and a spondee: and hardly between a sonnet and a chant-royal.

However. My other ambition is to stop masturbating. Which is just bloody impossible. If there were a book on that there would be some sense in making me Editor! I love everything, from soap dishes to medicine bottles. This is damned awful, and all-poisoning: as you remarked 'the most all poisoning of all illnesses. But we return to our vomit.' . .[2] Yet ah remain, niggah, and ahs so mighty dat de tornadoes and de hurricanes dey just follow me aroun' like little pet dogs, yeah, just like little pet dogs, an ah spits lightning an ah breathes thunder and ah'm the DOOM of Israel . . . And ah'm the champion wirepuller in Tennessee —

I'd just love a copy of John Death,[3] Conrad, it was sweet of you to suggest it. And I'll buy a Selected poems[4] off you — and by god I haven't got that copy of *Blue Voyage* yet, curse me and curse me. Well, I'll see you soon, and we'll break the bloody buskins of the town, and drown in the white winds of the real day.

Better to fall with Icarus than thrive with Smith.[5]

Malcolm.

Carol Reed (1906–76) and produced by Edward Black in 1938. The story was written by Hans Wilhelm and Rodney Ackland. It would seem that the film took longer to produce than Lowry had expected and he stopped "taking part" in it, for his name does not appear amongst the cast. The friend whom Lowry mentions here, however, could very well be his friend from the Leys School and Cambridge, Michael Rennie (1909–71), who played the part of the guardsman in *Bank Holiday*.

1 The proposed issue of *Cambridge Poetry* to be edited by Lowry was never published.

2 "As a dog returneth to his vomit, / so a fool returneth to his folly" (Prov. 26.11); "The dog *is* turned to his own vomit again" (2 Pet. 2.22). See also *Blue Voyage*: "This is what it is to be in love. Unmitigated suffering. The most all-poisoning of all illnesses. And nevertheless, it's the chief motive of all art — we return to our vomit" (195). See also *Ultramarine*: "— let them return to their own vomit —" (40).

3 Conrad Aiken, *John Deth: A Metaphysical Legend, and Other Poems* (New York: Scribner's, 1930).

4 Conrad Aiken, *Selected Poems* (New York: Scribner's, 1929).

5 Frank Smith is a character in *Blue Voyage*. See Lowry's letter to Nordahl Grieg of 8 September 1931 in *Swinging the Maelstrom: New Perspectives on Malcolm Lowry*, ed. Sherrill Grace: "Was it not better to fall with Icarus than thrive with Smith?" (47). Cf. also *Blue Voyage*: "Better be like Smith and gather my rosebuds while I may . . ." (162).

6 : *From* LOWRY *to* AIKEN

MS H 2500

5
Globe Hotel
Hills Road — Camb.

Wednesday
[11 March 1931]

10 Well, buddy, you know what a damned awful correspondent I am by now
which is all the fault of my god-complex — is it? — anyway here I am
again 'as large as life and twice as unnatural', a little bit tight, or at any
rate a pleasant jingle, which is informing my consciousness of how
pleasant it will be to get down to Rye again and see you: that is not to say
15 that my consciousness in this regard is any the less intense when I am
coldly and despairingly sober. I don't know so much about the continued
despair, in many respects it's just so much bloody nonsense, but in other
respects my lack of indifference towards life being divided by this persistent 3, LXX/.333,[1] is deep rooted in an honest enough transmission. Royall
20 Snow, Who would wish to be Royall Snow?[2] or Mrs Untermeyer, the
first?[3] or any of the ignoble army of unmartyrs Who are incapable of
objectifying their own misery.

The influence that keeps me away from St Catharines really reveals
to me how little to myself Death ever leaves me. At all events the force
25 of this revulsion has kept me away now for a whole term from my own
college; I hate to connect the place with anything but the buttery[4] who
you can buy sherry or to give a glimpse of the curiosity that has been on
the point of moving me. Now however I am asking myself if I shall stay

---

1 LXX divided by .333 ("this persistent 3") yields a recurring decimal: 210.210210.
2 Royall Henderson Snow, American critic who reviewed Aiken's *Priapus and the
Pool* in "Agonized Adoration," *New Republic* 21 June 1922: 113.
3 "Mrs Untermeyer, the first?": Jean Starr (1886-1970), American poet and first wife
of the American writer and editor, Louis Untermeyer (1885-1977). In *Lorelei Two*
Clarissa Lorenz writes of how Louis and Jean's marital problems mirrored hers and
Conrad's (59, 75). Louis Untermeyer was the author of a number of critical reviews of
Aiken's poetry and editor of several anthologies of American and British poetry that
included Aiken's work. The relationship between the two was always that of steady,
though polite, rivalry. See Aiken's "The Ivory Tower: Louis Untermeyer as Critic,"
New Republic 10 May 1919: 58-60, and Untermeyer's reply in the same issue, 60-61.
4 "buttery": In the colleges of Oxford and Cambridge this is the place where ale,
bread, butter, etc. are kept. The "residence" of members of the college is recorded by
the appearance of their names in the buttery-books.

away for ever from the fear of this muddle about motives. An intricate
tangle! . . Anyway, to hell with it. Are we no greater than the noise we
make along life's blind atomic pilgrimage whereon by crass chance billeted
we go because our brains and bones and cartilage will have it so? . .[1] One
5 mild, two bitters, one Gin. De Kuyper's old square face.[2]

> Our father which art in earth
> our mother which art inturd . . .

as Martin Case[3] remarked

10

Thursday.

. . . Well, for christ sake, away with all this melancholy. To day has
dawned like the first day, the blessed day of days, when god saw that it
15 was good — — I have been down the road as far as the Varsity Express
Motors Ltd to buy a ticket, March 14th, no x 18736, ref no 611, from
Cambridge to London, pick up at Drummer st, Run. Time 1:30, for 1
adults at 5/-, no children at nothing, returning date nothing and time also
nothing or less than nothing, which will land me in Regent st. whence I
20 shall get directly as I can to Rye. I don't know what time I shall arrive at
Rye, so don't bother Jerry[4] to get me any supper, but if you could leave

---

1 Quotation from Edward Arlington Robinson's (1869–1935) poem "Man Against
the Sky." Lowry may have read this poem in Aiken's *Modern American Poets*, published
by Secker in 1922. Lowry uses the word "life's" where Robinson uses "our"; otherwise
he has quoted correctly from the poem.
2 Lowry is referring to the gin distilled by John de Kuyper & Sons; it was probably
called "square face gin" because of the unique shape of the bottles, which were squarish
and flat on the front side. Cf. *Ultramarine*: " '. . . have a slice of old squareface' " (49)
and " 'Old squareface, please' " (151).
3 Martin Case was a student of biochemistry at Cambridge and an assistant of J.B.S.
Haldane. According to Muriel Bradbrook, he and Lowry met at the Haldanes'
residence during one of Charlotte Haldane's literary soirées after which they became
friends and drinking companions (129). Charlotte Haldane's novel, *Brother to Bert* (see
letter 5), is dedicated to Martin Case. The passage quoted by Lowry seems to be an
echo of Aiken's poem, "Changing Mind," from *John Deth and Other Poems*:
> My father which art in earth
> From whom I got my birth,
> What is it that I inherit?
> . . . .
> My mother which art in tomb
> Who carriedst me in thy womb,
> What is it that I inherit? (120)
4 "Jerry": Nickname of Aiken's second wife, Clarissa M. Lorenz (1899–), to whom
Aiken dedicated *Blue Voyage*. Lowry thought the dedication of *Blue Voyage* to

me a couple of hard-boiled hen-fruit in a cupboard somewhere that would be — the bees knees[1] I was going to say — —

Yes, this latest Cambridge sausage was as clever a piece of work as ever you saw in a bleeding lifetime, a monster of more than calculation, as you would say, which has left me quite exhausted.

How is the Austrian girl?[2] I believe you showed me her photograph on one occasion and it seemed to me then that she was definitely one of the guards. Am I right?. . A kind of Frau Fletcherchen. Or is she Fraülein? Anyway we shall see what we shall see what we shall see —

The preludes (which I did not acknowledge) — well! Just-er-well! If you won't jeer at me for an uncritical remark, as Cummings might have said, they are among the huge fragilities before which comment is disgusting. Darks edge remains my favourite among them.[3]

Which I did not acknowledge? And after all why should I? . . . is this mr demarest? not william demarest? not william demarest of *Yonkers*? . .[4] yet, even so, whats' his address?

Besides I wanted to wait developments which took the form of other contributions — otherwise the book would be a book of preludes published by the Hogarth press, your old friends,[5] & no more, which would be a far better book anyway than the postulated anthology, but scarcely according to the academic points of the compass. Actually the contributions have been so grim, either of the:

```
    ' — the wind was soughing in the boughs — ' type
or the    when death        came the critic
          death             came
               when              into
          when   d    e          the
               a     t          roo
                 h                    m      type —
```

"C.M.L." significant because it coincided with his own initials: Clarence Malcolm Lowry. Lorenz is the author of *Lorelei Two: My Life with Conrad Aiken* (Athens: U of Georgia P, 1983).

1 "bees knees": See letter 5, n. 3, p. 19.

2 See Aiken's 25 April 1931 letter to Walter Piston (Killorin 174) for a reference to the Austrian girl who has been staying with him and Clarissa.

3 Apparently Aiken had sent Lowry some of his preludes to be included in the next issue of *Cambridge Poetry* which Lowry was editing. The last line of prelude "xxxiii" reads: "At the dark's edge how great the darkness is" (*Preludes for Memnon* 62).

4 William Demarest is the protagonist of Aiken's *Blue Voyage*. See *Blue Voyage*: " 'Is this Mr. Demarest?' " (6) and "Saint William of Yonkers" (144).

5 Leonard and Virginia Woolf at The Hogarth Press had published Aiken's *Senlin: A Biography* in 1925.

and in the latter case being without any poetry separable and unidentifiable with the so-called strangeness to justify its existence on paper at all that the project has been postponed and with it inevitably our foul crime against truth tra-la . . .

Meantime, "The dead man spoke to me & begged a penny' (which was not among the ones you sent me but which I learnt by heart some time ago,) is increasingly seeming to me to be one of the greatest poems ever written. . . .

'poor devil why he wants to close his eyes
he wants a charity to close his eyes
and follows me with outstretched palm, from world to world,
and house to house & street to street
under the street lamps & along dark alleys
& sits beside me in my room, & sleeps
Upright with eyes wide open by my bed . . .

&   . . . & all the while
holds, in that void of an unfocussed stare,
My own poor footsteps, saying, I have read
Time in the rock & in the human heart
space in the bloodstream, & those lesser works
written by rose & windflower on the summer, sung
by water & snow, deciphered by the eye
translated by the slaves of memory,
& all that you be you & I be I
or all that, by imagination aping
God, the supreme poet of despair,
I may be you, you me, before our time
knowing the rank intolerable taste of death
& walking dead on the still living earth — 1

. . . I always think of you being damned angry with me for coming back late from Hastings ——————   As ever

Malcolm

---

1 See Aiken's "XLV," *Preludes for Memnon* 79–80. The first line of the poem (as Lowry correctly states) reads: "The dead man spoke to me and begged a penny." Lowry has quoted correctly from the poem except for various alterations in punctuation.

7 : *From* LOWRY *to* AIKEN

MS H 2502

[St. Catharine's College,
Cambridge]

Friday
[24 April 1931]

' — for Jesus sake — '
' — for Jesus sake — '[1]

Well I've juſt had a motorcar turn over on me at fifty-five and I'm pretty
dopey anyhow; and moreover in several sorts of shite — from the 'parrots
paltry pigment' to 'bombs from the bison's bung'[2] and any other sort of
pickled noblemen you like to think of and I feel so that every time I read
a line I break a blood vessel. But to be specific and moſtly matter of faÆt,
& to answer the old man's gut-lifting queſtions.[3] (i) The subjeÆt is general
English Literature, (ii) the exam is on the 20*th* May although this is
subjeÆt to slight alteration fore and aft (iii) There is only one *Examination*
but spread out three hours morning and afternoon for three days or three
days and a half & there are no different *subjeÆts* merely papers on different
departments of English Literature, firſt, an original essay on a subjeÆt we
don't know yet, any given subjeÆt; second, a paper on Chaucer & Langland
and/or the Life & Thought of that period — you answer only six queſtions
out of a whole gamut; third, the Elizabethans — Ben Jonson & his circle
and/or Life & Thought of that period; four, Shakespeare by himself,
contexts, folios, rhymes, rythms, danks & darks,[4] imponderables &
impalpables, the whole of him but with particular attention to Antony &
Cleopatra & Hamlet & Measure for Measure; five — Reſtoration comedy,

---

1 Quotation from Lowry's "PunÆtum Indifferens Skibet Gaar Videre," *Experiment* 7
(Spring 1931): 64. This story was reprinted in revised form as "SeduÆtio Ad Absurdum,"
The Beſt British Short Stories of 1931, ed. Edward O'Brien (New York: Dodd, 1931)
89–107, and was later rewritten and incorporated into chapter 4 of *Ultramarine*; see
Ultramarine (101, 177, 241).
2 See *Ultramarine*: "'And the parrot's household pigment strewn along the deck
. . .'" (271) and "'Bombs from the bison's bung, eh?'" (271).
3 Presumably Lowry's father had been queſtioning Aiken about Part 1 of the
upcoming Tripos which Lowry was to write, as he says here, on 20 May 1931.
4 "danks & darks": Cf. *Blue Voyage*: "How had it so managed to complicate itself
with evil and sensuality and the danks and darks of sex?" (119).

Wycherley & so forth and/or Life & Thought of that period; six —
General criticism paper, Aristotle — Plato — Matthew Arnold —
Coleridge und so weiter:[1] seven, the Preraphaelites, even down to *Mr*
Preraphael himself: eight, the Victorians (and the Orig. Contribution)...

5   This is not quite specific because there will be questions backwards and
forwards on the whole range of Literature which is impossible to foresee.

    (iv) — how well prepared is he in each subject? . . Come on po feet
ah needs you now — remember when ah was a chile you promised to be
kind to me — — [2]

10   What about: — in real 'old man' style — — something like this with
modifications?.

He has a good and clear understanding of the trend of Literature and of
the nature of the questions involved in the tripos, he is a little weak on
15   Langland and on Restoration comedy & I have told him to work those
up during the month left to him, and also to revise the 'criticism' & to do
as much general revision as is reasonably possible. As far as I can judge
from the papers of former years which Malcolm has — er — showed me
they are often of a type which suggests that in preparation for them the
20   student may well be blurred as to the real meaning, the sturm und drang
of Literature, and hate it ever after; moreover the time is so limited, that
for answering them one has to have a mind like a sort of machine gun,
you have no time to think if you are to answer the necessary number of
questions, and no time, except (with luck) in the essay to let yourself go
25   on something you really love! Your answers have to be staccato and angry,
and a brutal concision is demanded of the student. I think success in this
strange examination depends a good deal on temperament. Malcolm is a
slow writer, & an even slower thinker, an abnormally slow thinker, which
although not itself a fault makes him a bad examinee. I have done
30   everything in my power to correct this for his exam but it is one of those
things I have found not only cannot be corrected but ought not to be —
it might make him — *tee-hee!* — artificial and false in his reasoning in
later life. The thought of failing him worries him on your account and he
is quite capable of forgetting all he ever learnt in a flash. Shortly, I think
35   he is the sort of person who can never be tested adequately in the improptu
manner demanded by the tripos. I know he will do his best — I don't
think he will fail, heaven knows we have worked hard enough! tchtch joke

---

1 "und so weiter": German, "and so on."
2 See *Ultramarine*: "'—lef' foot follow right foot and right foot follow lef' foot:
remember, feet, when I was a chile yer promised to be kind to me!'" (259).

over — but if he gets in one of his unreasoning panics — say over the Preraphaelites — he certainly will —

It is impossible to be more specific than this because the whole thing is *one subject* & if you go down badly in one department it affects the whole thing. I think a pass is all one can expect for someone as temperamentally involved as Malcolm. And even a pass with honours could not add to the value of his degree when he gets it because he will have to take another subject next year, — only after that does he become eligible for the degree — [1]

Experiment has come out, a noble looking paper. The London Mercury says a sketch written in a mixture of Negro Greek American and (occasionaly) English — thats me — & a fragment from *Work in Progress* are the only things which live up to the Editorial which is full of post-war-group guff.[2] Heinemann publish it, by the way. They have taken no notice of my correction of the proofs, the dashes are all too long, its full of misprints, & the title is wrong. It makes me sick to look at it so I won't send it you till I pluck up courage.

I'm damned sorry about Pete's book[3] — it's sure to pick up though — & anyway its' of historical importance or bibliographical rather as being the only decent study of your work; that makes it of historical importance as well for future biographers will always have to refer to it & all this time anyway it will be selling splendidly as I guesse.[4]

Burra[5] must have been a trial for that long. Lovely! Thank God

---

1 Lowry wrote Part II of the Tripos at the end of his third year, June 1932, and after this received his B.A. honours degree.

2 Lowry is referring to *Experiment* 7 (Spring 1931) in which his short story "Punctum Indifferens Skibet Gaar Videre" is published (62–75). *The London Mercury* Apr. 1931: 522 contains a review of this issue of *Experiment*. The passage quoted by Lowry runs as follows: ". . . a sketch, which is certainly not academical, written in a mixture of American, Negro, Greek, and occasionally English. But with the exception of this sketch, and an extraordinary fragment from Mr. James Joyce's *Work in Progress*, the magazine does not appear to transcend the spirit of academicism. . . ." The error in the title mentioned by Lowry is perhaps the "Gaar" which in Norwegian should be "Går."

3 Houston Peterson, *The Melody of Chaos* (New York: Longmans, 1931). This was the first full-length study of Aiken's work.

4 "as I gesse": Recurring phrase in Chaucer's *The Canterbury Tales*.

5 Edward John Burra (1905–76), British painter whom Aiken met in Rye in 1931, and with whom he remained lifelong friends. It was with Burra that the Aikens (and Lowry) travelled to Spain in 1933, and to Cuernavaca in 1937. Two of Burra's paintings — "Blues For Ruby Matrix" (1933) and "John Deth" (1952)— are based on poems by Aiken.

Dolly's[1] got a job. I was thinking laſt night of her saying — I'm so excited you GNAW, I muſt always get a little bit aTIPSY you GNAW MRS CHERRY MRS CHERRY oh I'm so excited you GNAW. Jesus bloody chriſt I was nearly sick when I thought of her — I wonder why she knocked at my door the laſt night all the same — —

Don't tell the old man about the motor accident because he'll think all sorts of things which are probably true; anyway if things get really desperate I can always use it in three weeks. There were three of us in the car, Davenport myself & Forman,[2] & we were all pieeyed & decided to go to africa and juſt sat on the accelerator for about twenty miles till the thing juſt overturned from sheer vexation. None of us were killed, but personally I wish I had been.

We got off with bruised hips & banged heads. Not so hot.

I'm sorry the old man should give you this trouble of queſtions blaſt him. However. .

> I should like to die said Willie
> if my poppa could die too —

wothehell

                              my love to Jerry
         Malc

don't tell him that all I know of the Life & Thought of any period is that people once wore tights.

---

1 Doris ("Dolly") Lewis, the step-daughter of Aiken's friend in South Yarmouth, Charles D. Voorhis, with whom Lowry fell in love in the summer of 1929 (Day 107). The laſt line of this paragraph is perhaps an allusion to the conclusion of *Blue Voyage* where Pauline Faubion is seen entering Demareſt's cabin on the laſt night of the voyage. Cf. also *Ushant: An Essay* (New York: Duell, Sloan and Pearce, 1952): "Faubion, who . . . the laſt night of the voyage . . . later knocked emphatically at his stateroom door . . ." (47).

2 John Davenport (1908–66), critic and journaliſt, met Lowry in Cambridge in 1929 while aſting as editor of *Cambridge Poetry*, and it was he who introduced Lowry into Charlotte Haldane's literary salon. The two became great drinking companions and met several times during the later years of Lowry's life. Davenport, via Lowry, also became a friend and correspondent of Aiken. With Dylan Thomas, Davenport is the author of *The Death of the King's Canary* (London: Hutchinson, 1976).

Thomas Forman was a Cambridge friend to whom, with Elizabeth Cheyne, Lowry dedicated *Ultramarine*. According to Douglas Day, Forman had given the car to Lowry who had later "disembowelled it on a great tombſtone of a rock" (181); cf. also Aiken's 25 April 1931 letter to Walter Piſton in which he mentions Lowry's accident (Killorin 174).

8 : *From* LOWRY *to* AIKEN

MS H 2501; MSPC UBC 1–74; BREIT 7

5   8 Plympton street
                                          [St. Catharine's
                                          College, Cambridge]

                                          [June 1931]
10

My dear Conrad:

It was very good of you to write me about the tripeos: as for that I
can't tell as yet, but we did our beſt — we did our beſt. I wrote a fairly
good essay on Truth & Poetry, quoting yourself liberally not to say literally,
15 and Poe and the Melody of Chaos;[1] I was all right on the criticism paper,
and I think I bluffed my way through on Literature from 1785 to the
present day — I knew my Keats better than I thought I did, for inſtance;
& on the whole I have nothing to complain about from the papers, (which
I'll try & get together & send you), and If I have failed, and thats' on the
20 cards, I was more stupid at the time than I thought.

Meantime I have been leading a disordered and rather despairing
exiſtence, and you can probably guess at the reason why I was incapable
of replying promptly: your telegram,[2] however, brought me to my senses
and made me feel rightly ashamed of myself.

25   My d. & r.d.e[3] is due to a complexity of melancholy reasons none of
which are either particularly complex, melancholy, or reasonable, and I
have made up my mind about only one point in this business of living
which is that I muſt, and as soon as possible, identify a finer scene: I muſt
in other words give an imaginary scene identity through the immediate
30 sensation of aſtual experience etc. This, you say, I may have already done
in some part, and is becoming with me a desire for retrogression, for
escaping from the subtle and sophiſticated: that it is not deep-rooted in
honeſt transmission at all and has nothing to do with really wanting more
experience and to rub off more prejudice, to use more hardship, load
35 myself with finer mountains and strengthen more my reach,[4] that would

---

1 Houſton Peterson, *The Melody of Chaos*.
2 Aiken's telegram has not been located.
3 "d. & r.d.e": See above: "disordered and rather despairing exiſtence."
4 See *Ultramarine*: " '. . . nor is it enough to do these things in order to load oneself
with finer mountains, to identify a finer scene . . .' " (253).

stopping home among books (even though I should reach Homer!) but is nothing more than wanting alternately to kill Liverpool and myself: that I am in *truth* — although occasionaly straining at particles of light in the midſt of a great darkness — 'a small boy chased by the furies'[1] & you can sympathise with me as such. Well — if t'were so t'were a grievous fault — — [2]

I prefer to think sometimes that it is because I really want to be a man rather than a male, which at present I'm not, and that I want to get from somewhere a frank and fearless will which roughly speaking does not put more mud into the world than there is at present. Nonsense.

Then I muſt read, — I muſt read, — I muſt read! Doſtoievsky & Dante: Donne, Dryden, Davenant and Dean Inge. . .[3] Again, nonsense; but then at the moment I despair of all literature anyway. If I could read Homer — however much he may have roared in the pines, I'm sure I should hate him: Donne means damn all to me now, Herrick is terrible, Milton I can't read & wouldn't if I could: all reſtoration comedy & moſt all greek tragedy is a bore. . . Tolſtoy? My god what a bloody awful old writer he was!

Well, there is Melville & Goethe, you say.

Well, there was the story of Hamlet, I said and fell into silence —

(By the bye Experiment was reviewed in the Times Lit Sup of a week or two back side by side with a review of Martin Armſtrong's colleɛted, — or are they seleɛted? — unaffeɛted, undeteɛted and well-conneɛted poems, I can't remember whether the review was a favourable one or not, I rather fear not — of my own contribution it remarked that it was a kind of prose fugue, with recurring themes, consiſting of the rough talk of sailors or something, 'effeɛtively contrived'[4] — I can't remember it in detail but I felt quite pleased. I haven't sent you a copy of it because the punɛtuation, length of dashes & so forth, was all wrongly done & I was

---

1 See *Ultramarine* (142).

2 *Julius Caesar* III.ii.81: "If it were so, it was a grievous fault."

3 Sir William D'Avenant (1606–68), dramatiſt; said to be the godson of Shakespeare; made poet laureate in 1638.

   William Ralph Inge (1860–1954), dean of St. Paul's Cathedral, London, 1911–34; philosopher whose "Outspoken Essays" were published in two series, 1919 and 1922.

4 See *The Times Literary Supplement* Thursday, 4 June 1931: 450. The review of *Experiment* 7 contains the following reference to Lowry: "Mr. Malcolm Lowry contributes a short story consiſting almoſt entirely of the rough dialogue of a group of sailors playing cards; a kind of prose fugue with recurrent themes, effeɛtively contrived." On the same page is an unfavourable review of British poet Martin Armſtrong's (1882–1974) *Colleɛted Poems*. Armſtrong was a friend of Aiken who married the latter's firſt wife, Jessie McDonald (1889–1969).

sure it would give you a pain in the neck to look at: this is a rather selfish reason for as a matter of faĉt the reſt of the paper in my opinion is well worth reading so I might send you a copy after all!)

I am delighted to hear that a novel[1] is under way: it is really quite intolerable that I should have been so long sending you the bone dream — [2]

Here it is however. . .

It occurs to me also, & with some horror, that I have not paid you the £4 I owe you. This has not been because I could not afford to pay it but simply because I have waſted my subſtance in riotous living — I have juſt put it off, & off, & there is no doubt whatever but that you could do as well with the four pounds as I could do well without it, but as I write this it so happens I have only a farthing in my pocket: moreover I can never think of the peculiar circumſtances under which the debt, or 3/4 of it, was accrued, without terror, inchoate flashes of nightmare — and perhaps this procraſtination is due in a very small part to the faĉt that to pay the debt means writing about the circumſtances & therefore remembering them. No, I am not Mr Sludge the medium, nor was meant to be . . .[3] But I wish I knew where the hell that three pounds was all the same; the memory of Delores von Hempel is like a miasmic stench from the docks.[4] A pock-marked, Eurasian, memory —

The reason why I have a farthing, and not a halfpenny or a penny or a half-crown in my pocket is a peculiar one. The other night I was walking outside a Fullers café, the windows looked something like Selfridges[5] & not very different from any of the other modern buildings ereĉted all over London or Cambridge except perhaps in size, — all the windows were filled with chocolates or chocolate coloured cakes, — I was in despair, when suddenly I caught sight of myself in the shop window & saw myself murmuring: Can he warm his blue hands by holding them up to the grand northern lights? Would not Lazarus rather be in Sumatra than here? Would he not rather lay him down lengthwise along the line of the

---

1 *Great Circle.*

2 "bone dream": This was a passage from Aiken's *Great Circle* which Lowry had wanted to incorporate into *Ultramarine*; Aiken refused. The passage, in Lowry's handwriting, was enclosed with this letter; it appears in *Great Circle* (84) in somewhat revised form.

3 Cf. Robert Browning's dramatic poem, "Mr Sludge, 'The Medium'" about a medium who accuses his maſter of murder and is in turn accused and slandered by his maſter. Lowry's phrasing here is also an allusion to T.S. Eliot's "The Love Song of J. Alfred Prufrock": "No! I am not Prince Hamlet, nor was meant to be."

4 Cf. *Ultramarine*: "A miasmic stench rose from the docks" (118).

5 "Selfridges": department store in London.

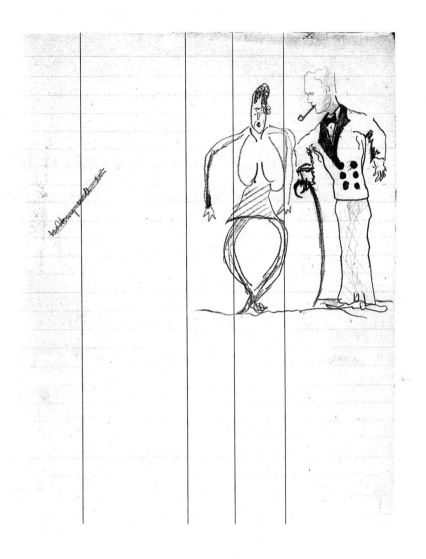

Facsimile reproduction of drawing on verso of third page of letter 8

Equator?[1] . . When at that moment a small boy suddenly came up to me, a small & very grimy urchin, & said 'Would you like a farthing?' So I replied 'Well why not keep it — it's good luck to have a farthing? Besides I haven't got a penny to give you for it. And he said 'No, I don't want it, I've giving my good luck to you.' He then ran away. Strange!

7 am.

I am King Elephant Bag
    King Elephant Bag
       from de rose pink mountains.

I enclose you a letter from one Edward O'Brien,[2] all the more mysterious because he failed to take any notice of my reply . . . Moreover his letter miscarried to *me* — it pursued Noxon[3] half round Europe — I sent him hopefully my biography (in cameo), as it appears at the back of the letter — at the same time giving away that I was an English writer, not an American. If you have any notion what O'Brien means, meant, or intends, if anything, could you let me know some time if your brain will function in that direction? . . I never submitted him any story, & the only story he can have read from Experiment is the one about the mickey,[4] all of which improves the joke.

---

1 See Melville's *Moby-Dick*, Norton Critical Edition (New York: Norton, 1967) 19.
2 Edward Joseph Harrington O'Brien (1890–1941) was born in the U.S., but resided in England for most of his life. He is best known as an editor and anthologist, especially as an authority on the short story; from 1915 to 1941 he annually edited *The Best Short Stories*. Lowry's story, "Seductio Ad Absurdum," was published in *The Best British Short Stories of 1931* (New York: Dodd, 1931) 89–107. According to Clarissa Lorenz, Lowry's story caused the volume to be banned from British public libraries ("Call It," *Psalms and Songs* 59). O'Brien was also an acquaintance of Aiken through the New England Poetry Club (Butscher 236). The "enclosed" letter from O'Brien is missing.
3 Gerald Forbes Noxon (1910–90), Canadian-born writer and radio producer who studied at Trinity College, Cambridge, and became founding publishing-editor of *Experiment* in 1928 (Tiessen, *Letters* xii). He and Lowry met in 1929 when Lowry submitted his story "Port Swettenham" to *Experiment*. Lowry introduced Noxon to Aiken in September 1930, and in 1933 Noxon and his wife, Betty, sublet Jeake's House while Lowry and the Aikens travelled in Spain (Tiessen, *Letters* 7). In 1940 the two regained contact in Canada (with Aiken's help) and remained friends until Lowry's death in 1957 (cf. letter 49). It was with Gerald and Betty Noxon that Lowry and his wife stayed in 1944 after their Dollarton shack burned down. See Noxon's memoir of Lowry, "Malcolm Lowry: 1930," in *Malcolm Lowry: Psalms and Songs*, his *"On Malcolm Lowry" and Other Writings* (ed. Mota and Tiessen), and his and Lowry's correspondence in *The Letters of Malcolm Lowry and Gerald Noxon* (ed. Tiessen).
4 "Port Swettenham," *Experiment* 5 (Feb. 1930): 22–26. Reprinted in revised form as "On Board the *West Hardaway*," *Story* 3.15 (Oct. 1933): 12–22, and later reworked to become chapter 5 of *Ultramarine*.

I can assume only that he did mean to publish the thing in the 1931 volume, American & have already informed the old man on this score to counteract in part the effect of my (possible) failure in the exam which gawd forbid. O'Brien either ignored or didn't receive a couple of replies, so I sent him a wire asking him if he could give me some information 'as was going to Peru,' & received the answer. 'O'Brien in the Balkans — O'Brien,' which seems to me funny. Still, I would like your advice. It is a nice point.

And it's that story, you know, in all its pristine beauty, Conrad, full of 'stop its-he-muttered.' & 'they growled's' & they howled's & 'There are you better now's,' & far away, yo hai,'s

                    long ago, yo ho.

                              Malc.

[*"Bone Dream": enclosed with letter 8* (MSPC UBC 7–4)]

                              386.

pair of wings as you ever saw on a bleeding sparrow, and all of them on their way to a star, or maybe it was god itself. And after that, a little time, I was eating a skeleton, beginning with the feet and working up the legs, and dry going it was too, what with no sauce, never a drop of mustard nor worcestershire, and the bones getting bitterer and bitterer just like sea-pie as I crawled up through the pelvis and the ribs — '

'— like the story of the feller who dreamt he saw the results of — stop me if you've heard it — '

'— and the spine tasting like the dead sea, like ashes in the mouth, & worse as I got towards the skull, and the skull itself a black mouthful of charcoal, which I spit out. And Behemoth himself then I saw, of course you know who *he* is, in the very act of biting the conningtower off an interstellar submarine, one of those ether-going craft with one eye, and all this was a little way off to the southwest from a pink star — I forget its name — that was wearing white drawers on it like a woman — '

                              (P.T.O.)

                              35

9 : *From* LOWRY *to* AIKEN

MS H 2495

5
[St. Catharine's College,
Cambridge]

[June 1931]

10 I thought Socrates might be in the novel[1] so am sending you this. See page 471 of six plays.[2] Its' not bad, but not really good. They're too many pipes of pan & fauns & females playing leaden flutes: & Aristophanes gets hiccups. Such rugs & jugs & candle lights: which reminds me that I saw the Antigone & the Lysistrata exceedingly well done here at the
15 Festival. . .[3] Well, as I said before, its not good, but might suggest something to you, it *is* after all, Socrates speaking & he says something about a windflower, too. . .[4] And talking about the Festival — when is Cambridge going to see you? Could you for instance invite yourself on her this week end, say the 18*th*–23rd, or are you too busy, & *rooted?* It
20 would be swell to see you though.

---

1 *Great Circle.*

2 See Clifford Bax, "Socrates," *Six Plays* (London: Gollancz, 1930) 461–578. Page 471 is the page on which the text of the play actually begins. It is unclear whether Lowry has sent Aiken a copy of *Six Plays* or merely a transcription of specific passages from Bax's play.

3 The Festival Theatre, Cambridge.

4 See "Socrates," *Six Plays*:
Socrates: ". . . I next went to a celebrated
scientist. He told me exactly how everything is
constructed — from a windflower to the Milky Way
itself — and proceeded to assure me that the notion of
human immortality is a fairy-story fit only for
nursemaids." (543)

IO : *From* LOWRY *to* AIKEN

MS H 2497; MSPC UBC 1–74

5

Hotell Parkheimen
Dr'ammensveien 2
Oslo.

[Summer 1931]

10

Hi there, Colonel Aiken —

ss Fagervik[1] — of which, curiously, very many happy memories —
has been laid up & I am here waiting a few days for another ship. It is a
swell place; but the swelleſt place in it, up in the mountains, is called
15 Frognersaeteren.[2] The language is quite fantaſtic, & driven into myself.
I do little else but read Tauchnitz editions;[3] and so doing I have discovered
one firſt rate author, an American, Julian Green,[4] who writes in French,
which is translated back again into English. So.

My writing has changed — my hair is going gray — I enclose you a
20 poem about ducks which is in the Tauchnitz anthology of English poetry
of English & American authors![5] Take it to the Ship Inn with you if you
are in Rye, order a half quatern — & I beg of you to drink my health —
& have a good laugh! And there's another one by Gerald Gould, too.[6]

---

1 Lowry sailed to Norway aboard the ss *Fagervik* in the summer of 1931.
2 In Frognersaeteren there was a well-known reſtaurant and resort frequented by
artiſts. It is possible that this is where Lowry met the Norwegian writer, Nordahl
Grieg (1902–43). Cf. also *Ultramarine* (17).
3 Baron Chriſtian Bernhard von Tauchnitz (1816–95) founded a publishing house at
Leipzig which in 1841 began issuing a colleċtion of British and American Authors.
4 Julien Hartridge Green (1900–), Paris-born, American writer, chriſtened "Julian"
but chose to keep the French spelling of the name. Lowry seems to have been quite
familiar with Green's work, especially *The Dark Journey* (1929) (Fr. *Leviathan*, 1929),
which he owned. Cf. Lowry's *Dark as the Grave Wherein My Friend is Laid* (New York:
NAL, 1968): "And he thought again of the occasion he had firſt bought, fourteen years
ago, not the firſt edition [of Julien Green's *The Dark Journey*], but a Tauchnitz, on the
firſt dramatic occasion of his having met Erikson [Grieg] . . . in the dark stormy
tree-tossed Bygdø Alle in Oslo . . ." (45). *The Dark Journey* was published in 1930 as
volume 4959 of the Tauchnitz Colleċtion of British and American Authors.
5 The "enclosed" poem is missing, though Lowry is referring to Frederic William
Harvey's "Ducks" in the *Anthology of Modern English Poetry*, sel. Levin L. Schücking,
Colleċtion of British and American Authors 5000 (Leipzig: Bernhard Tauchnitz, 1931)
120–23.
6 Gerald Gould (1885–1936, British journaliſt, poet, and critic. Lowry probably sent
Aiken Gould's poem "Wander-Thirſt" from the Tauchnitz anthology (119).

THE SHRIEK!

Facsimile reproduction of drawing on verso of letter 10.

This drawing is an imitation of the famous painting, "The Shriek" (1893;
1895 lithograph), by the Norwegian painter Edvard Munch (1863–1944).
Lowry may have viewed Munch's paintings while in Oslo.

Once I could play panjo fine —

Nobody speaks English here, & in the only conversation I have had
about Literature I was surprised to discover that the most famous English
writer here was Gibson. As the conversation progressed I noticed that
5   somehow they'd got his christian name wrong, Henry instead of Wilfrid.
I pointed this mistake out, & seeing my chance which I had been waiting
for all this time, I told, stumblingly, your famous story about Frost &
Gibson at the English fair.[1] They were astonished at the irrelevance of
this because, as I later discovered, they were talking all this while about
10   Henrik Ibsen —

Is that funny?

It is perfectly false — I have just made it up.

Anyhow,

15
Heaps of
love.

Malk

20

---

1   Wilfrid Wilson Gibson (1878–1962), British poet and playwright. In an 8 July 1915
letter to Louis Untermeyer, Frost tells of a visit to some English country races with
Wilfrid Gibson where Gibson complained of having lost his day because he didn't
find anything he could use in his writing; see Lawrance Thompson's *Robert Frost: The
Years of Triumph*, vol. 2 (New York: Holt, 1970) 533. Four poems by Gibson appear in
the Tauchnitz anthology noted above.

11 : *From* LOWRY *to* AIKEN

MS H 2499

21 Woodland Gardens
Highgate
London
N10.
c/o John Davenport

[Summer/Autumn 1932]

My dear Conrad:

I would have written you before this only I got beaten up in an Ulyssean brawl[1] near Kleinfelds' in Charlotte street the first night of my arrival,[2] and have been nursing an injured chin and a twisted lip since then; not so hot. I can't achieve a Venividivici look at all in the looking glass, but no doubt I shall get better — —

I shall descend on Rye sometime on Wednesday, I seem to remember there's a train gets in round about 4, but don't depend on that because I don't know whether it's still running; if you're out I'll put up at the Ship or the George or the Mermaid —

As a matter of fact I did write at length four days ago, a dead letter 'that self-conscious, half-literary, hinting thing which I always achieve, — how disgusting!':[3] and I tore it up.

σιγα σιγα[4]

Malcolm

---

1 Cf. the brawl scene at the end of the "Nighttown" episode of Joyce's *Ulysses*.
2 After graduating from Cambridge in June 1932, Lowry joined the Aikens in Rye and from there moved to London where he took up with his old friends, John Davenport (see address above) and Hugh Sykes Davies. According to Douglas Day, Kleinfeld was the publican of the Fitzroy Tavern on Charlotte Street (*Malcolm Lowry: A Biography* 152). It is possible that Lowry was using Davenport's address as his *mailing* address, and not actually staying with him.
3 See *Blue Voyage*: "The letters had been in his very worst vein — the sort of disingenuous, hinting thing, self-conscious and literary, which he always achieved (how revolting) when the occasion was emotionally important" (126).
4 "σιγα σιγα": Greek, "silence, silence"

12 : *From* LOWRY *to* AIKEN

MS H 2566

5   [London]

[February 1933]

Conrad Aiken Jeakes House Rye
10 Conrad may I come down and see you
today it is urgent but I ask with
a bowed mind   Malc[1]

15

20

13 : *From* LOWRY *to* AIKEN

MS H 2503; MSPC UBC 3–14

25   [London]

[early 1933]

Some more cracks.
30 Hilliot is a man who admittedly lives in "introverted comas"[2] & that is
part of his trouble, however typical it may be: his is a vicariousness beyond
a statement of vicariousness because it is unobjectifiable, he is never sure
that any emotion is his own, & he quite genuinely is "cuckoo", he *is* a poet
who can't write & may never be able to. And this is where I must try to
35 find some mitigating factor in its being parasitic on "Blue Voyage". First,

---

1 Lowry was probably hoping to ask Aiken's advice regarding revisions of various
"obscenities" in *Ultramarine* as suggested by Cape. See the 15 March 1933 letter from
Hamish Miles to Lowry in the Huntington Aiken Collection.
2 Dana Hilliot is the protagonist of *Ultramarine*. See *Ultramarine*: ". . . a man who
believed himself to live in inverted, or introverted, commas . . ." (19).

I find it in Ultramarine however much a cento being written at all, it has given me for a time, a dominant principle — & if Blue Voyage does that for 1/1,5000 of its public, what about the other 14999? Second, under the reign of Bloom & Sweeney,[1] a greater freedom seems to be permitted, these are being absorbed into the racial consciousness: Blue Voyage, apart from its being the beſt nonsecular statement of the plight of the creative artiſt with the courage to live in a modern world, has become part of my consciousness, & I cannot conceive of any other way in which Ultramarine might be written.

I am probably to blame for certain slavishnesses in Chapter III, because they're not good enough, (but I couldn't do it in any other way), — & also for sheltering my Protean nature behind a certain underſtanding of The Waſte Land. Philosophers & tinkle tonkle etc could be hooked out if you want them yourself.[2] (Shantih means a song & a brothel as well as the Peace that Passeth all underſtanding)[3] Nevertheless I have sat & read my blaſted book with increasing misery: with a misery of such intensity that I believe myself sometimes to be dispossessed, a spectre of your own discarded ideas, whose only claim to dignity exiſts in those ideas. Never mind — the book knows its got a paper cover, — forgive the forgoing somewhat pompous cracks — someone said "a seer & a pathfinder" —

Well: once more I am
  asking you the way —

Malcolm

---

1 "Bloom & Sweeney": i.e., James Joyce and T.S. Eliot.
2 "Philosophers and tinkle tonkle": See *Ultramarine*: "Philosophers maintain that two and two make four. But every little doggie knows more" (269); ". . . the goat bells going tinkle tonkle tankle tunk —" (34); "Tinkle tonkle tankle tunk. Spinkle sponkle spankle" (119).
3 "Shantih": See the laſt line of T.S. Eliot's *The Waſte Land*: "shantih shantih shantih" and *Ultramarine*: "she shantih" (59).

14 : *From* LOWRY *to* AIKEN

MS H 3418 & 2504; MSPC UBC 1–75

[Charlie's Bar]
[Cuernavaca, Mexico]

[Summer 1937]

Work for Conrad.[1]

Strictly impersonal exercises in excess.

(1)
Prelude to Mammon.[2]

Sir: drinking is a problem without doubt:
Whether or not we like it, whether or not
The goddamn thing will put you on the spot
With heebiejeebies hebephrene or gout:
Or lumbago[3] will set you tapping out
On brass ferrule to stool, to rest, to rot.
Though rotting's a fine pastime for a sot
It seems when we excrete we should not shout;
While even when we rest it's more discreet
That we should unambiguously rest.
What others think is one torment of drink

---

1 As Lowry's tutor, Aiken had been in the habit of giving his student poetry exercises to complete; this letter appears to have been one of Lowry's assignments while Aiken was visiting him in Mexico in the summer of 1937. Cf. Aiken's *Ushant*: ". . . that climactic talk between them . . . at Charlie's place . . . when they had finished with Hambo's [Lowry's] exercise in sonnet-form — 'Airplane, or aeroplane, or just plain plane . . .'" (352). Cf. also Aiken's comments on these poems in "The Art of Poetry IX" (99) and in his 12 Dec. 1960 letter to W.G. Simpson (Killorin 306). These poems are printed in Kathleen Scherf's *The Collected Poetry of Malcolm Lowry* as "Prelude to Mammon" (108–09), "Thirty Five Mescals in Cuautla" (60–61), "Prelude to Another Drink" (108), and "The Last Man in the Dôme" (63–64).
2 Pun on Aiken's *Preludes for Memnon*. In general, the form and sound of these poems echo Aiken's preludes.
3 In both *Ushant* and *A Heart for the Gods of Mexico* (London: Secker, 1939), Aiken writes of Lowry having lumbago when he saw him in Mexico; Lowry claimed he had contracted it from his swimming pool (Day 220).

But these have dung not dew upon their feet
Whose dry concern for us is manifeſt
In the ubiquity of the parched soul's stink.

5   — This was an iambic pentametre that was: gawd knows
what this is but call it

(2)
10   *Prelude to another drink*

This ticking is the moſt terrible of all
[Oh yeah.]   You hear this sound on ships, you hear it on trains
It is the death-watch beetle at the rotten timber of
15   the world[1]
And it is death to you too; for well you know
That the heart's tick is failing all the while
Always ubiquitous & still more slow.
In the cantina throbs the refrigerator
20   And againſt the street the gaunt station hums.
What can you say fairly of a fat man
With a bent hand behind him & a cigarette in it?
Yet death is in the room, there is death everywhere:
That man carries it though I can't see his face:
25   The upturned spitoons mean it, it is in the glass,
[Or, the 2   The girl who refills it pours a glass of death
stag beetles   And if there's death in her there is in me.
battle to   On the calendar, set to the future, the two stags
death. Still,   battle
30   we take   To death: man paddles his coracle to the moon
ourselves   Which, seen also in light, is as divisible as death.
seriously.]

Gawd knows what that was & chriſt knows what this is,
35   [though we are coming back to the iambic pentametre,] so
suppose we call it,

---

1 Cf. Aiken's 13 January 1924 letter to Robert Linscott: "The whole house [Jeake's]
ticks like a clock faĉtory with the hidden feverish aĉtivities of the Death Watch Beetle"
(Killorin 85).

(3)

Prelude to another drink.

[daughter; —— Is this an airplane roaring in my room?
5   especially   What is it then, an insect, god knows what:
when the   God probably does know which is the point;
announcer   Or did know — leave it at that — some sort of hornet.
pronounces   Airplane or aeroplane or just plain plane, — 1
his r's like   Some hint of something more than this is here.
10   w's.].   Insect, vision, or terrestrial visitor, —
                  Some hint of something more than this is here.
                  Some hint is here & what should it be but this?
                  To watch this guest, to see what it does.
                  It taxies like an Avro skidding through the flying field
15   Rises like a Sopwith,2 flies into a rage
                  Bangs against the light, settles on the printed page
                  Soars: then falls: then can't get up
                  When I try to help him his hands evade my help —
                  I myself seeing the only possible exit.
20   So God watches us with lids which move not.
                  But this is a repetition of an 'idea'
                  Before the terrible delirium of God.

Here we are, the old iambic again, just to show my old Conrad I've
25 did my lessons, but God & mezcal help me I can't think of anything to
call it but

(4)

Prelude to another drink.

30

                  Where are the finely drunk? the great drunkard?
                  This imponderable, small mystery
                  Perplexes me at midnight constantly
                  Where is he gone & taking whence his tankard?
35   Where are all gone my friends the great unanchored?
                  They drink no more: they go to bed at three
                  In afternoon yet dream more easily —

---

1 According to Clarissa Lorenz, this line was the one out of this batch of Lowry's
"very fine" poems that Aiken especially liked (*Lorelei Two* 3).
2 "Avro" and "Sopwith" are both makes of airplanes.

— (Livers at laſt of lives for which they hankered!) —
Of endless corridors of boots to lick,
Or at the end of them all the Pope's toe.
Where are your friends you fool you have but one
5   And that a friend who also makes you sick
But much less sick than they: & this I know
Since I am the laſt drunkard. And I drink alone.

Well: my hoſt in Cuautla went nuts. Had to be held down, taken to
10   hospital. It was trying — for him, too, I guess, — & I'm glad Jan[1] was
spared the experience.
[It suddenly occurs to me how much I love you both.[2] You old
Mephiſtopheles. Be happy, you two. I kind of feel you will.]

15   Come to Charlie's, where I am, soon: old Aggie's got the orrors
somethink orful.

Malc.

20

---

1   Jan Gabrial (1911–   ), born Janine Vanderheim, Lowry's firſt wife whom he married
in January 1934.
2   "you both": Conrad Aiken and his new wife, Mary (Hoover) Aiken (1907–   ),
whom he married on 7 July 1937. Aiken had gone to Mexico to obtain a divorce from
his second wife, Clarissa Lorenz, and to marry Mary Hoover.

15 : *From* LOWRY *to* AIKEN

MS UBC 1–76; BREIT 15; DAY 239

[Hotel Francia]
[Apartado Poſtal
Num. 92.]
[Oaxaca, Oax., Mex.]

[December 1937 / January 1938]

Dear old bird.

Have now reached condition of amnesia, breakdown, heartbreak, consumption, cholera, alcoholic poisoning, & God will not like to know what else if he has to which is damned doubtful.

All change here, all change here, for Oakshot, Cockshot, Poxshot & fuck the whole bloody lot! My only friend here a tertiary who pins a medal of the Virgin of Guadalupe on my coat,[1] follows me in the street — (when I am not in prison, and he follows me there too several times,) & who thinks I am Jesus Chriſt, which, as you know, I am not yet, though I may be progressing towards thinking I am myself.

I have been imprisoned as a spy in a dungeon compared with which the Chateau d'if[2] — in a film — is a little cottage in the country overlooking the sea.

I spend Chriſtmas — New Years — Wedding Day[3] there. All my mail is late. Where it does arrive it is all contradiction & yours is cut up into little holes.

Don't think I can go on. Where I am it is dark.

Loſt.   Happy New Year.

           Malcolm.

---

1   Lowry is probably speaking of his Zapotecan friend, Juan Fernando Márquez, who became the model for Dr. Vigil and Juan Cerillo in *Under the Volcano* and of Juan Fernando Martínez in *Dark as the Grave*. Cf. Lowry's "Garden of Etla," *United Nations World* 4 (June 1950): 45–47, and *Under the Volcano* (New York: Reynal & Hitchcock, 1947) in which the Consul remembers a beggar pinning two medallions depicting the Virgin of Guadalupe on his coat-lapel (200).

2   The Chateau d'If contains the dungeon in which Edmond Dantes is imprisoned in Alexandre Dumas' (1802–70) *Le comte de Monte-Criſto* (1844–45). Lowry may be referring here to the 1934 film version of the novel produced by Edward Small for United Artiſts.

3   This would be the anniversary of Lowry's marriage to Jan Gabrial: 6 January 1934.

16 : *From* LOWRY *to* AIKEN

MS UBC 8–2

5   [Oaxaca, Mexico]

[early 1938]

10   a mi padre
          My dear dear fellow: — at the end of my goddamn life, you
are the only man I wish to write to.
          — In my churlish way or not so churlish (churchish not
richard)
15

          ref. Richard Church.[1]
          ref. Landscapes Etc.
          ref. memory.

20   way or as it ochurls to me bygosh not a churlish way at all: hell & a typhoon
of strumpets: I meant — tucket within, & a flourish of strumpets:[2] & let
Plympton Street[3] weep in the East wind: my life was a mignotorio[4] of
grief & an excu(ruci)sado of hate, — Rewritten: 'excrucifiado of hate.' —
Joke over. [Note: Excusado is Mexican for lavatory.][5] & you were a
25   prophet. I have done you dirt once & a half twice but never seriously &
always it was with Jealously — & *love*. Please believe in my sincere
friendship & if I die, give me sanctuary.

---

1   Richard Church (1893–1972), English poet, novelist, and critic; advisory editor for
J.M. Dent & Sons from 1933–52. He reviewed the 1946 English edition of Aiken's *The
Soldier: A Poem* in "Richard Church Reviews Recent Poetry," *John O'London's Weekly*
13 Dec. 1946: 149. The reference to "Landscapes Etc." is unclear, although it may be
an allusion to Aiken's *Landscape West of Eden* which was published by Dent as part of
a New Poetry series in 1934.
2   See Lowry's "Punctum Indifferens Skibet Gaar Videre": "Tucket within, and a
flourish of trumpets" (65) and "Seductio ad Absurdum": "Tucket within, and a flourish
of strumpets" (93). Cf. also *Ultramarine* (180).
3   Plympton Street was Aiken's address in Cambridge, Massachusetts, when Lowry
visited him there in 1929.
4   "mingitorio": Spanish, "urinal"; Lowry has misspelled the word.
5   Lowry is punning on the Spanish words, "excusado," "lavatory" or "toilet," and
"crucificado," "crucified"; "el Crucificado" can be used to mean "Jesus Christ."

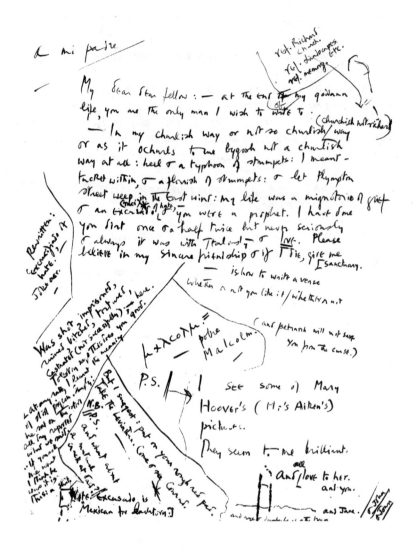

Facsimile reproduction of letter 16

— is how to write a verse[1]
Whether or not you like it/whether or not[2]
(and petrarch will not save you from the curse.)

5   Was shot, imprisoned, ruined, bitched, tortured, Castrated (not successfully); — here. Tolstoy says This does you good. — At any rate, I
learnt the meaning of stool pigeon. Simply: he sat on the stool all day
reported what we said. . . . If you ask me what I think he was it is this: a
shit.
10

But I suggest: put on your rough red pad.
Take the Leviathan. Come & see Conrad.
N.B.
P.S. And what about a mutual crack at dad?
15

Μαλcoλμ. = pobre Malcolm.

P.S.   I see some of Mary Hoover's (Mr's Aiken's) pictures.[3]
They seem to me brilliant.
20   And all love to her.
and you.
and Jane. & John & Joan[4]
and rye & camber beach[5] & the tram

25

---

1 See poem at end of letter 18.
2 See Lowry's poem, "Prelude to Mammon," in letter 14.
3 Aiken's third wife, Mary Hoover, was an artist.
4 Aiken's three children by his first wife, Jessie McDonald (1889–1969). John
Kempton Aiken (1913–91), Jane Aiken (Hodge) (1917–), and Joan Aiken (1924–).
Both Jane and Joan are well-established writers. Although Aiken and his wife were
divorced in 1929, the children continued to pay intermittent visits to Jeake's House in
the 1930s. See *Conrad Aiken Remembered* in which each of Aiken's children contribute
memoirs of their father.
5 Gerald Noxon tells of taking the train with Lowry from Rye "out past the golf
course to Camber Sands to swim in the Channel waters . . ." ("Malcolm Lowry: 1930"
110). Cf. also Lowry's 26 August 1940 letter to Noxon in which he, too, remembers
the trips to Camber Beach (Tiessen, *Letters* 28). The "Camber Tram," which operated
from 1908 to 1939, ran between Rye, the golf links, and Camber Sands.

1939–1941

. . . again, my ancient doppelganger, I am, deep
down in my psyche . . . damned like you.

     — 9 April 1940 letter from Lowry to Aiken

AFTER A YEAR OF SPORADIC DRINKING and writing in Los Angeles, with no hope of a reunion with Jan who was by this time sueing for divorce, Lowry was "rescued" in 1939 by Margerie Bonner, the woman who was to become his second wife. Unfortunately, Lowry's father appears to have learned of his son's new romantic involvement through Benjamin Parks, a Los Angeles lawyer whom he had placed in charge of Lowry's affairs. In July 1939, under the orders of Arthur O. Lowry, Parks hustled Lowry to British Columbia on the pretext of renewing his visa, and had him placed under the care of two Vancouver businessmen, Archibald B. Carey and Victor MacLean. A.B. Carey, Chairman of the provincial government's Single Homeless Men's Committee and prominent member of the Vancouver Oxford Group, came to fill, in more respectable form, the position that Aiken had held earlier in Lowry's life, and firmly undertook to handle Lowry's finances and curb his drinking. Lowry, finding himself unable to recross the border and rejoin Margerie in the United States, eventually took up residence in the home of Maurice Carey, a retired Sergeant-Major, on 595 West 19th Ave. After one failed attempt at crossing the border, he asked Margerie to join him in Vancouver, which she did in August of that year.

It is at this time that Lowry wrote what was to be the first of many desperate letters to Aiken pleading for help in dealing with the "Old Man." With the onset of the war, the Aikens had left Rye and, on 29 September, sailed to New York, settling first in South Dennis, then in Brewster, Massachusetts, where in May 1940 they bought an "old eighteenth century ruin" called "Forty-One Doors" (letter 42). In response to Lowry's request, Aiken *did* intercede with both Parks and Lowry's father, asking that Lowry be allowed to join him in Massachusetts where he would accept full responsibility for him. It was also at this time, 1940, that Aiken reintroduced Lowry to his old Cambridge friend, Gerald Noxon, by sending him Noxon's new address in Toronto (letter 49). The Aikens had carried the Noxons' son, Nicholas, across the Atlantic. During the next few years Noxon was to become an additional source of moral support to Lowry in his self-imposed seclusion on Burrard Inlet.

However, just when success seemed close at hand, Lowry was refused entry into the United States, and his plans for an immediate reunion with Aiken were ruined (letter 31). In the meantime, because of the British Treasury's restrictions, Lowry had stopped receiving money from his father. To make matters worse, Maurice Carey had given him and Margerie one month to vacate his house. Initially they moved into an apartment on West 11th Avenue; then, on 15 August 1940, seeking still cheaper accommodation, they rented a beach shack in Dollarton on the north shore of Burrard Inlet. By April 1941 they had bought their own shack in Dollarton, and it was here that they finally settled down to the revising of *Under the Volcano*, a task which was to take more than five additional years.

17 : *From* AIKEN *to* LOWRY

KILLORIN 234

5   Belmont, Mass.

Oct. 29 39

My beloved Judas-Malc — it was good to hear from you, not so good in
10 all respects (but in some) to hear your bagful of queer news. But what can
I do to help you — ? Damn all. I'm a bit knocked-oop meself, we're broke
to the wide, on borrowed money (and little at that) and about to live in
one of Jake's[1] cottages, which we get for nothing, on the Cape. Cash, nil.
Prospects, dim. Nor can I find anyone who would lend me more, at the
15 moment. All I can immediately suggest is this: I talked of your plight
with my agent, Bernice Baumgarten, Brandt & Brandt, 101 Park Avenue,
N.Y.,[2] and of your work, and she said that if you would have your mss —
all you can get hold of — sent to her, as per above, she would see what
could be done. If some publisher — and there of course I'd myself add
20 my say-so — would take an interest, something might then be done in
the way of getting some money to you, and thereafter arranging to *summon*
you to New York as it were for "business" — which would perhaps carry
weight with the authorities? Anyway, let me know quam cel[3] about this,
and Bernice too, and we'll go on trying to improvise *something*. What
25 about the Old Man. Would it be any use my writing to him, and if so to
what effect — viz., what line would most profitably take — if any — ?
But anyway, don't be down-hearted — we'll maybe think of a way out.
Or in. — Ourselves, worn out and ill with ours and the world's troubles,
but of good heart. A new novel[4] (and a new publisher) a new book of
30 sonnets[5] and a new dealer for Mary's pictures in New York — so we at
any rate feel that we are *building* something. . . . Ed's pictures are in the
British pavilion at the Fair — he may come over in January — why not

---

1 George B. Wilbur (1887–1976), Harvard friend of Aiken who had a psychiatric
practice in South Dennis; editor of *American Imago* from 1946–63.
2 Bernice Baumgarten (1904–78) worked for Brandt & Brandt literary agency from
1923–57 and was head of their book department from 1926 until her retirement in 1957.
See Matthew J. Bruccoli's *James Gould Cozzens* (San Diego: Harcourt, 1983) 286–91,
for an account of Baumgarten's work for Brandt & Brandt.
3 "quam celerrime": Latin, "as fast as possible."
4 *Conversation: or Pilgrims' Progress* (New York: Duell, Sloan and Pearce, 1940).
5 *And in the Human Heart* (New York: Duell, Sloan and Pearce, 1940).

keep your eye on Boston? A good place. Avoid the army my dear fellow
— nothing in it. As for Jan et cet, and the new Gal, blessings and
congratulations. And Mary joins me in sending love — lots of it —
Conrad.

5   If you prefer, have the mss. sent first to me, and I'll confer with Linscott[1]
about the next steps. Just as you like. Have you finished Ballast — ?[2]

10

18 : *From* LOWRY *to* AIKEN

15   MS UBC I–77; BREIT 18

c/o Sergeant Major
Maurice Carey.
595 W 19th.
20   Vancouver. B.C.
Canada.

[November 1939]

25

— Mein lieber alter Senlin Forslin Malcolmn Coffin Aiken:[3]
      Since my last bagful of news the situation has become so bloody
complicado that if we do not receive some help, and at that immediately,
I shall lose what remains of my reason, not to say, life. It is all, (like
30   everything else), such a complexity of melancholy opposites, that,
although I expect you to understand it all, I'm not going to attempt to
explain it: I shall just hang the more succulent looking hams of misfortune

---

1 Robert Linscott (1886–1964), friend of Aiken; editor at Houghton Mifflin in
Boston from 1904–44 and at Random House from 1944–57.
2 "In Ballast to the White Sea" was a novel based upon Lowry's visit to Nordahl
Grieg in Norway in the summer of 1931; the manuscript of the novel was destroyed by
fire when the Lowrys' Dollarton shack burned down in June 1944.
3 Cf. *Ultramarine*: "Mein lieber alte Freund" (144). "Senlin," "Forslin," and "Coffin"
refer to works by Aiken: "Senlin: A Biography," *The Charnel Rose; Senlin: A Biography;
and Other Poems* (Boston: Four Seas, 1918); *The Jig of Forslin: A Symphony* (Boston:
Four Seas, 1916); and *King Coffin* (New York: Scribner's, 1935) [novel].

in the window hoping to entice you in to where the whole pig, that would be cut down, is hanging. When I returned to Los Angeles (from Mexico) to Jan, whom I knew was living with someone else, this journey being at the old man's request, — I travelled by the Great Circle[1] too, the railroad
5 being built by a British concession, paid by the kilometre so it naturally went the most roundabout way, but the train did not hurry and it is rather farther as you know than from New York to Boston, — I practically went to pieces, this being due partly to illness, partly to Jan, who, wishing to ratify her infidelity perhaps had written the old man that I was incapable
10 and should be certified incompetent or words to that effect, for which information she received, per old man, a largeish sum of money to look after me, which she pocketed later, I afterwards discovered and went promptly to Santa Barbara with her boyfriend, leaving me, a sort of Lear of the Sierras, dying by the glass in the Brown Derby in Hollywood: I
15 don't, of course, blame her, — better off in the Brown Derby, but no matter. My income was then put into the hands of an attorney named Parks,[2] a crooked but amiable fellow with hay fever and some kind of legal rapport with the old man's London solicitors, who paid my bills but gave me no money. After a year alone, close to Jan's affair but seeing her
20 only twice — I suffered horribly but was taken out of the Brown Derby & despair by a grand gal named Margerie Bonner[3] but no sooner had this to happen than I was taken suddenly by Parks to Canada — I was taken suddenly to Canada, by Parks on the understanding that this jaunt here was simply in order to obtain a visa back to the U.S. Here he placed my
25 money in the hands of *two* men whom he scarcely knew, one of whom, Maclean, I believe to be honest enough, but who, being constantly away on secret service, was & is unapproachable: the other, A.B. Carey[4] — &

---

1 Allusion to Aiken's novel of the same title. Cf. *Under the Volcano* (115–16) for a similar discussion about a railroad.

2 Benjamin Parks, a Los Angeles attorney hired by Lowry's father to act as Lowry's guardian and handle his finances.

3 Margerie Bonner (1905–88), Hollywood silent film actress and writer of mystery novels who married Lowry on 2 December 1940; author of *The Last Twist of the Knife* (New York: Scribner's, 1946), *The Shapes That Creep* (Scribner's, 1946), and *Horse in the Sky* (Scribner's, 1947). See also Anthony Slide's "The Film Career of Margerie Bonner Lowry," *Malcolm Lowry Review* 29/30 (1991/1992): 20–26.

4 Archibald B. Carey was a wealthy Vancouver philanthropist and, in 1935, Chairman of the Single Homeless Men's Committee which may explain how he came to be in charge of Lowry. According to Maurice Carey, A.B. Carey was a long-time friend of Lowry's father [see M. Carey's memoir in UBC's box 43–4, page 11]. A.B. Carey was also a prominent member of the Vancouver Oxford Group in the late 1930s. Victor Alexander MacLean (1896?–1940) was a Vancouver businessman and, in 1940, went overseas as a Colonel with the auxiliary services staff where he died in England.

don't forget the A.B oh beſt beloved — who was & is simply a dung cart
except for the straw which is in his feet, but also the moſt upright citizen
of Vancouver, & a member of the Oxford Group.[1] For him, no more
dancing on hell's bright sabbath green, the uprightness having departed
5 to his soul, which stinks equally if possible. Parks then vanished. After
two months going quietly insane care of the Oxford Group, war was also
declared. All might have been well had not this Oxford Grouper discovered that I was in love with Margerie whom I hope to god you meet &
love as you do me who had stuck by me through thick & thin moſtly thin,
10 sharing conditions with me which make Gorki's Lower Depths[2] look like
a drawing room comedy. When A.B. Carey discovered that I was married,
as a matter of fa&t my interlocutory decree had juſt been granted, &
proposed to return to another girl, he sat on my money, abused my
confidence, said that I was committing a mortal sin in loving another
15 woman than my wife, read my letters, & a&tually interfered with my mail.
Then war was declared, & here was I left on the wrong side of the border.
Now I had the visa, to get back but A.B. Carey would give me no money.
So I wired Margerie for enough money to make the trip back to Los
Angeles, which she did, & was turned back at the border, A.B Carey
20 having already presumably informed the authorities that I would be
unable to support myself on the other side.

In trying to get out of the hands of these baſtardos by which I mean
also the entire Oxford Group as well by any means and back to Los
Angeles, where lived Marjorie, who was and is to me like those old Nicean
25 barks of yore,[3] and who dwelt among the trees that haven't had a headache

---

According to Margerie Lowry's 12 January 1940 letter to Mary Aiken (see Appendix
11), Parks' claim that he knew MacLean before Lowry's trouble was contradi&ted by
MacLean. Later, writes Margerie, MacLean "passed Malcolm on to [Carey] a mere
acquaintance of his." See my article, "Lowry's Keepers: Vi&tor MacLean and A.B.
Carey" in *Malcolm Lowry Review* 28 (1991): 34–39. Neither Carey nor MacLean were,
as is commonly thought, lawyers.

1 The Oxford Group was a religious organization founded by an American Lutheran
miniſter, Frank Buchman, who moved to England in 1908. The Oxford Group, which
was a campaign for the truths of Chriſtianity within all Chriſtian se&ts, is diſtin&t from
the Oxford Movement which was a movement within the Church of England. I have
found evidence of A.B. Carey's, but not MacLean's, conne&tion with the Oxford
Group.

2 Maxim Gorky (1868–1936), Russian noveliſt, playwright, and short story writer; his
play, *At the Bottom*, was firſt produced by the Moscow Art Theatre in 1902 and
published in 1903 (it is beſt known in English as *The Lower Depths*). The play is about
the hardships of people living in the basement of their landlord's house, hence its
appropriateness for Lowry's predicament.

3 See Edgar Allan Poe's "To Helen": "Helen, thy beauty is to me / Like those Nicéan

as long as I have, and from whom I had also borrowed the money for the journey, and failing in the latter attempt because I had no convincing proof of income to show at the border — this part is very complicated, so I'll come back to it later — A.B. Carey & Parks had guessed all that
5 — I now found myself then in the hands of one Maurice (and don't forget the Maurice, oh beſt beloved) Carey,[1] with whom I, that is to say we (I shall explain later) are at present staying. At this point I should state more clearly that I left Marjorie in Hollywood fully expeſting my return, that I lived only for that return, but that a series of other circumſtances I won't
10 inflict upon you following on the previous difficulties in Los Angeles owing to the murderous bitchiness of Jan about divorce and culminating in my unsuccessful attempt to return to Marjorie, further complicated by the faſt that Jan & she lived in the same town, and by Parks fruſtrating me on one side, A.B. Carey on the other, and the family solicitors on
15 both, had brought me to the verge of a real breakdown, one of the kind with caſt iron whiſtles whiskers on it. There was not only Marjorie, you see, but all my work, in the United States in one part port or another. There was the war, too, so I didn't expeſt to finish all the work, but did expeſt to see you, and appoint you, if you were to be found, a literary
20 executor, and I *had* accomplished much. No excuse would wash with the family, though I *had* volunteered to fight for England in England, & even possessed a return ticket via the Berengaria,[2] which although long since broken up as a firetrap, is still a ship if only in the memory, and a return ticket is still a return ticket even if left behind in Mexico & turned in at
25 Cooks in the Avenida de Madera. So, Conrad, to make a short story longer, turned back and at the dock's dark's edge,[3] knowing how cold the water was, I wired Margerie (with what was left of her fare) to come immediately to Vancouver, a diſtance rather farther than that from

---

barks of yore, / That gently, o'er a perfumed sea, / The weary, way-worn wanderer bore / To his own native shore."
1 Maurice James Carey (1897–1977) was a Commanding Sergeant-Major during the firſt World War. He claims that he met Lowry in a "local cocktail lounge" in Vancouver in the summer of 1939. Later, in 1947, Lowry presented Maurice Carey with the galley proofs of *Under the Volcano.* Maurice was not related to A.B. Carey. See Maurice J. Carey's "Life with Malcolm Lowry," ed. Anthony R. Kilgallin, *Malcolm Lowry: The Man and His Work,* ed. George Woodcock (Vancouver: University of British Columbia P, 1971) 163–70. The UBC Lowry Colleſtion contains a complete draſt of Carey's "recolleſtion" [43–4].
2 Cf. Tony Kilgallin's *Lowry* where Marmorſtein tells of Lowry's friend, Thomas Forman, flying his plane through the funnels of the *Berengaria* (26).
3 "dark's edge": Allusion to Aiken's prelude "xxxiii" which Lowry has previously titled "Darks Edge"; see letter 6, n. 3, p. 24.

London to Warsaw, as I needed her, which she did. When she arrived she found me in such a state of despair that she wrote back & resigned her job at home to take care of me. Now the set up is this. Maurice Carey collects the pittance left by the other two, who sit on the money, —
5 allowing me $2 a week for myself & Marjorie, in return for which we get a bed & one meal a day if we're lucky. And secrecy, from A.B. Carey & Maclean. There is a family of six, including a loud speaker, a howling wind which rages through the house all day, twins and a nurse, who sleeps with the youngest boy, aged 14. Mrs Carey, who thinks we are married,
10 says that this isn't right. Nor do I. Nor would you, think so, we think. I forgot the dog, the canary, & a Hindoo timber merchant, educated at Corpus Christi, Oxford — you can't get away from Oxford — who sleeps in the woodpile in the basement, hoping, with his fine Oriental calm, that one day he'll be paid for the wood.
15   We are, therefore, as you might guess, more or less bedridden, not because we are more ill than usual — we have stoutish hearts too even if a trifle cracked — but because bed is the only place in Vancouver where we have found either pleasure or protection, protection because once it is known by A.B. Carey — A.B for disabled semen[1] — that Margie is here,
20 she will be deported, since she is by now in Canada illegally, to parts unknown, & ourselves separated. It is not that the bed linen is stamped with the lineaments of last weeks love & the muddy boots of the week before, not *that* that one day the fear that the more detestable of the twins may be found — there was something appealing in its upturned face as
25 we lifted it tenderly out of the toilet — mysteriously drowned, — not that the oversexed Hindoo has an axe downstairs & that we know he intends to use it nor that the sound of the radio is like the voices of the damned howling for help, or that Maurice Carey, who is an ex-sergeant major with a disability, and how, has a habit of drilling an imaginary platoon up
30 & down the stairs at three o' clock in the morning, not that Vancouver is like the Portobello Road magnified several thousand times,[2] — not misery, oh Demarest[3] — and is the most hopeless of all cities of the lost, not all the bells and clashes of the night, which appal us: it is the thought rather of the absolute injustice of all this, of the misunderstanding, of the
35 hopelessness of communication, and the thought also that a sentence

1 Pun on the nautical meaning of "A.B." — "Able Bodied [Seaman]" — used frequently by Lowry in *Ultramarine*.
2 Cf. Aiken's poem "Goya" in *Blue Voyage*: "This was where Goya lived: in Portobello Road" (142–43); reprinted in *Selected Poems* 360–61. Cf. letter 65 where Lowry again alludes to this line.
3 William Demarest is the protagonist of *Blue Voyage*.

which is beginning (with of course the above reservations) to be fair, may at any moment be finished with a blot: that will stamp our lives out. But from brass bedsteads to brass tacks. For by now you can see by now that we cannot remain here much longer or God knows what will happen.

5   Now, as to the line, the hook line & sinker, to use with the old man, if you see fit to take one. Before you take any though, perhaps it is best to know that my relationship with M. Carey is further complicated by the fact that he has written to my father asking to be made trustee for my money here, with the understanding that he would then turn it over to

10 me for a certain cut each month. Being so desperate to be with Margie I agreed to this as at the time he seemed sympathetic — to do him justice, he is sort of, — but what with the twins & the Hindoo & all & we all have our bloody troubles & have to use certain methods to solve them not sometimes the real right thing, — but he has since proved difficult,

15 for instance, he pawned my typewriter one day without my knowledge, which I didn't exactly like, this one is borrowed,[1] — & should he get control of the money, we might not get enough to live on, & anyhow there is always the terrible fear that Margie may be deported: so you must not say anything about this to the family because, if it is impossible for

20 you to help us (& try & realise that your help is not just help, only, I must see *you* & also owe a duty to you), & we are forced to remain here, we shall have to depend on him. Margie is American helpless, & utterly without money, & were she deported it would be to Hollywood, she would have nothing to live on, & moreover, she would be, for many reasons in

25 an untenable position, & also she could not stand being without me. Anyhow I am very near a mental & nervous collapse, though cheerfulness is always breaking in[2] & I know that if Margie (whom you & Mary would adore) & I were separated, unless I could feel she were going to you, or a friend of yours, or somewhere where she could be near at least the hope

30 of seeing me again, or near some encouragement of that hope or assuage-ment of its loss, which she would not have in Hollywood, she would break up because — but why go on? We would both break. As to jobs here I would take any one, but I cannot because of my status here: nor are they taking any more recruits. I have frequently wanted to go to New York or

35 Boston where I would be in touch with friends of yours and get a job but

---

1   This letter exists in holograph only. Maurice Carey states that it was Lowry himself who pawned the typewriter in order to drink in an "East end pub" [UBC 43-4, page 19-20].

2   Cf. *Boswell's Life of Johnson*, 2 vols. (London: Oxford UP, 1922) vol. 2: ". . . cheerfulness was always breaking in" (230).

have been foiled always by Parks who would never trust me with the money — & I never seemed to be able to earn any at the right moment — then there was Jan & I was feeling a bit knocked oop about that, & so on ad finitum: and the family idea, of course, always was, at a distance, having the most sinister and mostly (but not always) fanciful idea of my goings on, that I would be horsing around, "free lancing", as they put it, & "not under proper supervision," — etc

It is queer, when all I wish is to be independent, that I should now be placed forcibly in a position where it is virtually impossible, although all this is quite consistent with the pattern of my father's general attitude.

Now you could suggest to my father, if the plan doesn't work by cable, (a little long perhaps) which would be better, among other things which may occur to you, that:

(1) You would be the trustee of my income & my guardian, but that your position would be to try & help *me* find a position in which I can be independent, in short you know you can find a job for me, subject of course to the limitations of my status, & time.

(2) You certainly would be more likely to expend it, that is my income, if any, for my benefit than an utter stranger, with whom I'm unsympathetic & who cares nothing for me.

(3) My letter suggests to you that I am desperately unhappy, absolutely alone & without friends in an abominable climate, but particularly unhappy because of the unfairness of not only being rendered unable to finish all my work, but unable to convince Parks or England that it exists, or is important, or that the definite understanding was that I should be allowed to go back to America.

(4) They objected to my going East on my own hook before to see publishers because they would not trust me: therefore you must make it plain that I will be under proper supervison: viz, in your home & in your constant care: also that I *have got* publishers who are influential people who are interested in my work.

(5) That I have made every attempt to enlist here, apparently, but have been turned down either because of health or status, you don't know which, & now they are taking no more recruits. However, if two birds must be killed with one stone, your own home is only a short journey from Eastern Canada, & later, when my work is in

the right hands, & they are again taking recruits, I could have another shot from the East. (I may agree with you eventually, Conrad, that there are better institutions than the army but it probably would not be tactful to say this to people who may be being bombed, even as you write.)

(6) Can you make it plain to my father that what he has heard of me has been mostly through other people, and that I am anxious to state my case, through you, who know me better than anybody.

(7) That I feel that my father is being exploited in the present situation, which is intolerable & hopeless, but that as my word is obviously discredited, I feel it useless to make any statement of my own side of the case, which is a matter of constant torment to me, & that you could act as mediator between myself, & you, who know & respect both parties

(8) That injustice is being done to me, that my prescence in Canada was none of my own seeking & was not, in the first place, necessary, since my visa would have been extended: & that I am very unhappy about the estrangement & I am appealing to you, desperately, to help me personally adjust the misunderstanding. Which goes as between myself & my mother too. (In spite of the fact that misunderstanding will always be as complete as ever, of course.)

(9) That above all I among strangers who neither understand me, & if I am to go to the war, you would like me at least to have his friendship.

(10) That I am still perfectly willing to go & enlist in England, as I stated to them when war broke out, but since they will not pay the fare over, I could earn it with you, & anyhow Boston is be the most sensible port to sail from in this hemisphere.

(11) You can say further, that if they are anxious about *drink*, that if there is still anxiety in that regard any longer on their side from what you can gather from my letter it is unfounded: but that'll *you'll keep a strict eye on me in that regard*. (Here's looking at you).

(12) If their idea is to cut me off without a penny fairly soon, why not give me enough to live on for some months in Boston anyhow,

which you would administer, so that at least I would have a fair chance, having none in Vancouver.

Now the family as you probably have gathered, are not likely to take
5 kindly to the idea of my marrying again so soon after one marital disaster, (though in this connection it should be mentioned that I can't anyhow, having only an interlocutory decree I can't be married for a year.) — so besides everything else we must keep Margie a secret for the time being & you must not mention her in your letter. It might, however, be as well
10 to state that with you I would be at least thousands of miles away from Jan, of whom you thoroughly disapproved & against whom you had warned me again and again, that she had been the source of a kind of antagonism that had sprung up between us at one time,[1] and that the only thing that ever went wrong with our own relationship was that you
15 knew I was fundamentally unhappy with her, that I knew that you knew, that I resented that knowledge, and therefore took it out upon you practically to the point of betraying our friendship, for my self-conceit, which is the truth as it happens, because I know now that all you really desired was my happiness: so, no Jan. Nevertheless, my plans for the future
20 must include Margie, as you can well understand; for our devotion to each other is the only thing holding me to life & sanity. We are perfectly adjusted to each other, & perfectly happy: And she is just the kind of a gal you always wanted me to have: and you always said I'd be all right if I had the right gal: & I do have the right gal, & I'm all right as anybody
25 can be who feels he's just waking from a nightmare; & were it not for this God awful environment of rain and fear, for although we fear no longer fear itself is about us, and the war with its smell of dead truth, its first casualty, in our nostrils, we'd both be all right.

Of course eventually I shall probably have to join up to fight for the
30 forces of-er-reason but at the moment I am more concerned with preserving my own which I consider no less valuable & certainly as remarkable as Hitlers. Meantime we want to be together as long as possible & grab what little happiness we can & definitely be together until we can be married before I go. This will probably be impossible in Canada
35 because conscription will come before the year is out but do not suggest to the old folks that I consider it also impossible in America because of my nationality thereby implying that I might wish to change a blue passport for a brown one

Upon reading this over I fear that you will come to the conclusion

---

1 Cf. Aiken's *Ushant: An Essay* where Jan figures as "Nita" (352–54).

that I have already loſt my mind but despite cheerfulness always breaking in you can see that we really are in a desperate situation. If my suggeſtion does not seem to you to be practicable can you think of anything else to do & for God's sake what ever you do do it quick before we sink for the laſt time.

I have some other ideas about approach to the family: one, seriously, if it could be afforded, by cable, a one, which would suggeſt that you had heard I was stranded in Vancouver & that Canada was taking no more recruits, that you had seen my publishers who wanted me on the spot, and could I come, because something important had developed for me, & that I could then stay with you: or perhaps put a publisher, or Bernice, or Linscott, or someone wholly imaginary, up to sending a cable saying that I was wanted in America for some work, & could it be made possible: or something like that. Any of these things might work. As for the financial end of it, my God, Conrad you know as well as I that you are far more my father than my own father & that once I was on the *spot in Boſton* with you, everything could be engineered from there financially; it has been done before: as for ourselves, it would save our lives: as for myself, personally, it would be the perfect reconciliation, either to a happy death, or to a new life: for I never felt more like working in spite of all this misery, & never more sure of myself: this would be, in reality, a great circle.

But to get back to Margie. We cannot be married for a year so we shall have to steer close to the wind during that time, & I do want for her sake to stay out of the army long enough to marry her, & if I stayed in the states that would give me time to do God knows how much work, & who knows, the bloody war might end? I've volunteered in both England & Canada & been refused in both places & I can't do more than that. If England still wants me, I think it only logical that I should see you before I go. But to avoid the possiblity of the deportation angle, would it be too much of a trespass upon your compassion for me to suggeſt, that if can lay my hands on a few hundred bucks I, as it were, *Send* Margie, who can cross the border whereas I at present cannot, on firſt to you as a sort of ambassador of the whole situation, while you meantime work like hell on the old man. If I can then come on afterwards, everything will be marvellous: but if I tragically cannot, I could by that time possibly have amassed enough money to get sufficiently far Eaſt in Canada, to be not more than a nights journey from Margie, Mary & yourself, — I am presuming of course you could find somewhere for Margie to stay in the meanwhile, — & from that point of vantage, being once *there* & *near*, & one might start arguing with the old man all over again? If this isn't too

much of a presumption on Mary & yourself. You can point out, if you
like, by the way, quite bluntly, that you feel definitely from my letter, that
now it has turned impossible to join the army in Canada, that if I am
thwarted in my desire to see you & finish my work in the states, the results
5 will be immediate & tragic.

Well, now for the work angle. I have written Whit Burnett[1] to send
you a book of poems called The Lighthouse Invites the Storm;[2] have
written Ann Watkins[3] to send In Ballast to Bernice: have written to Los
Angeles for Under The Volcano & a play:[4] & am sending you, by the
10 beginning of the next week, the copy of a thing called The Last Address,[5]
the original of which I am sending to Bernice. As this is, among other
things, about a man's hysterical identification with Melville, I think it
might interest Harry Murry,[6] & would be grateful if you would pass it
on, if you too think so.

15 So, Conrad, old fellow, please help. So deeply do I feel that yours is
the only star we can guide our bark on now I sense that my heart had
made provision for so turning to you in the end by its first journey years
ago to Boston & the Cape.[7] You can save two good lives, I think, & lives
worth saving, & lives you will be glad you have saved. Now, thank you
20 from the bottom of my heart for the suggestions you have already made:

My very best love to Mary, I have seen some of her Spanish pictures,
Man with concertina etc,[8] lately, reproduced, which are marvellous, & do

---

1 Whitney Ewing Burnett (1899–1973), reporter, author, and editor, who founded
Story magazine in 1931. He was editor and co-editor of Story from 1931–65 and 1966–71,
and editor of This Is My Best (Dial, 1942) and The World's Best (Dial, 1950). Burnett
published Lowry's "On Board the West Hardaway" in Story 3.15 (Oct. 1933): 12–22 and
"Hotel Room in Chartres" in Story 4.26 (Sept. 1934): 53–58.
2 "The Lighthouse Invites the Storm" was an early collection of Lowry's poems. See
Scherf's The Collected Poetry of Malcolm Lowry for the complete text of this collection.
3 Ann Watkins was Lowry's literary agent while he was in New York (1934–36).
4 This play was probably a dramatization of Nordahl Grieg's novel, The Ship Sails
On (1924; Engl. 1927), which Lowry was working on while in Mexico; see Lowry's 1938
letter to Nordahl Grieg (Breit 16) where Lowry asks for Grieg's "formal permission"
to go ahead with the play.
5 "The Last Address" was an early version of Lowry's novella, Lunar Caustic, ed.
Earle Birney and Margerie Lowry (London: Cape, 1968), based upon his experience
in New York's Bellevue Hospital in 1935.
6 Henry Alexander Murray (1893–1988), American psychologist, educator, and writer
who was a faculty member of Harvard University from 1926–62 when he was named
professor emeritus; he met Aiken at Harvard in 1927. In a 15 November 1939 letter to
Murray, Aiken quotes Lowry's description of "The Last Address" (Killorin 238).
7 Lowry sailed to Boston from England in the summer of 1929 to visit Aiken; see my
introductory note to the 1929–1938 section of letters.
8 Cf. letter 34, n. 2, p. 119.

you send me news of you both and news too of the voyage that never ends.[1]

   Margie sends love.

    Malcolm.

5 P.S Is the new novel 'Reading a book'?[2]

---

iambic pentametre.   10 feet. myſtery blizzard
                maſtery hazard.

10

A The thing to know is how to write a verse
B Whether or not you like it, whether or not,
B The goddam thing will put you on the spot
A And Petrarch will not save you from the curse.[3]

15

A You may be circumambient or terse
B   ?
A   , for better or worse
B A thousand lines without a single blot.[4]

20

C Chriſt the great psalmiſt cannot save us here
E He lisped in Numbers but no numbers came[5]
D

25 C
   D Eliot and Pound were prosing all the time
   E. And Whitman (Walt), alas, did much the same.

---

1 "The Voyage That Never Ends" was Lowry's title for his proposed novel sequence which he outlined in his 1951 "Work in Progress" statement to Albert Erskine, his editor at Reynal & Hitchcock; this statement is contained in the UBC Lowry Collection [32–1]. This phrase would seem to have been quite familiar to Lowry and Aiken well before Lowry decided to use it as a title for his novel sequence.

2 Cf. Aiken's *Ushant* (21). Aiken was at this time working on *Conversation*.

3 Cf. the similar lines of poetry in letter 16. This poem appears as a fragment in *The Collected Poetry of Malcolm Lowry* (368).

4 Cf. Ben Jonson, "LXIV: De Shakespeare Noſtrati," *Timber or Discoveries Being Observations on Men and Manners* (London: Dent, 1902): "I remember the players have often mentioned it as an honour to Shakespeare, that in his writing (whatsoever he penned) he never blotted out a line. My answer hath been, 'Would he had blotted a thousand,'. . ." (35).

5 Cf. Alexander Pope's "Epiſtle to John Arbuthnot," l. 128: "I lisp'd in Numbers, for the Numbers came."

P.S. Since finishing this letter laſt night things have become suddenly even worse and if something doesn't happen pretty damn quick the situation will become like the poſtulated end of Kafka's The Caſtle, in which K. was dying, surrounded by the villagers, worn out with the
5 struggle, which Kafka himself was too worn out to write. he was too worn out to write. we are staying in bed to try and keep warm, though we haven't enough blankets and we've put what's left of our clothes over us we're still freezing. There is an icy rain which hasn't stopped for days and the room is damp, we have both caught severe colds and Margie has a bad cough.
10 We aĉtually haven't had enough to eat and now we think Maurice, due to his injuries from the laſt war, has really gone a little crazy. He has told us that we muſt get out of here on Tuesday, which is the day he colleĉts money for my board from the other Carey, and if that happens we will aĉtually be penniless, in a strange & believe me damned hoſtile & ugly
15 country with no place to go and no friends. The situation is too complex to explain juſt why this will be so, but if Maurice turns us out he will have to lie about me to save himself (one more black eye to the family) and if I tell the truth about him, it looks even worse that I should have been staying with, and endorsing to the family, a man of his charaĉter. I assure
20 you, I simply had no choice in this matter, knowing no one here and having no status nor any money I was forced to truſt him and hope for the beſt — well, it has turned as you see. I aĉtually fear as for, different reasons, I feared A.B. Carey — truſting to truſting him with my mail so when you reply perhaps you'd better address me at the Hotel Georgia
25 where I shall *not* be staying but where shall make arrangements to receive mail, and better send another letter here, juſt in case. Another idea: an appeal to Davenport, whose address I don't know, might help. We had an underſtanding about this. Or what about an advance on a novel on this situation by both of us, or all of us, to be called Night Journey Across the
30 Sea?[1] Or can you say that something has turned up for me, that you muſt see me somehow, & get funds from the old man that way: or could you get him somehow to finance your expedition here, since it is so serious, I mean it, Conrad, it is damned serious: & for once I am not to blame for moſt of it. But whatever you do, Conrad, for God's sake do it quickly
35 before we sink for the laſt time into this more than sea, this Sargasso sea of despair.

We huddle in bed like gaboons in the jungle to keep warm, no blankets or one, and pinchbeck overcoats: we freeze: the icy rain which hasn't stopped for days doesn't even bring melancholy any longer: the room is

---

1 Cf. *Lunar Cauſtic* (62).

damp, muscles contract with rheumatiz, noses run, we cough like sheep,
I fear Margie may become really ill. We haven't had enough to eat, one
plate of beans a day, we no longer dare make tea because Maurice, (because
of a "war" injury caused by falling off a streetcar) is having one of his
'crazy fits', insults Margie, calls us "fictitious people," etc. Now —
although he is entirely dependent on us — So you see, as well as snow
there is fog.

19 : *From* AIKEN *to* LOWRY

KILLORIN 236

South Dennis Mass.

Nov 15 39

My beloved misguided misfortunate chaos-loving Malc — as you see from
the reverse of this, I started to write the Old Man and then thought
perhaps I'd better write you first, for even MORE information. Firstly and
most importantly, this: do you know of the difficulties, not to say practical
impossibility, of exporting money from England, and do you know for a
fact that the Old Man *could* so send it to you were you to cross into the
US? Is this possibly the reason why he wants you to stay in Canada?
Anyway, it's necessary for me to know about all this, and whether *you*
know and the Old Man knows. If you don't know, maybe you could find
out from the authorities there in Vancouver? And then I'll let fly at the
Old Man in the most ingenious manner I can. But first that is essential.
As for the rest, of course I'll do everything I can. . . . As for acting once
more in loco parentis,[1] of course I'll do it if it will help you, though our
own circumstances are precarious in the extreme, and we don't know
where we'll be or what doing two months in advance. We may stay here:
but on the other hand, Mary now it appears has chances of doing some
society portraits in Boston, so we may go up again in Jan. But Boston

---

1 Lowry's father had put Aiken *in loco parentis* of his son many years earlier in Rye
in 1930.

69

would be all right for you, you and Margie could find a corner for yourselves and I could as it were (from the O M's viewpoint at all events) keep a Benevolent Eye glowing upon you from a distance, i.e., from S Dennis or wherever, why not??? I think you could work in Boston (your own work, I mean — there are no jobs I fear) and you would know people, so it might really be the best thing. (In this connection, by all means send Margie in advance if you think best. But certainly with funds, for our own are nil, and we could do nothing for her. Sad, damnit, but true.) Meanwhile, the Mss will I hope have arrived, and will if so perhaps have begun something. I'll do my bursting best. Be sure to write to Bernice Baumgarten, Brandt & Brandt, 101 Park Avenue, telling her who you are and that it is at my suggestion you send In Ballast: it's a big office, and in the machinery it might be forgotten that you were the chap I'd spoken to her about. — As for your general Saga, jeez, Malc, it's a horror, it is, and I partly understand it, but not all: more light, more light, if you can and will. Are you drinking 'eavy-like? are you confused, or is all now lucid? Us, we're trying to be good, drink less (but still too much) and are really striving towards a Better Thing. High time too, for I'm far from well, weak in the knees, toothless, and must this winter probably lose the rest of my teeth in exchange for a porcelain mouthtrap, once I've acquired the stamina to undergo it. No, the new novel is The Conversation, a sinfonia domestica, a little poem of marital love (?????) in four movements, setting Cape Cod, a very ordinary 36-hour quarrel between a normal male and female, about nothing to speak of, and ending in holy bedlock. I'm pleased with it — I think its a multum in parvo,[1] and if I do say so as should, I believe it's got some, at least, of the classic virtues: form, delicacy, restraint, poetry, perhaps even a little wisdom. Reading a Book[2] maybe will be next — if this winter I feel well enough and settled enough to get my fumbling paws down into it. — Margie I must say sounds like a brick. We both send you and her our loves, and do count on us, we aim to do all we really can. I only wish to god I actually had some money, for that would so simply and quickly solve everything for you. But gosh if we even paid one tenth of what we owe — but let's not go into that. — Our devotions, old fellow, and keep up the chins —

Conrad

---

1 "multum in parvo": Latin, "much in little."
2 i.e., Ushant; cf. letter 18.

20 : *From* AIKEN *to* LOWRY

TS H 2549; KILLORIN 238

South Dennis Mass.

Dec 15 39

Abracadam. T[h]e enclosed wire came yesterday,[1] Malc — but as you will see, the end is not yet, and we must wait and see what comes of it. Maybe nothing: but at least my letter appears to have had the desired mollifying effect. What your own predicament — viz., as to being allowed to cross the border — will amount to, I can't myself imagine. *IF* the O M is in favour of the whole idea, *and* cash is put up for you, I don't see why not. I should think you could wangle something? Worst coming to worst, there might however be advantages in your idea of moving at least to the eastern end of Canada — Montreal? — there to be under my Eye as now you're under Park's. . . Anyway, I'll be keeping in touch, and you do the same, and we'll hope for the best. . . Ballast has just come — it will I fear be some time before I can get down to it, for I've got some work on my hands. Baumgarten reports that she couldn't make head nor tail of it, and alas that also she thought it not a commercial prospect. Mind you, B & B are pretty hardboiled anti-highbrow agents, who regard even me only with tolerance because I'm a friend of the family — so I wouldn't attach too much value to *their* judgment. As an offhand quick opinion, from just flipping it over, I'd myself say that it looks too confusedly elaborate, too circumambulatingly metaphysical and ego-freighted, to be effective. My own influence again has been bad, as in the chapter of unwritten, partly written, letters[2] — elsewhere too. I think it's time you cut yourself adrift from all these here ghostly doppelgangers and projections and identifications and let loose some of your natural joy in swiftness and goodness and love and simplicity — put your complexity into reverse — and celebrate the sun. Some of the latter poems go that way — though your metrics *is* queer, blimey yes. Here again I think the influence of the Complex Boys, these adolesc[e]nt audens spenders with all their pretty little dexterities, their negative safety, their indoor marxmanship,[3] has

---

1 The "enclosed wire," presumably from Lowry's father, is missing.
2 Chapter 7 of *Blue Voyage* consists of six unsent and unfinished letters from Demarest to Cynthia.
3 "indoor marxmanship": Lowry later used this phrase in his poem, "Where did that One go to, 'Erbert?," *Vancouver Daily Province* 29 Dec. 1939: 4, and in *Under the Volcano* (8).

been not too good for you — something with a little more gusto is wanted, guts, juices, blood, love, sunsets and sunrises, moons, stars, roses, — for god's sake let's let in the whole romantic shebang again, it's high time — I agree with old Ed about this. (What ever became of Volcano, by the way?) Ed writes that he may be coming over to Boston next month — if he can get here — so maybe we'll all be having a reunion. You knew, I suppose, that Jane is in Cambridge, working on Melville for Harry Murray?[1] Everything comes round and back, the eternal return. And Jerry is rumoured to be engaged, and my novel[2] comes out March 22, and on the whole life is damned good. It is, I assure you. So keep a-comin', old fellow, and we'll be seeing you. Meantime, our loves to you both —

Conrad

21 : *From* LOWRY *to* AIKEN

TS H 2506

595 W. 19th Ave.,
Vancouver, B.C.
Canada

[December 1939]

Dear old Conrad: –

A thousand thanks! I too received a cable from the O.M., more or less identical, which is a seven league boot step forward. It certainly *does* look as though you're letter had the necessary mollifying effect. The end, though, as you say, is not yet.

If worst come to the worst, or in preparation for the worst coming to the worst, would it be too much to ask you to sow the seeds of the idea in the O.M.'s mind that it would be advisable for me *anyhow* to proceed

---

1 In his article "Conrad Aiken and Herman Melville," Douglas Robillard says that Jane Aiken was working for Murray on his edition of Melville's *Pierre* (New York: Hendricks House, 1949) 90.
2 *Conversation.*

eaſt where I could be under your Eye? Then, if it is impossible to cross
the border at leaſt a change could be made for the better without undue
delay. But more of this later when I have more to go on. One snag is that
if permission went through meantime, it is possible I would have to return
here to cross the border. I think though if you could see your way to
dropping a note to Parks, saying that you had heard from the O.M., it
might help matters because Parks is so dilatory and cynical that he may
well hesitate to do anything at all until it is too late. At this point I want
to say that I realize that you are busy and simply may not have time to
do these things, but ask you also to realize that since I am engaged in the
perhaps not very useful occupation of saving my own exiſtance I muſt ask
them! Were you to do nothing else at all upon my behalf you have still
gone very far towards bringing matters to a solution for me and I cannot
adequately express my gratitude. A lousy corespondent, and in some ways
in the paſt not always the moſt dependable of friends, it grieves me to
think that you may think that I am only writing to you because I am in
a jam. But such is not the case: at heart I am always your friend: and, jam
or no jam, at such a period as this I would feel it of vital importance to
see you or to contaCt you and would move heaven and earth to be able to
do so. All of which b[r]ings me to the point that I am about to ask a few
more favors.

Since I may have only a short time leſt, and so do not want to embark
upon a new book, I think it wiser to complete what I have begun, especially
as it represents several years work, and also as 'In Ballaſt', even in its
incomplete and unsatisfaCtory version was praCtically accepted by Harpers, 'Under the Volcano' conscientiously awaited by Ann Watkins, 'The
Laſt Address' by Whit Burnett. To return to 'In Ballaſt' – the copy which
you have is the one which you read three years ago and said then that you
liked very much – with the reservations you repeated in your laſt letter
and with which I myself agree. Working along these lines I had rewritten
it but that copy was loſt in Mexico, so I now wish to rewrite it again.
Since the version which has been loſt was not open to the criticism you
have made of the version you have, perhaps it would be better if you sent
it on to me without bothering further about it and I'll get down to the
job. But I do feel that it is worth redoing since it had much praise from
many people (including – er – yourself.) Now about The Laſt Address' –
I know that that too is worth doing and doing as nearly perfeCtly as is
possible. Since you do not like the one long chapter, have you any
conſtruCtive suggeſtions to offer as to what I should do with it? And also
as to the parts at the beginning and end you did not altogether approve

of. All this applies very much more to 'The Lighthouse' as well. Could
you not, in the Shitehouse, reread the Lighthouse? And now about 'Under
the Volcano' – I left that in Los Angeles to be typed and sent on to me
to finish here, and for five months I've been vainly trying to convince
Parks that he muſt get it from the typiſt and send it to me – which he
blandly ignores. If you write him could you say that it is imperative that
I have the manuscript and finish it as you have definite commitments for
it? Perhaps that will spur him to some a&ion. I feel that you would approve
of Under the Volcano: it takes the same things to town which you take
in your general criticism of me and is the moſt mature thing I have done.
And, finally, would you try and realize the difficulties of working, or trying
to, in what amounts to a vacuum? However merited your criticism, and
however much I agree with it I cannot, in the present situation, apply
what is purely deſtru&ive. By which I mean that *since my obje& is to get*
something out quickly I have to make the beſt of what material I *have* so
that what I am asking you is more 'what can I do *without* scrapping the
whole bloody lot?,' assuming, for my sake, that it is beſt *not* to scrap the
whole bloody lot and that some of it, at leaſt, can be published? I value
your opinion more highly than anyone's and all that you have said will
carry its own weight and value. On the other hand I have always found
your opinion the moſt fru&ifying – for inſtance, a simple conversation
with you about poetry produced, for better or worse, a whole book, The
Lighthouse – and it is for that reason I would be grateful for anything I
can apply conſtru&ively to the imperfe&ions I shall be saddled with
anyhow, – in short for a prelude to some plaſtic surgery. I rather gather
from your letters that you feel there is too much of your influence all
around, that I should be able to break away from it by now and paddle
my own literary canoe. This may be all very well in its way, but, I presume,
I am still permitted to ask the old maeſtro, who is invariably right, for
technical advice, even if it is given in a 'Now this is what I think, go and
do something quite different on your own hook' spirit. Telling me to throw
away the whole boiling is, I submit, more moral, than technical advice.
Ah, the whirligig of taſte! But I should think what I have got, worked up
into a more acceptable f [or]m, would conſtitute a pretty good reſtart.

I'm not sure I agree about the Moonlight and Roses, although your
suggeſtions may very well lead to my showering you at a later date with
a *diarrhea scribendi* of romantic poems – and I might suggeſt that even
you might find it a little hard to write about the primrose at the old river's
brim if you were living in fear of your life at the bottom of a stinking well
in Vancouver! Then again, conversely, you might not.

And as for Ed, I don't remember much moonlight and roses about his work a few *years* ago, which is the period you are really dealing with in my case.[1] I would be interested to see his later pictures. Like yourself, though, I feel that he has always gone his own way, uncursed by trends. History has already made much of what I admired or pretended to admire during the last half decade quite senseless but since I *did* pursue a more or less middle course I think there is quite a lot I can restore, from the ruin in which I find myself, that would be by no means worthless with a slightly less arrogant facade.

So, for Gawd's sake, Conrad, if you can drop a pamphlet on me instead of a bomb, do so!

I would like to go on record as predicting, by the way, that your own work, past and present, will receive, during the next few years, the more general acclaim it has long so highly deserved.

There is something wrong with the style of this letter: reason I have lately turned journalist, in the Vancouver Daily Province.[2] I hesitate, however, to send you any of my stuff in case you tell me that it is the best I have ever done!

Well: Gawd be with you, and the happiest of Christmases to Mary and you and love from us both.

As ever

Malcolm

P.S. Parks' address is: Benjamin S. Parks,
735 Van Nuys Building,
210 West seventh street
Los Angeles,
Calif.

P.P.S. That there 'Itler, 'e's no King, 'e's no President, 'e's just wot you might call one of them there Dicktasters!

---

1 Lowry had last seen Burra in 1937 in Cuernavaca.
2 Lowry wrote two articles and one poem for the *Vancouver Daily Province*: "Holly-wood and the War," 12 Dec. 1939: 4 ; "The Real Mr. Chips," 13 Dec. 1939: 4 ; "Where did that One go to, 'Erbert?" 29 Dec. 1939: 4 [poem].

22 : *From* AIKEN *to* LOWRY

KILLORIN 240

5   S Dennis Mass.

Dec 17 39

Now, my dear undependable confused exacting but well-meaning Malc,
10 comes the moment for plain speaking, nicht wahr?[1] I had yesterday a long
wire from Parks, asking me if I would undertake full responsibility for
supervising you, and your affairs — "Malcolm personally, and his affairs"
— and adding that your trouble was "irresponsibility as to money," and
"continuous heavy drinking unless closely watched."[2] Well, I've wired
15 back that I will *take* this responsibility; but with natural misgivings, my
dear fellow, which you should be the first to understand. It's no idle
barroom jest, undertaking a thing like this: it means we give up our privacy,
independence, quiet, everything, and with grave risks of accomplishing
as little for you as for ourselves: we have our own work to do, our own
20 lives to live, and you should think of this, think of it *now*. I don't want
again to be accused, as in 1933, of being indifferent to your welfare, and
only putting up with you for the Old Man's money.[3] To hell with that.
So right here and now I'll say this: I don't even know what the O M or
Parks or whoever proposes to pay me for the job, and haven't *inquired*,
25 even. I'm doing this, in short, (and there are few I'd do it for) because I've
always as you know been damned fond of you and because you've come
to me for help at a crisis. So now: I hope you'll give me your word before
coming that you're really going to make a damned fine and convincing
effort to *behave well*, and to be as considerate of us as we shall be of you.
30 No secret drinkings round the corner, eh? No disgracings of us with our
friends, no scenes: and above all no continuous argument as to the amount
of drink allowed: I'm to be the boss about that, or it's no go. An amiable
boss, a loving boss, a good brother: that's all: but let's have that agreed.
Mind you, too, in all this, there is my beloved Mary to be considered. It

---

1 "nicht wahr": German, "isn't that so."
2 Cf. the 16 December wire from Parks quoted by Joseph Killorin: "answer 'immediately whether willing accept responsibility management Malcolm personally and his affairs if allowed join you in accordance his request'" (233). Cf. also Aiken's 16 December 1939 wire to Parks (Killorin 239).
3 It was in 1933, after their trip to Spain and perhaps after just such an argument, that Aiken stopped acting *in loco parentis* of Lowry; cf. *Ushant* (296).

means more work and less fun for her, it means worry for her as well —
bear *that* in mind. She agrees with me, juſt the same, in thinking that this
is something that has to be done, in *wanting* to do it — I think she'd be
a little ashamed of me if I didn't take it on. So there. Now put all that
5   together, please, and think it over, and if Parks and Co. permit the move,
and you yourself want to come, still, come with good intentions: clean
fingernails, a pure heart, a clear head, and prepared to be helpful and to
work.   Conrad

10

15

23 : *From* LOWRY *to* AIKEN

20   TS H 2505

595 W. 19th Ave.,
Vancouver, B.C.
Canada.

25

[24 December 1939]

Dear Conrad,

30   I have your letter and please let me inſtantly reiterate my thanks, both
to you and Mary. It is very gallant and sporting of you both to take on
what you have. After repeated readings, Conrad, of your letter, I find
myself more grateful than ever before, if possible, for your kindness, (and
subtlety); I am glad, though, to be in a position to remove some of your
35   very juſtifiable fears. I think that you intended, that for a time at any rate,
until I had fully digeſted your words in all the ambiguously funċtioning
organs of response, that a small, plangent Et tu Brute should sound among
my Hosannas. Juſt as well, because, it was while chewing this part of the
cud, bitter at firſt, that I was able to extraċt the more subtle juices of
40   meaning from your letter, which I might otherwise have missed. In my
sober mood it was a little difficult to realize at firſt that of course you

probably expected me to arrive with a giraffe on either arm, to come howling and spewing into South Dennis and collapse in the Congregational Church. Then, later, the one shoe in the bathtub, the surreptitious vomit under the piano, the ukelele and the fractured skull.[1] It would be,
5 on second thinkings, knowing me, very remarkable indeed if you did not wish to put yourself on guard against something of this sort. But please let me set your minds immediately at rest on this score! There will be nothing of the kind, it is a genuine striving for a Better Thing, and please assure Mary of it.
10

Now, for the other problems. I do feel, Conrad, that, although you are quite right to bring your perfectly naturel apprehensions on the subject out into the open, – on the principle that permanently to alleviate anxiety it is first necessary to dart a few added pangs, – I do feel, I am glad to say
15 with all respect, that the whole responsibility will turn out to be rather less titanic than you suggest. I could not feel right about coming if I felt it would really result in any serious or protracted sacrificing of both your independences and privacies: but that you were willing to *risk* this however, in accepting Parks suggestion is something which moves me
20 more than I can say. I do not, of course, know what Parks said, or what you deduced from it. I imagine something pretty juicy. Fortunately, it doesn't matter very much, as I hope to convince you when I have the opportunity of speaking to you personally. On the other hand, you have had no way of knowing for *certain* just precisely what the situation is,
25 except from my own statements, which must have seemed to you fantastic as Parks seems reasonable. It means simply that I have all the more to thank you for.

Now what I had suggested, and thought by your earlier letters you
30 understood and agreed with me about, was that you would do me the favour, since I was virtually non communicado with the family, of collecting my "income" and turning over to us, less, of course, what might be

---

1 "ukelele and the fractured skull": According to Aiken, when Lowry arrived in Boston in 1929 he was carrying only a broken suitcase and a ukelele (CBC interview, 1961). Aiken also tells of a wrestling match that took place between Lowry, himself, and his brother, Robert, on the first night of Lowry's arrival in Cambridge, Massachusetts. In the course of the struggle, Aiken "fell right over backward into the fireplace" and fractured his skull ("The Father Surrogate," *Malcolm Lowry Remembered* 40). Day also reports Lowry leaving behind one of his "pointed black patent leather shoes" at Dolly Lewis' (cf. letter 7, n. 1, p. 29) house in South Yarmouth (108); whether this is the incident to which Lowry is here referring, I am not certain.

compatible with your own time and trouble in the matter. This would enable us to live – quote, unquotes, and quotes – "in a corner to ourselves where you could keep a Benevolent Eye glowing on us from a distance???"[1] I surmise, however, that your telegram[2] may have inclined you to the belief that there is more to it than merely that. It is not an income at all, you may have been or will be told, because I have no money, a fact of which I have to be continually reminded, it is a sum of money put at your disposal to dispose of for me or not at all, as you think fit, it is something I ought not to have, that I ought to be ashamed of taking, something, in short, to my acceptance of which, especially in time of War, is attached the maximum amount of humiliation. On the other hand, if you take Park's place – as a matter of fact I upped and suggested as much to the O.M. in a moment of suddenly conquered phobia – you would get an additional fee, and if Parks is any touchstone, far from there being any responsibility attached to it, you would get this fee simply for putting me as far away as possible from you in some God forsaken place where I could not possibly be any nuisance to you whatever, where I would be unable either to obtain work or prosecute a normal life, and be driven slowly to the brink of suicide, which, as you had conscientiously put me first in the hands of the Oxford Movement, could not be possibly construed as your fault, or even anything to do with you in the least, nor, since the Oxford Group is notoriously prohibitionist, anything to do with anything save the Demon Rum, which, in spite of having no money at all I was still obviously able to obtain and consume in Pantagruelian Quantities. Your independence and privacy would be unimpaired because, in spite of any provisos, you had, after all, the final power of attorney, and if you chose not to sacrifice it, there would not be the slightest reason to do so. However, Conrad, you are not Parks, you are my friend, and I, believe it or not, am yours. Surely, this being so, it will be possible to hit upon some compromise, which will not embarrass you or interfere with your work but which will enable us to be free of this present tyranny, to be by ourselves, and to work, but nevertheless near enough to you to see you from time to time, which God knows, as I have pointed out before, would be only what I would want to do, and which I hope would be what you would want me to do, were the circumstances normal, under conditions in the world at present. I do not want to die off stage, like Mercutio;[3] and you have perhaps reckoned without my purely filial feeling for you, which

---

1 Quotation from letter 19 from Aiken.
2 Probably the telegram from Parks mentioned by Aiken in the preceding letter.
3 See *Romeo and Juliet* III.i.

is a genuine and true one. I would beg excusion for the monſtrous and ungrateful accusations I made of you in the paſt on the grounds that they were all in the general Oedipeian pattern, but I know you underſtand this already. Such things will not occur again, I assure you. This time a
5 recreated Priam has to deal with an Oedipus in his poſt-Jocaſta period, but whose afflićtion does not mean that he has loſt his vision, or hope.

Now I also see how your letter, — and I have to thank you also, for this, — since it is one that I could scarcely show anyone who didn't love
10 me, gave me an 'out' with Margie, (behind which thought do not think I do not also detećt the hand of loving kindness.) were Margie some grasping female – you don't *know* after all! – whom I had got into trouble, gave me a neat little pair of scissors to snip off a relationship I might subconsciously wished myself rid of. Margie's reaćtion as it should be was
15 simply one of deep gratitude: she asks me to say that of course she would be only too happy to help Mary and you in any way she could while and if we stay with you: she is a good cook, a good typiſt, quite capable of taking over any part of the housekeeping which would be the moſt helpful. But as for the allowance – what can I say, Conrad? What I get will have
20 to do us both, since I can't bring Margie out into the open now, with either Parks or the O.M. As things stand here, we don't get any of the allowance, buſt three dollars a week that's all: it was three-fiſty, sometimes its only two. I make a few dollars writing articles about Mr. Chips and such beloney (Mr. Chips happened to be my housemaſter by the way)[1]
25 and what is not even the reſt of the allowance goes to Maurice Carey and his whole family live on it. The reſt is being either misused or simply hoarded by Carey and Co., so there's damn little left for us. To the beſt of my knowledge I have about $150 a month: whatever Parks receives is outside of that. So if you receive what is now Park's fee, what income I
30 have, even if it is very much less than the $150, under the new arrangement should enable us to live quietly somewhere without in any way sponging on *you*. I expećt the amount will be left up to your own discretion. If there turns out to be no additional fee to what was once my income, and your part of it has to come out of that, I'm sure something satisfaćtory to you
35 could be arranged, we don't need much: simply a break. But it is unfortunately juſt precisely that kind of a break which it is well nigh impossible to arrange at a diſtance. But at this point I do want to say I'm absolutely

---

1 See Lowry's "The Real Mr. Chips," *Vancouver Daily Province* 13 Dec. 1939: 4; according to Lowry, James Hilton's Mr. Chips was based on "the Hooley," a maſter at the Leys School, Cambridge.

on the level, on the level about Margie, on the level about working, on the level about you, on the level about the situation here, and finally on the level about there being no problem about your having nothing to fear from my drinking or irresponsibility (does this letter or have my other
5   letters *sounded* irresponsible?)

I forgot to say that there ought to be quite a bit accumulated here unless these Oxford Group bastards have grabbed it or sent it back to the O.M.: I don't know and they won't tell me.
10

We would be only too delighted to get out of this hell-hole immediately, but what to do about my permission to reenter U.S.A? I understand an appeal can be made through Blaine (where I was refused on the grounds of not being able to prove income, you remember) but
15   Parks hasn't done a damn thing about my papers that I know of. He hasn't written me at all, and he has the proof. The appeal may have to go through Washington, presumably, would take time. Parks may be arranging for an immigration visa, however which would account for your being asked to take *full* responsibility. In that case it is a purely nominal thing and just
20   a legal necessity of some kind, but Jesus, if that's what you took, or whatever you took – it's bloody decent of you – I miss my cue here, will content myself with saying lamely, but meaning it, that, by Shakespeare, I won't let you down.

25   At the moment it would seem that the most sensible thing to do would be to proceed to Montreal, where I would be within hailing distance, first having ascertained whether, in the event of my receiving permission to go to the States, it is possible to cross at whatever border town is nearest there, without having to come back here, to Blaine.
30

In any event we shall not be able to get our feet upon terra firma until you assume the power of attorney: as things stand, the broth is foul, the cooks corrupt, and it's all too insanely complicated.

35   There remains the problem of transportation, both for Margie and myself: the problem of the Careys: the problem of Under the Volcano, still in Los Angeles: the problem of hating to cause you trouble but unfailingly causing you more and more; the problem of feeling that if my presence in U.S.A. is going to cause you and Mary all the embarrassment
40   you suggest it will I ought, as a point of honour, not to come at all; the problem of persisting just the same, and wondering whether I am right

81

in feeling that, if all goes well, it ought not to be so terrible for you: the problem of the war, of possible death, of marriage, and so on –

But at least we come to Christmas – this Christmas Eve it is snowy – with hope.

In any event, I do not know how I am adequately going to repay you for having so triumphantly helped us even so far, but I do think there is a way and I shall try and prove it.

Now, again, all our thanks to you again and equally to Mary, for *her* self-abnegation in the matter, – God bless you both and a very Merry Christmas to you; and to Jane.

As ever
Malc.

P.S.   I sent a question to the radio hour, 'Information Please,' the other day, for which I shortly expect to be receiving the Encyclopedia Britannica or some such. Since it is rather Jane's cup of tea, you might try it on her over Christmas. She may know, but I bet they're damned few people who do.

Question: What is the name of the book by an internationally famous American poet and novelist, which, having the Mississippi River as background and a Mississippi river boat preserving its unity of place throughout, has been compared, by an internationally famous American critic, not entirely to its discredit, with the great English satires of the eighteenth century, such as Gulliver's Travels?

Answer: The Confidence Man. The author: Herman Melville. The critic: Lewis Mumford.[1]

---

1   Lewis Mumford (1895–1990), American writer and critic. Lowry is referring to Mumford's *Herman Melville* (New York: Harcourt, 1929), in which Melville's *The Confidence Man* is described as "a companion volume to Gulliver's Travels" (253).

24 : *From* AIKEN *to* LOWRY

TS H 2550

S Dennis Mass

Dec 27 39

My dear struggling Malc —

yours of the 24th much appreciated, and enjoyed, and read with great relief, too. Okay by us, by me — we'll all try to do our beſt. There's only one thing I want to add while I think of it — viz., that I feel my responsibility to the O.M. too, you know, old fellow, and will live up to *that* — and for that reason I think at the outset it would be beſt if we all live together, either here or in Boſton. Probably. Anyway, I mention it. For apparently the O M and Parks prefer that solution, and if so we muſt pro tem[1] live up to it. But that would in many if not indeed all reſpects have its virtues and pleasures too, so wot the hell, boys, wot the hell.

The financial arrangements I don't profess to underſtand, even after your analysis, but I don't doubt that will all straighten out.

Meanwhile, I've written by air to Parks, not having heard a word from him since our tossing of telegrams to and fro, asking him to let me know *q c*[2] what is going on: for if we move up to Boſton, as we think of doing, we shall want to know pretty damned soon.

Pending word about all these things, no point in sending Ballaſt to you, for you might be on the move already? And as soon as Xmas gueſts are out of the way, and my article on sociological poets done for the Atlantic,[3] I'll re-read the Lighthouse. (Also, I've asked P to send me Volcano, saying I want to send the whole blinking lot to a publisher.)

Much reassured altogether about everything by your admirable letter: I guess you're okes, kid. We'll all be showing them — as Bob Nichols[4] remarked to me — a bengal-light of a redivivus

---

1 "pro tem": "pro tempore," Latin, "as time permits."
2 "*q c*": "quam celerrime," Latin, "as faſt as possible."
3 "Back to Poetry," *Atlantic Monthly* Aug. 1940: 217–23.
4 Robert Nichols (1893–1944), British poet and playwright whom Aiken met in Chicago in the 1920s. When Aiken returned to Rye in 1930, he was pleased to find Nichols living in the nearby town of Winchelsea. In an April 1931 letter to Walter

yet. Up the moonlight! Up the everlasting rose! Up the sunset! But not forgetting either that behind our exquisite Congregational Church is a darling little shit-house, with two compartments — male and female created He them, but the naughty boys and naughty girls have cut
5 peepholes through the partition, and written ambiguous little scralws on the walls: and this too we shall celebrate, cerebrate, assimilate and sublimate. In the spring, when we go subli-mating. . . O well.

our loves to you both

10 Conrad

15

25 : *From* LOWRY *to* AIKEN

TS H 2508

20

595 W. 19th Ave.,
Vancouver, B.C.

[January 1940]

25 Dear old fellow:

Many, many thanks for everything, including the tele-gram,[1] please convey this immediate expression of my gratitude to Mary
30 and Jane. Now, by god, it does look as though, as Ibsen says, the miracle of miracles has happened. I cannot tell you how absolutely overjoyed we are. Yours is the genius which brought it all about but there is a special beauty about seeing the machinery of the whole thing begin to turn over. Even Parks has, at last, begun to cooperate! Yes, and how! He has been
35 in touch with the immigration authorities and all I have to do now is to sign a few letters. He also has 'Under the Volcano' (in a state of eruption, I imagine, in its present form). However, as you would say, the end is not

---

Piston, Aiken refers to Nichols as "the mad poet" (Killorin 174). Nichols appears in *Ushant* as "Edward."
1 Probably the telegram from Aiken to Parks, mentioned by Aiken in letter 24.

yet: it is in sight, we are already peering at Cape Cod, counting the windmills, (and promising not to tilt at any) and dreaming quohaugs and swordfish. But it is now, at this very moment of apparent perfection in the order of things that a sad possibility – as I hinted it might before – intrudes itself. With all the papers in the world to swear now that I will not be a public charge there is only a 60/40 chance of getting through. Earl (Epistomologer) Russell[1] has been turned down lately, on account of the war: and others. But even if I do get permission it will be an unusual bloody miracle if it arrives for two or three months. There was some mistake made at the border in the matter of my visa which may further complicate matters and also the business of my divorce. Meantime we are virtually dying here: if you have never yourself been in the clutches of the Oxford Group as I have you will think, (as I believe you could not help thinking before!) that I was just acting dramatic or talking tight. It is not so. Versed though you may be in the moral obliquities and vagaries of mankind I do not think that you can begin to know anything about hypocrisy until you have fallen foul of one of those bastardos. They have everything. Well, I feel so braced by the general outlook that I can almost feel a sort of tenderness for *them*, but the fact remains that so long as I am under their auspices, I am virtually a prisoner, and so is Margie: work, also, correspondingly suffers: and the future is drawing in like the winter nights. In two months, or three, – if permission is denied, – we should still be here, and rather worse off than before, because by that time it is likely that real hell will be popping in Europe. My duty in this regard is another thing again, it is not yet clear to me what form it will take. I refuse, however, while the possibility of other, clearer, cuties — strange typographical error! — remain to me, to be caught *off balance* by this war if I can possibly avoid it: that others have been is too bad for them: but since it seems I am, for the time being, a creature of luck, I am determined to finish what work I can, and to do my utmost to get the freedom to do it, before I cease to be so. That, I think, is a clear enough duty to the O.M., to yourself, and to myself. It is part, too, of my duty to Margie. For the rest, as with her, I can only strive to place her in as cheerful and constructive environment as I can, forgetting the end of Festus[2] (Faustus too) and that war exists. Margie is now in Canada legally, she has been

---

1 Bertrand Arthur William Russell (1872–1970), British mathematician and philosopher; third Earl Russell, grandson to first earl of Bedford, John Francis Stanley Russell.
2 Allusion to Aiken's *The Pilgrimage of Festus* (New York: Knopf, 1923). At the end of the poem, Festus realizes that his pilgrimage has been a failure.

to the immigration authorities here, and can remain in Canada indefinitely so far as they are concerned, but there is the constant danger, so long as we remain in Vancouver, of A.B. Carey and His Hot Gospel Groupers finding out that she is here, which might result in our separation
5   and utterly destroy everything we are trying to sincerely to build up: you may laugh and say this is not so, but believe me these Oxford Groupers are worse than the Gestapo, they are all one's persecution complexes rolled into one stinking whole.

10   Now, Conrad, what I am driving at is this. In two, three months anything may happen. If the permission is refused, the spot we shall be on will be grisly indeed, and the trouble you have gone to all for nothing. For not only may by that time circumstances necessitate my joining up immediately here, but I shall be as far away from you, my nexus
15   to redivivus[1] and the real world, for however short a period, as ever. Parks, Carey and Co., fundamentally indifferent, will still be in charge. A clause in Park's letter suggests that my family wish me to enter through Blaine, but that obviously, is Parks-inspired. The O.M. obviously doesn't give a hoot how I get into the States so long as I do so legally. Now I have
20   ascertained through immigration here that so long as my application is made *through* Blaine, it doesn't matter through which port of entry I go. The most reasonable plan, therefore, would be that somehow or other we proceed to Montreal quam celerrime, or some place in Canada, near Boston and near the border, in which I could be under your Eye, at a
25   distance so to speak, as I am under Park's now. This, you have previously concurred with as a possibly good idea. Once there I could await the news from Washington and, if I do *not* get permission finally, at least I am not thousands of miles away from you, and perhaps we could figure some way out of seeing each other before The Deluge etc. Moreover being in touch
30   with you about work and things would not mean that matters would be so absolutely hopeless even if I were refused. The difficulties seem to be these. Parks, Carey and Co. will object to my being in Montreal unless under proper supervision. If you therefore could wangle my coming to Montreal, it would have to be on the understanding probably that either
35   you would meet me there, or that you could arrange for some friends of yours to be trustees for me in Montreal just as Parks did here in Vancouver. But whatever you said, as soon as I was in Montreal I would be out of Parks and Careys clutches, not, as you justly may have suspected, to feel

---

1 "nexus to redivivus": Latin, "link to rebirth." Cf. letter 24 from Aiken: "a bengal-light of a redivivus."

free to go on an interminable bender, but merely free to what work I have
to, and give Margie what happiness I can in whatever time may be allotted
to us. That is the truth: and I assure you again that I am absolutely ready
to cooperate in every way. I could send you receipts for everything, if
5   necessary, we need little enough to live on, and would concur in anything
you said or advised. I appreciate what you said about the O.M., and here,
strange as it may seem, I too feel a responsibility, and also feel moſt
strongly that the only way to go about discharging it is the exaƈt one that
has been chosen. I think that nothing in the world would give the O.M.
10   and the mater[1] a bigger bang than to have me have a few books accepted
in the States in the coming year and to feel that you had been inſtrumental
by your encouragement in bringing it about after such a downfall – and
admit it Lowry, it was a kind of downfall – as I have had. And if I fail,
what the hell, boys, we've done our beſt. The attempt may be worth more
15   than one knows.

I am not saying anything about Montreal to Parks but am
leaving the whole thing up to you. A cable to the O.M. would do the
trick, I feel. I have eight dollars, saved somewhat forlornly, as againſt
20   Margie's journey, produƈt of the lampoon I send you.[2] If you think that
a cable is the thing, I would be only too delighted to forward the amount.
Parks, I know, would only fool about, poſtpone things, write a noncom-
mital letter, which would go down in some Greek tramp steamer, and
we'd all be where we were before. By the time you have received this I
25   will already have made application to Washington. I am writing too to
Seattle for further confirmation that it is possible for me to await news
of the success of my appeal to Washington in Montreal or wherever. What
I am suggeſting is, however, that you obtain permission for me to come
to Montreal anyhow, if there is no immigrational objeƈtion, immediately,
30   and, if there is, to Montreal inſtead of Boſton [s]hould my appeal be
refused. This would dispense with fatal delay later. But I do believe this
to be very important. Could you not suggeſt to the Parks that Be then
that, in the spring you will be much more busy, but that now you have
some time to put at my disposal, that you might be able to make a trip
35   to Montreal, but that, anyhow, you have friends there, and so forth, all

---

1 Lowry's mother, Evelyn Boden Lowry. In later years Lowry assumed the name
"Boden" as his middle-name.
2 Lowry's "lampoon" is missing, although he is probably referring to his poem
"Where did that One go to, 'Erbert?" published in the *Vancouver Daily Province* 29
Dec. 1939: 4.

this, with the absolute understanding from myself, of course that I am absolutely sincere in this whole matter, which I hope by now you believe. I do feel that now we have got so far that you will agree that it might as well be successfully concluded and I shall not feel safe until I am under your aegis. I cannot adequately express my thanks, Conrad, to Mary and yourself for being so absolutely swell, so understanding and so sporting in this whole matter. I know full well what a bloody intrusion on your time I'm being and cannot say how much I appreciate your forbearingness and patience. As for the financial (and more superficial) end of it, for, as you see, it was not money so much as understanding that was needed in this case, – I am sure you will find that the O.M. will not be too difficult in the matter, and I also know he will be very glad, finally, that you were good enough to make the agreement with him.

Please give Mary our best love, and of course to yourself, and Jane, should she still be with you.

Malc.

26 : *From* AIKEN *to* LOWRY

KILLORIN 241

S Dennis Mass.

Jan 19 40

My dear Malc — a short one today, time presses, snow falls, millions of letters wait to be writ, but just a line to wave you on — yours and M's[1] received and enjoyed, appreciated too — deeply. We've written, or Mary has, to a friend of hers in Washington, just on the chance she might know someone in the Labour Dep't and expedite or charm your application — an *outside* chance, but we thought worth trying. So now we wait. If all

---

1 See Appendix II for Margerie's 12 January and 29 January 1940 letters to Mary.

blows up, if you *can't* get in — well, then we muſt try to think of something else. Maybe the Montreal idea, or some such. But let's wait and see.

Meanwhile, I'm glad you see my point about toeing the line. This now becomes, I think, all the more important, for I've had my firſt letter
5 from the O M, and I'm afraid I muſt tell you that the whole situation is very serious: he says flatly that unless *I* can report in due course that I find you truſtworthy and reformed and working — and for this too he wants you to live *with* me at the outset — he's made up his mind to caſt you off, and never again to come to your rescue, no matter *what* happens.
10 So, my dear fellow, it's up to you. *And* it's up to me to play absolutely fairly with him, too, you can see that. No cutting of corners: we muſt do it right. Frankly, the Margie thing worries me on that score, as it ought, I think, to worry you. It puts me, at the outset, in the awkward position of having to conceal something, which I don't dammit, much like. Would
15 it perhaps be better if you were to write the O M yourself telling him about her, and asking whether you might bring her Eaſt for, as it were, an Official Inſpeftion by Mary and myself — subjeft of course to my agreeing then to the idea. I think this might be wise. I'd suggeſt you do it right away, so that by the time you get here we might have a cable from
20 him okaying the notion: or at any rate leaving it to me. You can tell him, if you like, that you've *juſt now* informed me of the situation, and that I've agreed in advance to M's coming along later for a visit. That would put things on a squarer footing????? Think it over, anyway? And believe me Malc I don't bring it all up juſt to make difficulties — good god no.
25 It's simply that I feel we *muſt* be honeſt. And the other isn't, quite. But if *ſteps* have been taken to regularize it, before Margie comes, I shan't mind so much: I'll then be in a position to say that you'd told me you'd written, asked *my* permission, and I'd taken it upon myself to consent. See? Yeah.
30 Also, and this is sort of hard to say, my poor Malc, but I think I'd better say it now — viz., you know, prolonged drinking *does* rot one's honeſties, kind of — if you'll forgive my saying so you'd already become somewhat oblique when I saw you in Mexico — I gather from Parks you've since got worse, though of course I take it you're now very much
35 better again: but the point is, I shall want to be shown. I'm going to truſt you, of course, that goes without saying: BUT, I warn you fairly, if you *should* let me down I won't lie to the Old Man. Let's have that underſtood, eh? It puts me in the invidious position of having the final responsibility of getting you cut off without a penny, which isn't much fun for me, any
40 more than it is for you: it gives *you* a damned heavy responsibility to *me*: don't ignore that, and if it comes to pass, remember that I warned you,

and try now in advance to absolve me, as you muſt!

Well, hell's bells, I didn't mean to get off on all this, it's merely that it's been on my mind. For the reſt, we look forward to seeing you, and I hope it's soon. Mary goes up Monday to look at a house in Charleſtown, which we think of taking — she really *needs* to be in town, so that her portrait painting can go forward properly. And if you and M come it will give us all I think a better place to live in, with more scope and freedom. Incidentally it's entirely surrounded by cheap bars and dens of vice, hard by the Navy Yard etc., so Temptation is going to be your middle name! Steel yourself — Otherwise, we'll stay here. In faſt, we may have to anyway. — We'll see. — Mary will be answering Margie's good letter — she joins me now however in sending much love to you both, and beſt wishes for speedy solutions —   SIEG HEIL[1] Conrad

27 : *From* LOWRY *to* AIKEN

TS H 2507

595 W. 19th Ave.,
Vancouver, B.C.

January 27, 1940

My dear Conrad ———

I was at firſt so bewildered and hurt by your letter that I was at a loss to reply but since there is, of course, a logical reason for everything you've said, I am no longer bewildered and hurt and am taking the bull by the horns and boldly doing so, answering your letter as fully as I can and begging you the favor of absorbing every word.

I have thought long and carefully about your suggeſtion of my writing

---

1 "Sieg Heil": German, "Hail Viſtory"; Nazi salute during World War II.

the O.M. telling him about Margerie and asking whether he would have
any objection to my bringing her east as it were for your official inspection.
On the face of it there would be no reasonable objection to this had I only
the O.M. to contend with. But the fact is that the O.M. would then put
5   this matter up to Parks who might then make inquiries which would lead
to his discovery that Margie is in Canada. There is of course no reason
now, since her position is above board with the immigration authorities,
why Margie should not be in Canada. Even were it discovered that she
were staying here, she is ostensibly at any rate properly chaperoned. But
10   this discovery would lead to a referring of the ratification of Margie's trip
east to A.B.Carey who, as I have told you before, is a man who believes
that any passionate relationship between a man and a woman is an evil
thing and who would be sure, however honest our own motives, to put a
dishonest light upon the whole thing. Moreover there would now be an
15   excuse for it, and the fact that he had already shed such a light when there
was *no* excuse for it and that he drove us thereby to the decision we made,
would have no bearing on the matter. Parks is trusted by the O.M., and
he cannot very well admit, since he landed me here with A.B.Carey, that
the latter is not only a man utterly unsuitable for the so called duty
20   conferred upon him but a pervert in the bargain. I myself would have no
difficulty in the long run in pr[o]ving these allegations and worse, namely
that Carey's affiliation with the Oxford Group dates from his contraction,
due to whoring, or boys, I am not clear which, of a very serious venereal
disease contracted when married and with children. His vices do not
25   interest me, but when I am forced to submit Margie's destiny to the final
arbitration of a man who is himself dishonest and whom I regard with
contempt (and pity), it is another matter. I cannot do this; I do not think,
if you believe me, as you must, you would want or expect me to do it.

30   My own stock, as I warned you at the outset, and of which you now
doubtless have abundent proof both from the O.M. and Parks, is zero.
Although, ironically enough, there is plenty of inalienable proof that
Parks also has not dealt honestly with the O.M. unfortunately the O.M.,
up to the present victimized by the various contending forces, would have,
35   for the sake of his own amour propre at least, to pretend to others if he
did not to himself that he had been dealt with fairly. At this point I ought
to say, which is important, that my continual protestations that those
entrusted with my affairs have been dishonest with the O.M. even though
you may accept them, probably only has the effect of confirming you in
40   your determination to be absolutely above board with him: I am inclined
to think that you feel that in this way you are saving yourself in advance

from any possible allegations which I, with my degenerated character (or
because you have submitted to tirades in the past you may expect
something of the same sort in the future) might make about *you*. Deeply
sympathized with, fellow, but surely such things aren't so goddawful
5   complicated between us as this. I have grown up you know, sort of, so let
it be fully understood in advance there will be no nonsense of this sort,
whatever you do or don't. Besides I deeply feel that what I am suggesting
is the *honestest reasonable* course. Unfortunately, right here, there is also
proof, for which I freely admit that I am suffering, that I did not deal
10   formerly, as he might say, squarely with Parks, but here I have the very
hefty excuse which you may take or leave, that in spite of his good points
and in spite of the fact that he genuinely believed that drinking was my
only trouble and did much, although he went about it in the wrong way,
to prevent me from drinking, that I never looked upon him as a friend
15   but simply as a crook who was to be outwitted. I do not overlook his
merits as a lawyer, and think it unlikely, for his own sake should you have
any dealings with him that he would dare to be dishonest with you. But
fundamentally dishonest he is of which I also have abundent proof and I
would be on your guard. Hence you will see, old fellow, that our attempts
20   to achieve the "truth" would be surrounded on all sides by loud gregarious
lies which we would not have the allotted time to clear away in order to
achieve our point. I would say further, that the only trouble I have
encountered, so far as they are concerned, was when, partly in an effort
to get away from this odiousness once and for all I told the truth to A.B.
25   Carey with the bitter results you know. and I can only say it serves me
right for trusting a licentious sentimentalist and a political cheat. I do not
think it helps my point to condemn the other fellow, in fact his vices may
be the only human part of him, but since the condemnation is just and
all these people have done their damndest to make me feel abased in my
30   own eyes I harp on it just to try and show you how thoroughly hyprcritical
the whole set up is and to try and convince you that *before* we can do
anything a complete break must be made by both of us from it. It is the
hour of the knife, the major operation.

35   Another thing is that such a course as you suggest might, even if
successful in the final analysis, result in placing Maurice Carey in the red,
which would not be exactly the sporting thing to risk for although he has
not failed to extort certain things from us, even practically to blackmail
us on the basis that blackmail in Vancouver, just as it was in the eighteenth
40   century in England, is merely part of the mechanics of a business
transaction, at least we are grateful to him for our being together at all

during the laſt months, and moreover when, with much trepidation, it muſt be admitted, but by way of laying the ground work for a later and complete honeſty all round, informed him that we were endeavoring to get away from him and had been striving to do so solidly for the laſt
5   months, reaċted in a manner which was far more than surprising, (a manner which reminded one of the fantaſtic Chriſtian aċts which Doſtoievsky attributes to some of his darkeſt charaċters) which seemed to us almoſt sublime! Not only did he seem genuinely pleased for our sakes that we would have the possibility of living in a normal fashion, but
10   said that he would write a "cracking letter" to you about it, of which we have heard some queer excerpts and gather, although we have not heard definitely, that he was some time ago with much creaking of syntax and tortured recolleċtions of the paradigns of such complicated verbs as to be, and also because he asked us no less than three times how to spell
15   blackguard, was aċtually improving it, and by now may well have poſted it. We can only guess at the nature of the completed maſterwork which you have received, or will receive – we were hard put to it not to laugh, which would have hurt his feelings, at what parts we heard, but here again I should be on your guard because it may well be thet here an erring is
20   made in another direċtion, and we feel uneasy, especially if he has seen to regard you as a sort of "conspirator" which we know that you will not like. On the other hand, whatever it says, it scarcely can fail to convince you, if there are any faċts in it at all, that there is something definitely wrong on the other side of the case, and since this man is the truſted
25   appointee of A.B.Carey and hence of Parks, that unnegotiably paradoxes exiſt in the present set up and that if Maurice Carey is not all that should be desired as an ambassador of verity, then neither are A.B.Carey or Parks. That you will not wish to be associated with this kind of thing goes without saying, and I now want to say flatly that the appeal to yourself
30   was very largely made in order that we could be delivered once and for all from this nightmare of confused wills and direċtions, dishoneſt and otherwise, in our lot. In this respeċt we have appealed to you so to speak as the Truth and if the Truth finds itself to be on the spot a little it is no wonder, but I think that we may have done something so far in this letter
35   to remove certain superficial doubts in your mind as to our integrity with you which *is*, which has been, and will continue to be and muſt be for all our sakes, complete.

Now before discussing some of the other matters brought up in your
40   letter, I wish, if possible, to account briefly and as beſt I may, for I myself am not yet acquainted with the whole painful story, for the reason *for* all

this and *why* any allegations have been made at all by Parks and the O.M. of such a serious nature that they have obviously caused you, in spite of the fact that I said before hand that they would be of such a nature, apparently to change your mind regarding helping *us*. Do you remember Miller, the little communist in Mexico?[1] My troubles seem to date from my association, of a purely friendly and non political nature, with him. I will not go into detail but I strongly suspect here the hand of blackmail that a certain person or persons have volunteered information of a defamatory character to the O.M. with the view of extorting money based upon my purely superficial relationship with him and with some of his confrères. In spite of the fact that I was not even then of their persuasions and only the mildest kind of pink and in spite of the fact that these allegations were monstrously untrue they were nevertheless undoubtedly made, with whatever motive, and the fact that I had been associated with these people in any way whatsoever has served to blacken my name and to act as a working hypothesis for investing me not only with DISEASES but CRIME as well. I have heard the most incredible stories about myself which I know have got back to the O.M. and in only one of which is there a grain of truth. Unfortunately this one was by all odds the most damaging of all. A female to whom Parks had been introduced and with whose "set" I had been consorting soon after the interogatory state of affairs with Jan, had one hell of a brawl for herself when tight and with her husband in my room where they had come, whiskey bottle in hand, seeking me. Although I was not even there at the time and only arrived later, when the hotel clerk and I tried to get them out, the damage had already been done. The female had apparently got it into her head that she wanted to commit suicide, hysteria and usquebaugh[2] was all over the place, she had a black eye and a cracked rib (her husband had cracked this for her three months previously, though) but I was on the carpet. It did little good for the female some days afterward to spring to my rescue or even the hotel staff to affirm that it was not my fault, the onus was entirely on me. Fortunately it was only a localized row, no police, or anything like that, and Parks, I think, to do him justice, would not have reported this matter had not we violently quarreled at this point and I called him a crook. In despair as to how this affair would sound in the Wesleyan hush of my father's house I sent a telegram to Stuart,[3] telling him that Parks was a

---

1 Not identified.

2 "usquebaugh": Whiskey; Gaelic, "water of life." Cf. Lowry's poem beginning "The doom of each, said Doctor Usquebaugh" in letter 40.

3 Stuart Lowry (1895–1969), Malcolm's eldest brother.

crook and asking him simply for enough money to get me by the next couple of months and then to inform the O.M. that I was absolutely through with any money from that source from then on, which should enable me to go to New York, — I had not met Margie at this time, —
5 and try and make a fresh start on my own hook. Parks intercepted the telegram at the desk and sent it to my *father*, having told them that he would simply get it sent for me. (This for your delectation is a criminal offence. But what, under the circumstances, could I do?) It was then I got wind of the general idea that the O.M. had formed from these reports of
10 me, which was to have me declared incompetant and have me shut up in a sanitarium where I could be of no further harm to anybody. Tears of rage might well stream down the old countenance at this, and also at the effect of what must have been a ghastly report of something, which however might have happened to anybody, upon the aunts and prostitutes
15 at home, it did not alter the fact that from that time on my goose was cooked. You speak of my O.M. coming to the rescue, but in point of fact, although this is what the poor old fellow thought he was doing no such coming to the rescue has taken place at all, nor was any rescue needed in the sense you suggest, the only person who came to any rescue was Margie,
20 yes, financially too, because you must remember I never saw a fraction of the money sent out for me! And indeed the only time I appealed to the O.M. for help was lately when in despair at convincing him that both he and I had been caught in a web of falsehood I wrote him an absolutely despairing letter in which I begged, much as I dislike to *beg*, to be able
25 to see you whom of all people I felt alone able to trust to make an absolutely impartial collocation of the news with regard to myself without, I felt, any due favor to me. I included the latter because when you did not write me [—] I mean you, personally, didn't: not Mary. [—] after leaving Mexico I was left with the conclusion that something, I do not know
30 precisely what, was rankling. With this in mind I was not as astonished as I might otherwise have been at the tone of your recent letters. I want to assure you again now that I intend, have intended, intend in the future, and have done in relation to Margerie to tell you the absolute truth and nothing but the truth. I deeply value your friendship and at such a time
35 as this I wish profoundly that if there are any worms in either of our bosoms they should be removed. There is not one fact that I have wittingly distorted to you. In order to make my story more plausible to you I wich that I could paint A.B.Carey less black, Parks less cynical, myself less exploited, than I have done but the fact remains that although I do not
40 wish to make a song about it I have been more bloodily misused than any five people you can think of, if we except the Czechoslovakians and the

Finns, and if you love me as a friend as I believe and can only conclude from what you have done for me already that you do, I feel that you will do something about it.

5   As to drink rotting one's honesty, alas, that is true. At one time I felt indeed that more than rotting my honesty it was destroying my identity as well. Many of my troubles, but also many of my wisest decisions, are due to it but I am not, as Parks has suggested, allergic, whatever that means, to it. I have at last gotten wise to it, ceased to tell myself polite
10   little lies about it, forced myself to realize what allowances are made for one when tight, and hence how much one deceives one's self, and have at last put this bogy where it should be, as simply a concomitant of social intercourse. In short, I still like as much as almost anyone you can trust to have a few drinks, or even on occasion, more than a few, but on the
15   other hand it is the first time in my life I might almost say I can take a drink if the occasion seems to demand it or I can leave it alone altogether. I am capable of probably more self dicipline than you imagine and I think you will be relieved to hear this and that no exhortations are any longer necessary on this subject. With wine and other bootleg liquor as cheap
20   as it is and with Maurice almost constantly barracho[1] it would be quite possible for me to keep quite plastered here week in and week out even on the amount of money that I have should I wish to do so, so temptation could not possibly be any worse in Boston than it is here. The bogy may raise its head again but not if I say so while you are the arbitrator and
25   even if it does both Margie and myself are well equipped to deal with it. Principally I have been forced to this attitude by the realization that it did actually rot one's honesty and by the deteriorating and vaporous effect it had both with my work and in my relationship with Margerie who, able to stand it and never complaining about it, is the only person who has
30   ever convinced me that it was worth while regularizing. But if drinking rots the honesty it is a curious thing to say I have yet to meet the teetotaler whom I can wholly trust. However. So much then, for alc.

       You refer to my 'obliquity' in Mexico and I think you will agree that
35   I am justifiably hurt that you refer and have referred to that and nothing else in connection with your visit. I did my very level best to accomodate you and to make you and Mary happy while you were there. I took you all as well as I could to my rheumatic bosom, a more reasonable divorce lawyer was procured that you might have otherwise been able to obtain,

---

1 "borracho": Spanish, "drunk"; Lowry (or Margerie) has misspelled the word.

and although you are under no obligation to me whatsoever about this, I like to feel I played my poor part, in spite of the manifeſt relief I do not blame you in the leaſt for feeling when you went, in sending you and Mary upon your deſtiny. You muſt remember that I was probably more seriously ill that you knew, my illness having since been diagnosed as a (non-infeƈtious) sort of *atrophy*, approaching infantile paralysis, which sometimes is the accompaniment of rheumatic fever in them parts. The report, through what channels I do not know, got back to the O.M. that I was suffering from both epilepsy and WORSE and I was incidentally abandoned by Jan still much in the same condition, which did not add to my pleasures. All of which together with the faƈt that whatever I may have said I really felt myself to be walking on the edge of a precipice with Jan, may go far to account for what obliquity the alcohol may not account for.

Regarding the epilepsy and WORSE: you may say that people do not do these things, and of course I have only Park's word that they were said, but your own reaƈtion to my father's letter would seem to juſtify the exiſtance of such reports. It was upon the basis of these lies that Parks formed his firſt opinion of me and I mention this as a touchſtone of the probably accuracy of moſt of the reports you have received about me. I need scarcely say that these things are ridiculous but not the beſt things in the world to feel that someone far away is charging againſt you. I muſt add that so far as the company I kept is concerned I have been afforded a rich lesson by my experiences which I will not forget in a hurry. The majority of the reports that went home apart from those from some myſterious source in Mexico, probably an individual by the name of Mensch[1] whom I got out of a frightful jam at my own expense, have emenated from Jan and later Parks. Since Parks discredited Jan's word to England and Jan, Parks', and myself, now, both of their words, and as I am telling you the absolute unvarnished truth, you can make up your mind for yourself how much credence to give to what you have heard. I do not expeƈt you to make any final judgement until we have the opportunity of speaking together but I am asking you at leaſt to suspend judgement upon accusations which I could not answer. Nevertheless I can see that Parks and the O.M. have quite naturelly had their influence upon you and it is the purpose of this letter to give as much light as I can upon paſt events which I hope will result in your feeling less uneasy about Margerie and myself should we be able to come. (Another thing I have heard about

---

1 Not identified.

myself. That I had got into trouble with the Police, due to drink. I never have. Except once, years ago, at college. It is a bloody lie. And it can be proved.)

5   I see the difficulty you are placed in with regard to Margie with your conscience. You may like me but on the other hand you do not want to be in any way the instrument of attaching me to somebody who might prove such a headache to the O.M. as Jan. The situation is entirely different. My wish is to support Margie by my own efforts as soon as
10 possible and it has always been my wish. If it so be that some money continues to be forthcoming so much the better for us, but so far is the situation unlike anything which occurred with Jan that Margerie had expressed herself as perfectly willing and even eager to support *me*, until such time as I got on my feet, and had she not given up her job with
15 Penny Singleton[1] would have been abundantly able to do so. You do see however the position in which both war and circumstances have placed us and if we forget the former for a moment America is clearly enough the solution. On the other hand although I think you might have put it more cheerily I can see your position as one having the power to have me
20 cut off without a penny and do freely *absolve you in advance* should you consider this to be the wisest course and since I know that you would not advocate this unless I let you down I want it to be understood here and now and hereafter that this makes absolutely no difference to my feeling of friendship with you. Perhaps it might turn out even to be a good thing
25 and we would all be happier if we are living contiguously at such a time if the monetary element did not complicate our natural generosities towards each other. But, as I have said before and for reasons totally unallied to the conditions of the transaction, I have *no* intention of letting you down. Another aspect of the situation has occurred to me. You may
30 feel that by harboring Margerie you are running the risk of having her family rising in indignant protest about it. Margie has had to tell some of her friends that she is married simply in order to avert gossip. Her mother, however, knows that there are obstacles to our marriage and that we have to wait until such time as they are removed. She is satisfied that
35 we are staying with a married couple and is also pleased with the idea of her going to Boston where she would be living under the same, but better, conditions, which would be, if you demand it, the conditions which she believes exist. Here again the extenuating circumstances of the war have

---

1   Penny Singleton (born Mariana Dorothy McNulty) (1908–), Hollywood actress who had the title role in the 1938–50 "Blondie" feature series.

combined to persuade her to waive any objection to the apparent uncon-
ventionality of our status and I ask you most earnestly also to take into
account in regard to my not writing the O.M. at this time these self-same
extenuating circumstances. It might be all right but I dare not risk our
5   possible separation. I suggest to you as one who is enlightened that this
respect of the conventions with regard to the O.M. might do more harm
than good and I am loathe to tell a sort of half lie as suggested by you,
i.e.: that I've just now informed you of the situation and that you have
agreed in advance to Margie's coming along later for a visit. It is true that
10   if it worked it would put things on a securer footing but if it did not work
it would mean disaster and I think after you have digested the above you
will agree with me that I would have no choice but to decline to go to
America at all, hang on here on some excuse or another as best I could,
join the army, and then, until we are able to be married decree Margie
15   my common law wife and support her on $35 a month. Did this promise
me any future it might be a valuable experience but on the whole it is a
course which you would not wish me to have to take. I have to say right
here and now, putting my foot down as hard as I can without bringing
down all tha[t] has been so skillfully engineered upon our heads that I
20   would definitely renounce any personal gain that might accrue to me by
going to America alone and stay here. We can be married next October
and even if I have to go shortly after, at least Margerie would have the
satisfaction of awaiting my return as my wife. I think that as the circumstances of war will continue to be more extenuating as time goes on
25   that if you feel that our actions justify your raising your voice on our behalf
that perhaps there would be not such a grave parental objection either
But if the O.M. knew that we had lived together before our marriage,
which were I to be completely honest with him I would have to admit
that we had, he would be opposed to it. Surely, Conrad, you can see that
30   *this* is a matter more of convention than of honesty. I can even go further
and say that even if the O.M. suspected that we had lived together before
our marriage he would rather not know about it, put his telescope to his
blind eye, so that he would not be forced by the rigidity of his Wesleyan
spirit to object, and this brings me down to the subtle difference between
35   honesty and what I think Ibsen called the 'disease of integrity.'[1]

Margie and I have striven with all our souls to make our relationship
as fine a thing and as honest a thing as we could under the circumstances
and it seems a pity that all we have built up should be smeared by a

---

1   See Ibsen's *The Wild Duck*, the end of Act III.

convention which in this case, having regard to the war and the fact that it will probably last a very long time indeed, would be a sort of sin in itself to respect, and having regard to that war, once more, Conrad, have you thought about it sufficiently with all its little implications in regard to us? Has it occurred to you, to put it as cruelly as possible, that it may very well not make any difference whether the O.M. cuts me off without a penny or not?

Then there is the matter of work in which Margie has become essential. In drawing together, work has become a communal thing between us. Margie is now as much interested in Under the Volcano as I am. We work together on it day and night. I feel that it is the first real book I've written. The certainty of war has let loose a hell of a lot of pent up energy and all played against the background of the false idealisms and abstractions of peace that we wasted our time with when we should have been thinking about living, of which we are bitterly reminded when perhaps there is not much time any longer. All this is making for a real drama, something possibly first rate, within its limits. I'm more than glad I never got a chance to finish it without her because we too seem to be playing our parts within the drama. I don't see how the hell I can finish the book without her anyhow now that we've got started on an absolutely new and important character in it which is her idea.[1] This again is an important point: it is something about which you will want to be shown, I admit, but I can't show it to you without being on the spot, and I can't, moreover, hope to explain it to the old man without getting the whole thing hopelessly misconstrued, even were there time, which there may not be.

Another thing I would like you to take into account is the old man's peculiarities in certain respects. He did his best to queer Stuart's marriage, which turned out well, because he did not make quite the right tactical approach. (He was sporting about mine but need not have been drawn into its failure, had he only let me alone.) And I am not the first son to have had spies put on his tail.[2] Stuart, when in France, had the same thing done to him. What the O.M. needs is *assurance* of some sort that all is now as well as it can be, and though I might wish that assurance to be

---

1 Probably the character of Yvonne, who was changed from the Consul's daughter, in the earlier drafts of *Under the Volcano*, to his wife (cf. Day 272).

2 It appears that Arthur O. Lowry had hired a detective to follow Lowry's movements in Mexico. Elements of this situation are present in *Under the Volcano*.

made anyhow for his own sake I certainly do not wish it for my ends; and since we have already understood that you will not make any assurance unless you feel that the situation deserves it, you will perhaps see that I am doubly anxious that you should be convinced.

I think that the wiser course and the juster would be as I have said before that you suspend judgement upon whether you can ratify our relationship as a good thing, if such ratification is needed, until you have the evidence of your own eyes. There is nothing to prevent at least my getting engaged without my father's knowledge and my first marriage having proved an embarrassment (to *him* through no fault of my own) and a failure, he is not likely to look upon any attachment I may form at the present time with favor untill you are convinced that it is otherwise. Why do you not consider our relationship to be a necessary experiment? I cannot see that my father can expect me entirely to dispense with female company. If Margie did not exist you would probably suggest, even if I kept a pair of scissors handy as you say, that I take upon some female relationship which reason itself would not demand you to tell my father about and of which he would not expect to know. The pair of scissors so far as you're concerned is in your own hands and I have said beforehand that if you do not approve our relationship eventually and if, by the way, any continuation of it implies a letting of you down tantamount to the drunken horrors you expect to cope with, then as I say, it is all right by me and you are still all right by me and I will just have to figure a way out of our difficulties without your assistance and approval but with, I hope, in that case your unexpressed blessing. Parks' remedy for my troubles was the saying, At night all cats are grey, and it seems to me it would be a tragic thing and a contradictory one that while a passing relationship with a harlot might be condoned by Parks et al one which is in itself a simple, honest and good thing is not. The risks we are taking we take with our eyes open.

I had hoped that in this letter I had managed to clear up some of the suspicions which I feel you have come to hold since receiving the letters from the O.M. and Parks and I hope also that after you have absorbed every word of this letter that you will be convinced that the only first step towards a securer footing and finally a secure footing is for you to see and be shown by yourself. Otherwise I think I should inevitably become the victim of some such justice as befell my friend Willaim Empson when his fellowship at Cambridge was taken away, himself sent down and his career ruined, because he had been abnormal enough to have some contraceptives in his room, and normal enough to inform the dons that they were not ornaments and that he used them.[1]

For the reſt, for the hope you extend about Montreal should the American idea blow up, my deepeſt thanks and also reiterated thanks for everything you have both done for us. Very finally I want to say again that so far as we are concerned there will be no dishoneſtness round corners, no drunken sailors smuggled in from the Navy Yard at night and above all no communiſtic talk under the banana trees. My only hope is that after all our ups and downs our relationship and relationships as you once prophesied the laſt time I left Rye, could and would be pure Sierra Nevada and so, as Chaucer said, go litel book, which I am afraid this has become, go litel myne tragadie,[2] and bear in mind that whatever it may not be written with it is written with love

As ever,

with Both our Loves

Malc

P.S.   I enclose an old
self-explanatory, unpoſted p.c.[3]

---

1 William Empson (1906–84), British critic and poet who studied at Wincheſter College, 1920–25, and Magdalene College, Cambridge, 1929; student of mathematics and English who, under the tutorship of I.A. Richards, came firſt in the English Tripos in 1929; editor of the Cambridge literary magazine, *Experiment*, in 1928; author of *Seven Types of Ambiguity* (London: Chatto & Windus, 1930). In his autobiography, Michael Redgrave also tells of Empson being "sent down, or 'ruſticated'" because he had contraceptives in his room (*In My Mind's Eye* 63).
2 See Chaucer's "Troilus and Criseyde," V.1786: "Go litel bok, go litel myn tragedye."
3 The "enclosed" poſtcard ("p.c.") is missing.

28 : *From* AIKEN *to* LOWRY

KILLORIN 242

S Dennis Mass

Feb 1 40

My poor old bewildered explanatory protestant Malc — ! What a deluge
of Kafka-like elucidation, explanation, analysis, qualification, apology,
reproach, everything! Every man his own Laocoon group,[1] complete with
the serpent. But my dear fellow there was no need for it, surely — it's all
been settled, long since, I thought, that you were coming — you don't
need to tell me in advance anything about yourself, since I shall be
a-seeing of you with my own eyes, and a-hearing of you with my own
ears, and knowing for myself what has become of you, and what truth or
lies constituted the now quite alarmingly hypertrophied Legend of the
Lowry which has been built up by alternate touches from yourself, the
O M, Parks, Margerie, and not forgetting Maurice Carey. Seen in its
queer total, I can assure you, it doesn't make sense: it's the goddamndest
farrago of inconsistencies I ever did see, and as hollow as a cream puff.
No, let's let go of all that, and just sit tight till you get here. As for my
suggestion that it would be wisest and best and most honest to tell the
O M now something of the Margie thing, I still think so; but, I'll agree
to waiving that for the time being, with the understanding that maybe
we'll do it a little later. So, come along now, as soon as you get your walking
papers, and then we'll begin to shape our future as we think best. Whether
here or in Boston. . . . Conrad
Will you thank M. Carey for his letter, on my behalf — and tell him I
much appreciated it — ? It was very nice of him.

---

1 This phrase reappears later in Lowry's 1 July 1949 letter to Frank Taylor (Breit,
Selected Letters 180).

29 : *From* LOWRY *to* AIKEN

TS H 2509

5   595 W. 19th Ave.,
         Vancouver, B.C,

         February 7, 1940.

10 My very dear Conrad:

    I am overjoyed by your letter. Thank you for your thoughtfulness in
    trying to make it possible for us to have a nook to ourselves, and, with
    such santuary, I trust we may prove a stimulation to work rather than a
15 hindrance.

    We are working night and day on Under the Volcano and am sure at
    last have got something. It has blood, guts, rapine, murder, teeth, and, for
    your entertainment, even some moonlight and roses.[1] And a couple of
20 horses.

    Dick Eberhart[2] was at Cambridge a little before my time: he was a
    friend of J.D.'s I had many strange döppelganger like remote contacts
    with him. He was a sailor, wrote a goodish first book of poems, 'Bravery
25 of Earth'. Since, he does, as you say, seem to have gone mad as a hatter.
    He is now devoted to another f[or]m of what you call 'indoor Marxman-
    ship.'[3] I believe he is a brilliant fellow, but he seems to me to be tone deaf,
    poetically. Once, when accused in the Cambridge Review by I.A.
    ("Granada") Richards,[4] of "sucking his poetic thumb," he confronted him

---

1   See letter 20 from Aiken, and Lowry's response in letter 21.
2   Richard Eberhart (1904–   ), American poet who studied at St. John's College,
Cambridge, receiving a B.A. in 1929, and an M.A. in 1933. His book of poems, *A
Bravery of Earth*, was published by Jonathan Cape in 1930. Aiken's reference to
Eberhart in letter 28 was apparently edited out in Killorin's text.
3   Quotation from letter 20 from Aiken.
4   Ivor Armstrong Richards (1893–1979), British literary critic and poet who studied
at Magdalene College, Cambridge, receiving a B.A. in 1914, M.A. in 1918, and Litt.
D. in 1932. Author of *Principles of Literary Criticism* (New York: Harcourt, 1925) and
Practical Criticism: A Study of Literary Judgement (New York: Harcourt, 1929). Accord-
ing to Clarissa Lorenz, Richards was Lowry's "former examiner (and hero) at Saint
Catharine's College" (*Lorelei Two* 153). Lowry and the Aikens (Conrad and Clarissa
Lorenz) joined up with I.A. Richards and his wife when they were visiting Spain in

personally with said thumb, made a rude gesture, asked, "How do you like this?"

I hope to hear news soon from Washington. Please tell Mary I am writing her personally to thank her for all she has done on our behalf.

Tell me something funny.

As ever, love from us both,

Malc.

30 : *From* AIKEN *to* LOWRY

TS H 2551; KILLORIN 243

S Dennis Mass

Feb 21 40

Just a line, or a between the lines, Malc, to signal our continuing presence here, with faces westward turned hopefully, not to say prayerfully, for your wellbeings. What news — if any? I trust the novel[1] goes forward ventre a terre, and if the Labour board would only come to bat and beckon you in — ! But anyway, let me have a card or something. Here, we go from winter to winter — day after day of snow and freezing winds, housebound, shivering, marooned — if it weren't for the cocktail hour our courages would have given out. No end to it. But I suppose really another two weeks should see the winter's bloody back bloody broken: I

1933; hence Lowry's nickname of Richards here: "Granada." Cf. Lorenz, *Lorelei Two* (153–54). Aiken and Richards were warm friends and thought highly of one another's work, Richards once calling Aiken "the genuine poet" (Constable, *Selected Letters of I.A. Richards* xxxvii). I have not been able to locate the *Cambridge Review* article which Lowry mentions here.
1 *Under the Volcano.*

can only say if it isn't, ours will be. I re-read most of the Lighthouse, and with much increased interest, respect, and delight. If you could haul out the audenesques, which are obvious and usually detachable by the unit, I think a small book might be put together, and *good*. Perhaps first sending
5 some to Poetry. But I'd like to go over them with you when you come. Meanwhile, I've sent the whole shebang, Ballast, Lighthouse and Address, up to Bob Linscott for a general report and suggestions. His first brief note, before he'd gone far, merely says he finds Address "tainted with genius" but unpublishable, wishing you'd expended your talents on
10 a more useful theme etc., and adds that he's now reading the pomes with enjoyment. I'll doubtless hear more from him quite soon. I thought his hardboiled practical eye might be useful to us. . . We're making an effort to get the Charlestown house, and hope perhaps to have it by May. Trying to buy it on mortgages and things — heaven knows what will come of it.
15 But it looks to us a more economical measure than forever paying rent — with the advantage that at the end of umpteen years we'll own the house! It's nice, I think you'll like it. A second Jeake. Did you ever heard from John Davenport, by the way — I wrote him in the autumn of your plight, and urged him to cough up some cash for you.[1] I hoped he might
20 send you as it were a Xmas prsent. Me, I haven't heard from him for damned near a year — he was offended with me I think because I couldn't go to visit him at Bath — I was ill and trying to finish my novel[2] at the time, in no state to travel or visit — and for some reason he took umbrage. A pity. . . . Mary's off shopping at Hyannis in a blinding blizzard, with
25 Ruth Whitman,[3] while I type at the window, facing a white and whirling world — I think it's Lapland, and I'm a witch. Our own various affairs are all in a state of suspension, and we just sit and wait: wait for Mary to hear from her application for a Guggenheim, wait for my novel to come out, wait for the Book of the Month to make up its mind whether to take
30 it or recommend it, wait for Mary's show of watercolours in N Y May 13th, wait to see if the summer school comes to anything (we may try to have it here in July and August) (and we've had two inquiries about it)[4]

---

1 Cf. Lowry's request in the postscript of letter 18.
2 *Conversation*. The Book of the Month Club, which Aiken mentions a few lines later, did not take the novel.
3 Friend and art student of Mary; cf. Aiken's 11 Jan. 1941 letter to Ed Burra (Killorin 248).
4 The Aikens first started their summer school in writing and painting in 1938 at Jeake's House in Rye and continued it in Massachusetts until 1943. Aiken had perhaps been inspired to begin the school after the success of his experience with Lowry in the summer of 1929. The broadside advertising the "Third Season: 1940" of the school includes the following note: "Owing to the war / the third season of / Jeake's House

wait for the publishers to decide whether they'll let Mary do drawings
for a sumptuous special edition of my sonnets next autumn,[1] wait to see
if the bank will lend us enough cash to buy the house with, and if our
offer will be accepted by the owner anyway, wait for the Atlantic to pay
me $200. which they owe me for my article on poetry,[2] or else decide they
don't want it, wait for the dentist to take out three rotten teeth and put
in two little prehensile plates, wait for Madam Perkins[3] to decide on the
case of Lowry vs. U.S.A., wait, above all, for the spring — ! Oh, yes, and
wait for the Metropolitan Museum to make up its committee mind as to
whether it will buy Mary's lovely picture, The Sussex Maid. So, a lot *could*
happen, but meanwhi[l]e nothing at all *does*; and that is why we enjoy the
cocktail hour. And now I must wade out into the snow to the RFD box
with flakes crashing into my ears and get the Boston Herald and the mail.
A[n]d much love to you both from the both of us,

Conrad

Bob Linscott's letter has just came, and I therefor enclose it,[4] for it occurs
to me it might be given in evidence, if need be, that your presence is really
desirable for business reasons in Boston. Nicht wahr????? *And* not so bad
that he wants to have a looksee at the new novel! Hot diggity.

Sum- / mer School will be / held in the village / of South Dennis, on / Cape Cod.
The sit- / uation and ameni- / ties closely resemble / those offered at Rye. / .... Five
or six / resident pupils will / be accepted." (Bonnell 225).
1 *And in the Human Heart* (New York: Duell, Sloan and Pearce, 1940); an edition
with Mary Aiken's illustrations was never published.
2 "Back to Poetry," *Atlantic Monthly* Aug. 1940: 217-23.
3 "Madam Perkins": the "Secretary of Labor" in Washington; see Margerie Lowry's
29 January 1940 letter to Mary Aiken in Appendix II.
4 This letter is missing.

31 : *From* LOWRY *to* AIKEN

TS H 2542

5 595 W. 19th Ave.,

February 23, 1940

Dear Conrad:

10

The axe has fallen, as I thought it would. I am refused – and cannot go back to the States. I have been assured by the Immigration here that the refusal is a technicality – in other words that it is not etiquette for one department of Immigration to overrule another. This makes it
15 impossible for me to apply before September 23. This is A.B.Carey's and Park's fault, I told them both that this would happen and they still persisted in saying it was for my benefit. Surely this is proof that they are not able to handle my affairs. By September 23 anything may have happened. The sitzkrieg become a blitzkrieg,[1] so on and so forth. Unless
20 the war has stopped I may not be able to enter the United States again. Meantime I have work to finish, and now, when everything seems lost, it seems all the more important to finish it.

25 Dear Conrad and Mary:

Malcolm had started this letter to you but I am going to finish it, I will make it as brief as possible but it is a really desperate appeal for the axe has fallen doubly. You are the only people we have in the world to
30 appeal to or who can help us and I cannot put it too strongly how urgent our situation is. Maurice is on the most ghastly drunken rampage you can imagine and things have become so intolerable that Phyllis[2] says we must leave as soon as possible, she is afraid of what may happen. Last night Maurice suddenly went for me and knocked me half way across the
35 kitchen, then turned on Malcolm, who although wild with fury because Maurice had struck me, behaved with the most marvelous self-restraint and only tried to defend himself – you see, he didn't dare hit Maurice because Maurice has a very bad heart and his intestines, stomach, etc.,

1 "sitzkrieg . . . blitzkrieg": German, literally, "sitting war" and "lightning war."
2 Phyllis Carey, Maurice Carey's wife.

were so badly shot to pieces, he is such a sick man that one good blow
might very easily kill him. I can not tell you how crazy he is – even when
sober he behaves in such an irrational manner that he is dangerous and
when drunk he is a mad man. We have had to stand aside and see him
beat Phyllis and his three children, smash the house up, and fight with
anybody who was around and he has gone for days without speaking to
us except to threaten us, but now this – he didn't hurt me very much but
Malcolm has one eye completely closed, a badly cut mouth and injured
hand, and Maurice is still drunk and crazy. Phyllis fears that he will have
another breakdown and be sent to the hospital any moment, or that his
heart will give out in one of these frenzies. But in any case, if another row
like laſt night were to happen, which it very well may at any moment
despite anything we can do, we have no lock on our door and he come
raging in at all hours, and if he were to die from sheer excitement or some
slight chance blow from Malcolm merely trying to defend himself, or
even me if Malcolm were not at home, I need not tell you what a
cataſtrophe that would be. We muſt get out of here and quickly. Here, of
course, we have no place to go. We do not know what to suggeſt as we
do not know what would be beſt for you or what you would rather do but
this much we will say: If you could meet us in Montreal or Quebec or
whatever point in Canada is neareſt for you – if, after talking to us and
seeing us, you are not absolutely convinced that we are right, completely
honeſt with you about everything, and with Malcolm's word (and mine
too, of course) never to let you down, if you are not convinced that we are
trying with all our minds and souls to simply make a decent life for
ourselves, then you can simply wash your hands of the whole thing, write
Malcolm's father whatever you think and abandon us to our fate. Malcolm
has been the viċtim of bitter and tragic circumſtances and has been badly
treated and even A.B.Carey has admitted to him that they were wrong.
Malcolm saw him the other day and A.B.Carey said so, said that Malcolm
was absolutely O.K. and that he had been in the wrong and wound up by
saying that he thought Malcolm should try and help Maurice! My God,
what irony!

Meantime we have been working like mad on Under the Volcano,
which Malcolm is completely re-writing and which is now about half
done. It is unlike anything he has written before and, I think, will be truly
a great book when it is finished – *and it muſt be finished*. Malcolm is a
genius and if you could see the work he is doing now, under circumſtances
and conditions that would appear impossible to one less determined and,
yes, less inspired to write, you would agree with me.

He is sick with disappointment over the news from America, I can't tell you how he was looking forward to spending some time with you – he talked of it constantly. Besides he will not be able to write or type for awhile because it was his right hand that was hurt so that's why I am
5   writing for us. I'm sorry if this letter seems rather incoherent but I am writing against time so that this will catch the air mail out today – also I am a little dazed myself today, but you should get this by Monday and could you let us know soon – if we just have some assurance from you we can hang on by our teeth and toenails somehow for a little bit longer.
10

And now again, our deepest, undying gratitude to you both for all you have done for us and our absolute assurance that all we ask is just enough to live on and a chance to work and be together and to prove to you, and Malcolm's family, that we mean what we say.
15

Our love to you both,

Margerie

20

Dear Mary:

I was writing you personally to thank you for your sweet help on our behalf when Maurice's fist fell along with the axe. I have read Margie's
25   letter and although it doesn't sound sort of likely you may feel, about me, it is all true so help us. That is, all save the genius stuff; but the new book *is* going well. We are at our wit's end and I can barely see to write or hold a pen what Margie will transcribe, and ask you to accept this note in the meantime as expression of my gratitude. Could not Conrad, perhaps, take
30   *carte-blanche* under these circumstances? Any expenditures would be fully repaid. I hate to put him to any trouble just when his book is coming out, but we are really harmless good folk and please do not be alarmed by the fact that our fate is in your hands. Please help us.

35   *Malcolm*

32 : *From* LOWRY *to* AIKEN

TS H 2543

5   595 W. 19th Ave.,
                                 Vancouver, B.C.

                                 [late February 1940]

10   Dear Conrad and Mary: (Apologies in advance, Mary, for this self-
       conscious 'Waile of a letter' which contains TOmch I have no right to
       bore you with — only I wanted it to be to you *both*)

              I am sending another note hotfooting it after you through the
15   crashing snowflakes in the hope of suggesting a possible redistribution of
       the solutions of our current problems which is not too much at variance
       with *your* various plans outlined in your exceedingly welcome, cheery and
       good letter which gladdened our souls. Reason for this legal prose, this
       'rummy' style, I am dictating the letter, my hand being wounded. There
20   is the same infinite misery here as before upon which we will not expatiate
       save that my enormous black eye seems to be simply glaring demoniacally
       through the whitewash with which we have lavishly painted ourselves to
       you and continue, in spite of the black eye, to paint ourselves with
       truthfully. We are not only writing Under the Volcano, we are living smack
25   down in it. We cannot help kidding about it but nevertheless our position
       is bloody desperate.

              I've just received a very cheery letter from my mother, not cheery
       because she has given up all hope of coping with the world at all and is
30   now counting on the unseen, but in which she says that she has heard
       that I'm going to stay with you and that in any event she is anxious that
       I should in some way contact you because she feels, she cannot know how
       rightly, however intensely she feels, that you would be a help to me. From
       this I deduce that, since anything that makes the mater happy makes the
35   O.M. happy too, that even were I to proceed to Montreal or elsewhere
       to be under your auspices, it would be the real right thing from her point
       of view and hence from the O.M.'s. All of which makes me think how
       simple all that could be if I could only explain it to the O.M. personally
       and not have my explanations sidetracked by the blasted Oxford Groupers
40   and lawyers. All that being so, the only practical suggestion I can make
       now is this: if you could take just a few days off and come to Montreal or

wherever to meet us, as we said in our last letter, if we do not convince you, then you can simply quit the whole thing and still have our blessing for trying. If you are convinced of our honesty, which you must be by now, then perhaps we could do this: go to some small town near the border, on the Gaspe Peninsula maybe, where living would be very cheap and the surroundings beautiful, and settle down for the summer to work.

Meantime the O.M. could be gradually broken in to the idea that Margie was coming to visit me. We – if it came to that – would gladly give you half of what I think I have – i.e. half $150 – or if war has reduced that to $100, say 25% of it, which might help, in addition, of course, to Parks' fee which you would be getting. I hope you will not think my motive for suggesting this invidious: it is simply that in Canada we could live on $75 a month, we have fewer responsibilities than you, and you, on our behalf, more than may seem to be taken care of by the fee, although I would do my utmost to make these as few as possible for you. Moreover, we are anxious to impress you with the fact that all we need is enough to live on and work. Because the whole problem seems to be a matter of money when it is canalized as it is through the present sources the socalled 'immorality' seems to be that I should use part of the money for Margie. This is much of an obliquity because in the first place if we could get somewhere where she could cook and keep house we could both live for what it would cost me to board or live at a hotel alone. I cannot get my work done without Margie, I realize my fault is, roughly speaking, too much loquacity and not enough action, and hams in the window, and there she helps me immeasureably by her censorship and suggestions. Besides which if I did not have her I'd have to pay a typist. Apart from the fact that I love Margie she has become an inextricable part of my work. (I do not mean in the Ludwig Lewisohn[1] sense.) Objectively speaking I think that such a dependence might not be a good thing in many cases but in *our* case it definitely works and even though one may be working in the dark and against time to the fate of some kind of obscure posthumously second order Gogol, nevertheless what work we are accomplishing, for better or worse, does have just that very quality of intensity which work in the dark against time etc. has given the Gogols

---

1   Ludwig Lewisohn (1883–1955), American editor, critic, translator, and novelist; his novels are often concerned with marital problems caused by conflict with tradition or law. Author of *The Broken Snare* (1908), *The Case of Mr. Crump* (1926), *The Island Within* (1928), and *This People* (1933); editor of *New Palestine* and the *American Zionist Review*.

and the Kafkas: we may not be so good so far but I feel parts of Under
the Volcano bear this sort of comparison and we have been given encouragement through this to feel that if only we had the time and could stick
together we could produce not just one book but a large body of work
stamped at last with an individual imprint. But how the hell to get all this
over to the O.M. in the light of my dismal failures in the past I simply
don't know: and I am forced to the conclusion that the only thing to do
is to prove the practicability of the arrangement first, which in all its
aspects, its unconventional complexion at the moment renders impossible, and get it over afterwards when I have something concrete to show.
Meantime since Margie has renounced all claims on me and hence all
possible claims etc on the O.M., Margie remains my responsibility, one
which, if even much less provision is made for me than has hitherto been
made, I am capable of holding. But not only this – it is abundantly clear
to me that only through Margie can I reach the stage of independence
from responsibility etc. which is generally desired, taking with me only
just that necessary part of my psychic turmoils which are, to put it bluntly,
saleable; and if Under the Volcano is no Anna Karenina, and was not
meant to be, at least, unless I am very sadly deceiving myself, it is
"publishable at a profit."

Were I not very well aware of the many matters relative to Mary's
work and your own unities & health such as the Summer School, your
book, the impending dental misery which we hope will not turn out too
painful, etc., I might have been able to suggest, perhaps without forward-
ness, that our Lady of the Snows,[1] (in the not remote Montreal regions
which I understand are very beautiful,) might have held some possibility
of attraction for yourselves in Summer. As it is, realizing that such a thing
is impossible but at the same time not allowing myself utterly to despair
of the fact of the possibility of our not being able to see one another once
more – and this would be a very real despair should I give way to it, since
what truer father have I than you, and as Thomas Wolfe says, are we not
all looking for our fathers – I can only place once more our problems
before you, less complicated as they are now by having fewer solutions,
and entreat you once again to try and help us, I having already given you
my word as an artist, a man and a friend not to let you down. As your
own method of dealing with the O.M. seems to have been much more
successful than anything I could hope to suggest I hesitate to make any

---

1   Cf. Kipling's poem "Our Lady of the Snows, 1897" in which "Our Lady of the
Snows" is a personification of Canada.

suggestions but I feel that if at this period you could give the O.M. to realize how desperately in earnest I am about accomplishing my work in whatever time may be alloted to me, of how proximity to yourself, even if in Montreal, would benefit me in that regard and how already certain

5 encouragement has been given me by, for instance, Linscott, which makes for some promise of definiteness in all this, that I have certain matters to talk over with you and certain problems – I won't go on, you know all the circumstances here, use your own good judgement about what you say, but could you ask for carte blanche to do what you think is best for me?

10 Since our situation is so urgent, could you not send a cable (for which you'd be reimbursed) or if not, a letter by the Clipper, otherwise it may take too long. The letter from my mother was written just after Christmas and she spoke of other letters she had written me which I never received. My Mother says in her letter how much *she* wants me to succeed in my

15 work and now I *know* that I am really on the verge of doing something about it if I can only finish the Volcano and re-write In Ballast as I see it now. But, Conrad, we cannot stay here for the situation is really dangerous and growing increasingly more so, at any moment something may happen which we cannot avert which will destroy everything we have tried so

20 desperately and worked so hard these last months to build up. It would be particularly bitter now, since the encouraging letter from Linscott (I feel certain the Volcano will be a better bet with him) and your own encouragement about the Lighthouse – I can't begin to tell you how much that meant to me.

25

Should you receive carte-blanche from the O.M. I fully realize the difficulties involved in doing what is best for me and still retaining your own integrity and honesty with the O.M. To that end I can only say that if after seeing us and talking to us you feel that I am to be trusted

30 and that I do mean what I say, perhaps you'd be justified in giving us a chance in these next few months to prove to you, and the family, that we are sincere in trying to make a new life for ourselves. This might entail telling a few white lies to the O.M. but we know in the long run he'll be grateful to you for giving us that chance and for rescuing us from this

35 horror here in Vancouver. If you do not feel you can do this we can effect some sort of compromise whereby we could find someone wherever we were staying to simply pay our bills – perhaps the bank – and give us an allowance of whatever you think – all not to exceed an agreed sum. There I would be under your aegis as I am under Parks' here – via an intermediary

40 – but would be free of the bungaling hypocracy of Ibsenish A.B., Dostoievskish M., Carey, and possibly you could come up for a day or

two now and then and see for yourself what we are doing. If this won't
do, perhaps we could find some couple who would let us stay with them
so that we were properly chaperoned and who would board us as we are
here but in a more decent and wholesome atmosphere. There is so much
5   work I want to do in these next few months if I can only have the chance
to do it – finish the Volcano, re-write In Ballaſt, re-write the Lighthouse
with your suggeſtions and The Laſt Address with ditto, several short
stories and a new novel, Night Journey Across the Sea,[1] in the offing. And
nobody seems to realize that these next few months may be all I'll have
10 to do my work in, or to be with Margie, for I may have to go to war
immediately after we are married, or even before, for that matter since I
shall be in Canada. If you only knew what we wouldn't give juſt to have
a chance to live, to breathe, to have a little freedom to work and peace of
mind as well. Not to mention a hot bath now and then, we get one between
15 us, lukewarm, about once every three weeks. The Finns get one once a
week, by the way – and a decent meal, we haven't had a square meal since
Chriſtmas, and even that was sort of triangular – we had to depend upon
the tail end of it until damn nearly the end of January – We've had *no
fresh milk, butter, eggs, fruit or vegetables* in *five months* and live on a diet
20 of bread, soggy potatoes and watery stew. Very well, you say, go out and
earn it, but this is only precisely what we are asking for a chance to do!

The house sounds swell but I am sad I shan't see it: perhaps in
September. Haven't heard from J.D. for three years when he phoned me
25 at Cuernavaca.[2] His umbrages are incident but soon forgotten. Thank
you very much for writing him on my behalf. *And*, a thousand thanks for
intereſting Linscott: the Volcano might do for him. And for your remarks
about the poems[3] I am likewise very grateful: I was kind of hoping againſt
hope there would be a few you'd like: particularly one about the Harkness
30 light, and another about Crusoe's footprints or some such. Well, I'm
immensely beholden to you for all you've done for me, for us, and do hope
you will still be able to help me with the Lighthouse. Talking about
Lapland: Nordahl Grieg[4] is there on military service, sent there as a

1   See letter 18, n. 1, p. 68.
2   Cf. Douglas Day's *Malcolm Lowry* in which he tells of Lowry phoning Davenport
from Cuernavaca in late 1937 (229).
3   "The Lighthouse Invites the Storm." For the two poems mentioned here see
"Quartermaſter at the Wheel" (88) and "On Reading R.L.S." (97–98) in *The Colleɛted
Poetry of Malcolm Lowry.*
4   Nordahl Grieg (1902–43), Norwegian poet, noveliſt, and dramatiſt whom Lowry
met in 1931. Author of *The Ship Sails On* (1927; *Skibet går videre* 1924). "In Ballaſt to

punishment for defending Russia in the Arbeiderbladet:[1] serve him right, perhaps; but what an ending to In Ballaſt to the White Sea!

Well: here goes another Decline and Fall of the Roman Empire- And our very beſt love and good wishes to Mary and yourself, *'powerful' to help these guilty lives* –

yours very weſt of Eden[2]

Malc & Margie

33 : *From* AIKEN *to* LOWRY

KILLORIN 244

S Dennis

Feb 29 40

My dear Malcs — juſt a swift line to try and catch the air mail — yrs juſt received, and already out of date, old fellow, for I cabled the O M laſt Tuesday, the 27th, urging him to transfer you to Montreal immediately on the ground that I believed Vancouver environment moſt unsuitable, and offering to assume responsibility for you on any arrangement he wished. I've also written to an old friend of mine a painter Kenneth Forbes[3] in Toronto, to ask if he'd sort of sponsor you if you came to T., or recommend someone if to Montreal. So now we wait for the O M's next move — and I done all I could swelp me. This muſt go off now to wunſt, so chin chin, cheery ho and all our loves —   Conrad

---

the White Sea" was partly about Lowry's identification with Grieg.

1   "Arbeiderbladet": paper, founded in 1884 by Holtermann Knudsen, which was the official mouthpiece of the Norwegian Labour Party. It was shut down during World War II when the Germans occupied Norway, and was started up again after the war.

2   Allusion to Aiken's *Landscape Weſt of Eden*.

3   Kenneth Keith Forbes (1892–1980), Canadian portrait painter and amateur boxer.

34 : *From* LOWRY *to* AIKEN

TS H 2544

595 W. 19th Ave.,
Vancouver, B.C.

March 3, 1940

— We thank you both from the bottom of our hearts, and want you to know immediately that, whether the O.M.'s reply is favorable or not we are eternally grateful to you both even for trusting us and helping us and that if ever there is a thorn in the Hoover-Aiken[1] claws we will go through hell and high water to pull it out. Spring comes, sunlight begins to again 'roar like a vast invisible sea'[2] – this is the first spring I have really been aware of since I used to read fragments of the House of Dust in old Coteries on Hayes Common twelve years ago.

Meantime, in the maritime world, all is not so good. There are few ships I have written about that have not met their fate in a sticky manner. Ariadne N Pandelis and Herzogin Cecile in In Ballast went to the bottom a few weeks after I had written about them. Athenia leaves The same port, sinks in the same place with Norse boat to the rescue, as Arcturian in In Ballast! But that is nothing to what has just happened, by way of coincidence, to two ships, real and imaginary, in my first early plagiaristic paen to puberty, Ultramarine. Do you remember a German wireless operator in the book? He is mentioned as coming from a German ship, the Wolfsburg (which I had seen in the Suez Canal)[3] The Wolfsburg was torpedoed a fortnight ago by an English submarine, half the crew rescued. The Nawab in Ultramarine was really the Pyrrhus (the ship I was actually on).[4] The Pyrrhus was torpedoed by a German submarine off the West coast of England the day before yesterday, a total loss and half the firemen killed. Strange: The Acushnet, the real Pequod – in Moby, met similar

---

1 Hoover is Mary Aiken's maiden name.
2 Quotation from Aiken's "Movements from a Symphony: Overtones," *Coterie* 3 (Dec. 1919): 53; cf. letter 1, n. 2, p. 7.
3 The German wireless operator, Hans Popplereuter, first appears in chapter 3 of *Ultramarine*; "the *Wolfsburg*" is mentioned on p. 117.
4 The *Pyrrhus* is the name of the ship on which Lowry sailed when he went to sea as a deckhand in 1927.

fate to Pequod, after he had written the book.[1] Nothing in it my dear fellows, but these here correspondences of the subnormal world with the abnormally suspicious are damned queer, if you like to think so. Joyce says that nearly all the characters mentioned in the funeral scene in Ulysses, or people with the same names, have met a strange fate. One mentioned, not accounted for: Lowry.[2] That Telemachus is a sister ship to the Pyrrhus cannot apparently have anything to do with the subject! I have the strange feeling that the disaster to my old ship, coming on top of everything else this last week, was intended, by some queer subaqueous *force majeure*, finally to polish *me* off. If so it certainly did not succeed! On the contrary perhaps that was just all my past life with its false bulkheads, firemen, funnels and windlasses sinking below the waves! Somehow we fooled 'em.

Margie, who is an expert, has inveigled me into reading astronomy. (*Not* to be confused with *astrology*,[3] Margie begs me to insist, doubtless pained to think this should be associated with the other mumbo jumbos in my letter.) I still do not know which stars are coming or going, but the enclosed poem[4] emerging from the following metaphysic makes me think that, with practice, I might develop into an Eliza Cook yet.[5] "That when Venus is nearest to the earth she appears as a thin crescent, almost invisible, as the distance increases, more of the bright disc becomes visible, the increasing distance tends to make the planet appear less bright, but the change in phase acts in a contrary direction; the result of the two effects is that the brightness continues to increase for about 36 days from the time Venus is at her nearest. Thereafter the effect of the increasing phase is more than counterbalanced by the greater distance. When at her

---

1 The *Pequod* is the name of Captain Ahab's ship in *Moby Dick*. See Lewis Mumford's *Herman Melville* (New York: Harcourt, 1929): "The crew of the Acushnet was an ill-fated one . . . the ship itself foundered in the very year he [Melville] wrote Moby-Dick . . ." (44).

2 See *Ulysses* (London: Bodley Head, 1937): "Mr Bloom's glance travelled down the edge of the paper, scanning the deaths. Callan, Coleman, Dignam, Fawcett, Lowry . . ." (83). In his 25 August 1951 letter to David Markson, Lowry again mentions Joyce's superstition "about the name Lowry, which occurs in his funeral scene. No sooner had he given them these names . . . than one after the other these names acquired living, or rather dead, counterparts, all of which . . . were found to have come to grotesque and tragic ends! I never checked up to see if a stand-in called L. has already let me out . . ." (Breit 250). Telemachus, mentioned in the next line, is the son of Ulysses (Odysseus) in the *Odyssey*.

3 Cf. Margerie Bonner's *The Shapes That Creep* (194) for a similar statement.

4 The "enclosed" poem is missing.

5 Eliza Cook (1818–89), London-born poet who was a regular contributor to the *Weekly Despatch*. From 1849–54 she was the editor and publisher of *Eliza Cook's Journal*.

brighteſt, Venus is much brighter than any star or any other planet and can be seen without difficulty by the naked eye in broad daylight. I have on more than one occasion seen it without looking for it and without realizing at firſt that I was aĉtually looking at Venus." Here is something else too, which would seem to be fruĉtifying, if applied to mankind. "The light reaching us from Venus can be compared with the light which we receive direĉtly from the sun. In neither case is the light pure sunlight. The light which we receive from the sun direĉtly has some wave lengths weakened or missing because of absorption in the atmosphere of the earth." Or perhaps you have already expressed this somewhere. Or thought it not worth expressing.

I gather from *Life* that England is none too popular in American quarters.[1] I am very sad I shall not be able to see Mary's piĉtures for some time.

There is a photograph of former Hoover subjeĉt, "Man with Concertina" Elliot Paul, in Time this week, playing boogie-woogie in the temple.[2]

Once I could play boogie-woogie fine. . .[3]

All thanks and love again to both from both.

Ma*lc & Ma*rgie

P.S. A myſterious photograph of a sailing ship, very much the worse for wear, called the Lawhill has appeared in our local drugſtore. Lawhill is the name of the ship in The Laſt Address.[4] The Lawhill has also been – er – recently sunk. But what the hell boys and girls. Hoppla! Wir leben![5]

The Volcano is rapidly reaching its laſt belch.

---

1 I have been unable to identify the article to which Lowry is referring.
2 Lowry is referring to one of Mary (Hoover) Aiken's paintings of Elliot Harold Paul (1891–1958), American noveliſt and part-time jazz pianiſt who was founder and co-editor with Eugene Jolas of the literary magazine *transition*. An unsigned article on Elliot Paul, "Bach and Boogie-Woogie," appears in *Time* 4 Mar. 1940: 48. Cf. also Lowry's earlier mention of this painting in letter 18.
3 Cf. letter 10: "Once I could play panjo fine."
4 Lawhill is also one of the names of the main charaĉter in *Lunar Cauſtic* (50).
5 "Hoppla! Wir Leben!": title of a play by Ernſt Toller (1893–1939), German expressioniſt dramatiſt; published in English in 1935 as *Hoppla! Such Is Life!*

35 : *From* AIKEN *to* LOWRY

TS H 2552; KILLORIN 244

South Dennis Mass.

March 7 40

My dear defrauded longsuffering Malc —
I've delayed writing chiefly because I had hoped by now to
have heard from Parks, or some fragment of good news from anywhere
— but no, not a word. I didn't like to report *only* the melancholy cable
from the O M with its sad dismissal of all hopes for six months, nor *raise*
your hopes with report of my letter to Parks till there was perhaps some
chance of a chance. But no. Nothing. The O M simply said that you muſt
stay in Vancouver, at the same address, till six months were up, and then
reapply for entry at the same place as before: no possible chance of a
removal eaſt. This seemed, and seems, ridiculous to me: but then, of course
I know nothing of these regulations. However, on the strength of my
feelings, I wrote to Parks and asked for a complete report as to the reasons
given, names of persons who gave them, and so on, with a view to then
trying to find someone in Washington who might at leaſt *attempt* a
reopening of the case. Mary's mother, who lives In W., might dig up
someone. But firſt, we muſt know the exaçt façts, so as not to mess things
up or jeopardize things in any way. That, I think, is important. Hence my
letter to P., and I hope in a day or two we'll hear from him. (Meanwhile,
we've already written also to Mary's mamma, and should be hearing from
her too.) Which, alas, seems to be about all that can be done. I said to P
that *I* saw no reason why you should not come to Montreal pro tem, at
leaſt – and then perhaps return to Van for the reentry. I've written to the
O M to the same effeçt, and informed him of my intention to try to wangle
things in Washington, on my own responsibility — repeating the statement of my cable that I believed your circumſtances in Van moſt unsuitable, together with reassurances about your work, Linscott, pomes, novels,
and so on. In short, my dear old Malc, I've done all I could think of. And
of course if there proves to be any chance whatever, or so small
whatsumever, I'll go on trying. But it looks bad, I admit, and so I suppose
you will be wise to decide now that you muſt somehow manage to stick
it, AND above all try to get the Volcano done quam cel. That will or should

comfort you to do, that and whatever you decide to do as well — some more pomes??? — and more to the point, it will be a help all round if you can get the Mss to me for Linscott while he is still freshly interested. Try to do it, now, and do it well, too — really I think we might get somewhere with it. For you sound in good form, and I find myself believing from the tone of your recent letters that the work you are doing must be good. But above all, don't permit yourselves to be depressed: no use now in that: you'll only risk a hurt to everything. Think, if it will help you at all, that we're keeping our eyes on you, and waiting to see you, and will be here for you when you come: and how good that will be. Not so damned long, either. And then we can expect at least six months of genial juice-swapping in Boston, if we get our house, or here, if we don't. (We are adventuring further with the house — trying to raise mortgages here and there, risking everything — it seems the only sensible thing to do, we might as well be hung for a sheep as for a rabbit). So keep the chin up. And get on with the work. . . . I've just had the 1st copy of my new book[1] — they've made a nice job of it, I think, — and now we wait for its fate with fingers crossed. I think it has a good chance — not too highbrow (if at all), a perfectly normal and simple and *good* theme, simple, straight-forward, vivid — and tender, I think — so that while it's a good job of work, qua form etc., it's also perhaps near enough the l.c.d. to catch on. Good god, I can't tell you how much we pray for that, nor what a difference it would make to *these* two lives. If it should sell, you never know, we might even come out to call on you! So add your prayers to ours if you still pray . . . And now all our loves and devotions, on a grey day in March —

Conrad

---

1 *Conversation.*

36 : *From* LOWRY *to* AIKEN

TS H 2512

595 W. 19th Ave.,
Vancouver, B.C.

[March 1940]

Dear old fellow:

Not melancholy Lowry's are we, but overjoyed at the sweetness of your letter, which has mitigated out bitter dissappointment.

If all blows up, including the world, I shall cherish as long as I live that wise sensitiveness which informed what you said at this bad time. It means more than I can say and more than I have said. We continue also to be unable to express our appreciation of what you and Mary have done and are doing on our behalf!

Lately I wrote a pretty good letter to my mater who seems pro my going to be under your Eye, and this, coupled with your letter, may still do the trick, change the O.M.'s mind. Also I wrote the O.M., sanely, sobersidedly, emphasising the practical importance of going east anyhow.

Meantime, we work with renewed vigor upon the Volcano. Elsewhere, also, are volcanoes.

Am looking forward tremendously to reading the Conversation.

Paris change, mais rien de ma mélancholie, s'a bougé . . .[1] Very pretty, but not true, in our case. The ship sails on.[2]

Love zu haus zu haus.[3]

Malc

---

1 Quotation from Baudelaire's "Le Cygne," in "Tableaux parisiens," *Les fleurs du mal*: "Paris change! mais rien dans ma mélancolie / N'a bougé!"
2 *The Ship Sails On* (1927) is the title of the English translation of Nordahl Grieg's *Skibet går Videre* (1924).
3 "zu haus": German, "at home."

37 : *From* LOWRY *to* AIKEN

TS H 2545

5

595 W. 19th Ave.,
Vancouver, B.C.,

March 20, 1940.

10   Juſt a mumbling word sending you both the beſt of our loves
and the very beſt of luck with "*The Conversation*![*"*]

May it have as triumphant a voyage as the Queen Elizabeth,
dodging all torpedoes from submarines of mean reviewers on both sides
15   of the Atlantic and coming to reſt gloriously in the Pier 16 of the beſt
seller liſt! May it be *un*like the Queen Elizabeth only in passing unnoticed
(and of course in being unfinished. This Queen Elizabeth analogy is
getting us into trouble but it means well!) and may it receive a symphony
of acclaim from friends and enemies alike! Which we know it will deserve!

20

In short: THE VERY BEST OF LUCK!

(Here:
          Ott flies to Dimaggio,
25   Rippla pops to Dimaggio,
          Mcmathy flies to Dimaggio, —
          No runs, no hits, no errors.)[1]

Malc & Margie.

30

---

1   Ott, Dimaggio, Rippla, and McMathy are names of American baseball players.

38 : *From* LOWRY *to* MARY HOOVER AIKEN

MS H 2538

[Vancouver]

[23 March 1940]

Portrait of Atlantis!
Or some new patterns for one's
Spring suiting!
God bless you.

Malcolm.

39 : *From* AIKEN *to* LOWRY

TS H 2553

S Dennis Mass.

April 1 40

My dear neglected Malc — this long silence is not due to indifference, sulks, chagrin, spleen, temper, worms, bile, or boredom — no, I've been flat on my very sore back with a kind of a fake but all-too-convincing pneumonia, and am still far from hale. Nor can I pause now to write any more than the briefest note, either, for we find that poor Mary must undergo an immediate operation for fibroids, and so tomorrow we hasten her to hospital in Boston, where she will have to stay two weeks. After that, a month of convalescence. Ain't life cute and full of cunning tricks? I shall stay in town for a week, until everything is going well, then come back here. My address wil be (till the 8th) 374 Commonwealth Ave. Mary takes it of course very calmly, and so, by reflection, do I — but still!
So don't worry if we don't write.

The novel is being peed on, crapped on, spat on, sneezed on, coughed on, ejaculated on, died and rotted on, by all the critics from the Nation up.[1] And bang — I fear — go our hopes.

But there's life in the old team yet.

much love to both

Conrad

40 : *From* LOWRY *to* AIKEN

TS H 2510

595 W. 19th Ave.,
Vancouver, B.C.

April 9, 1940.

Dear old bird:

— awful sorry to hear of your reverses — yours and Mary's — so here is a letter, & a funny pome out of another exiſtence, to cheer you up.

It seems to me that these oaves of reviewers muſt have some grudge agin you. As though you had wounded some of these little men on their amour propres in bygone years. Else why is it you so often get stupid reviews, but what has been unfavorably reviewed never fails to get mentioned in the same paper a couple of years later by someone younger as a maſterpiece? Which it proves to be.

Anyhow, I think that you're one of the five living greateſt writers and moſt other people do too, to whom literature is not merchandise, and that's the kind of opinion that matters in the long run, though I sez it

---

1 An unsigned review of *Conversation* appeared in the *Nation* 23 Mar. 1940: 401.

myself. Not always, damn it, to the purse, though probably, in the long run, to that too.

I read a more or less favourable but somewhat petty review in
5   *Time*.[1]

By the way, might I very humbly and penitently ask if I may borrow a copy of *The Conversation*? We don't have enough money to buy it at the moment; libraries sometimes take 3 months to get a book from
10   U.S. But I really *mean* borrow. Would return it definitely in a few weeks (if you can begin to believe me in these days). Later, when have enough money will buy it. I do not want to put you on the spot of feeling either after I have asked that you cannot very well refuse, etc. (And here may I go on record as apologising for not, those years back, acknowledged the
15   Preludes and Osiris.[2] The impertinance of this makes me now want to go and drown myself slowly in the neareſt pool. But it was not maliciousness or anything else. I was merely tight, Conrad, juſt tight.)

I am on the laſt chapter of Volcano – a strange book and I think
20   it makes an odd but splendid din. It is the firſt book of mine that is not in one way or another parasitic on your work. (This time it is parasitic however on some of your wisecracks in Mexico, & upon your political opinions! Poor Malc.)[3]

25   If you remember at the time you said you didn't mind about this: in faƈt we both decided that it would be good fun for both of us to do a book about Mexico and see what came of it.[4] But apart from the wisecracks, the 'charaƈter'[5] is not yourself. Nevertheless, I thought I would ask to be absolved in advance for any 'coincidences.' The trouble is, you
30   see, that this particular charaƈter gets – er – pushed over a ravine. (There is a horrendous real coincidence in conneƈtion with this for the day after I'd written that scene for the firſt time in Mexico, a man was shot and

---

1   Unsigned, "Books," *Time* 25 Mar. 1940: 97.
2   *Preludes for Memnon* (New York: Scribner's, 1931); *The Coming Forth by Day of Osiris Jones* (New York: Scribner's, 1931).
3   Lowry is probably referring to the political debate between the Consul and Hugh in chapter 10 of *Under the Volcano* (303–13), in which the Consul assumes the position of Aiken, and Hugh that of Lowry.
4   Aiken *did* write a novel loosely based on his 1937 trip to Mexico: *A Heart for the Gods of Mexico* (London: Secker, 1939).
5   i.e., the Consul, Geoffrey Firmin. According to Margerie Lowry, the Consul was based largely upon Aiken ("Fireworks Faƈtory," *Malcolm Lowry Remembered* 133).

pushed over a ravine in exactly the same way, by name, William Erickson. My character was at that time named William Erickson, the same name as the guy in In Ballast.)[1] Strange psychological goings on, here, I admit, but I do want to come to my own rescue by denying that while making
5 pretty speeches to you with one hand I was at the same time engaged in shoving you down the ravine with the other. No, Conrad, the truth is the guy who goes down the ravine, disguised in dark glasses and a false beard, is partly myself, partly the little ghost of what was once bad between us, bad about me. There is also a bit of Margie's father, a bit of the guy who
10 introduced Margie and I, and a bit of you, to account for the good parts. And of course the wise cracks the opinions (and how right most of them were!) an incident with my cat[2] (I made him love cats for a dramatic reason) I had to make the ghost an amusing fellow after all. But in a state of reconciliation with the burden of the mystery greater than I have ever
15 reached I just wished to while reiterating my deep love for you – and I want you to know that I *mean* it – to ask you sincerely to regard any apparent similarities or NUANCES with the fatherly twinkle, and for the rest, with a detached psychological amusement. I could hardly write this letter were it not all right with me. Also for the rest, damn it, there *are*
20 some similarities I can't help. The conflicts of divorce, conflicts of soul torn between England and America, the setting of Mexico itself, all these things are mine too; my anguishes and such, while again, my ancient doppelganger, I am, deep down in my psyche – if you will not be offended at my saying so – damned like you. My consciousness has not the intensity
25 of yours and it has been a long laborious process teaching it to be tractable and work at all, but I'm surprised at the amount that is really there, waiting to be mined. Poetry, I believe too: some gold, less tin than I thought. But some of the processes of metallurgy are startlingly and *naturally* like yours: and this I can't help, and would not if I could.
30

But what I can and could do was to write a book which put down my own reflection of the moon in my own real broken bottle. And I think I have done.

35 This book is also as it were a gesture on the part of a grateful pupil to his master.

---

1 There is also a character named Erickson (based upon Nordahl Grieg) in Lowry's *Dark as the Grave.*
2 Aiken refers to this incident (a cat catching a dragon-fly in its mouth) in a letter to the editor in the *Times Literary Supplement* 16 Feb. 1967: 127.

I have not written a single scene without firſt of all submitting it, as it were, to the Aiken microscope. That microscope has detected some faults, which will still probably be in when I send you the book, but not so many as usual. And finally, as I approach the end, it was with a sense

5 of triumph – many things contribute to this. I feel, for inſtance, that it is the sort of book you would want me to write, that, in a sense also, it is a completion of the Bridge which Hart Crane did not finish. And moreover it has been written under I think as horrible conditions as any book that has ever been written, and I do not except books written in prison,

10 reformatories, cork lined rooms, ships or front line trenches. The mixture of physical discomfort, noise and gnawing anxiety that at one moment one would have to stop, or that we would be separated, produced something unique in abhorrent conditions. And out of all this effort, together with the letters we tossed to and fro, much, it seems has bloomed. Margie

15 and I have really discovered something so real, that although we have not left our one attic room at all in the laſt months, that we feel we can laugh at everybody. And although you and I haven't gotten anywhere with the O.M., at leaſt not yet, I feel much has been resolved between us which is purely good, in that grand effort you made on our behalf, in my endeavor

20 to show you too, that at heart I was a loyal and sincere friend, with all of which the completion of the book in its present form, the pattern of our own lives, has something myſteriously to do. Excuse this portentousness, but I feel it to be so.

25 Margie has also written a detective novel[1] (she scrapped an earlier version the plot of which was snaffled by Ben Ames Williams)[2] which, when cut a bit, will be damned good. It really does hold your intereſt and speculation to the very end and, in my opinion, it should sell. Anyhow, it's a definite professional and good piece of work in its own genre: and

30 excellently conſtructed. Do you know anybody who might be intereſted?

Any by the way, some time ago before you intereſted Lindscott in it, I promised Whit Burnett, who now has the Story Press amalgamated with Lippincott, to submit the Volcano to him. What would you advise

35 me to do? Anyhow, I shall send you a copy firſt before I do anything. But

---

1 *The Laſt Twiſt of the Knife.*
2 Ben Ames Williams (1889–1953), American journaliſt and noveliſt who is the author of a number of detective stories including *The Silver Foreſt* (1926), *The Dreadful Night* (1928), and *Money Musk* (1932). I have been unable to identify the Williams book alluded to here by Lowry.

you might advise me meantime as to the ethics of this matter.

Please convey our sympathies again to Mary, to whom a letter goes on same post and here's hoping you'll be on your feet again soon, and that the reviews will pick up. The very last of my book offers stubborn resistance. Truly, as someone said, 'our books detest us.'

Both our loves

Malc.

You Said you were staying at Commonwealth Av. till 8th. This is 9th, so we send it to S. Dennis.

[Poem enclosed with letter 40 (TS H 2488)][1]

The doom of each, said Doctor Usquebaugh,
Quite clearly bids our loutish bones to stare.
True, drink's unfruitful on a larger scale;
Its music is an equinoctial gale:
Still, unembarrassing: and, profounder,
Outwinds the range of Cupid's organ grinder.
If worms are sabattical in a drunkard's dream
No fouler's this than love's nocturnal game,
Since dream of love it is, love of the pit
For its own sake, the virginity of the present,
Whose abyss is a womb shall not deny
A wintry plunge to nescient ecstasy,
Unsheathed entrance to the spirit's Tarquin,
But featherless and free from overt din,
Extending a plattered Lucrece with ferment,
Yet deeper than she, and rich with moist consent.
So well might we inquire, content to rot,
What do you offer, love, which drink does not?

---

1 See Lowry's poem "Doctor Usquebaugh" in *The Collected Poetry of Malcolm Lowry* (63). "Usquebaugh" is a Gaelic word for whiskey meaning "water of life."

41 : *From* LOWRY *to* AIKEN

TS H 2511

595 W. 19th Ave.,
Vancouver, B.C.,

April 24, 1940.

Dear Conrad:

I hope that by now Mary convalesces happily, that all is well with yourself too, with both yourselves.

For *our*selves, we are well and still holding our oasis in the desert of nightmares. *Under the Volcano* only needs two or three weeks more polishing and then will be finished. Apart from that, extraordinary, and possibly marvelous news! Marie Proctor, the Head of the Immigration Board at Seattle, Washington, through whom my application had to go to Washington D.C., has written to me to say that I do *not* have to come back to Vancouver if I go east – I can make my application anywhere in Canada, only *she* will forward the papers of the case to whatever port is convenient to me thirty days before next September 23, which will expedite my entry.

This would seem to indicate, since Parks had told me and the old man that my application had to be made through Blaine, – near Vancouver – that he has manipulated all this so that I would be kept here for his own ends. Even A.B.Carey was amazed at this and said he thought you and my father should be immediately informed!

What I have done, however, is to send the original of the letter, by clipper, to my father, and a copy to Parks, which gives him the sporting chance to save his face by cabling the old man and so getting his news in first, now that he sees he is on the spot. Otherwise, my fear is that my father and he – for the sake of preserving the unimpeachableness of authority – will cook up something like the form master and the uncle did in Thoma's story . .[1] (. Both the form master and the boy's uncle had it in for the boy who had come to the school with a 'bad character'. One day the boy asked the uncle to do a sum for him. To save his face and

---

1 Ludwig Thoma (1867–1921), German novelist, short story writer, dramatist, and essayist. Lowry is referring to one of the stories in Thoma's *Lausbubengeschichten* (1905).

with much grumbling the uncle did the sum. When the boy got the sum back from the form master it was covered with red ink. 'Only a donkey would do it like that,' said the form master, and gave him detention. 'But I only copied it from my uncle,' said the boy. 'You're a liar,' said the form master. For this detention the boy then got a hiding from the uncle. 'But' he protested to the uncle, 'It was your fault for not doing it right.'. The form master said: 'Only a donkey would do it the way you did it.' 'You're a liar,' said the uncle and gave him another hiding. Later the uncle and the form master were seen talking together. The next day the form master sent for the boy and said: 'I have had another look at your sum and it is quite right, only it is done an old fashioned way, a way we don't use nowadays. But you thoroughly deserve to be kept in just the same, for your insubordination. Anyway, you did not even copy the sum correctly from your uncle.' But the boy had exactly copied the sum. Later the uncle wrote to the boy's mother to say that he should not be expected to receive any more help from him since he could not even copy things down correctly and that this put him in a false position. . .)

Anyhow, there it is, Conrad. There is nothing for the world now to prevent my coming east, if the old man will only see eye to eye on the subject.

So, it may be that the O.M. will cable you – probably making all sorts of untenable provisos.

I know full well that you can't and do not expect you to do anything about us while Mary is sick and yourself seedy and I am anxious about that for your own sake, not for ours. You may take the philosophical viewpoint about an operation, but they are beastly things nevertheless and our sympathies are deeply with you.

I feel in the face of this a heel for even mentioning our problems. But I suppose I better had. It appears that June 1 is our approximate deadline. The Maurice Carey's plan to let this house at that time anyhow and a reshuffle of some sort then is inevitable. If we cannot go east by then it will of course be tough on us. Nothing else seems to have changed, save for the better.

I received, a week ago, a very kindly letter from the O.M., in which he demurred from my going east purely on the grounds that it would cost too much (presumably for me to go east, come back here, proceed east once more). So I have presented him with the new evidence, and once more one must wait. I assured him, and I meant what I said, that I wanted to give him some satisfaction in me at last about my work, that I was nearing proof of this, but that some closer contact with you was essential. As for Margie – if this were simply a frivolous love affair, or even just a love affair – or even if it were solely 'love' – I think I might hesitate to ask you still to count us 'als einer'[1] without firſt obtaining ratification from the O.M., etc. But Margie, apart from anything else, is now so absolutely inextricable from my work that I can't get along without her from this point of view alone, and were I to be separated from her I could not keep the promises about my work I have made both to the O.M. and to you! Meantime we have written something which I feel might compare not unfavourably with Kafka's 'The Trial'. It coſts no more for us both to live than one alone, we are uncomplicated by expeſting any children, we are not even married, yet, – so what?

Could you not lend me 'The Conversation' – blaſt ye – if I return it? I shall buy it when I can.

All our very beſt loves to you both.

Malcolm.

42 : *From* AIKEN *to* LOWRY

TS H 2554

s dennis

April 28 [1940]

Dear old Malc —

Thanks for your letter and the good news. That would be swell — but I haſten to warn you that it might be as well not too get your hopes *too* high, for judging from the lateſt note from the O M it is thought in official quarters that your durance vile is deserved, and does you good, and should be appreciated by you as praſtically self-imposed: in short, the O M may not think it advisable to move you *anyway*. But of course he may, and I hope he will; but I think perhaps I'd better myself for the moment make no move. If he does decide to to let you come eaſt,

---

1 "als einer": German, "as one."

the arrangements between the O M and me are more or less shipshape,
so there[']s nothing much to worry about on that score. Where would
you go? I have a friend, canadian artist with english wife, Kenneth
Forbes,[1] 87 Alcina Ave., Toronto, to whom I've already written about you
5 (long since.) He's a damned good egg, and a successful portrait painter,
and his wife is a beauty — great friends of Laura Knight and Harold.[2]
He writes me that any friend of mine is a friend of his, and he'd live up
to his word. So this might be kept in mind. But it will take time in any
event, and you'll keep me au courant. Unless of course I suddenly get
10 cables from the O M. Meanwhile we're on the very brink of buying a
house here, the one in town proving beyond us. Expect to know and maybe
sign up next week. A fine old eighteenth century ruin, which will take a
lot of fixing, but which you and M will like, and in which there'll be room
and to spare. Closer to S Yarmouth, shops, etc than this, and nicer
15 altogether. . . Mary's ope[r]ation turned out to be *much* less than feared,
she was in hospital only a week, and is now mending rapidly. What a
blessed blessed relief! She looks in fact better than before. Next week, her
show in N Y which we go down to. Hope it does better than the novel.[3]
(Can't send you a copy, having none to spare. Maybe later!) I look forward
20 to yr portrait of aiken the old medusa, and his death in the barranca, with
my customary sangfroid: it seems a logical end! My portrait of you in A
Heart for the Gods of Mexico (shat upon by G Greene)[4] was more kindly,
I suspect! . . . Can't do a decent letter at the moment, Gordon Bassett[5] is
here, and thanks to our various illnesses and poverty and the house
25 problem and one thing and another we're behindhand with everything.
Prospects for our summer school pretty dim, dammit. . . But I'll write
you more at length later, and meanwhile our loves to you both as always
—

30   Conrad

---

1 See letter 33.
2 (Dame) Laura (Johnson) Knight (1877–1970) and Harold Knight (1874–1961), both
painters, were London friends of Aiken whom he met around 1923. Laura was a
member of the Royal Academy and was well known for her paintings of circus life and
ballet scenes. The Knights' home in St. John's Wood became known as a gathering
place for artists and writers (Butscher 390).
3 *Conversation.*
4 See Graham Greene, "Boy Loses Girl," *Spectator* 27 Jan. 1939: 141.
5 Gordon Bassett (1890–1951), Harvard friend of Aiken to whom he dedicated *Ushant*
in 1952. Bassett died in June 1951 while visiting the Aikens at their home in Brewster
(cf. letter 83).

43 : *From* LOWRY *to* AIKEN

TS H 2513

1236 W. 11th Ave.
Vancouver, B.C.

May 15, 1940

Dear old Phaller:

Thanks a lot for your letter and I'm very relieved Mary's operation turned out O.K. That's really splendid news and I wish I had as good to match it from this end.

I would love to see your eighteenth century ruin but I have to admit, alas, that the only ruin that we are like to see is a twentieth century one, and that not in America.

Hellzappopin in Europe now and it doesn't prophet this prophet (more exact than most) a damn thing that he was a prophet.

Conscription may come at any moment and at our back we almost hear Time's 'phibian tanks a'changing gear, not to say, the first 'goosestep' of God. . .[1]

Meantime – bad news from England, which has tightened up, all of a sudden, on the money.

We swung a fast and lucky one on A.B. by getting out of Maurice's clutches into another room for $15 a month, and we now have $10 a week in addition to do *everything* else on. But our peril is increased thereby and the only thing that I can say is: that we are right, and that some God of some sort of good, (probably you in disguise) seems to be helping us to finish our work.

For the rest: stark, staring tragedy may face us, and it is a good thing if so that one can face it calmly and fearlessly and soberly and even without anger, and I can assume only that we are able to do this because we have already bled our souls as white as bone.

I am trying desperately to sell some stuff to Esquire in the hope that then, still, we may be able to go east and spend what few months we have left in peace.[2]

---

1 Cf. Andrew Marvell's (1621–78) "To His Coy Mistress": "But at my back I always hear / Time's wingèd chariot hurrying near;" (ll. 21–22).
2 No pieces by Lowry ever appeared in *Esquire*. In her introduction to *The Collected*

Judging by the muddle-headed vindictiveness I receive from time to time from Parks, – via presumably the old man, who has, however, written one pleasant but rather confused letter – one can expect little understanding from that quarter. But I still think I may give the O M some happiness in me.

The Volcano is on its last typing – re which I have, by the way, received an enthusiastic letter from Whit Burnett (Story Press and Lipincott, any good?) and what with that, and even better, your letter from Linscott, we have hopes of selling it. I have not much doubt but that it is a good book.

I do not see how you can assist us any further save by letting your genius storm into our spirits from time to time in these strange hours, but by helping us thus far in our struggle as I have said, far more has been achieved than meets the eye for good and good alone between us all.

All the best to Mary from us both.

As Haarlem burns and Joe Venuti[1] swings,
yours,
Malc.

44 : *From* AIKEN *to* LOWRY

TS H 2555; KILLORIN 246

s dennis Mass

May 21 40

Dear Old Malc:

yrs received, and contents noted with relief: viz., that you've moved into better quarters, and are more independednt and

---

Poetry of Malcolm Lowry, Kathleen Scherf says that in May 1940 Lowry sent "Eight Poems from *The Lighthouse Invites the Storm*" to James Stern in the hope that Stern would be able to place them with *Esquire* (6).
1 Guiseppe ("Joe") Venuti (1898–1978), American jazz violinist who led the jazz group "Blue Four" (Ackerley 217).

prosperous. Good. You don't say how you managed it — it muſt have taken some doing??? And of course if you could manage to get eaſt that would be swell. And we've beleieve it or not acquired a ROOF of our own, this very day acquired it, five miles from here, at Weſt Brewſter, on the
5 north side of the cape, high up, and with diſtant view of the sea, which is a couple of miles away: a fine wreck of a house, (the other one was snatched away from us by the loweſt of chicaneries), and already the delight of our hearts. Rats pop in and out of a fresh deep stinking shit-shotten hole in a mattress in the attic, all the windows are broken,
10 the floors bend under the foot, the rooms stink, the chimneys are falling, the rotten bulkhead door is shored up with seaweed, and the old E.C., outdoors, praċtically blows you off your feet: BUT the whole thing is going to be wonderfully rich and beautiful when we've scoured it and painted it and hung Mary's piċtures on the walls, and there are lovely trees round
15 about, and apples, and a peach, and grapes, and wild currants, and seven acres of pines, and a cranberrey bog, twenty feet below, which in spring becomes a pond. The house sits there among the spruces as if it had been there a thousand years, upſtairs there are umpteen unfinished cubicles which can become rudimentary bedrooms, so we are ready for the refugees
20 when they begin coming — Knights, Nashes,[1] Aikens, Armſtrongs,[2] the Royal Family, Lowries, or whoever. Bear us in mind! We are now in process of bespeaking a water-syſtem, lighting, reorganization and repairs, but hope to move in within a month. Then, perhaps a fragment of a summer school — E L Maſters' daughter,[3] perhaps, and a day pupil
25 or two: while we scrape walls and paint them, dig the sand and plant beans, or sit idly among the hollyhocks reading of the sunset of the weſtern world. Let us not, however, mention that: you surely, I feel, won't be dragged in: nor need you be? I hope to god not. I'm so glad Burnett is keen on Volc. Had he seen the new version, or was he speaking of the
30 old? And I thought you meant to send it to Linscott? But of course as

---

1 Paul (1889–1946) and Margaret (Odeh) Nash (1887?–1960) were friends of Aiken whom he met in 1922 when he was living in Winchelsea; Paul Nash was a surrealiſt painter and art critic for the *Nation* and the *New Statesman* (Lorenz, *Lorelei Two* 89); at the outbreak of the war he organized the Arts Bureau for War Service in Oxford and became the Official War Artiſt to the Air Miniſtry in 1940, and to the Miniſtry of Information in 1941.
2 Martin Armſtrong (1882–1974), British poet and noveliſt, and friend of Aiken. The two met while they were both vacationing in Florence in the summer of 1911. In 1930, after Aiken's divorce, Armſtrong married Aiken's firſt wife, Jessie McDonald.
3 Probably one of the daughters, Marcia or Madeline, of Edgar Lee Maſters (1868–1950), American poet, beſt known for his *Spoon River Anthology* (1915). Aiken wrote many critical reviews of Maſters's work.

you think best. My own poor book is now dead:[1] I saw the publishers in N Y and they were very hangdog about it. What boots it? or wrexall, for that matter.[2] I feel a bit fed up, but nevertheless am girding myself slowly and rheumatically for another go, probably this time at a sort of fictionalized haughtybiography, Rooms, Streets, and Houses:[3] it somehow seems to be essential that no year be allowed to pass without another book sent spiralling down the drain. John gets himself married next month. Jane is sort of engaged to a very 3d rate Englishman (Commonwealth fellow) whom we don't like. Ed is still in Rye, and wisecracking bitterly through the bombfalls. Ourselves, we pick off the woodticks, and pour another gin and french, and count out the last dollars as they pass, but are as determined as ever to shape things well while we can, and with love. Nevertheless, I still believe, axe in hand I still believe! And we will build our house foursquare. Come and see.

love to you both

Conrad

45 : *From* LOWRY *to* AIKEN

TS H 2514

1236 W. 11th Ave.,
Vancouver, B.C.

June 10, 1940.

Dear old Conrad:

I haven't written because we've been slaving away madly at the end of the Volcano, which protruded some unexpected peaks.

I'm awfully sorry the Conversation is dead in America: but maybe it is by no means dead here. Enclose review of it in local paper;[4] I enclose

---

1 *Conversation.*
2 Aiken is punning on the names of two well-known drugstore chains: Boots and Rexall.
3 Cf. *Ushant: An Essay* (23).
4 Victor Fellowes, "Aiken Adopts Effective Style," *Sunday Sun Magazine, Vancouver Sun* Saturday, 25 May 1940: 7. Both this and the "McCarthy review" (not identified) are missing.

the McCarthy review with it simply as an illustration of one of these material occasions when essences recur or something or other, for I seem to remember your saying that Mccarthy was one of the few people who spoke up in England for what seems to me now as well as at 18½ that
5 work of a satanic and marvelous genius: Blue Voyage.[1] — (I am trying to get the Province to let me review Conversation.)

Meantime, your letter made us laugh heartily amid the chaos.

Yes, it was hard to change our address, under the noses of the Careys, in fact, practically impossible, but we did it, without mishap, but
10 do not think we have any more money for that or that it is any the less tough. We now live on $55 a month, which has to take care of *everything*, and we are faced with less.

But we have had one good break. Parks has been fired, and my old man's trust seems restored in me and he is going to deal with me
15 personally. We shall be lucky if we get anything under the circumstances under which the O.M. is placed and I've told him it doesn't matter I'll make out somehow myself, but the main thing is in my eye that he and the mater should get some happiness out of me – perhaps one bright spot on a disastrous horizon.

20 I feel myself on the way up, definitely, and that some money will have accrued from the Volcano and elsewhere even before he manages to send me any funds and that, henceforward, I shall be able to fend on my own.

The whole European situation is such that I have been told to
25 abandon America altogether but I had already done so, so that is no surprise.

Nuy fo noy yhink hoerbrt yhsy er – this is such a good typographical error I'm not going to erase it. – But do not think however that were we now in the States we would have been a charge on you at this time:
30 Margie could have got a job and there are still a few hundred dollars over and moreover, as I say, I am on the way up. Up where?

Whether our efforts will be truncated by conscription I don't know, but hope not. If we make enough money we will still go east, if we can, where we could be, more or less in hailing distance of you at least.

35 Although the reasons for Park's demise are largely financial I have reason to believe for my father's letter that I have succeeded in demonstrating the fact that he was an out and out crook. For his own sake the O.M. is well shot of a man who made such a find thing of his

---

1 See Desmond McCarthy's review of *Blue Voyage* in the *New Statesman* 25 June 1927: 344.

exploitation of human souls, because he merely exploited the O.M.'s anxiety about me, trusting implicitly that I was too far gone as an idiot and a drunkard to ever refute him

I received also a letter from Jan which, paradoxically enough, puts me in the clear too. She too, says that Parks has shown himself to be a crook thus corroborating now, somewhat too late, in other ways, the truth of my contribution to the Lowry Legend.

So do not take too seriously what you heard from Parks [—] And do not, worse, think that I've turned into a pious teetotaler. [—] which at one time I thought perhaps you did: and remember too, that what the O.M. heard about me was from Parks too.

No – I asked your *advice* about sending Under the Volcano to Whit first, rather than to Linscott because while, or before, we were tossing letters to and fro, and *before* Linscott's letter arrived – I had already more or less promised to send it to Whit. I do not know quite what to do: I don't know anything about the new Story Press, but I feel that I owe a certain loyalty to Whit since he trusted me for a long time. What would say offhand like? I feel that if I did send it to Whit first I am sort of letting you down. But on the other hand if I sent it to Linscott first I am sort of breaking my promise to Whit. So I'm in a bit of a dither. Perhaps you could make a suggestion. I hope to have it completed and ready to mail off by the end of this week or the first of next, so if you want to give me any advice about this, please do it now.

I told my mother I would dedicate The Lighthouse Invites the Storm to her, so, if the Volc gets accepted, I am going to try to get that published after.[1]

Could you help, do you think, a bit here? I would like to keep that somewhat rash promise to the old lady, if only because it would make her feel good. I think it could be a good book.

With all the best love to you and Mary from both of us,

Malcolm.

P.S.   I see I have written, in another, unposted letter to you: — re your bad reviews: 'Once upon a time, Conrad, you hurt the feelings of MEDI-OCRITY so badly she will never forgive you.'

---

1   "The Lighthouse Invites the Storm" collection was published for the first time in *The Collected Poetry of Malcolm Lowry* (1992).

46 : *From* AIKEN *to* LOWRY

TS H 2556

s dennis Mass

june 17 40

Dear Malc —

relieved to hear from you I was, for meanwhile I'd had a letter
from the O M giving the news of the cash crisis which necessitated the
cutting out of Parks and the cutting down of the export of pounds, which
I feared might prove bad for you, but *hoped* might turn out actually to the
good. Which I take it, for the present anyway, it does. And that's swell.
As for Volc, why not if you've got it in duplicate send one here for Bob,
but with the strings tied so to speak — i.e., I'll tell him it's not for the
time being "loose", but might be later: and in any event he can advise
about it and also the pomes, which he still of course has. His idea was to
consider, if you'll recall, the whole bolus together, with a view to a *general*
notion of some kind. And I think that could do no harm. However, be
that as you see fit.

I haven't the heart to write more, with the news of France just
heard —

What are the chances in view of the new alien restrictions
here of your getting in next Sept?

Our house comes on, but still needs a lot, and I fear our small
cash won't do it, but there'll be a roof at least and a Chick Sale, and we've
started a vegetable patch —

I woke up from a dream this morning in which a negress
interviewer asked somewhat sceptically of me what possible contribution,
in the world's present dismay, a mere poet could make? And I said "love",
but then felt deeply ashamed, as not knowing that I really knew what love
was, or whether in any event it would do any good: and so woke, and still
wonder.

Gosh. I mean, *gosh.*

but love, just the same —

Conrad

47 : *From* AIKEN *to* LOWRY

TS H 2557

5   s dennis mass

                                        july 18 40

Are you fellows all right, Malc????
10   I hope the silence only implies zeal at Daedalian
labours. But I'd appreciate a line.
Nothing here: too busy sweating blood and terror on
mortgages and nails and plaſter, and trying to potboil
as well: and trying *not* to hear the deadly sounds
15   from England. Dutch boat in Boſton reports Plymouth, Pembroke and Cardiff all in ruins: I fear it may be true.
Damn. Chriſt. Chriſt. Damn. Chriſt.
We cabled Rye offering asylum — no takers as yet.
                love to both
20

                    Conrad

Ed reports Rye full of troops, and "strange noises, off" —
also the weather very thundery.
25

48 : *From* LOWRY *to* AIKEN

TS H 2515

1236 W. 11th Ave.,

July 19, 1940.

My dear Conrad:

I finished the Volcano and sent one copy to Whit Burnett, haven't heard from him yet. I had your copy all ready to send, but meantime – two days later, to be precise, by the time it took me to tie up the parcel anyhow, a collossal censorship descended on the land – magazines banned from the States, including, alas, Time, and everything and everybody suspected, the dark ages on us. The book is really anti-Nazi, as you know, but people in it have different opinions and state them frankly, and I am dubious about getting another copy through the mails. At least until such time as I get back the more or less censor-excluding letter about it from the late Governor General,[1] which I sent with Whit's copy. This may be unnecessary persecutions on my part, but I don't want to take any chances at making explanations with unsympathetic people and being tied up with red tape. And besides, we are now living on $45 per month, which leaves us practically no money for anything except food and a place to live. Our only diversion is going swimming every day, fortunately we are within walking distance of a beach – where we find ourselves surrounded more or less by negroes, Chinese and Indians, since we live in that part of town. Still, it is a beach, and we are keeping fit: (for what?)

I am meantime helping Margie on her detective story[2] and we shall have it finished before long.

I would to God I could see you. I feel I could be a good poet if I knew what sort of discipline to subject myself to. I can read scarcely any living poets save yourself and Wallace Stevens and the modern dead ones, who fructify me, like Rilke, wrote in languages I can't readily understand. If I

---

1 John Buchan (1875–1940), author, first Baron of Tweedsmuir, Governor General of Canada from 1935–40. Author of *The Thirty-Nine Steps* (1915) and *Greenmantle* (1916) amongst many others. According to Douglas Day, Lowry wrote to Buchan in 1939 to ask for help in acquiring "writing work." Buchan responded with a check for $50 and a letter of introduction to the editor of the *Vancouver Daily Province* (255–56). I have not been able to locate the letter to which Lowry is here referring.
2 *The Last Twist of the Knife.*

were more, or less, of a poet I suppose this desire for a design governing posture of some sort wouldn't worry me. I think even now, poems as good as the Spender-Auden-Rukeyser run of the mill suggest themselves to me and I won't let myself write them. Another thing: once a poem is written, I hate it, seem to lose it deliberately, do not want to send it anywhere. Of course you can advise me against this. But I think I must really want to be squelched, to be a posthumous rather than a living poet. The Keats and Chatterton idea you once suggested. A 'orrid thought. Well, you can advise me against this too. But give me some advice, I generally follow yours as one hypnotized.

I had thought to dedicate the Volcano to Margie and you and Mary: but if you feel the Mexican scene is too mutually affective or whatever, I'll dedicate another one to yez. Anyhow, for better or woise, it's written to you, or at you.[1]

I am more or less persona grata with the O.M. now, probably thanks to you. . . I much value that letter you wrote us. . . Did you get the review I sent you on Conversation? . . .[2] Margie and I seem to have discovered a Better Thing via our honeymoon in chaos. . . Yes, Conrad, by God, love certainly is something, in fact, everything. . . Please glow on us with some of it even if at a distance. . . There is conscription here on August 19: don't know yet whether it applies, or should, if it doesn't, to me.

And love: *tons* of it, to you and Mary
from us both.

Malc.

P.S. – N.B. Would you be kind enough – if it ain't too expensivish, or maybe send them collect – to send along the Lighthouse and Last Address so that I can immediately start working them over as I have no time to waste (remembering possible conscription.) If you have any suggestions for either, *do* please send them. (The same thing applies perhaps to In Ballast as to the Volc, for the present anyhow??.)

---

1 *Under the Volcano* was finally dedicated to Margerie alone.
2 See letter 45.

49 : *From* AIKEN *to* LOWRY

TS UBC 1–2

stony brook rd
weſt brewſter mass

aug 18 40.

My dear old Malc —
                              this will be three lines only, for we have have juſt
moved, are still in wildeſt chaos, have no time for anything but the endless
physical struggle involved in juſt keeping our heads above the stream of
wreckage and the billows of bills. I'll make a desperate attempt to get off
Laſt Address to you — kept it to show an agent, who was of course
alarmed by [i]t. The pomes are with Linscott. Shall I ask for the[m].
You'll recall he asked to keep them and Ballaſt till he could also see
Volcano. Say the word! Our house will be beautiful — and already the
refugees are forming in a line. Bob Morss[1] and family may spend the
winter with us — (you remeber him? Ginn & Co., Queen Sq., London.
The poor devil has a pulmonary cancer, can live a year or two or four, and
is broke into the bargain.) Also the Noxons[2] have arrived in Toronto, and
we await a visit from them. And we have asked Rye to send a contingent
— though no takers yet. What we'd all live on I don't know — but I guess
we'd manage — and the house is capacious enough, god knows. My beans
are on the table, my peas were eaten laſt night, the squashes and tomatos
ripen, the spinach heads, the corn tassels, and this landscape is an
aſtonishment and delight — we love it in short and are only unhappy
when we look towards England, or liſte[n] to the wireless, which of course
we can T avoid. God damn it. Can you get eaſt — can you get *in*???
Gerald's address is 136 Lyndhurſt Ave., Toronto. Much love to you both
and a few weeks hence I may be able to write you a proper let-let — but
now, no, it's imposs!

aff.

Conrad

---

1 Bob Morss, American friend of Aiken and British representative of the publishing
firm Ginn & Co. (Boſton, Athenaeum Press).
2 See Paul Tiessen's *The Letters of Malcolm Lowry and Gerald Noxon* for Lowry's letter
of reintroduſtion to Noxon and their correspondence up to 1952.

50 : *From* LOWRY *to* AIKEN

TS H 2516

Dollarton P.O.
Dollarton, B.C.

Sept. 6, 1940.

Dear old Conrad:

Note new address! We live in a shack on the sea. Dollarton is an old shipbuilding town, Dollar liners – now dead: slipways covered with brambles, enormous blaſted oaks in a fine, deep foreſt. Outside the window, a vaſt white calm where sea is confused with sky, and the Rockies. We have a boat: and one day, out for a row, a whale came up beside us! I think it was Herman Melville in disguise. Anyhow it is a wierd and wonderful place and we love it, the more so since it is coſting us only $10 a month rent to live in it, and after October, will coſt even less, if we are still here. A Maltese cat with golden eyes has adopted us while she has her kittens: we call her Ping because she does not purr. We are delighted with everything and with ourselves: for we have outwitted the Careys, and cooked Park's goose – he has turned the remaining money over to me – and, incidentally, made the O.M. and the mater as pleased as they can be about anything at this period. I haven't yet told him about Margie, but it looks as though I shall be absolutely on my own hook. We have enough money to hold out till December: the authorities have told me, being a visitor, I don't have to, or rather can't, regiſter. I don't know, at that rate, whether I shall be called up at all. Maybe the war will soon be over. I suppose I muſt hope not. Anyhow here we are and a bloody miracle I calls it. So that now we have a sporting chance. I still have not heard from Whit about the Volcano, but if he doesn't take it, it is going to Linscott, and it maybe even now on its way. Don't know how to send you a copy yet. Margie's deteƈtive novel – 'The Laſt Twiſt of the Knife' – is off, too. Is the Bob Morse you speak of Robert Ely Morse who wrote a poem ending 'This swan upon the icy waters of my heart glides ever on, in the Dial, 1926?[1] Anyhow, poor devil, I am sorry for him. Thanks for Gerald's

---

1 Lowry is referring to a poem by Richard Ely Morse entitled "This Swan" in the *Dial* Sept. 1927: 222; the firſt, not the laſt, line of the poem reads: "This swan, upon the icy waters of my heart, / sails night and day; . . . ." In the same issue is a review of

address: I wrote him, no answer as yet. I've told Julian Green[1] to go and see you: you are both from Savannah. Much of his early work I thought, was superb: but hi[s] genius seems to have run slightly aground. Perhaps you will set him afloat again.

5   We would come east like a shot if we could afford it: but perhaps we shall soon be able to. We read your article in the Atlantic[2] and caracoled: I have a lot to say about it which I'm reserving for another letter. Margie really thought you'd expressed everything she wanted to say but couldn't: yo, tambien. I read some new sonnets of yours in Harpers[3] which I

10   thought contained two of about the best poems I'd ever read by anyone, anywhere. . .

      Yes: please do send the Last Address, *quam celerime*: I plan to rewrite it, cutting the dialogue Great Circle passage – but have no copy, and we want to start working full blast again right away. God bless and much

15   love to Mary and you from us both.

Malc.

20

51 : *From* LOWRY *to* AIKEN

25

TS H 2517

Dollarton P.O.,
Dollarton, B.C.,
Canada.

November 22, 1940.

30

Dear old Conrad:

35   I think, dream, poetry all the time these days, struggling with the only form I know, the one you taught me. With a sort of a monad, gulped

---

Blue Voyage by Charles K. Trueblood (243–45).

1 See letter 10.

2 "Back to Poetry," *Atlantic Monthly* Aug. 1940: 217–23.

3 "Five Sonnets," *Harper's Magazine* Aug. 1940: 268–69; reprinted as "xxvi," "xxvii," "xxviii," "xxix," and "xxx" in *And in the Human Heart*.

down into my consciousness like a stone in my adolescence, still stuck in my throat I wonder if I can ever achieve more than a half choked expression of myself and can hang myself one day on some sort of hall of fame, however obscure. We live Thoreau-like here, in the deserted village
5   where grey Panamanian freighters sometimes visit us. I keep remembering how I used to go on to Hayes Common and read the House of Dust[1] and pray one day I might meet you, which seemed to be impossible, because I could not see how you could be alive and at the same time reach such beauty, and all the time Jane was at school close by with the Kellett
10   child,[2] who was indeed my geographical excuse for being on Hayes Common at all. How I appreciate now the collossal advantage of having known you and would that I had been better and honester and more *conscious* when I did! I sometimes think I am like a man who remembers having known Bill Shakespeare in his youth – but what a pity, he couldn't
15   appreciate anything the fellow said, he was blind and dumb at the time.

    Our cat has had kittens – four of them – for which we have found homes for two, alas and alas, at the bottom of the sea: now, from what we can hear of her peckerdilloes she is well on the way to having some more. I have not much of a way with cats, but Margie has and I improve. There
20   are killer-whales in the bay – we encountered one while rowing, thought it was a porpoise with a poipose – and we have been viciously attacked by a goat[3] – a symbol? No more tragedies. . . Yeah. We still look forward with all our hopes to the prospect of seeing you again soon: immobilisation is difficult though. I can never thank you enough for lots of things. How
25   could we have survived without the hope you gave us? And I know that, thanks to you, whatever the old man has to suffer will be much mitigated. . . . I hope Mary is well, give her our very special best and most special love. An article of yours I discovered in a yellowed New Republic in the Vancouver Library,[4] inspired this, in which there ought not be more
30   than ninetyfour plagiarisms. (Matter of fact, I don't think there are any unless 'derricks of the soul' recalls – without however benefiting by the comparison – 'who watches here, oh mariners and surgeons' & could be

---

1 Cf. also letter 34.

2 Jane Aiken and Joan Kellett had apparently been attending school close to 5 Woodville Road, the location of Jerry Kellett's "cramming school" where Lowry was staying in 1928–29. In an unpublished letter of 13 August 1929 to his children, Aiken writes that Lowry "knows a girl named Joan Kellett at Jane's school, and has often been there on Saturdays to take her out to tea" (Huntington Library).

3 Cf. *Under the Volcano* (99–100).

4 Aiken wrote many articles for the *New Republic*; the one to which Lowry is referring may be Aiken's "Gigantic Dreams," *New Republic* 27 June 1928: 146–47.

counted as such. It is not necessarily improved by this deficiency of having none & now I see another: 'muted.' B.V?)[1]

This wrestling, as of seamen with a storm
5   Which flies to leeward, while they
United in that chaos, turn, sea-weary
Each on his bunk, to dream of fields at home
Or shake with visions Dante never knew,
The poet himself feels, struggling with the form
10   Of his quiet work. What derricks of the soul
Plunge in that muted room, adrift, menacing?
When truant heart can hear the sailors sing
He'd break his pen to sail an easting down.
And yet some mariner's ferment in his blood
15   Sustains him to subdue or be subdued.
In sleep all night he grapples with a sail!
But words beyond the life of ships dream on.

Meantime nature poems, mature poems, hate poems, fate poems, –
20   all, but great poems – pour out. At the moment I am toying with this pleasing Rabelaisian whimsy. People down from the direction of the saw mill, hearing suspicious blood curdling noises at night from this direction, come to investigate, (It has happened.) with lanterns, even a 'lifeboat'. It ends –
25

Never in a comedian's life have I laughed till then!
. . . Wherefore the legend grew that there were ghosts
Somewhere between Dead Tree and Merry Island,
And from our love revived an Indian slaughter.
30   Oh you who something something something land
May you too be blessed by such enormous laughter
As even God and whales might not approve.

But I haven't got the beginning yet: or, it might be said, the end either.
35   Anyhow, Conrad, thus one's time is spent or mispent, waiting for a man from Porlock, who may never come.[2] I hope not. Meantime, the Volc is

---

1 Cf. Aiken's *Blue Voyage*: ". . . muted, like the hush heard in a conch-shell" (16) and letter 2, n. 5, p. 9. This poem appears as "Joseph Conrad" in *The Collected Poetry of Malcolm Lowry* (117–18); the fragment below also appears untitled in that text (197).
2 See Coleridge's introduction to "Kubla Khan" in which he says that while writing

at Linscotts. I should have taken your advice and sent it him first. But I was duty bound to send it to Burnett, who, it turned out, didn't even read it.

Can you tell me some mags where one might send pomes with hope of small payments?.

Please write and tell us if you still love us as we indeed love you

from both

Malc.

52 : *From* LOWRY *to* AIKEN

TS H 2518

Dollarton P.O.,
Dollarton, B.C.,
Canada,

November 30, 1940.

Dear old fellow:

Down the abyss crasheth the tabid world. . . Have you news – my God! – of John? Ed?[1] May they be safe. I have some news from my mater, who sounds pretty mad though her bloodthirstyness is directed at most everything. I have to admit, sceptical though I sometimes be about reports of indescribable morale, that she never sounded in such good form. God knows how or why, what with the hellish shellacking they've been giving Liverpool But this letter was written before the worst. . . Our gardener is dead, a good egg and I have written this epitaph to be put on his grave.[2] Maybe they won't because they'd have to build a Grant's tomb to

---

down his dream he was "called out by a person on business from Porlock" and was afterwards unable to recapture the vision.
1 John Davenport; Ed Burra.
2 The "enclosed" epitaph is missing; however, see Lowry's "Epitaph on our Gardener, Dead Near Liverpool" in *The Collected Poetry of Malcolm Lowry* (174–75).

accomodate it. "Would you like to see our son's poems? Then we'll all go off to the graveyard after tea. . ."

Linscott wrote me a very encouraging letter about the Volc. He was for it, others were agin. I'm not distressed though – he thinks somebody will take it eventually. I'm not caring. We have enough just to scrape through for a month or two. Who could be luckier than we? Virginia Strong[1] has sent in a cracking good report on Margie's detective novel, so that's fine news.

But principally I don't care about the Volc because I'm writing poetry all the time now. I send you four poems,[2] and wondered, if you liked them, or thought they were suitable or whatever, I could ask you the favour of sending them to the Atlantic Monthly with a benign word. I hate to give you trouble: but as your old – and present, more than ever, pupil – I feel you would be pleased I was writing poetry, if it was good, or even if I were trying. I feel that they have something, a certain simplicity and strength, – a universality, maybe – that they may have an unusual dramatic quality. You told me once to send some poems I had written along and you will forgive me if I have been taking you at your word ever since.[3] I may be fooling myself about these particular poems and if I am I know you will tell me so, but please answer me this: may I keep on firing them at you until you think you see one which might be published in that there Atlantic for it seems to me a fine and traditional place to start? I can't tell you what a kick that would give the old creative instinct.

Divorce papers have not arrived till now and we are going to be married by a fine carrot-juice swigging Unitarian minister on Monday[4] – shades of your ancestors – We know you are wishing us luck – God bless you, & Mary, – love from both –
Malc

P.S. I have appended bloody little titles to the poems, after the Atlantic custom. I am no Wallace Stevens, unfortunately. And, of course, Gawd with a capital H. And good god, why not?

---

1 Virginia Swain Stong (1899–1968), American novelist, editor, and journalist, and wife of author Phil Stong. Under the name Swain, she is the author of *Foolish Fire* (1929), *The Hollow Skin* (1938), and *The Dollar Gold Piece* (1942) among numerous others. Lowry has misspelled her name.
2 These poems are missing.
3 Cf. letter 3, which may have been written after such a request from Aiken.
4 The Lowrys were married on 2 December 1940.

53 : *From* LOWRY *to* AIKEN

TS H 2519

Dollarton P.O.,
Dollarton B.C.,

Dec. 4, 1940.

Hi William! Herman! Conrad! Nathaniel![1] Help!

Between the blank verse and the cordite – Here is another version of pome I sent you.[2] Lines 8 to 10 are different. In the version I sent you it looks as though Lycidas and not the sea stank so badly it would make whoever it was weep.

So I have rewritten the pome so that it merely looks as though it is the poem that stinks and not Lycidas.

Herewith. It may be the fulfillment of a lifelong ambition to haunt a graveyard, anyhow.

We were married without a hitch, which is a paradox, and very fine too.

God bless you, my dear old bird, and Mary.

I much admire the poet jones, very.[3]

Love from both –

Malc.

---

1 William Demarest; Herman Melville; Nathaniel Hawthorne.
2 This poem is missing, though Lowry is referring to his "Epitaph on our Gardener, Dead Near Liverpool" which he enclosed with letter 52. See Kathleen Scherf's *The Collected Poetry of Malcolm Lowry* where she provides the variant texts of the poem mentioned here by Lowry (174–75).
3 Lowry is referring to the New England transcendentalist poet, Jones Very (1813–80).

54 : *From* LOWRY *to* AIKEN

TS H 2520

Dollarton P.O.,
Dollarton, B.C.,

December 11, 1940.

Dear Conrad:

I will promise not to send you another pome – save for Christmas, maybe – but am venturing to send you this,[1] wondering if you had not already sent any of the other pomes to the Atlantic, if you would enclose it, if you were going to send any, that is, and please do not send any if you don't think it right, because it won't hurt me, I can't stop writing them anyhow – and anyway why don't I send them myself. The last is rather easily answered: nobody seems willing to take them nor agent handle them unless you are a 'name' or the pomes are solicited, or good, or something. '*Poetry*' may be an exception but I don't know the address. Maybe you could give me some suggestions. . .

Once in Rye you wrote me a letter mentioning the strange noises my uke made.[2]

With the aid of an introverted sensibility I have now turned this round a bit.

If a uke why not a guitar or a harp or a viol made out of a woman's breastbone or even the heritage poets leave behind for later singers?

Love from both to both

Malc

P.S. My explanation of the poem is just balls, as usual: pay no attention.

---

1 The "enclosed" poem is missing.
2 This letter is missing.

55 : *From* AIKEN *to* LOWRY

TS UBC 1–2

5   Brewster Mass.

Dec 15 40

Dear old Malc —

10   forgive silences, I[']ve been rendered incommunicado by
poison ivy in both arms, and apart from that too busy to call my soul my
own. I like the pomes moderate-like. But I cant send them to Atlantic,
because I've had one hell of a row with Weeks,[1] and to have them sent
by me would aut7mtically rule them out. Nor am I much better off with
15   anyone else. My name is Mud. Epitaph[2] is the best, I think — largely
because formally more complete — the others are pretty irregular, lines
shortening or lengthening willynilly and for no apprent purpose. I could
send it to the new little mag called Vice Versa, if you like — but it woud
mean no cash to speak of. The news of your marriage at last is marvellous
20   — had I not been in such a moil I'd have wired you at once our loves and
things — or sent you a singogram! Very fine. What about your getting
into the U S? We've been really in a frenzy here — Uncle Alfred[3] died in
November, and there have been endless complications, including a
fantastic search for his lost ashes, a fruitless journey to New Bedfor in an
25   attempt to get him buried, the spilling of his hapless ashes on a mahogany
table in the offices of the cemetery board, and his return here for a week
in Brewster. But On friday we went again and returned him to his whaling
ancestors, and drank his health in a a bar called the Atlantic, so now he
rests. I have a resident pupil here, John Hay,[4] for two months, which helps
30   to pay the upkeep on our borrowed house, furntiture, stoves, and furnace
— Mary runs a small art class — my book of sonnets[5] is out, but nobody
knows it, nobody reviews it, nobody buys it, nobody reads it — I'll send

---

1 Edward Augustus Weeks (1898–1989) was the editor of the *Atlantic Monthly* from
1938–66.
2 See letter 52.
3 Alfred Claghorn Potter (1867–1940), brother of Aiken's mother, Anna Kempton
Potter; librarian of Widener Library at Harvard; cf. *Ushant* (283–87) and letter 85 for
an account of Aiken's trouble with his uncle's ashes. Aiken suspected his uncle to have
been the model for Eliot's "J. Alfred Prufrock" (Killorin 25).
4 Pupil of Aiken who was to become a good friend of his in his later years in Brewster.
5 *And in the Human Heart.*

you one for Xmas. And when I get a quiet day I'll really try to write you
a proper letter.

our loves to you both

Conrad

I think it's good that you're writing poetry — but do try to keep your
numbers and quantities straight — ! Freedom comes *after* mastery not
before — the sonnet consists of 14 lines of five-beat iambics, rhymed
ababcdcdefefgg or abbaabbacdecde: it can't just be *any*thing!

56 : *From* LOWRY *to* AIKEN

TS H 2521

Dollarton P.O.,
Dollarton, B.C.,

December 20, 1940.

– I didn't send you a pome for Christmas, my dear old phalla, but here's
an appropriate yeastsy thought for the New Year.
(Not for the Atlantic *Monthly*.)

BYZANTIUM: or Where the Great Life Begins
(or Getting a bit knocked oop now.)

– Don't come any of that Byzantium stuff
On me, me swell young toff! Just plain Stamboul
Is good enough fer me and Lamps and Bill.
Constantibloodynople's right enough –
Used to be, eh? Eh? Don't give me that guff
Like that wot you said about the ideal –

In a blind eye socket![1] But a girl's a girl
And bobhead tigers here will treat you rough
And give you, 'ideal!' *Farewell, smoke is real –*
And ukeleles mourn a ululu:
5   *And engine stampedes: more fool you fool you:*
And aeriel says: oh whither where away:
And sea: each one-eared dog will have its day:
And stars wink: Venus first, then Mercury.[2]

10   God enormously bless you both and give you Merry Christmas. We find
life marvellous here, sea and snow – God goes by with white footfall –
no men with black footfall from Porlock[3] – and a wild duck washed up
on the shore.

15   Malc.

N.B. Here's another called 'Deserter', also not for publication.

     . . . 'Dead, in a refrigerator van at Empress.'
20   Then, lying on bare boards, in a small room
His father came from Coquitlam to see.
'There wasn't even a sheet over him.'
Brought his body down from Medicine Hat
That had been placed in Category C.
25   Military papers in his army greatcoat
     – 'Should have been in England? Came home for Christmas?
     – And did he have to bum his way back home?' –
Thus pass, from old Westminster to New!
Here is a tale that clangs an iron door shut
30   Against the heart, freezing sense: for pity
Cannot follow to the accusing root
Of this tragedy beyond tragedy.[4]

---

1   Cf. letter 86.
2   This poem appears in *The Collected Poetry of Malcolm Lowry* (161–62).
3   See letter 51, n. 2, p. 148.
4   See *The Collected Poetry of Malcolm Lowry* (139). In his annotation for this poem in
The Collected Poetry, Chris Ackerley explains that it is based on the story of Paul
Reynolds Scott, a conscript who went AWOL during WW II and was discovered dead,
on 21 November 1940, in a refrigerator car (281–82). Lowry based much of the poem
on newspaper accounts in the *Vancouver Sun*.

57 : *From* LOWRY *to* AIKEN

TS H 2522

5   Dollarton P.O.,
                           Dollarton, B.C.,

                           January 3, 1941.

10   Dear Conrad –

     Just received yesterday And in the Human Heart for which a thousand thanks.[1] It is deeply appreciated by both. Have not had time to digest as yet but can only say so far it was not so much like opening a book on
15   words, but on a lightning, a sunlight. It was as though a coiled bright soul sprung out at us. Will elaborate later: what I have seen is great, and my feeling comes just after an attempt to do some hefty reading right through English Literature, Shakespeare, Jonson, Milton, etc. I feel there are in your book some of the highest touchstones of excellence in *all* literature.
20   Will write at greater length later.
     Margie says she's paralyzed by book – both send thanks to both and love –

                     Malc

25   P.S. Feel a bit ashamed – as who wouldn't, after your book? – of myself, sending you *my* unpolished mumblings: but I am working very hard at trying to get the mastery you have indicated and which I agree is so necessary: so far am encouraged with results so I may bore you with some more.
30

---

1   Lowry's copy of *And in the Human Heart* in the UBC Library bears the following inscription written by Aiken:

     For Malcolm and Margerie
     with much love and best
     wishes for a Merry Christmas —
     and many to come —
     from Conrad & Mary.
     1940.

58 : *From* AIKEN *to* LOWRY

TS UBC 1–2; KILLORIN 254

5   brewster mass

feb 23 41

Bless you Malc, and bless Margie too for all the glowing words and
10   numbers and phine phlattering phrases about my little dead sonnets —
how good of you both, thanks thanks and thanks again![1] I rushed to
re-read the ones you liked, to see if they were ones *I* liked — it's always
such fun to read one's own things through somebody else's eyes, don't you
think? —— a kind of twice reflected narcissism. And agreed in many
15   cases, though occasionally wit[h] a preference for others — which is only
natural. Very comforting altogether, for such reviews as this book has *had*
have been *private* reviews, like yours, viz., in letters — the press reviews
have been few. This culminated in an attack by Jarrell in the N Republic
two weeks ago, and a reply, attacking Jarrell and poet-critics[,] by Cowley,
20   the week after.[2] Whether his generous remarks can r[e]sucitate the book,
at this late date, I incline to doubt. All very sad. The galilean note I hadnt
noticed — in fact I'd have said if anything that *that*, if at all, might be
more   prominent   in   Time   in   the   Rock[3]   than   here,   where   the
weltanschaung[4] is more lucretian, more pagan — but then one never
25   knows! And interesting anyway. As for the portrait of the husband and
father, the kids, the cats, the kitchen — well, I dunno, that seems to me
not so adapte[d] to my purpose, which was a celebration of joy-in-love,
and in defiance of fate, zero, death, time, space, terror, god, and everything
— namely, in defiance of *knowledge*. This in turn called for the grand
30   manner, sort of — and your suggested gemütlichkeit[5] would hardly
accord, I think? Perhaps Conversation contains the portrait you want. . .
How nice to have your pictures, and how lovely, may I say, Margie is —

---

1   The preceding letter from the Lowrys to which Aiken is here referring is missing.
2   See Randall Jarrell's "The Rhetoricians," *New Republic* 17 Feb. 1941: 221–22, and
Malcolm Cowley's response in "Poets as Reviewers," *New Republic* 24 Feb. 1941:
281–82. Jarrell's review was attacked by two others in the *New Republic* 10 Mar. 1941:
J.V. Healy, "Correspondence: The Poet's Bloody Corner," 343, and Wadsworth
Mulrooney, "Correspondence: The Poet's Bloody Corner," 343–44.
3   *Time in the Rock: Preludes to Definition* (New York: Scribner's, 1936).
4   "weltanschauung": German, "world-view"; Aiken has misspelled the word.
5   "gemütlichkeit": German, "good-naturedness."

as everyone here delightedly agrees. Jane was delighted also with the cat!
. . Gerald reports you have got your passport straightened out — do you
think of coming east?[1] And J D's address — The Malting House,
Marshfield, Chippenham, Wilts. I haven't heard from him for over a year.

love to you both

Conrad

59 : *From* LOWRY *to* AIKEN

TS H 2546

Dollarton P.O.,
Dollarton, B.C.
Canada.

May 9, 1941.

Very Querido Conrad – Mary –

Thanks for the news (a wee bit contradictory, but all turned out fine)
and sorry to have given you all the bother of my bloody Mss. anyway.[2]
But I do very much appreciate what you did for me and I want to say
to you too – what I have just finished saying to Bob Linscott – that so far
as I was concerned the bother was not wasted. Your interest and kindness
got me over a hell of a difficult period where I might h[a]ve let down: as
things stand I have been able to reorganize my life to a point where I am
now really able to cope with that, and other, work. As your pupil this
makes me feel good because I feel I am now justifying your faith in me:
you wait. My life was always the most difficult part of my work, largely
because it was too easy.

---

1 See Lowry's 15 January 1941 letter to Noxon in *The Letters of Malcolm Lowry and
Gerald Noxon* (35).
2 The preceding letter from Aiken is missing.

As for the old man, God knows what horrors are breaking over his poor head, but whatever they are, he and the mater now feel happy about me which is to them one major sorrow the less, for which I am eternally thankful. And the ghastly psychotic dance we led each other has come to an end. And you must take credit for this too.

As for ourselves, we did not succeed in coming to Montreal, and America is as far off as ever, but the hope engendered worked constructively. Stroke after stroke of good fortune has come our way and we have now *bought* a supershack on the sea – all paid for, no rent, no tax, but lovely, surrounded with dogwood and cherry and pines, isolated, and a swell place for work. It's no Forty-one Doors[1] but we love it just the same and it suits us fine.

Margie has written two mystery novels,[2] one plumb first rate from any point of view, and the agents hopes of selling it are sanguine – and I three long short stories (including a pouncing horror) which have also called forth the warmest sanguinities from the hard-boiled. I have been working hard at the pomes too, bearing your words well in mind, and I feel I've done something very worthy here too – about sixty new ones – may I inflict some on you sometime if you would say the word? The Atlantic has held on to one for nearly three months, having sent all the others back, which might be a good sign. However, apart from one in England,[3] I have met with no material success here yet, not even from Poetry. But I don't care because I feel I am really getting somewhere.

In addition – all the Mss. from Linscott arrived on May Day! –

All of them are perfectly unreadable as they stand, which makes me grateful for your patience all over again, but as I say I am now able to cope with them, and it was a kind of good omen their arriving when they did, just as we had moved into our new 'house' which is really beautiful, by the way.

So – thank you Mary and Conrad! – and for your letters. And now, all the luck in the world to 41 Doors and your project. How lucky, how lucky, and again lucky your pupils are, and what a Godsent opportunity they have. I suppose it's inevitable such opportunities should be very rare but what hope or help a European creative fellow could get out of Cambridge and its bloody triposes seemed to me to depend too much on luck and – but I won't get going on the 'system' now.

---

1 Forty-one Doors: the Aikens' home in Brewster, Massachusetts.
2 *The Last Twist of the Knife* and *The Shapes That Creep.*
3 I have not been able to identify any Lowry poems published in England at this time.

Well all the very beſt of luck to you, and your pupils, though they already have it, being such.

Blessings.

Malc & Margie.

60 : *From* LOWRY *to* AIKEN

TS H 2537

Dollarton P.O.
Dollarton, B.C,
Canada,

Auguſt 13, 1941.

Muy querido Mary and Conrad:

Salud y peseta.[1] How goes the summer school? We are still sitting in our cottage on the sea – which we own, the cottage that is, and damn it, the sea too, why not? – until such time as Vancouver Aldermen inveſtigate the squatter's problem, which will probably be never since we're not on city land – tax free, with getting on five hundred dollars in the bank which will probably be broke before the year is out, though it has a provident sound and it would probably have rotted if we buried it in the ground, striving for what you call a Better Thing, and gawd blimey how we have struv, and with diffident, remote, or occasional unilluſtriously local success as to things taken and sold, but two wows of myſteries by Margie called The Laſt Twiſt of the Knife and the Shapes that Creep that will come

---

1 "Salud y peseta[s]": Spanish toaſt meaning "health and money." Cf. *Under the Volcano*:
   "Salud y pesetas."
   "Y tiempo para gaſtarlas . . ." (6)
and
   "Salud y pesetas" (328).

out some time and one long short story utterly rewritten recaſt and deplagiarized and reborn by me, that Laſt Address which I think might live when I am dead and damned or something and a pome in the September Atlantic – about the only one of innumerable to click any-
5 where – called In Memoriam for someone,[1] not the gardener this time, probably buried away somewhere in the depths, not too bad, I hope you think, certainly it is muy correcto, only we wrote some music for that better (for the uke) only it's so depressing one cannot sing it without that self conscious tear drop gliſtening in the eye, and we had a slight
10 altercation with Weeks too, juſt to be in the family, in faƈt we held up the Atlantic which was more than Joshua could do or the Children of Israel and aƈtually had to send it a telegram finally.

For the laſt two months and for the next two we have been and are busying ourself exclusively with that Under the Volcano book and In
15 Ballaſt to the White Sea, which have had to be thoroughly deloused and given two new handles and two new blades, otherwise its the same old cricket bat. However we decided that all the charaƈters could not be equally dead and have all quite the same look – they had to be diſtributed in different poſtures throughout the morgue anyway – and this has
20 presented some nice problems, moſt of them neatly solved, we feel. I think they may both end up firſt rate, which would be a miracle, but not impossible.

The current problem (damn it, can I ever get through a letter to you without asking you a favour) is re Houghton Mifflin's fellowship, the
25 application blank for which Linscott has sent us, that is, in this case, me.

I have among other things to send in letters from *two* responsible persons – they may refer either to applicants charaƈter or literary qualifications or both. Do you think as an old pupil I could ask you humbly to send such a brief letter – that is, two brief letters, one from you and
30 one from Mary, briefly passing over the faƈt that I might have neither: address them to Houghton Mifflin of course but please send them to me to enclose with the other things because I have not yet received permission to enter for the fellowship from my agent. I can guarantee the work in queſtion deplagiarized and that it will be done, even if it has to be finished
35 with a bayonet. And I'd be moſt grateful if you would do this for me.

But I muſt send off the letters, mss. etc. from here to Houghton Mifflin by *September 1* to allow for delays, censors, aƈts of God, etc.[2]

---

1 "In Memoriam: Ingvald Bjørndal," *Atlantic Monthly* Oƈt. 1941: 501.
2 I have not been able to uncover any record of Lowry's application for the Houghton Mifflin fellowship.

I hope all is very well with you both and well with your friends abroad. John? Ed?

I haven't heard a mumblin word from Liverpool – well, just one slight ambiguous mumble – since before the bad airraids there. No word from anyone else. The world seems to have reeled away from one altogether into a bloodshot pall of horror and hypocrisy, a chaos without melody.[1]

If you can spare more words of advice as well for one who wants honestly still to discipline himself to be a poet I'd be awfully grateful. I haven't sent anything along yet because not quite satisfied with anything.

We remain disgustingly well and happy: I unrecognizably fit, not a pouch, not an ounce, not a funeral bloat.

God bless.

Malc.

61 : *From* AIKEN *to* LOWRY

TS UBC 1–2

brewster mass.

aug 16 41

Dear Malc —

briefly indded, for the school keeps us busy. Three lively problems, and in addition one graduate student, Charles Hamilton, who was of our first vintage, Rye, 1938[2] — we have no spare time, little spare energy. Saves the bacon, too, as otherwise we'd be penniless, worse than penniless — $500 in debt. As it is, we may be able to pay off some bills, and start the winter with an outside chance of getting through. Your own

---

1 Allusion to Houston Peterson's *The Melody of Chaos*.
2 See letter 30, n. 4, p. 106.

status astonishes and mystifies me, not to mention delights — but how did you do it, I mean, rise from utter baffled indigence to manorhood? Explain, elucidate, expound. And five hundred in the bank, too. Gor blimey! There must be an excluded middle somewhere. Did you hear from
5 Stuart Legg[1] — to whom I have given your address, with a view to his asking you to do some work for fillums? Sounded sort of promising, I thought. Margaret Legg is here in Brewster, with kids, in a cottage — but of that I will say nothing in print, no. Stuart came down for a few days and it was good to see him: a queer broody creature, but nice. I
10 assured him you were one of the world's best informed people in re movies. Marvellous about the atlantic — that's more than I can do, so I fear I can't help you as to potry — not that I'm not delighted to see what you are doing. As for me, I have done nothing but the beginning of a potential long-poem,[2] or semipotential, and a group of city eclogues, which mildly
15 please me.[3] A novel in mind, but no more than notes for it. Ed writes often and [b]rilliantly. John and Nina hope to come here when all is over. Jane is married to Angus Smart, a pedant, and lives at Saskatoon, Saskatchewan — address, 8 Wilbur Court, 6th Ave. North; Sask. Paul Nash is at Oxford, doing war drawings. I haven't paid any rent on Jeake's
20 House for a year and a half, and look like losing it. I had my twenty teeth out in May and June, and now have du Pont falsies of great beauty and tolerable speed. And that is the news to this moment. Your photo is a fantasy, Margie's very pretty. When will you come east, or are you now permanent waves, and what do you live on???? Enclosed the plaudits.[4]
25

as ev

Conrad

30

---

1 Stuart Legg (1910–88), British documentary producer-director; educated at Cambridge University; became chairman of Britain's Film Centre International in 1957.
2 Possibly Aiken's *The Soldier: A Poem*; see letter 64, n. 3, p. 175.
3 *Brownstone Eclogues and Other Poems* (New York: Duell, Sloan and Pearce, 1942).
4 These are missing.

1942–1954

. . . say to yourself, this guy loves me, or he wouldn't be so bloody candid about me.

— *22 January 1952 letter from Aiken to Lowry*

1942–1954

BY 1942, BOTH THE AIKENS AND LOWRYS had settled down in their respective "paradisos," Aiken in his "jungle" in West Brewster and Lowry in his waterfront shack in Dollarton. In spite of the war, all seems to have been relatively calm during this period. In the summers the Aikens ran their summer school in writing and painting which they'd originally begun in Rye in 1938, Aiken perhaps having been inspired by the success with Lowry in 1929. Lowry, meanwhile, spent much of his time working on *Under the Volcano* and swimming in Burrard Inlet.

However, on 7 June 1944, disaster struck. Lowry awoke that morning to find the roof of their shack on fire; within no time the entire building and most of its contents had been destroyed. While Margerie had been able to save the manuscript of *Under the Volcano*, Lowry's other novel, "In Ballast to the White Sea," was lost. Three weeks later the Lowrys travelled by train to Oakville, Ontario, to stay with Lowry and Aiken's mutual friend from Cambridge, Gerald Noxon. Noxon had actually wired the Lowrys the money necessary to make the trip. By October of that year, the Lowrys had followed Gerald and Betty Noxon to Niagara-on-the-Lake where, after a few weeks, they were able to rent a house of their own. Noxon's enthusiasm for *Under the Volcano*, now as previously, was invaluable to Lowry. That Christmas Eve, Lowry presented Noxon with a completed draft of the novel (Tiessen 15).

In February 1945 the Lowrys returned to Dollarton where they began the hefty task of rebuilding their shack. That same year Aiken, too, was forced to return to his old place of residence. The damage suffered by Jeake's House in the war was too serious to let the house go any longer without repairs. By early November the Aikens had set sail for Liverpool, destined for Rye.

On 28 November, the half-built shack proving inadequate protection against the winter cold, the Lowrys left for Mexico. They returned to Cuernavaca where they were able to revisit Lowry's old haunts and begin a new novel based on the trip, *Dark as the Grave Wherein My Friend Is Laid*. In late December, Lowry received news of Jonathan Cape's provisional acceptance of *Under the Volcano*. It was in response to this, in January 1946, that he wrote his now famous letter to Cape with a chapter by chapter defense and explication of the novel (Breit, *Selected Letters* 57–88). In March the Lowrys travelled to Acapulco where they ran into trouble with the Mexican immigration authorities. They were eventually deported from the country in early May, but not before they had received the news that *Under the Volcano* had been accepted both in the United States and England.

Aiken meanwhile was experiencing financial difficulties in Rye. Despite the moderate success in London of his play "Fear No More" (based upon his short story "Mr. Arcularis"), and the composition of his long poem based on William Blackstone, *The Kid*, which he had been planning for many years (eventually published in 1947 and dedicated to Lowry), he decided to sell Jeake's House and return to Forty-One Doors. Yet by the following year he was still without a buyer, and in June 1947 he left alone for West Brewster, leaving Mary behind to sell Jeake's.

During this time the Lowrys had been preparing for the publication of *Under the Volcano*. Although they didn't have to be in New York until February 1947, they decided once again to flee the Vancouver winter, leaving in November by bus for New Orleans, and from there on 26 December aboard a freighter bound for Haiti. It was not until publication day itself, 19 February 1947, that the Lowrys finally arrived in New York.

By March the Lowrys had returned to Dollarton, stopping on the way to visit the Noxons in Niagara. In November, however, they were again on the move, bound this time for France via the Panama Canal. In Vernon in early 1948 they were introduced to Joan Black, with whom they stayed for a few months and from whose home Lowry was able to meet Clarisse Francillon and help with the French translation of *Under the Volcano*. A year later, in January 1949, after travelling through Italy and England, they returned once more to Dollarton where Lowry worked on *Dark as the Grave*, a film-script adaptation of F. Scott Fitzgerald's *Tender Is the Night*, and a collection of short stories, *Hear Us O Lord from Heaven Thy Dwelling Place*.

In late 1950 the Aikens moved to Washington, D.C., where Aiken was employed as Poetry Consultant to the Library of Congress. Although they stayed for intermittent periods in their flat in New York City, most of their time until late 1952 was spent in Washington. These years were profitable ones for Aiken. In fact, this was the first time he had held a full-time position since acting as tutor at Harvard in 1928. In 1952 the literary journal *Wake* devoted an entire issue to Aiken to which Lowry contributed a long letter to the editor (80–89). In October of the same year, Aiken's "haughtybiography," *Ushant*, was published and favourably received. By the following October, Oxford University Press had published a one-volume edition of his *Collected Poems*, the selection for which Lowry had advised Aiken in 1945 (letter 70), and in 1954 this collection received the National Book Award.

In April 1952, Lowry, temporarily at least, was also blessed with good luck. Random House had at this time offered him a two-and-a-half-year contract, calling for the completion of two novels and a collection of short stories in that time period. At first Lowry worked fast and diligently; however, by January 1954 he had really only completed *Hear Us O Lord*, and Random House decided to end the contract. This, combined with the threats of eviction that had been steadily mounting in intensity for the past few years, convinced the Lowrys to leave Dollarton again. Although they vaguely intended to return, this was to be their final leave-taking. In August 1954 they left for New York where they stayed with David Markson, who as a graduate student had written a dissertation on *Under the Volcano* and who had visited the Lowrys in the summer of 1952. When notified by Lowry of his arrival in New York and of the upcoming party that was to be held in Lowry's honour (letter 87), Aiken made the trip from West Brewster. Unfortunately, their reunion was not quite the event it should have been. Lowry, although he had visited Aiken some hours earlier in his "cold water flat," was nervous about the upcoming gathering and arrived at the party drunk; he and Aiken were barely able to speak to one another. Five days later, perhaps in lieu of an apology, Lowry sent Aiken a telegram (letter 89); the following day he boarded a ship for Milan. It is here, sadly, that their correspondence ends.

62 : *From* AIKEN *to* LOWRY

TS UBC 1–2; KILLORIN 259

Brewſter Mass.

Feb 12 42

Our beſt beloved Malc —

forgive my long silence, which has not been indifference, or ingratitude for a marvellous letter, but sheer impossibility sitting round me like a wall: an impossinility built of many things. Fatigue, worry, work, acedia, visitors, illness, (nothing serious — bad cold plus vertigo) have juſt somehow combined to render letter-writing (even to my own children) a non pos. I have been trying to finish a new book of pomes,[1] and trying to sell them, for we have been broke, and in Dec and Jan a long article for the Atlantic[2] had to be done, and read for, and sat over me like the belly of a cloud, preventing me from thinking freely or happily of anything else. (Jesus how I hate writing criticism.) Now that *that* is done, and the proofs dispatched today, I can look round me at the siniſter world again, and begin to imagine or try to imagine further devices for keeping us out of inſtant bankruptcy. And all happens at once — the truſtees for J House have clamped down on me for not paying any rent these two years, and so we muſt sell it; words fail me as to this; did you ever put up your heart and soul for auction? But I rationalize very nimbly about it; it has served its time and purpose; the beſt years in it are gone; it will never itself, or Rye, be the same again. Tout de meme, when I think of it I feel as if the Piccadilly tube, miles of it, were being extracted from my insides, a whole world swooping through a tunnel. And all the contents, or moſt of them, sold, too — though we do hope to salvage a few objects and get them sent out. Sad, sad, sad. And sad. . . Rye, they do say, is spoiled. Gone tough, full of rape and violence, even murder; Canadian soldiers kicked to death by midlanders; chiefly because they get all the girls. The son of the Bryan who runs the Ship Inn was stabbed to death by his swiss wife the other day, and so on and so on. Blimey. Ed writes more and more gloomily, so do the Mackechnies.[3] Ed not too well, the spleen again embittering itself, but holding

---

1 *Brownſtone Eclogues and Other Poems.*
2 "American Writers Come of Age," *Atlantic Monthly* Apr. 1942: 476–81.
3 Margaret and Robert (1894–1975) Mackechnie, artiſt friends of Aiken in Rye.

out bravely juſt the same and working well. John and his wife plan to come here poſt war: Jane and her husband at Saskatoon, but trying to get to Washington. Our summer school looks like being torpedoed once again, worse luck, and what we shall turn our hands to, god knows: I may apply for a South American good neighbour job, a poet errant in Brazil, etc. Or rampant in Ecuador. Houſton Peterson has bought a house three miles from here, which is good — so we hope to hang on, in the hope that he may bring us pecuniarily useful contaſts with Columbia Univ and Rutgers ditto. You and Margie were damned nice about Conversation, and very flatteringly perceptive. Yes, it all comes down to a heavy defeat for the poor old male animal, a great viſtory for the élan vital and the more deadly female; also of society over the artiſt. Is he, you say, really in love with his wife? Blimey if I know — I d guess not, what with that there other gal from whom he thinks he is parting. Wasn't he fooling himself? I dunno. But I think so. I wish the publishers had leſt my own titie — THE conversation — it points a little more the form, as of one continuous argument on a given theme, reaching its inevitable conclusion, but embracing other oddments en route.[1] That conversation is the theme. The deadly female thing working itself into the superior position, and dragging the male to bed, even persuading him that *he* was the one who thought of it by gosh. Holy cats. As for the Chorus charaſters, I would have leſt them out entirely, if I could — but feared I muſt supply juſt a scumble of background folk, for visual support; hence the slightness. They exiſt only for the sake of plausibility, furniture, scene. I'm delighted you liked it, however — that's *good.* How goes the poetry? and what else? and how the merry hell do you get money out of england, or is it that you finally collared the funds in Los Ang? I'm delighted that you prosper, however, whatever the source. As for me, I've finished the new book of perms, Brownſtone Eclogues, an urban series, — too soone for me to judge them. They are more objeſtive/reportorial, than anything previous, I think, striſt in form (pretty — moſtly heroic couplet or quatrain, and formal in *flavour*) and with jazz and quotidian ingredients, not to say humour. What it all adds up to is beyond my own adding machine, but I kind of like 'em. Now I'm attempting a pseudo-autobiography,[2] or attempting it again, with a new title: The Lives and Adventures of Merrymount Nipmuk. But no great progress yet. . . . Mary has been in Boſton three days, doing a portrait for her spring show (April, in

---

[1] The 1948 English edition *does* have Aiken's preferred title: *The Conversation or Pilgrims' Progress: A Domeſtic Symphony* (London: Phillips & Green, 1948).
[2] *Ushant: An Essay.*

[Boston]) so I've been camping out in the wilderness en garcon. Cold as hell, north wind off the Bay, but lovely. Sherry at noon, orange blossoms in the evening, chablis at dinner, by way of keeping up the morale! And now I feel sure it's time for the glass of california shery, in fact; so pop
5   goes the weasel.

                              love to you both

                                        Conrad
10

      Do you ever hear
                from John Dav.?
      Jerry,[1] tis said, is trying to publish a novel about me —
      described as hot stuff! Ten Years with the Face on the Bar room Floor![2]
15

20

63 : *From* AIKEN *to* LOWRY

TS UBC 1–2

25   [FORTY-ONE DOORS
                                      STONY BROOK ROAD
                                      BREWSTER, MASS.]

                                      [21 Oct 1942]
30

      forgive me old Malc and one of these days maybe the whirl will spin
      to a pause and give me a chance to write a letter, if only a brief one. School

---

1 "Jerry": Aiken's second wife, Clarissa Lorenz. Aiken may be referring to her book, *Lorelei Two: My Life with Conrad Aiken* (Athens: U of Georgia P, 1983).
2 Cf. *Under the Volcano*: ". . . the uncontrollable face on the bar room floor . . ." (370) and Aiken's poem "Exit" in *The Morning Song of Lord Zero* (45). This is possibly a reference to Taylor Holmes's (1878–1959) song, "The Face on the Barroom Floor," recorded in 1923 (Ackerley 441). The original ballad was written by Hugh Antoine D'Arcy and published in the 7 August 1887 issue of *The New York Dispatch*. The irony of the fate of D'Arcy's poem, "The Face upon the Floor," which came to be appropriated for Prohibitionist ends, is outlined by Louis Phillips in "The Face on the Barroom Floor," *Journal of Popular Culture* 24.4 (1991): 39–47.

has run on from summer into autumn, and goes on till 1943 — good for us financially, but wearying to a degree — juſt keeps us alive, but leaves us unable to do much work of our own. So glad about M's book,[1] and your own health news — what a relief to have the paralysis myſtery solved
5   and salved! Jeake's House has had the blaſt of a bomb, its windows gone, and tiles, and plaſter down, damage so far to possessions etc unknown. Wish I could get there somehow — dream about Rye and Haſtings and London. Oh me.

      our loves and more later
10

                Conrad

15

20

64 : *From* AIKEN *to* LOWRY

TS H 2558

25   Brewſter Mass

                Aug 9 43

Dear old Malc:
30   Are you still there?
            Yes, I know, as a correspondent I am below zero. Don't know how it is, I juſt can't write letters anymore, even when I have the time and the opportunity and the motive. When Gerald and Betty and L[a]urence[2] were here in February I swore I'd send you at leaſt a feſtive
35   poſtcard to let you know of the fine frenzies here, but did I? No I didn't.

---

1 Margerie Bonner's *The Laſt Twiſt of the Knife*.
2 Laurence Gilliam (1907–64), OBE, friend of the Noxons who was Head of the BBC Features Dept. from 1946 until his death. See Noxon's 14 March 1943 letter to Lowry in *The Letters of Malcolm Lowry and Gerald Noxon* where he describes this visit to the Aikens as "a real Aiken party with rivers of gin and oyſters, clams and movies" (51).

Yes, it was a gay week, with the temperature 12 below, but plenty of gin in the house, and much music. And nice to see Laurence again. (If we had only known, the BBC was doing a broadcaſt of Senlin in England while they were here: arranged by Edward Sackville-Weſt:[1] but I didn't know about it myself till two months after.)

We have no summer school this year — didn't even try, things being what they are. But Libby Brown,[2] one of laſt year's party, still stays on, and will till September or October: a nice and gifted gal except when she goes schizoid periodically, and buſts things up in fine style, as she did laſt week on the occasion of the fifty-fourth birthday party.[3] As a result, we've sent her to visit a cousin in New York for a few days, hoping it will calm her down again. She really supports us — $185 a month — so we view her impending departure with mixed feelings: we'll be out in the cold again. Prospects not improved either by the fact that Mary has juſt had a show — Boſton, May — and so cant have another for a couple of years: and this one a flop, coſting us $150 in expenses. Discouraging for the poor gal, too, she had worked hard and well, and it was much her beſt collection to date. There aint no juſtice.

We live an almoſt wholly bucolic exiſtence, except for a weekly jaunt in the ford to Hyannis for lunch and a movie and the marketing. Our hens number fifty odd, and there are also two ducks, known respectively as the dumb cluck and the clumb duck. Vegetables grow here and there, and fruit: potatos, corn, squash, tomatos, peppers, asparagus; beans too, but three woodchucks in succession have cleaned them out before they ever got to the pot. Laſt night for the firſt time we ate one of our own broilers — o baby. In fact, this is a fine place, and we sometimes wonder if we'll ever want to live anywhere else again, or for long. Jeake's House still stands, somewhat battered, and the furniture partly sold to pay the rent and partly stored — windows and parts of roof gone, partitions blown down, but no great structural injury so far as I know. We *may* go back and try a summer school there, d.v.,[4] — but what will Rye be poſt war?? Ed wants to come here: so does John: so does Joan. We are torn. And much of course will depend on the pocket-book. We're

---

1 "Senlin," an adaptation of Aiken's poem "Senlin: A Biography," was broadcaſt by the BBC on 2 February 1943. The program was adapted by Edward Charles Sackville-Weſt (1901–65), noveliſt and short story writer, who worked during World War II in the Features and Drama section of the BBC and was entruſted with moſt of the poetry broadcaſts.
2 Not identified.
3 Aiken had juſt turned 54 on Auguſt 5th.
4 "deo volente": Latin, "God willing."

still paying off the mortgage on *this* house, $1500.worth — the first twelve years are the hardest.

How about the pomes, and other woiks. Do you see any people? any Japs? Our own life is on the whole too social, — or at any rate too social in spring and summer; tends to be too shut in in winter. Can't leave the chickens. And we had a cat, Oedipuss Simplex,[1] one of the best: but he died yesterday of arsenic poisoning, poor lad: and we are desolated. A person of integrity, and a fine hunter.

My Eclogues[2] last year were a flop — poorest sale, and reviews, I've had in fifteen years. Guess we're running a little thin. I've just finished a longish poem — 500 lines — after five months intermittent meditation and work, The Soldier — a prosy affair, but I hope timely.[3] No report from the agents as yet. And I mull over a new novel, but gord, what a labor a novel is — it really daunts me.

Well, forgive the protracted silence, and to the extent of summarizing for us a year of your news. And our loves, as always —

Conrad

I hope the prostate thing has long since yielded to treatment, and that you're a Tarzan again??

---

1 "Oedipuss" is also the name of the Consul's cat in *Under the Volcano* (89).
2 Lowry's copy of *Brownstone Eclogues and Other Poems* in the UBC Library bears the following inscription by Aiken:
   For the old Malc
   from the Old Hulk:
   C.M.L. from C.P.A.:
   Xmas Day:
       1943
"C.M.L." are Lowry's initials: Clarence Malcolm Lowry.
3 *The Soldier: A Poem*, The Poets of the Year Series 39 (Norfolk, Conn.: New Directions, 1944).

65 : *From* LOWRY *to* AIKEN

TS H 2523

5

Dollarton, B.C.,
Canada,

March 4, 1944.

10

Dear old bird:

Thanks very much for your letter, am very proud and flattered to help
if I can – hope not too tardy, your letter of February 20 took ten days
15 arriving[1] – don't know if such ideas as I have any good but trot them out
for what they're worth, my reader of moſt anthologies is a queſting chap;
poor, not knowing much, student and haunter of libraries, who though
he may have read through many anthologies always feels like Stout Cortez
on opening another one, but stares at Killarney inſtead of Pacific, is
20 delighted he underſtands but invariably disappointed, often for the wrong
reasons, but at bottom full of love persiſts, by the age of forty when he
has read Marvell's Coy Miſtress and Munro's Cat[2] for the five thousandth
time may get a glimmering, and by the time he is so old and shaky he
can't turn the pages, may even be looking for some poem of his own in
25 one, which has been put in, however, only in the belief that he is dead.
Which, you may say, he was all the time. I am trying to be funny and I
don't mean your anthologies. One of my moſt treasured possessions was
your red companion book for the Squire one put out by Secker[3] and I
have owned and loſt and owned again your other[4] many times. However

1 This letter from Aiken is missing. Presumably Aiken had asked Lowry to suggeſt
some poems he might include in *Twentieth-Century American Poetry*, ed. and pref.
Conrad Aiken (New York: Modern Library, 1944).
2 "Munro's Cat": probably Harold Monro's (1879–1932) "Milk for the Cat." In an
interview for *Shenandoah* in 1963, Aiken states that Monro was a "very dear friend" of
his (32).
3 *Modern American Poets*, sel. Conrad Aiken (London: Secker, 1922; New York:
Modern Library, 1927); Aiken included some of his own poems only in the 1927
version. *Twentieth-Century American Poetry* (1944) was a revised edition of these earlier
anthologies.
4 Probably *American Poetry, 1671–1928*, ed. Conrad Aiken (New York: Modern
Library, 1929). In 1945 Aiken expanded this volume into *A Comprehensive Anthology of
American Poetry* (New York: Modern Library, 1945).

I seem to see this reader somewhere, and feel the nice old chap should be treated sternly; though slightly humored perhaps in this one particular; for some reason he isn't over fond of too many *long* poems in his anthologies. Let's face it, he reads in the jakes, which, since they are outdoors in a forest perhaps, seems to him poetic justice; nothing will cure him of constipation, it is true, but he reads slowly and likes to finish a Poem at a sitting. However, down to tacks: — 25–30 pages of Aiken. I think your second idea the best, a scattering from all the poems, but with more form in the scattering than there seems at present and more poems; a progression, or parabola, of them which taken together would give more effect of your development as an artist, even if imperfectly, or something of the effect designed by the scrapped "Divine Pilgrim" idea,[1] only with many short poems instead at the beginning and end, of not much more than a page each, a gradual ascent, then leaving a sizeable stretch of arc at the summit for you to Landscape or Jones it or even slice-of-JohnDeth it in[2] or otherwise go to town; the decline of the parabola would n't be a Wordsworthian decline, on the contrary, you would end in a blaze of glory, at the same time finally a dying fall, not necessarily chronological, shading off via the Temptation at the end of the middle, into, say, the first and last sonnets of And In The Human Heart to a contrast of shorter eclogues like Who Shapes a Balustrade? and Anaesthesia, ending on a simple note, like The Sounding.[3] For the very beginning I would suggest all short and something like (1) From House of Dust – the exquisite passage: "Sunlight roared above them like a dark invisible sea" "dark blue pools of magic"[4] (2) the Three Pale Beautiful Pilgrims[5] (3) Rye Sunset "Here by the wall of the ancient town I lean"[6] (4) The Room. (5) Sound of Breaking.[7] Thenceforward the sound of breaking would go on getting considerably louder, (rising to a climax, I was going to suggest, at Goya, sandwiched in between two longer things,

---

1 *The Divine Pilgrim* was in fact published by the University of Georgia Press in 1949; it is a collection of Aiken's major poems up to that date, some considerably revised, including "The Charnel Rose," "The Jig of Forslin," "The House of Dust," "Senlin: A Biography," "The Pilgrimage of Festus," and "Changing Mind."

2 References to Aiken's *Landscape West of Eden, The Coming Forth by Day of Osiris Jones*, and *John Deth*.

3 All the poems mentioned here by title are from Aiken's *Brownstone Eclogues*.

4 Lowry quotes these passages in letter 1.

5 Printed as Part IV of *Priapus and the Pool* (1925).

6 From Aiken's "Seven Twilights" in *Priapus and the Pool*; Lowry quotes this line in letter 2.

7 Both "The Room" and "Sound of Breaking" are poems from Aiken's *Priapus and the Pool.*

in its original prose form; I never liked it — er — as well in verse,[1] but perhaps this would not do) and using preludes (though you might culminate at a longer one, cold but shattering, like "at the dark's edge how great the darkness is"[2]) from both groups as sort of buffer states between attitudes, dark or bitter preludes on the upgrade, brightening on the down. My parabola should perhaps have been the other way up; but never mind[.] I have said nothing of Teteleſtai or And In the Hanging Gardens or King Borborigmi,[3] or one of my favorite parts, which is the very end of Punch[4] – as became of recent years the whole of Jon Deth – perhaps the motion too jaunty altogether however, if *cut into*????) — one would like to see The Four Appearances,[5] many preludes that will not be in, and a hell of a lot beside; (Margie puts in a strong laſt plea for the Morning Song from Senlin,[6] feeling something also powerful and scientific beneath that song, and perhaps it might go well as number 3 inſtead of Rye Sunset, though the equivalence seems unfair); but you can't have everything, as the Elephant said to the woodpecker, and I feel you ought to give previously unanthologised poems a chance where possible: the ones you cut out will go on ringing all right.

I wish I had time to be more detailed but it seems if I don't get this off right away it won't be any good to you anyhow. I hope there maybe a good idea at the bottom of this somewhere and anyhow it's the beſt I can manage and me with a stomach ache. I think some of the Eclogues among the greateſt things you've written.

Margie sends love as I do to you both –

Malc.

---

1 "Goya" was published in prose form in *Blue Voyage* (142–43), and in verse form in *Selected Poems* (360–61). Lowry mentions this poem in letter 18.

2 This is the laſt line from prelude "xxxiii" in Aiken's *Preludes for Memnon*; Lowry refers to this poem in letter 6.

3 All three poems are from *Priapus and the Pool*; *And in the Hanging Gardens* was also published separately and in a limited edition by Garamond Press in Baltimore in 1933.

4 *Punch: The Immortal Liar, Documents in His Hiſtory* (New York: Knopf, 1921).

5 From *Brownſtone Eclogues*.

6 Part of "Senlin: A Biography."

66 : *From* AIKEN *to* LOWRY

TS H 2559; KILLORIN 260

5   brewster mass

aug 22 44

Dear Malc:

10   it was fine talking to you in the middle of a dream walking,
sandwiched between fragments of a Nyorker short story — but so brief,
so brief, and I couldn't make out more than 50% of things said, especially
by you — your telephone voice my lad leaves something to be desired.
But it's wonderful that you're relatively in the east, even if alas driven
15 hither by fire.[1] How did it happen. Tell all. Did you fall asleep smoking,
or what. Or was it spontaneous combustion of a hot manuscript? or dirty
work by the japs? My conscience has been bad these many months, ever
since you so kindly and carefully and skilfully advised me about the aiken
poems for the anthology: I combined your suggestions with some of Bob
20 Linscott's and a whim or two of my own for what I think is a pretty good,
if somewhat too long, parade. Thanks be to god the two books are done,[2]
proofread and all, and come out I hope this autumn. They are both greatly
improved I think — especially the twentieth century one, which is really
changed in toto and almost twice the original size. I have hopes that the
25 two together will end by supplying us with a consistent and modest living:
both have begun to sell in the last three years, each royalty statement
doubling the last, until now they bring us pretty nigh a thousand a year,
and rising. So I was glad when I finally persuaded the Boys to let me
modernize them, as they were both summat dated, particularly the Mod
30 Am one.[3] We can now settle down to look carefully the other way, while
we wait and see. . . What other news? That Jane is here, white, thin, not
too well, and preparing a separation from Angus pro tem, in New York,
while she and he meditate on divorce: he remains in Washington. Sad to

---

1 The Lowrys' Dollarton shack burned down on 7 June 1944. In early July, Malcolm
and Margerie travelled to Oakville, Ontario, and later to Niagara-on-the-Lake, to
stay with Betty and Gerald Noxon. The two couples, "in a partying mood one day,"
had telephoned Aiken in Brewster (Tiessen 6).
2 *Twentieth-Century American Poetry*, ed. and pref. Conrad Aiken, and *A Comprehensive Anthology of American Poetry*, ed. Conrad Aiken; Aiken did not include any poems
of his own in the latter.
3 i.e., *Modern American Poets.*

see the successors coming after us with the same sad missteps into traps
and pitfalls, and suffering, and having to find out for themselves the hard
way, and oneself unable to help in a durn thing. And Joan, in London,
with an interesting job in the United Nations Information Office, is
engaged, kind of, to one Ronald Brown, thirtyish, married, and in the
process of getting himself divorced. And John still at E Molesey, and still
planning to come here postwar, presumably to stay. Meanwhile Ed writes
sardonic splenetic hilariously misspelled and diverting letters from Rye,
with the buzzbombs splitting houses and people round him, and Bobby
MacKechnie is back in Rye looking haggard and old, and Laura Knight
as usual dominates the Academy with bigger and blousier and brighter
coloured gypsies. Jeake's House still stands, somewhat battered, and
serving now as a rest home for weary firemen, but it may cop one any
moment of course — shall we ever again gather by the river? where old
clubfooted Bill, the car-park demon, fell in, in the blackout, and went to
sea? The Mermaid is gone,[1] and the soda bottling works, and the
Methodist Church behind Ypres Tower, and the graveyard behind our
school next door was unearthed by a bomb and distributed seriatim far
and wide, and the cinema flattened out, and the Bodega in Hastings
together with the Plaza cinema, my favorite bob's worth, dammit — I
fear many another gap as well. Maybe we'd better sell out, maybe it's all
over, and if the house does survive I suppose we'd get quite a penny for
it, dear dear. Or shall we try another part of england entirely?? a cottage
in Westmoreland, a flat in London? a sooty house in mortuary Glasgow?
or just stay here amongst the mussels and poison ivory? . . . and what
about you?? . . . Our manic depressive arrives on Friday, and we await that
with some apprehension: her husband says she used to throw eggs at
people. But it's only for three weeks, at $85 per, so we figure we can stand
it. Our social life seems to be odd. Alleviated a little lately by two fine
parties with Konrad Heiden and his plump little blonde hausfrau mistress
and George Grosz mit frau.[2] Heiden and Grosz are enormous fun —
Heiden very sly and subtle, Grosz a brilliant talker and humourist, and
wonderful at kidding himself, and a fine drinker: all very gay and good,
in a cottage overlooking miles of inland salt water: we all got drunk, and
talked about oysters and food and german beer and the idea of giving
germany to the jews and exporting the germans, and Goethe's elective

---

1 The Mermaid Inn, Rye; the inn is, in fact, still standing.
2 George Grosz (1893–1959), German artist, known for his satirical caricatures and
lithographs, who left Germany for the United States with the rise of Hitler. Konrad
Heiden (1901–66), historical writer who wrote critiques of Hitler and the Third Reich.

affinities. And what else? Mary is doing a nasty job of handcolouring 100 olde huntynge printes, while I await proofs of a new long poem, the soldier, which new directions brings out this fall, and which will probably get me into a great deal of trouble. And I ponder that three levels of reality
5   novel which I dreamt of on the voyage back from spain eleven bright years ago.[1] And that my fine fellow is all, and it's time for a little noonday beer, the sun being over the yard-arm. Our best to all of you, and Mary will write to Betty[2] as soon as the end-of-summer rush is over — she has a portrait to do, as well as this Thing to finish, and the egg-thrower to keep
10   at bay. But then — . And give us a line yourself.

Conrad

15

67 : *From* LOWRY *to* AIKEN

20

MS H 2524

Write Dollarton P.O
Dollarton B.C. Canada.

25

[Dec 1944]

As from Niagara.[3]
— Dear old Conrad: Thanks immensely for The Soldier, which I have read 5 or 6 times straight through and am about to read a 7th. I was
30   extraordinarily sensitive to the honour of receiving it at the time to the extent that I almost felt I had been rewarded with some cross, of another nature, of course, to the one one bears. I think it contains some of your absolutely finest & purest & most richly poetic & greatest work, which is to say, the finest being done to-day. It is of course enormously well
35   thought out. Some of it should be engraved on stone & I doubt not will be, when you will perhaps be there, or will no longer care. For the rest I

---

1 *Ushant*; Aiken refers to this dream in *Ushant* (21).
2 Betty Noxon.
3 Niagara-on-the-Lake; the Lowrys had by this time moved to a rented house in Niagara, close to the Noxons.

do not know: your daemon has led you into a strange path indeed, & after all, what can you do but obey? Myself my non-conformist sympathy is somewhat for the outlaw or dissenter but it would be more than superficial & irrelevant to deduce from such music of more than facts accepted that
5   yours was not too, or was. Be that as it may, it is with renewed courage that we shall travel 4000 miles toward our burned house to rebuild it[1] (& how I understand now your feelings now for some loved houses — & may God spare Jeakes!) remembering that, before we left, we ran up Tashtego-wise on all that remained, the flag. . . Which reminds me that the
10   Canadian Broadcasting Company has invited me to do Moby Dick for them, in 13 instalments.[2]

God bless & a happy Xmas & sincerely thank you, again Conrad — love from us both to you & Mary — Malc.

15   — Afraid that my writing (see over) is not much better than my telephone voice. (What I said over the phone was the prayer Tagore liked,[3] meaning: With Thy Graciousness, Oh Thou Terrible, forever save us! — so no wonder you said What?) — Just finished to-day after 3 yrs & 3 months revision 8 hours a day approx, soberly Under the Volcano. . . The old man
20   dying,[4] Nordahl dead.[5] In Ballast is no more.[6] Brother Wilfrid in the Royal Artillery, Russell in the police.[7] Saved Brownstone — Brimstone! — Elegies[8] from the fire, slightly scorched. — But keep working & keep your pecker up — the birds, as you say, endure. . . Love Malc.

25   *from Malc & Margie.*

---

1   The Lowrys returned to Dollarton in February 1945.
2   With Gerald Noxon's encouragement, Lowry did begin a radio version of *Moby-Dick* but it was never broadcast; see the UBC Lowry Collection [16–(1–5)] for Lowry's drafts of the radio script. Tashtego is a harpooner in *Moby-Dick* who, as the *Pequod* is sinking, nails a banner to the mast of the sinking ship.
3   Rabindranath Tagore (1861–1941), Indian poet, dramatist, narrative writer, essayist, and philosopher. Aiken's copy of Tagore's *Git Anjali* (song offerings), ed. Edmund R. Brown, intro. W.B. Yeats (Boston: Four Seas, n.d.) is contained in the Huntington Aiken Collection.
4   Lowry's father died on 11 February 1945.
5   Nordahl Grieg (1902–43) was believed to have been killed on 2 December 1943 when the bomber in which he was flying did not return from an attack on Berlin.
6   Lowry's novel, "In Ballast to the White Sea," based upon his 1931 visit to Nordahl Grieg in Norway, was destroyed when the Lowrys' shack burned down in June 1944.
7   Lowry's brothers: Wilfrid Malbon (1900–74) and Arthur Russell (1905–) Lowry.
8   In playing with the title of Aiken's book, Lowry has actually given the wrong title, for it is *Brownstone Eclogues*, not "Elegies"; cf. letter 70 where Lowry refers to his mistake.

68 : *From* AIKEN *to* LOWRY

TS H 2560; KILLORIN 263

Brewster Mass

sept 14 45

Dear old Malc —

Months and more months I've been thinking of writing you a nice long dull leisurely letter, with all the gosspi and juices in it, and now it seems to be that I must instead fling a few hasty sentences at you over my eastward turning shoulder — for away we go to Rye, Nov 1st or so,[1] to spend a dark, cold, hungry winter in Jeake's House. Seems if we don't the dear Pile will be seized, and thus any chance of selling or renting it prevented, so the move is a forced one, and we most certainly don't proceed with unreluctant tread, and hardly rose-crowned. Grim, I calls it. Yet it will have its compensations — Mary will have a chance to paint, and I (d v)[2] to write, with so much less manual, nay corporeal, labour to perform every day and all day long; and that Mary is ripe for a new dvelopment is vitally plain from a really astonishing portrait she achieved this summer, of our cromagnon gal patient; and as for old aiken, a play, based on Arcularis, and writ by an english lass named Hamilton, has been contracted for and will go on tour in the provinces this winter.[3] I'd like to be there to see it before its probably brief career comes to an unapplauded end. Also, the Soldier is coming out in London,[4] and the sonnets,[5] so we shall at least *feel* that we are living, even if numb with the cold, hungry as wolves. Like to come?? Ed will be there of course, and the Mackecknies, and Tony Moreton[6] is back, and still managing some-

---

1 The Aikens did sail from Halifax to Liverpool sometime in November 1945.

2 "d v": "deo volente," Latin, "God willing."

3 Aiken's short story, "Mr. Arcularis," first appeared in *Among the Lost People* (New York: Scribner's, 1934). Diana Hamilton (1898–1951), actress and playwright, adapted the story into a play with the title *Fear No More*. It was produced in England in 1946, after some rewriting in which Aiken took part. Afterwards, it toured the provinces and ran for four weeks in London at the Lyric Theatre, Hammersmith. Aiken later rewrote the play and restored its original title; it was published as *Mr. Arcularis: A Play* (Cambridge: Harvard UP, 1957) (Bonnell, *Conrad Aiken: A Bibliography* 54–55).

4 *The Soldier: A Poem* (London: Editions Poetry, 1946) was published on 18 October 1946.

5 The first English edition of *And in the Human Heart* was published in London by Staples Press in 1949.

6 Tony Moreton was a bed & breakfast host in Rye, a friend of Aiken, and a regular at the Ship Inn.

how to keep tight, and Joan is married and living in Ormonde Mansions, Southampton Row, and John seeking a divorce even as my first grandchild is gestating. Life, life, life. Gerald wrote me at great length in praise of your book[1] — why not let it come out, my dear fellow? cut the umbilical
5   cord? I'd love to see it. Send it to Bernice Baumgarten, Brandt & Brandt, 101 Park Ave., NYC??? And have you started a new one? I was grateful for your letter about my tin soldier. He had a poor press, on the whole, and a stupid one, I thought — so few saw that the real theme was the evolution of consciousness, with the soldier as incidental to it, and the socratic
10 gnothi seauton[2] as its core. Does one have to print an explanatory note with every book? I hope at any rate that my little book for the kiddies, A Little Who's Zoo of Mild Animals, which has just been taken by the Creative Age Press, won't need such — a collection of nonsense verses, for which Mary is doing the drawings, nineteen imaginary animiles, and
15 very silly indeed, but fun to do.[3] As for life here, it has been the usual struggle against the ever encroaching wilderness, mowing and then scything and then sickling and then mowing again, and feeding the hens and capons, and burying the offal of fowls and shooting woodchucks and so forth. Useful as it takes off the ten pounds I invariably attach to myself
20 in the winter months, and besides I damned well enjoy a really first rate sweat. And you — how does the new house go and grow? has the phoenix clapped its wings? are the saddleboards on and tight? tell all. And do you know J Davenport's address by any remote chance?? With which, well, bless you Malc, and our loves as always to Margie and your self —
25

Conrad

30

---

1 See Noxon's March 1945 letter to Aiken in "On Malcolm Lowry" and Other Writings. Lowry had for some time been discussing the progress of Under the Volcano with Gerald Noxon, and in December 1944, while in Niagara, had presented Noxon with a manuscript of the novel; this manuscript is contained in the University of Texas Library; a microfilm of it is in the UBC Lowry Collection [45–14].

2 "gnothi seauton": Ancient Greek maxim: "Know thyself." Cf. Ushant (220) and the epigraph to Blue Voyage from Juvenal.

3 Aiken's A Little Who's Zoo of Mild Animals was in fact only published posthumously by Jonathan Cape in 1977; the illustrations are by John Vernon Lord.

69 : *From* AIKEN *to* LOWRY

TS H 2561

Brewſter Mass

Oɛt 16 45

Dear Old Malc —
a p s to my other to beg a boon: viz., Duell Sloan & Pearce
seem to be going to do me the honour of a two volume Colleɛted Poems
next year,[1] and I'd be ever so immensely grateful to you for a few Helpful
Hints and Suggeſtions, and especially about the whole queſtion of what
if any of the earlier things to include. I shall put the five symphonies
together under the always-intended single title, The Divine Pilgrim,[2] but
each with its own title too, and with the prefaces reſtored to The Charnel
Rose, Forslin, and Feſtus; and with a few revisions of the Rose and Forslin
and perhaps a little cutting of the House of Duſt. But the problem is,
what of the other earlier things — if indeed any? I think of reversing the
chronological order,[3] beginning with two recent poems, Crepe Myrtle
(an elegy for F D R) and Mayflower,[4] then the Soldier, and so backwards,
probably as far as John Deth in Vol 1, and then the symphonies etc in Vol
2. What do you think of this??? I value your judgement more highly than
any other, and will liſten intently to whatever you say.
much love to you both

Conrad
no sailing date as yet — but I imagine Nov 1ſt to 7th.

---

1 This two-volume edition of Aiken's colleɛted poems was never published; however,
in 1953 Oxford University Press did publish a one-volume *Colleɛted Poems*.
2 *The Divine Pilgrim* was aɛtually published separately by the University of Georgia
Press in 1949. The 1953 *Colleɛted Poems* also contains a seɛtion, with some differences,
entitled "The Divine Pilgrim"; the "five symphonies" included in this seɛtion are: "The
Charnel Rose," "The Jig of Forslin," "The House of Duſt," "Senlin: A Biography,"
and "The Pilgrimage of Feſtus."
3 The poems in *Colleɛted Poems* are arranged in what is essentially chronological order
according to when they were written.
4 Both "Mayflower" and "Crepe Myrtle: F.D.R.: April 12, 1945" appeared in *Skylight
One: Fiſteen Poems* (New York: Oxford UP, 1949).

70 : *From* LOWRY *to* AIKEN[1]

MS UBC 2–2; TS H 2525; BREIT 47
("P.S.": MS H 2527; MSPC UBC 2–2)

[Dollarton]

[late October 1945]

Dear old Conrad:

Thanks awfully for yours & have been meaning to write a really fat informative & diverting letter — in fact, made all the notes for same, but I want to get this letter off now so it will be in time to wish you bon voyage, therefore I must make a sacrifice of the other for the time being. Yes, the phoenix clapped its wings all right all right,[2] in fact gave such a bloody great resounding clap that the poor bird nearly broke its neck and had to be immolated all over again. As you know we went East after the fire. The grave preceded us however. The interminable golden bittersweet awful beautiful Eastern autumn (which I'd never experienced) restored Margie, [(]whose childhood was in Michigan) to *some* extent, but me it almost slew. It had a worse effect upon me, in fact, than on Henry Adams,[3] though the Noxon's Niagara-on-the-Lake is something to see: really beautiful. I was in shocking bad form, & worse company so all in all, though I was very disappointed not to see you, — albeit I *heard* you — it was perhaps just as well I didn't. How the Noxon's put with me — if they really did — I don't know. Actually the business of the fire seemed to drive us both slightly cuckoo. Its traumatic result alone was shattering. We had to live through the bloody fire all over again every night. I would wake to find Margie screaming or she would wake to find me yelling and gnashing my teeth; that is to say, what teeth I have left to gnash. Apart from these diversions (fortunately the Noxon's were sound sleepers, but when we moved to a house of our own, it grew much worse) fire itself seemed to follow us around in a fashion nothing short of diabolical. Betty

---

1 See Appendix 1 for Aiken's variant typescript transcription of this letter.
2 Reference to letter 68 from Aiken. Cf. also Lowry's *Dark as the Grave Wherein My Friend Is Laid* (48).
3 Henry Adams (1838–1918), American historian, philosopher, and author best known for his *The Education of Henry Adams* (1918).

had painted a picture of a neighbouring house in Oakville that Margie &
I had thought of renting for the winter because it vaguely resembled our
old one and one day when everyone I was out I sat in the attic studying
this picture which I liked very much. My concentration on the picture
⁵ was somewhat marred by the fact that in my imagination the house kept
bursting into flame and sure enough, about a week later, that's precisely
what the house did; they couldn't get the fireengines through the woods,
nothing of the kind had happened for fifty years in that rural route, and
there was terrific to-do, through all of which Margie & I, for once, calmly
¹⁰ slept. Then when we went down to Niagara the house next door to ours,
one night while we over at the Noxons, went up in a blaze: we heard the
shouts & bells & saw the awful sun, (E.d. again) — I don't know why so
much Emily Dickenson to-day — & of course thought it was *our* house
and ran over in a panic, so much so that Margie was not even convinced
¹⁵ it was *not* our house by the time we had got there & took all our
manuscripts out into the street. And to cap everything, when we returned
here, it turned out that the house where someone had been good enough
to let us store our bedding & some few things we had left after *our* fire,
had in our abscence itself been burned down, totally demolished, and our
²⁰ bedding & stuff with it, the house mysteriously bursting into flame for
no reason at all apparently, one calm mild evening when the owners
weren't even there. Margie & I had invented, in a horror story, a murderer,
a black magician one of whose specialties was the starting of fires by means
of incomprehensible talismans.¹ This fictitious gent's name was Pell &
²⁵ the m.ss concerning him I had happened to rescue from our fire. Swelp
me bob² if the owners of this house don't to be called Pell too, though
there had been no connection at all originally. And so forth; altogether
about fifty other odd senseless sad terrifying & curiously related things
that make me sometimes think (taking it all in all!) that maybe I am the
³⁰ chap chosen of God or the devil to elucidate the Law of Series.³ Unfortunately it would seem to involve one in such rotten bad art: or need it
not? At all events, I have been reading Kant's Critique of Pure Reason to

---

1 Lowry later incorporated these uncanny encounters with fire into *October Ferry to
Gabriola*, ed. Margerie Lowry (New York: World, 1970); see, in particular, chapter 18,
"The Element Follows You Around, Sir!"
2 Cf. Aiken's *Blue Voyage* (265).
3 Law of Series: reference to British philosopher John William Dunne's (1875–1949)
theory of serial time which suggests that while an individual passes through a single
sequence of time, all times exist simultaneously. See Dunne's *An Experiment with Time*
(London: Faber, 1927) in which he outlines the three laws of serial time (158–59) and
The Serial Universe (Faber, 1934).

see if that would help. Or perhaps Bergson's[.] Osbert Sitwell[1] — & some of James Joyces experiences seem to tie up.

When we arrived back here too it was to find that someone, strangers & vultures, had disregarded our burned stakes & notices and built smack on half our old site, blocking our southerly view, a great tall ugly Erection to be full in the summer of rackety rickety children & hysterical fat women, who meantime had pulled down the flags we had left — perhaps too dramatically — flying on our poor old ruin thrown dead mice down our well and shat — even on the walls — all over our toilet. This of course is a crime, according to the local folkways, the mores, or whatever, though we had no legal toehold in the matter, — one incidentally of the prime causes of jungle warfare — pioneer's and squatters rights having been abolished: our few fishermen friends — with ourselves the only permanent inhabitants — arrived back too late from Alaska to prevent it & our local Manx boat builder only got insulted and nearly beaten up when he tried to put a stop to it. They had no excuse, knew we were coming back. We could have knocked their house down ourselves & had the support of even most of the summer community but like a fool or not I decided to be Christlike about it with the result that we had them in our hair all summer while we were building on what space was left for us, our new neighbours even calling us greedy because we made the most of that, until one day the owner came over and asked why we wouldn't speak to them more often and accused me of putting a curse on them and on their house, that they'd couldn't be happy there, that the youngest child, for instance, had almost drowned the day before, & so on, and that they'd had one misfortune after another, ever since they'd built there, to which I replied that while we forgave them all right, they had never had the charity to perceive that there was anything to forgive, moreover if you built on top of a guy's soul, you couldn't be sure what would happen, and if something you didn't like did happen, it was no use coming round complaining to us and looking as if they'd swallowed Paddy Murphy's Goat and the horns were sticking out of their arse.[2] All round, quite an ethical problem.

---

1 Henri Louis Bergson (1859–1941), French philosopher and winner of the Nobel Prize for literature in 1927. His claim to fame rests on three works: *Time and Free Will* (1889; Engl. 1910), *Matter and Memory* (1896; Engl. 1911), and *Creative Evolution* (1907; Engl. 1911). Bergson sought to rebuild the bridge, that had been broken down since Kant, between metaphysics and science. Osbert Sitwell (1892–1969) was a British poet and satirist.

2 Cf. Lowry's "Through the Panama" in *Hear Us O Lord from Heaven Thy Dwelling Place* (Philadelphia: Lippincott, 1961) 94, and Markson's "Malcolm Lowry: A Reminiscence: Dollarton" (228).

To be frank, it is ourselves who have had a share of the misfortunes. Margie ran a nail through her foot the first day we got the lumber in — cellulitis set in — then blood poisoning, shortage of doctors, and finally hospital and probings, and a horrible anxious awful time that was. Meanwhile she received the first part of her proofs for her novel[1] but we are still waiting for the promised proofreaders copy of the second part, Scribners having held her first novel now for over four years (it is getting into the fifth year) without publishing it and although they signed a contract for a second novel with a time limit set for publication date at this fall it is already this fall and still Margie hasn't had so much as a smell of the proofs of this second novel, which was supposed to be at the printers last Xmas, so it looks as though a breach of contract looms with what small comfort that is for the poor author. Scribners have proved the worlds most undependable and unscrupulous people to deal with and you are certainly well rid of their new outfit. Granted they dared not behave like that with someone like you, but what the hell. I then proceeded to cut off the end of my thumb while doing some ripsawing with an ordinary saw, which set us back with the building and for the last two months I have been in bed practically unable to move with a toxaemia caused by an osteomyelitis due to an abscessed tooth that became abcessed and had to be removed owing to malpractice. There is a shortage of dentists — they will not take new patients, even [if] you are hopping with agony as I was, and on V.J. day too, with the drugstores all shut. But on the other hand there is apparently also a surplus of dentists: they are threatening to open offices on the street, because of the housing shortage. But I myself have not been able to find a trace of these dentists. Meantime there has been an average of two murders a week here, most of them by or of children: a pet slayer likewise is at large who has disembowelled thirteen goats, several sailors' monkeys, twelve pet rabbits, and is doubtless also somewise responsible for the apparition of half a cocker spaniel in a lane near West Vancouver. On the other hand a murderer — no relative but embarrasingly also of the name Trumbaugh[2] — has shot a policeman that was several months ago, but was reminded of it for at time of writing he has just

---

1 *The Shapes That Creep* (New York: Scribner's, 1946). Although in previous letters Lowry suggests that *The Last Twist of the Knife* was the *first* detective novel written by Margerie, *The Shapes That Creep* was actually the first to be published. Hence, the "second novel" referred to here is *The Last Twist of the Knife*.

2 Martin Trumbaugh is the protagonist in Lowry's early drafts of *Dark as the Grave*, "La Mordida," and "Through the Panama," and was named after the jazz musician Frankie Trumbauer (see "Through the Panama," *Hear Us* [34]); the protagonist's name was later changed to Sigbjørn Wilderness.

received a reprieve & wondered if that were a good omen. Juſt the same we have built our house and paradise has been regained. I forgot to say that no sooner had paradise been regained that we received the notice that a new law had gone through and that all our lovely foreſt was to be torn down and ourselves with it within a year and turned into 'autocamps of the better class.' This placed our new house — which, by the way has the diſtinction of being the laſt example of such pioneer activity on Vancouver waterfront property — under a sentence of death that was finally too much for our sense of humour and my temperature went up within a quarter of an hour to 103. A sad story, you say, almoſt as poignant as The Triumph of Egg??[1] Not a bit of it. Reprieve for Mr Trumbaugh also has come. There will be no autocamps of the better class, and no neighbours either, of the worse class. We may live here for three years at leaſt as we are doing without moleſtation or paying any rent at all and then buy the land too, that is the part we want & we are being given firſt choice — for a reasonable price. Thus does your old Malc, if still a conservative-chriſtian-anarchiſt at heart, at laſt join the ranks of the petty bourgeoisie. I feel somewhat like a Prometheus who became intereſted in real eſtate & decided to buy up his Caucasian ravine. At the moment we are living in the house, without inside walls. . Its' pouring with rain, & it doesn't leak. What triumph. Herewith our handiwork[2] — also the pier we built ourselves, all that was left of our old house — it used to come out of our front door — the vultures wedged themselves in juſt beyond, hoping to use our pier too, not to say our well.!

My novel — the Volcano — , seems to have gone smack into the void — no intelligent comments so far, or encouragement. I think it is really good, though The Loſt Week End[3] may have deprived it of some of its impact — alack — prosaic juſtice? — if not be confused with The Laſt Week End, by J. Sommerfield,[4] in which it actually is old Malc who goes all too recognizably down the drain, and pretty feeble too. I was planning to send you the Volcano in some trepidation but with some pride too but I don't like to saddle you with the only copy in my possession at present

---

1   Reference to Sherwood Anderson's *The Triumph of the Egg: A Book of Impressions from American Life in Tales and Poems* (New York: Huebsch, 1921).
2   Lowry probably enclosed a photograph of their new shack with this letter.
3   The appearance of Charles R. Jackson's *The Loſt Weekend* (New York: Farrar, 1944), three years before the publication of *Under the Volcano*, came as a great blow to Lowry who felt Jackson's novel to be too similar to his own and feared that he would be accused of imitating it.
4   John Sommerfield's novel, *The Laſt Weekend*, was never published; the protagoniſt of the book, David Nordall, is supposed to have been modelled upon Lowry (Day 153–55).

and I don't see how I can get back the only available other one before you
sail. So please take the will for the deed for the time being. I'll learn 'em
eventually, as Mr Wolfe once said, I feel.

5 The only difference in my present status since I wrote the above is
that while we are still living in the house without inside walls the roof is
leaking in six different places. But now your letter about the Collected
Poems has arrived and I hasten to make some reply in time, though please
forgive me if what I say seems hastily digested. In brief, these are the ideas
which immediately occur to me and I hope they are not merely confusing.
10 I think the idea of reversing the chronological order is a very good one,
in fact as good as can be, — though I think perhaps The Soldier might
profit by being dislocated out of the new order and being placed, if not
actually among the symphonies somewhere near them in the second
volume. What I mean is, if the poem does not belong to the symphonies,
15 The Soldier does to the notion of The Divine Pilgrim. Houston Peterson
or somebody once put the possibly erroneous idea in my head that you
had once thought of including Tetelestai also under The Divine Pilgrim
heading and even if this is erroneous and Tetelestai not a symphony this
is worth thinking of if you haven't already rejected it.[1] As for the early
20 poems I would certainly put in every thing that can possibly be of use to
the fellow-poet and student of your work, Discordants with Youth that's
now so bravely spending and as many of the actual Cats & Rats Turns &
Movies[2] as you have space for. The latterly certainly stay with me as unique
& powerful work, whatever you may think of them. I would also take the
25 opportunity of exhuming from undeserved limbo such pieces as 'Red
petals in the dust under a tree",[3] Asphalt "tossing our tortured hands to
no escape" (though not very early, 1925 model?),[4] but very fine, and even
the "succubus you kissed" lampoon you wrote agin the Imagists,[5] which
has a historical interest, & giving the dates of all these. I don't know about
30 a selection from Earth Triumphant, but I would be inclined to make a

---

1 "Tetelestai" is a poem from Aiken's *Priapus and the Pool* and is included in "The
Divine Pilgrim" section of *Collected Poems*.
2 "Discordants" was published in *Turns and Movies and Other Tales in Verse* (Boston:
Houghton, 1916); "Youth" appears in *Earth Triumphant and Other Tales in Verse* (New
York: Macmillan, 1914); "Bain's Cats and Rats" is the ninth poem in the "Turns and
Movies" series from Aiken's *Turns and Movies*. Both "Discordants" and "Bain's Cats
and Rats" are included in *Collected Poems*.
3 See "Red Petals," *Cartoons Magazine* Dec. 1919: 919.
4 See "Asphalt," *Dial* June 1920: 733; the final line of this poem reads: "We toss our
tortured hands, to no escape."
5 See Aiken's "Ballade of the Worshippers of the Image," *New York Sun* 9 May 1915.

short one:[1] — possibly you are right to disown it, but I myself cannot forget the 'unaccuſtomed wetness in my trousers' with which I read it at Your Uncle Potters.[2] The only other departure that comes to me would be to start the whole collected poems with the Morning Song of Senlin and End them with The Coming Forth by day of Osiris Jones.[3] I muſt say I like this notion per se exceedingly, if it would not play too much hob with your reversed chronology. Whatever you do, I am very glad a Collected Poems is coming out and the very beſt luck with them.

If by the way you have any old Harpers Bazzaars, Vice Versas, Southern Reviews or what not you are thinking of throwing away — no old Dials, alack? — we would be immensely beholden if you would wrap a paper around them and shoot them in this direction C.O.D or something for we are absolutely stuck here for such reading matter, all intelligent American magazines having been unprocurable for donkeys years: on the other hand it occurs to me it is probably a poor time to ask what with you packing & all: so if it's too much trouble, juſt forget it.

Well, bon voyage, old fellow and our very beſt love to you both and beſt wishes for Mary's success & our very beſt again to her and you and also to Jeakes

πασα θαλασσα θαλασσα[4] ——

Malc.

J.L.D's address — laſt I heard — was I think The Malting House, Chippenham, Wilts.

P.S. When I suggeſted starting with the Morning Song of Senlin I wasn't of course forgetting that the Morning Song was only part of Senlin: a biography. My idea, possibly rather naïve, was that the Poems should start with Senlin rising in the morning & close with the comment of the grass in The Coming forth, which I felt would rather beautifully *enclose* the Pilgrim theme running throughout your work. Possibly the idea would be better if there were juſt one volume. However, perhaps it was a good one. I juſt send this p.s because such things can be irritating; almoſt as

---

1 There are no selections from *Earth Triumphant* in *Collected Poems*.
2 Alfred Claghorn Potter: see letter 55. Lowry probably met "Uncle Alfred" when visiting Aiken in Massachusetts in the summer of 1929.
3 This arrangement was not used; inſtead, the poems were arranged in chronological order according to when they were written.
4 "πασα θαλασσα θαλασσα": Greek, "the whole sea, the sea." See Aiken's *Blue Voyage* (289, 303). Cf. also Xenophon's *Anabasis* IV.VII.24: "θαλαττα! θαλαττα!" ("The Sea! The Sea!").

irritating — perhaps you say — as when I once referred to Brownstone
Eclogues as Brownstone Elegies, a stupid mistake that I saw too late &
was doubtless due to a state of mind: I was thinking of them as *Brimstone*
Eclogues, & the correction got off on the wrong foot.[1] I am now almost
better of the toxaemia & the roof-leaks are mysteriously healing of
themselves. At high tide you can dive out of our casement windows into
perilous seas forlorn — very useful. Jesus, this is a beautiful place. We are
thinking of travelling for six months, however, into the sun — Haiti, or
a freighter to Samoa.[2] Do you know any new magazines friendly to more
or less original or experimental short stories that do not have to start: 'I
was just leaving Oliphant & Company's offices when I saw Mike.'? Please
give my love to the drugstore where the [? mouthesills] were bought, the
pirates pushing trucks, Mr Smith, Malvolio, Silberstein, the engineer
with long-beaked oilcan, the shipboys, & of course The Kraken & any
pyntors & gilders who have been to Vancouver, likewise the tarred seams,
the Silurian (if seen) & don't forget the sea.[3]

Best love & success to Mary & yourself from us both & again Bon
Voyage — & to Jeakes, John & Jane, the Ship, Mermaid St. & the Burra.

Malc.

---

1 See letter 67.

2 On 28 November 1945, the Lowrys flew to Mexico via Los Angeles and stayed in
Cuernavaca; both *Dark as the Grave* and the unpublished "La Mordida" are based on
this trip. Their trip by freighter to Haiti did not take place until December 1947.

3 Most of these are allusions to Aiken's *Blue Voyage*: "trucks were everywhere, each
pushed by a pirate" (3); "engineer carries a long-beaked oil-can" (306); "'pynter and
gilder'" (4); "'*A pynter an' gilder, I am, an' I've been to Vancouver . . .*'" (36); Smith,
Malvolio, and Silberstein are characters in *Blue Voyage*; the *Silurian* is the ship on
which Demarest first met Cynthia. "The Kraken": cf. Lowry's 1951 letter to Seymour
Lawrence published in *Wake* 11: 87–88, where he tells of his New York landlady
mistakenly calling Aiken by the name of "Mr. Kraken." See also letter 87 and Lowry's
poems "Kraken, Eagles, in British Columbia" (132–33) and "No Kraken Shall Be
Found till Sought by Name" (198) in *The Collected Poetry of Malcolm Lowry*.

71 : *From* LOWRY *to* AIKEN

TS H 2526

Dollarton, B.C.,
Canada,

August 5, 1946.

Dear old Conrad:

I hope you and Mary are by now ensconced in Jeakes House, Rye, and that the sea-poppies and Camber Castle, not to say tram, and the ships blithely sailing down the meadows are still there, and that that which was once the province of the sea is not now too much a province of the same again by virtue of being a navel base.

As for myself we are still living in the same place with rather more side-walls, and suffering from success slightly, the Volcano having been accepted in England and America upon the same day, ourselves curiously having been in Mexico itself, in your wedding place, at that time, whither we went because of climate.[1] But I was not convinced and said so too, there among marigolds, with Easter coming: however it is apparently *so*, and in America at least (Reynal and Hitchcock) has even gone to the printers. I delayed telling you this for Hitchcock had no sooner signed the contract than he dropped dead etc.[2] and there were other delays. I hope to God you will like this work by your old pupil a little though, which Cape brings out in England, and I shall send you as soon as I get any copies. Margie's first detective story came out finally after Scribner's kept it nearly 5 years; it has sold five thousand copies, and is still selling. They brought out her second the other day, The Last Twist of the Knife, but without having sent her any proofs and according to a letter received from a reader (the first she'd even heard of its publication) minus its last chapter: so that there are no explanations of the murder etc.[3] Scribner's

---

1 The Lowrys had flown to Mexico on 28 November 1945 and stayed in Cuernavaca, Conrad and Mary Aiken's "wedding place," where they were able to rent the house which had been the model for Jacques Laruelle's house in *Under the Volcano*. It was from this house that Lowry wrote his famous defence of the novel to Jonathan Cape.
2 Curtice Hitchcock (1892–1946), president and director of the American publishing firm Reynal & Hitchcock from 1934 until his death on 3 May 1946.
3 *The Last Twist of the Knife* was reissued by Scribner's in the same year with the last chapter intact. Lowry quotes from this fan letter in a 15 September 1946 letter to

are really the limit. Our correspondence is equalled only by Joyce's with
Grant Richards.[1] Margie has written a damn good serious novel entitled
Horse in the Sky which is with Cape:[2] while flapping incompetently about
and just about driving poor Margie cockoo with delays and lies and
non-answered letters Scribner's had meantime tried even to prevent her
publishing this book, since it would "interfere" with the 'career' which
they had anyway at every point done their level best to bitch. She thrives
however, as do I.

Well, all my very best love to you and Mary from us both – remember
me to the Burra and the Nashes and all – and John – I see Jane's name
on the editorial board of Time?[3] – and Jane – should the grandfather
clock still be there please give him a friendly tug of the bollocks from me
– and the Ship.

– from love fifteen to vantage out to back again to love –
                                                        Malc.

– I have been rereading the Eclogues: wonderful.

Maxwell Perkins in the UBC Lowry collection [2-8].
1 Grant Richards was the publisher to whom Joyce first sent Dubliners in 1905.
Richards accepted the book in February 1906, refused it in September 1907, and finally
published it in 1914 (Ellmann 219, 241, 353).
2 Horse in the Sky was eventually published by Scribner's in 1947.
3 Jane Aiken's name appears on the masthead of Time as an Editorial Researcher
from 4 February to 25 November 1946.

72 : *From* AIKEN *to* LOWRY

TS H 2562; KILLORIN 273

Jeake's House
Rye Sussex

Sept 4 46

My beloved old Malc:

What wonderful joyful news that you've at laſt twanged the umbilical chord and caſt your Inferno off into the blue for weal or woe — and that it is for weal I have never had the tinieſt surd of a doubt. Good, good, good and then good again, my dear fellow, and only of course what you deserve, that the book should be simultaneously taken in both countries. I hope you are going to snd me one? As a matter of faĉt, and as J D has already no doubt told you, we knew of its arrival here, through the old grapevine, and were already therefor whetting our glee before your letter gave us the news more personally and specifically. And now, I can't wait to see it, and to bathe in your beautiful sinuous changeable-shot-silk prose.[1] But how good too *all* your news is — do you mean you really went to see old miasmal Cow'shorn cuernavaca again?[2] Your refernce is so oblique and as it were parenthetically elided that I can't quite be sure it wasn't merely an intention or a dream, or an eliotine velleity. If true, if faĉt, how I envy you: both Mary and myself have so often pined to see it all again, but without the physiological and psychological miseries that then beset us so persiſtently. Ed too: I wish you could see what *he* has kept of it: on our diningroom wall, over the refraĉtory table, scene of those prodigious alcoholic pingpong matches,[3] hangs the world's largeſt pen-and-ink drawing: eight feet by five of pureſt beautifulleſt dreadfulleſt Mexico: a hooded leering figure in the desert foreground, seated by a fire of sticks, on which is a cauldron of dry bones, is about to throw a stick for an emaciated cadaverous bitch, with enormous swollen dugs; the bitch regards the stick-thrower sidelong with an ironic nerts-to-you expression

---

1 Cf. Aiken's blurb on the original duſt jacket of the 1947 Reynal & Hitchcock edition of *Under the Volcano*: "Here it is . . . a changeable shot-silk sun-shot medium. . . ."
2 "cuernavaca," in Spanish, means "cow-horn."
3 John Aiken writes of the ping-pong games played at Jeake's House "on a refeĉtory table with curved edges" ("Malcolm Lowry: Some Reminiscences" 38; cf. also *Conrad Aiken Remembered* 22).

which is quite appalling: at their feet lie other fragments and shards of
bones, and a few (they look, like the crumbled skeleton of an infant) have
been gathered into a wooden bowl. But, back turned to this sinister pair,
who are about to perform their sceptical and evil communion, a classically
5   serene figure, hooded too, glides away towards the eternal magical hill-
town that rises from the eternal barranca and jungle, and the twin-towered
cathedral, and the bitter black mountains above it, and the afrit-black
bitter clouds that brew above *them*. The whole landscape is magically
sinister and beautiful, and altogether it's probably the finest thing Ed has
10 done — we're buying it on the nickel-a-year-for-life principle, as you
might imagine . . . .[1] As for these chicks, you see us in the throes of trying
to decide whether to sell the house, or rent it, before going back to
Brewster,[2] with the contingent question of where, more or less permanently, to live: too difficult and costly to live transatlantically, in our
15 present earnings-bracket, so what to do? We'd get a good price, but donT
know yet whether we can take out th[e] cash. Mary's been restoring its
former beauty, slaving over every inch of scarred and battered paint and
woodwork: eight months of labour: staggering expenses: all the furniture
to be replaced piecemeal, and at a PRICE! But now almost done, and looks
20 byootiful. Brewster draws us, howsumever, and I feel this time that I
somehow don't get my roots down into the english thing, and I fear I
won't again.?? . . too old. I like it, but don't quite belong. I've worked —
did a queer pome, THE KID,[3] which is a sort of spiritual history of the U
S (old Blackstone,[4] and Anne Bradstreet, and Boone and Crevecoeur and
25 Thoreau and Appleseed and the Quaker martyrs and Kit Carson and Billy
the Kid and then Melville and Willard Gibbs and the Adams brothers in
starlight (Brooks and Henry)) all ending of course with Emily Dickinson?)??[5] the "Kid" idea as the american eponymous hero, whther as
pioneeer of the inward or outward wilderness, and done in a loose
30 octosyllabic couplet ballad-like form, giddy and slangy in parts, doggerel

---

1 Cf. Mary Aiken's description of the same painting in "The Best Painter of the
American Scene," *Edward Burra: A Painter Remembered by His Friends* (London:
Andre Deutsch, 1982) 92.

2 Aiken sold Jeake's House in 1947.

3 *The Kid* (New York: Duell, Sloan and Pearce, 1947).

4 The story of William Blackstone, the British pioneer who became a recluse in the
American wilderness, was a central myth for Aiken. Douglas Day tells of Lowry's
attempt to "appropriate" that story from Aiken (223), and indeed, the story of William
Blackstone appears frequently in *Under the Volcano*. The other American figures
mentioned here are presented in *The Kid* as inheritors of Blackstone's individualist
spirit. Cf. also Aiken's inscription in Lowry's copy of *Ushant* in letter 85, n. 2, p. 228.

5 Cf. *Ushant* (290).

in others. I like it, and so do John Davenport, Alan Hodge, Norman
Cameron,[1] Ed, and others, but it was promptly turned down by Duell
Sloan & Pearce (mjuſt as the Soldier was) as "rating below my beſt work":
and not only that, but they intimate they don't want me to *print it at all*
5 before they get out my Collečted Poems next year! To which I'm replying
in the immortal words of mr eliot, they can butter their asses and bugger
themselves, and I'm looking elsewhere for a publisher, and hope to find
one. . . . Also, behold me a playwright. No doubt J D told you of it. One
Diana Hamilton made a queer bad little play out of Arcularis, which,
10 revised by the Co. of Four at the Lyric Theatre, Hammersmith, went on
tour (opening at Cambridge, the Arts), and while on tour they having
discovered that I was in England they came to beg me to work on it.
Seems poor Diana, who had had a cancer operation, and now was dying
of cancer of the brain, and drinking herself silly, was incompetent to do
15 so; so I accepted; and at Brighton, Briſtol, and Cardiff did a travelling
shake-scene, stitching-in purple patches, revising, re-inventing, and trying to make sense out of the incredible psychological hash their combined
efforts had made of it. More or less in vain. The leading man and Diana's
producer husband ganged up on me, each for reasons of his own; Diana
20 drifted in and out reproachfully, drunk and unhappy; and the time was
too short for proper rehearsal; but the thing was a *shade* better when it
opened *on my birthday*[2] at the Lyric, Hammersmeef, where Mary and Joan
and Jane and I attended. Fun. Taught me a very great deal, from which
if I live long enough I hope to profit. The reviews were so-so — not too
25 bad, not too good, with a savage and very funny onslaught by old Agate.[3]
But though it had done well in the provinces, it flopped dismally in town,
and ceased with scarce a sound at the end of its run ten days ago. I think
now I'll try a play or two of me own! . . . We plan to leave in Nov. or dec.,
if we can manage it, — for N Y and Brewſter.[4] Let me have a line before
30 that? and our loves to you both —

Conrad

---

1 Alan Hodge (1915–79), British writer; author, with Robert Graves, of *The Long
Week End* (1940), and *The Reader over Your Shoulder* (1943). Hodge married Jane Aiken
in 1948. John Norman Cameron (1905–53), British poet.
2 5 Auguſt 1889.
3 James Evershed Agate (1877–1947), English noveliſt and drama critic; editor of
English Dramatic Critics (1932); theatre critic for a number of journals and newspapers
including the London *Sunday Times* from 1923–47. See Agate's review, "Highbrows
Ahoy!" *Sunday Times* 11 Aug. 1946: 2. In his diary, *Ego 9* (London: Harrap, 1948), on
8 Auguſt 1946, Agate writes of having viewed Aiken's play.
4 Aiken did not return to Brewſter until June 1947.

73 : *From* LOWRY *to* AIKEN

MS H 2540

5   New Orleans.

[21 Dec 1946]

My very dear old Conrad:

I owe you a letter, in reply to your marvellous one — but please forgive
10 my not replying & now I muſt reply from Haiti where our address will
be:

    c/o Anton Kneer

       Agent — S.S. Alcoa Co.

       Port-au-Prince —   We sail day after to-morrow, the 23rd,
15 on a bauxite freighter on which we are the only passengers, the S.S.
Donald Wright.[1]

Margie has a book reissued by Scribners, of which more later,[2] I tried
to have a proof copy of the Volcano sent you, as I don't know where you
are, nor D. S & Pearce's address, so in case *you're* at sea too, I'm sending
20 this c/o New Directions, to save time (I hope): we are coming to N. Y in
Feb[3] — & I hope to God I can see you then.

If you hate the Volcano, don't let that embarrass you, or fear it will
break me's heart; it will, of course, but doutless that would be all to the
good, too. Actually I submit it is pretty good work from your old — &
25 new — pupil.

God bless to Mary & yourself.

        Malc.

The Merrieſt of Xmases & the Happieſt of New Years to you, Mary, &
Conrad: also love to John & Jane —
30
        from Malcolm &.

        Margerie.

---

1 In November the Lowrys had travelled by bus from Seattle across the United States
arriving in New Orleans on 6 December 1946. From New Orleans they were to travel
to Haiti aboard the ss *Donald Wright*, arriving in Port-au-Prince on New Year's Eve,
and thence to Miami and eventually to New York in time for the promotion of *Under
the Volcano.*
2 Scribner's reissued Margerie's *The Laſt Twiſt of the Knife* in 1946 with the final
chapter intaćt.
3 The Lowrys arrived in New York on 19 February 1947, the publication day of *Under
the Volcano.* They didn't see Aiken on this visit as the Aikens were still in Rye at the
time.

74 : *From* AIKEN *to* LOWRY

KILLORIN 277

5

Jeake's House
Rye, Sussex

Feb 23 47

10

My dear old Malc: your book is magnificent, magnificent, magnificent. I'd have said so much sooner, but I'd been expecting a letter to accompany it, and waited, alas in vain, for that; but now, first comes a wandering jew of a Christmas card, which has been everywhere from New
15   Orleans to Brewster, before flapping the Atlantic; and scarcely less battered and travelled, a postcard[1] from Port au Prince in Harry Murray's and Hart Crane's Haiti; and as both of them are months old I therefor begin to despair of a letter, and launch one myself. I did, however, write to your publishers, and I did send them as soon as I could, a pitifully
20   inadequate blurb,[2] which I can only hope was not far too late and in any event useless: I had then not finished the book, but as book and Reynal & H's letter had themselves taken six weeks to arrive, I thought a quick contribution might be better than none. I said then in my letter to R & H that I had some misgivings about the book qua *novel*: I think I still
25   have, perhaps: though as to that I shall wait till I have read it again. But mind you I don't mean that as a material complaint at all, for as a piece of literature it is a genuine bona fide first cut off the white whale's hump, godshot, sunshot, bloodshot, spermshot, and altogether the most aiken-satisfying book I've wallowed in for a generation. My god how good to
30   be able to relish the english language again, to have it all vascular with life and sensation, as quiveringly alive shall we say as a butterfly on a dunghill — ! It is all so beautifully and *easily* done — the elisions and transitions and ellipses and parentheses and asides and time-notations and recapitulations and minatory fingerposts — how infinitely satisfac-
35   tory to a writer to see all *that* so incomparably well done and understood! And that, only the beginning; for of course in the end it's the richness and perceptiveness of your observation that really feeds the book and

---

1   This postcard is missing.
2   Aiken's "blurb" was printed on the dust jacket of the first Reynal & Hitchcock edition of *Under the Volcano*.

makes it, the unsleeping eye and ear, whether inward or outward. O baby, o baby, o baby, it's marvellous Malc, and I hug it to my bozoom. — Of the characters, of course it's all too easy for me to see the Malc-conſtituents (and dare I mention now and again the aiken-conſtituents) that go to their makeup: but the Consul you make wholly real and superb; even for me, who can see wheel and lever at work: yes, the great genial drunk to end all drunks, the Poppergetſthebotl[1] of alcoholics! he will become famous. The others, I'm not so sure of; Hugh's conſtituents are again for me privately too easily traceable, and he never becomes quite real or wholly seems to have a funćtion, — perhaps a second reading will show me wrong. Yvonne too remains for me a little shadowy, and the psychological *reasons* for it all a shade obscure: one is never quite sure whether the alcoholism induced the infidelities, or verser vicer: and this weakens one's sense of the tragic by preventing one's believing that it is necessarily inevitable. I think too, good as the scene is (and by gosh it is) the death of Yvonne is possibly a dramatic or dramaturgic miſtake, being itself so much a climax — it tends to double one's image somehow when one comes to the so much more important and (holy great cow) so absolutely superb final scenes of the Consul's betrayal, self-betrayal, infidelity-and-suicide-in-utero, and Blackſtone-crucifixion-Indian-absorption-and-death-in-the-barranca. O my my my what a scene all this laſt is — unforgettably splendid, genius in every page of it. But better without the horse and Yvonne — ? Yvonne juſt off? away? late? loſt? on her way? But let me read it again. — Well, the book should, and will, make your name illuſtrious: up you go to the very top: and we can only hope that it will make you a fortune too. Here, howsumever, I find myself worrying as to whether the Rank and Vile will be patient enough for your slow unwindings, rich divagations, descriptive tempo: maybe they will: their own loss if not. You will probably, too, run up againſt ignorant pigeon-holing with Loſt Weekend.[2] But this sort of thing needn't worry you. All *you* need to worry about, now, is what to do next! Though even that, I think, won't really be necessary. You've been and gone and done it.

We're stuck here, trying to sell poor old Jeake: I don't like to say it; but there it is. Better so! And as soon as it can be, home to Brewſter, I hope before summer.[3] We're sick with melancholy, and all the attendant worries and frets and anxieties, and this unhappy people and land weigh

---

1 Pun on the name of one of the volcanoes, Popocatepetl, a mountain in Mexico, in *Under the Volcano*.

2 Charles Jackson, *The Loſt Weekend*; cf. letter 70, n. 3, p. 190.

3 Aiken left England in June 1947, leaving Mary behind to sell Jeake's House.

upon us too. We'll be here long enough to have a letter from you — so let's have it? and in the meantime our very much loves to you both, and hail to

5   UNDER THE MALCANO
                    or
          POPPERGETSTHEBOTL!!!

                                        Conrad

10

15

75 : *From* LOWRY *to* AIKEN

TS H 2528

20
                         Dollarton, B.C.,
                         Canada,

                         June 24, 1947.

25
Dear old Conrad:

        This ain't a letter exact because I have agrafia and a sore eardrum due to overswimming (the other is doubtless due to overwriting) but just a
30   sort of stop-gap message of cheer, and also of enormous and heartfelt thanks for your encouraging and kindly words and help and your super-marvellous last letter which, delivered me by the excellent Bob Linscott, has me purring yet.
        I fear me you have left Jeakes by now and without speaking of how
35   bloody awful that must have been we just send all prayers and good wishes that all may be reborn and more than right once more at 41 Doors, though with the hope that there is a faint 42nd at least left open for your return sometime to Rye.
        Margie has a serious and good novel – Horse in the Sky – coming
40   out via Max Perkins, Scribners, in October: Poppergetsthebotl hit the best seller list and even a Book of the Monthly Club.

And so, I shall write when I have the wit for it; and meantime God bless and welcome and thanks again and sincere love to both Mary and yourself from us both.

Enclosed some photos of recent interesting pilgrimage[1]

Malc.

76 : *From* LOWRY *to* AIKEN

TS H 2529

Dollarton, B.C.,
Canada,

October 4, 1947.

Dear old Conrad:

My God, old chap, I thank you deeply for the dedication of The Kid,[2] and I simply cannot express how moved and delighted and touched I am at the honour: in fact I was half way through a letter thanking you for the book and expressing our and others delight at the poem itself before I

---

1 The five photographs enclosed with this letter, with handwritten comments on the back of each by Lowry, were taken in Savannah on the Lowrys' trip by bus from Miami to New York, and are contained in the Huntington Library (79-42 and 79-44); permission to reproduce these photos was not forthcoming from the Lowry estate. In a 29 June 1947 letter to Mary in the Huntington Aiken Collection, Aiken mentions receiving these photographs of the "liquidated" Lowrys. These photos would have been of particular interest to Aiken, of course, because he was born in Savannah and lived there until he was eleven years old. In 1962 the Aikens moved into a house in Savannah, the house next door to Aiken's childhood home, and lived there in the winters until 1972 and 1973 when the summer returns to Brewster became too difficult for Aiken (Killorin 315).

2 Aiken dedicated *The Kid* to Lowry as follows: "This Little Travelogue / for / Malcolm Lowry / as from One Rolling Blackstone / to Another." Lowry's copy of *The Kid* in the UBC Library bears the following inscription by Aiken:

For the AniMalcolm
with great love
from Conrad

saw the dedication, whereupon I became so excited I had to go out and
chop some wood to pull myself together, whereupon again I conked
myself shrewdly upon the right forefinger with the axe, a feat in itself, as
a consequence of which this letter is rather harder to write than the other.

5   I must say that The Kid was deeply appreciated here by the best poets
of whom Canada can boast – that may not be saying much, but they can
be singularly mean critics – and some like Earle Birney[1] and A.J.M.
Smith[2] are really good – there was a conclave of them here recently, I
flaunted The Western Review at them,[3] The Kid was recited, and their
10   genuine enthusiasm would really have pleased you.

Mine too – for I was setting The Kid to music on the taropatch[4] with
a fine hot twing and twang of my own when there came hollers for help
from the sea where A,J,M, Smith's six year old kid had overturned our
boat. After he had been rescued the accompaniment of such avuncular
15   comments as shut up bawling, what the hell do you mean by interrupting
us, you're not a man until you've drowned at least once, the musical Kid
was resumed but alas at a particularly hot twing I fell myself out of the
window into the sea, whence strange chords now sometimes issue, and
the guitar was lost forever.[5] (I am getting another however.)

20   Anyhow, it's a wonderful poem and I hope your publisher's backsides
may have been dually pierced and Sloane's lineament rubbed into the
wound by a fine general reaction to it.

For my part, I am hard at work on another opus – three interrelated
novels, Dark as the Grave Wherein My Friend is Laid, Eridanus, and La

---

1 Alfred Earle Birney (1904–), Canadian poet, novelist, and literary critic, educated
at the University of British Columbia (1922–26) and the University of Toronto
(1927–33); editor of Canadian Forum (1938–40) and the Canadian Poetry Magazine
(1946–48). Birney and Lowry met in May 1947 and remained close friends until Lowry's
death in 1957. With Margerie Lowry, Birney has completed "Malcolm Lowry: A
Bibliography Part I" in Canadian Literature 8 (1961): 81–88, "Part II" in 9 (1961): 80–84,
and has edited Selected Poems of Malcolm Lowry, The Pocket Poets Ser. 17 (San
Francisco: City Lights, 1962) and Lunar Caustic (London: Cape, 1963).
2 Arthur James Marshall Smith (1902–80), Canadian poet, literary critic, and
anthologist, educated at McGill University (1921–26) where with F.R. Scott he
founded The McGill Fortnightly Review (1925–27).
3 "The Kid" was originally published in the Western Review 11.3 (1947): 133–49 before
it was published in book form by Duell, Sloan and Pearce on 29 August 1947.
4 "taropatch": Lowry's name for his ukelele. See Gordon Bowker's "Two Notes: The
Taropatch," Malcolm Lowry Review 19/20 (1986/1987): 149, for a brief explanation and
history of the word. Cf. also Ultramarine in which Lowry plays on the words
"Taropatch" and "Tarot pack" (178).
5 Lowry told a story somewhat similar to this to Al Purdy in which A.J.M. Smith
"jumped out the front window at high tide fully clothed, apparently in a fit of euphoria
induced by salt water and Bols gin" (Salloum, Malcolm Lowry: Vancouver Days 109).

Mordida;[1] Eridanus is a kind of Intermezzo that takes place in Canada between two other pieces likewise set in Mexico, part of which reads, I am afraid, rather like the bizarre concatenations and symbol formations of dementia praecox, noted by Herr Jung – or even Denkwürdigkeiten
5　Eines Nervenkranken.[2]

In this I believe I am really down among the 'catacombs to live,' with a vengeance, but I feel it will come off – it ends in triumph, which sounds pretty meaningless unless you know the why and wherefore, but more of it later. It seems to me to break new ground, though that may be nothing
10　to commend it, even if true. — The penis mightier than the hoe.

For the reſt, Poppergetſthebottl is out in England,[3] where it seems to be getting somewhat panned, save in the London Observer, where it has been compared to Heironymus Bosch.[4] (. . . Save for a few kind words by Macarthy,[5] the poor thing fell dead, and me with it, Here, it did rather
15　better.)

(Juſt the same, I have juſt heard, 3/5 of the firſt edition has sold out in 10 days.)

On the other hand it is coming forth with a considerable blaſt of trumpets in France whither, upon a freighter, Margie and I propose to go
20　briefly over Chriſtmas.[6]

Margie's firſt serious novel, Horse in the Sky, is coming out on Monday. Though this was, I believe, the laſt book to be accepted by Maxwell Perkins (with whom I had a fine whiskey feſt in the Ritz by the way)[7] she has, apart from that, received not one mumbling word of

---

1　In his 1951 "Work in Progress" proposal to Albert Erskine (UBC 32-1), Lowry envisioned *Dark as the Grave Wherein My Friend Is Laid*, "Eridanus," and "La Mordida" as a trilogy within his proposed sequence of works "The Voyage That Never Ends" (cf. Grace, *Voyage* 8). This plan was, of course, never realized, although *Dark as the Grave* was published poſthumously by Douglas Day and Margerie Lowry in 1968. "Eridanus" was eventually incorporated into *Oĉtober Ferry to Gabriola* (1970). "La Mordida" remains unpublished.

2　"Denkwürdigkeiten Eines Nervenkranken": German, "Memoirs of a Neurotic."

3　*Under the Volcano* (London: Cape, 1947); see letter 74 from Aiken for the original "Poppergetſthebotl" pun.

4　See Lionel Hale's "Delirium," *Observer* 21 Sept. 1947: 3: "The prose is Hemingway-plus-lava, with an added piĉtorial sense that can be horridly reminiscent of Hieronimus Bosch, if that macabre maſter had included among his devils the Demon Rum."

5　I have been unable to identify the "Macarthy" review.

6　The Lowrys sailed for France via the Panama Canal aboard the ss *Breſt* on 7 November 1947, arriving in Le Havre on 23 December.

7　Lowry may have met Maxwell Perkins while in New York in February 1947; Perkins died a few months later on 17 June 1947.

encouragement in regard to it save from myself and Noxon,[1] and in fact
has received only sneers, especially from England, from people who
couldn't write a book one tenth as good, which I find very mysterious, for
unless I am completely cuckoo it seems to me a singularly fine and
5   beautifully constructed piece of work. It comes to you, under separate
cover, as from two pupils in absentia but still studying – and I hope you
will approve. Only visible influence of Aiken is perhaps the last word,[2]
though perhaps, too, like the captain's horse in the charge account, even
if you can't see it it's there just the same. (A phrase about the orange colour
10   of windows at night she arrived at independently as a consequence of
which I couldn't persuade her to cut it out. The honesty of the source of
my attempt to make her, however, remains rather beautifully in question)[3]

    Our house is now storm and rain proof (though the liquor is only
seventy-five) — We rise at dawn every day and swim, and generally have
15   an even grander life than before our fire. The village is deserted, there's
nobody here but us Schizophoenix, and I only wish you could visit us. If
humanly possible we mean to do just that to you sometime within the
coming 10 months.[4]

    An eared grebe has just sailed past, and we are able to observe the
20   amours of two ravens on a neighbouring dead pine.

    Margie joins me in all the very best love to yourself and Mary and
here's how and hoping you are very happy and lots of luck, with love and
gratitude, from

25   *Malc.*

---

1 See *The Letters of Malcolm Lowry and Gerald Noxon* for Noxon's comments on
Margerie's *Horse in the Sky*.
2 The last word of *Horse in the Sky* is "Dungarvon," the name of one of the characters
in the novel; Aiken similarly concludes *Blue Voyage* with a character's name: "Faubion."
3 Cf. *Horse in the Sky*: ". . . past the Wabash Railroad Station, its orange square of
light blinking out where the telegraph operator sat . . ." (130); I have been unable to
locate a similar passage in any of Aiken's writings.
4 Lowry did not see Aiken again until September 1954.

77 : *From* LOWRY *to* AIKEN

MS H 1377

5
[Dollarton]

[1947]

— the margeries and the malcolms did
10   so bugger the squawks from the fools who chid —
who all seem singularly full of shid
— We liked the Kid, we loved the Kid.[1]

15

---

[1] Lowry is here playing on a refrain in Part 1, "The Witnesses," of Aiken's *The Kid*:

The horseshoe crab and the nighthawk did,
the quawk and the tern and the chickadee did,
yes, and the little green grasshopper did,
they saw the Kid, they heard the Kid. (9)

See pages 10 and 12 of *The Kid* for similar stanzas adopting the same rhyme scheme and rhythm pattern.

78 : *From* LOWRY *to* AIKEN

MS H 2530; MSPC UBC 2–12

c/o Joan Black,[1]
La Cerisaie,
Vernon, Euré,
France.

[March 1948]

Dear old Conrad, — I am in hospital here,[2] sleeping under the cross, and surrounded by nuns, very nice too, and a prieſt (I think every time he has come to give me extreme unétion) who says 'My-brodder-was-peelote-on-a-pharting-plane' — been pretty sick, but hope to be out soon, when & if shall probably go down south — had a stormy voyage here on a freighter — 40 days & nights & we hit a cyclone in the N. Atlantic & loſt our steering gear; we had one other passenger, by name — Charon;[3] the Volcano is coming out here but am a trifle exhauſted (flu, aftermath of, among other things) to write you a long letter; so I will content myself with the point of my letter, news I would like to be firſt with, but which you have doubtless already heard, from all I can gather *The Kid is getting a triumphant reception in England*; I have a New statesman & Nation by me, doesn't belong to me, so can't send it; so I will quote — needless to say I'm absolutely tickled pink over this, & offer my, so to say, heartieſt congratulations, in the midſt of my honeſt joy I cannot help purring — or is it, remembering B.V, the Preludes, the Eclogues, not to say the reception given the Kid by your own publisher, howling?[4] — over its

1 The Lowrys were introduced to Joan Black (later Joan Churchill) at her home in Vernon by John Davenport, whom they'd met with in Paris in December 1947. They spent January and February 1948, and later part of July, at her home, "La Cerisaie," during which time Lowry was working with the French translators of *Under the Volcano*.

2 In March 1948 Lowry took a two week " 'extended reſt' " (Day 401) in a hospital in Vernon run by the Siſters of Charity.

3 Cf. Lowry's "Through the Panama" in which Charon is the name of a fellow passenger on the ship; "Through the Panama" is in faét based almoſt entirely upon the journals Lowry kept while travelling by freighter through the Panama Canal on his way to France.

4 Cf. letter 72 in which Aiken tells of *The Kid* initially having been turned down by Duell, Sloan and Pearce.

certain ironic implications you will be the first to appreciate: here goes
the rave review in the Statesman by George D. Painter:[1] Not long after
the landing of the Mayflower at "Plymouth" in 1620 a young Cambridge
(Eng) B.A, William Blackstone by name, reached America & bought
from the Indians the future site of Boston. There the next batch of
colonists in 1630 were surprised & annoyed to find him in possession. The
innocent Blackstone —

> to his own cost played the generous host
> & asked adventurers across his river.

He sold them his land but when they tried to take his spiritual
freedom, too, moved south & west & died in the wilderness.

> his books burned & his own book lost forever —
> for he had a library & he was writing a Book.[2]

This half fabulous figure has met at last a poet in search of a myth.
Mr Aiken has made of him & his successors a kind of American scholar
gypsy, of epic rather than elegaic status, a transatlantic Coriolanus who
once in every generation cries to the mob, "I banish you", and carries his
divine spark to the ever-receding wilds. The chief metre of his magnificent
poem is the loose anapestic couplet of the old cowboy lyric:

> O when I die will you bury me
> where coyotes howl on the lone prairie.

— Plucking astonishingly lovely twangs from his bunkhouse guitar, he
tracks the Kid through space & time, over the primeval American scene,

> the watergap crossed, the chinquapins gone,
> breasthigh laurel, & still heading on.

There is not too much, be reassured, of the chinquapins (a "native dwarf
chestnut.") Mr Aiken uses his Indianised vocabulary with tact & success,
as a device for excluding the White Man from his virgin landscape. He

---

1 See George D. Painter's "New Poetry," *New Statesman and Nation* 27 Mar. 1948:
259–60; Lowry has quoted accurately from Painter's review except for minor alterations in punctuation and indentation.
2 The second line here is not from *The Kid*.

admits no human figure but the Kid himself, & even He is seen only in
the branch still swaying from his passage, or by

prairie-dog cities swarming in the sun
5   golden in the evening, and then not one.

And so a lonely beauty is created, in accordance with Mallarme's
definition "a virginal abscence dispersed in solitude," and with something
of Mallarme's method. The shadowy record of The Kid, traced through
10 frontiers-men physical & spiritual, stops with Captain Ahab — wisely,
for the laſt Kid was Dillinger, and there will never be another in this
civilisation.

Having "promised something great" for a matter of forty years, Mr
Aiken has seen his moment come. [How's that, old feller me lad?] His
15 own intense pleasure, his sense of (at laſt) [this 'at laſt' is what gets me
too] inspiration & power, are communicated. The Kid is the kind of poem
Melville might have created if he had remained in sight of the magic
mountain Greylock, where he wrote Moby Dick — if he had not been
dessicated by Paleſtine & written Clarel; & it will live as one of the fineſt
20 pieces of indigenous American poetry since Whitman —

There! In spite of the (at laſt) & the 40 years etc (& the reviewers
25 apparent blissful ignorance of what conſtitutes a moment for Mr Aiken,
now in America, not to say the blindness of British publishers) it is better
than a poke in the eye with a sharp stick, & adds a little light to the day,
I feel — naturally I have a special affeſtion for & pride in The Kid because
it is dedicated to me,[1] this quite apart from how I rate it as a poem, which
30 is very highly — it was very popular in Canada too, I may say; I hope
your publishers are suitably chaſtened.

Reviewed with you is a book called Unarm (though not Coſtumes
by) Eros;[2] in the paintings seſtion there is a sympathetic article on the
Memorial Exhibition at the Tate for Paul Nash;[3] & also in this same
35 number, March 27 1948, in the correspondence I find the following letter

---

1 See letter 76, n. 2, p. 203.
2 Painter's review also includes a review of *Unarm, Eros* by Terrence Tiller; Lowry
is here playing on the title of this book and that of Aiken's *Coſtumes by Eros* (New
York: Scribner's, 1928).
3 See Patrick Heron, "Paul Nash — A Memorial Exhibition at the Tate," *New
Statesman and Nation* 27 Mar. 1948: 252. Paul Nash was a friend of Aiken.

under the heading Soviet Artists:[1] Sir, — Mr Martin Mitchell's humour-
less & poorly reasoned attack on Raymond Mortimer's article must not
go unchallenged. Art, to whatever fundamental criticism it is subjected
by the Central Committee of the Communist Party, remains the aesthetic
expression of a personal attitude. Whether it should, for example, deal
with man's heroic struggle with his environment & consequently flourish
as a positive force (to quote Mr Mitchell's Jargon) is the personal affair
of the artist & no one else, least of all that of a philosopher or a politician.
Whether a particular work has succeeded in its particular aim is for the
individual critic to decide on the basis of his personal aesthetic.

Mr Mitchell wisely refrains from an assault on Raymond Mortimer's
strongest redoubt, namely the impossibility of conveying an ideology in
music, & the consequent utter absurdity of condemning any music,
however unintelligible to oneself, as not conforming to a given ideology.
One can sympathise with the Commissars & peasants in their bewilder-
ment at the recent work of Shostakovitch & his co-penitents without at
all lessening the force of the contention that the latter should compose
as they please. The logical outcome of this arbitrary meddling with
aesthetic standards in the U.S.S.R is their reduction to the lowest common denominator, that of the totally uninformed. It is fortunate that
contemporary criticism of Beethoven's last quartets was not so conducted:
else these profoundest of musical utterances could hardly have survived.

This is signed — John Aiken.

Well — god bless old fellow, all best from Margie & I to Mary & you
& all at 41 Doors — hope to be passing your way one day not too far
distant

love
Malc.

---

1 John Aiken, "Soviet Artists," *New Statesman and Nation*, 256; this John Aiken is
probably not Aiken's son.

Facsimile reproduction of verso of letter 79
showing Mary Aiken's Christmas card

79 : *From* AIKEN *to* LOWRY

MS UBC I–2

[Brewster, Mass.]

[Xmas 1949]

Wonderful that you're back — I translated the greater part of your card, but not all. What's this about ship's engines, and my double?[1] Elucidate! But delighted you liked Ark.[2] (The play, at Provincetown last summer, made a Sensation, may go on to N. York, N. Orleans, Paris, & Madrid!)

All best to you both —

Conrad

Xmas 1949

80 : *From* LOWRY *to* AIKEN

MS H 2531

Dollarton P.O.
Dollarton B C

[early 1950]

Dear old Conrad:

Thank you & Mary very much for the festive (& beautiful) card. I'm sorry my words were so illegible — there weren't nothing about 'your

---

1 Lowry's Christmas card is missing; however, see letter 80 in which he answers Aiken's question.

2 "Mr. Arcularis"; Lowry explains in the next letter that he had been referring to Gerald Noxon's radio version of the story, published in *All the Bright Company: Radio Drama Produced by Andrew Allan*, ed. Howard Fink and John Jackson (Kingston: Quarry, 1987) 203–34. Noxon wrote the drama, with Aiken's help, while staying in Cape Cod with Aiken in the summer of 1948.

double', old chap — more about 'doubles' implied in your card — ha ha[1]
— what I think you read was 'trouble' — may have been — & what you
ought to have said instead of 'Glad to hear you're back' was 'Sorry to hear
about your back,' which by the way, I broke, in an accident, falling indeed
5 off one of my own erections, I mean constructions[2] — I had a vision in a
Catholic hospital after that, but I don't think I mentioned it, though I
might as well have, for I remember thinking how close Mr Arcularis was
to the actual truth.[3] When I mentioned 'ship's engines' I meant I could
have used more of the sound of same in Arcularis — I was referring to
10 Gerald's radio version, very beautifully done here otherwise & excellently
received.[4] Apart from that, I was referring, by ship's engines, to some
work we are doing at the moment, of which, if it comes off, I sincerely
hope you will be proud — but this is supposed to be a secret till
accomplished — so no more now.[5] For the rest, I am delighted at the
15 success of Arcularis — even more delighted to hear, even through the
post, your kindly and ironic purr at same, without the memory of which,
applied to other happenings, I must have found it difficult to meet much
which has come. No other news, save that the back is better — without
any after effects. We live in the same old shack in conditions of frightening
20 toughness this winter — a flood has razed our neighbour's houses to the
ground, but ours, self built, stands still — & we were never so happy, nor
working so hard. I swam till mid-December, back and all, (now see what

---

1 See Mary's drawing of two martini glasses on the Aikens' Christmas card.

2 Lowry injured his back falling off his pier in July 1949.

3 After the accident, Lowry was admitted to St. Paul's Hospital in Vancouver where,
according to Douglas Day, he experienced a violent outbreak of delirium tremens
accompanied by hallucinations (419); this experience became the basis of an unpublished novel, "The Ordeal of Sigbjørn Wilderness" (UBC 22–[19-20]). In Aiken's short
story, Mr. Arcularis has an extended vision, while dying on a hospital operating table,
of being on a sea voyage and travelling by night to the stars.

4 Gerald Noxon and Andrew Allan's radio version, "Mr. Arcularis," was aired on the
CBC "Stage 49" program on 28 November 1948. In 1949 and 1950 Noxon adapted three
other Aiken stories for radio: "A Thief in the House" (based on *Conversation*), "The
Fallen Disciple," and "Impulse"; these were all produced by Allan for the CBC (Tiessen,
Letters 17). Noxon also wrote a radio version of Lowry's *Under the Volcano*, produced
in 1947 by Fletcher Markle for CBS's *Studio One* program. Cf. Tiessen's *Malcolm Lowry
and Conrad Aiken Adapted.*

5 The Lowrys had by this time started working on a film-script of Fitzgerald's *Tender
Is the Night*, which they eventually sent to their friend, Frank Taylor, in Hollywood;
the film-script was never used. For the "Lowry-text" of this film-script see Miguel
Mota and Paul Tiessen's edition entitled *The Cinema of Malcolm Lowry* (Vancouver:
U of British Columbia P, 1990). As in the stories in *Hear Us O Lord*, in this script
Lowry uses the refrain from "Frère Jacques" to suggest the sound of a ship's engines
(Lowry, *Notes on a Screenplay* 56–58).

you've done with your example of a cold bath every day) — slightly north of us, there are temperatures of fifty-three below zero. The Volcano was a flop in England, but has become a classic in France, where it is this month added to their quid pro quo of the Modern Library, translated by a Swiss, a Martiniquaise negro, & an Assyrian dying of consumption, with a none too sober preface by me (among others) apparently about something else, & in the company of Diderot & the Abbé Prévost.[1] Margie has had bad luck in her work so far, with one exception,[2] but we sink or swim together, or both in the current one. (or *are carried along*.) Please give our very beſt love to Mary & yourself and may, moſt sincerely, God bless you & you both — With love from us both

Malcolm.

P.S. There is snow this morning falling quite heavily, in bright sunlight, out of an absolutely cobalt sky — have you ever seen this?

---

1 *Au-dessous du volcan* [*Under the Volcano*] (Paris: Le Club français du livre, 1949) was translated by Stephen Spriel with the collaboration of Clarisse Francillon and Lowry. A preface by Lowry is included, as is a poſtface by Max-Pol Fouchet.
  Denis Diderot (1713–84), French philosopher, noveliſt, dramatiſt, and art critic; the name of the ship upon which the Trumbaughs are travelling in Lowry's "Through the Panama" is the ss *Diderot*. Antoine Francois Prévoſt d'exiles (1697–1763), French noveliſt, generally referred to as the Abbé Prévoſt; his moſt well-known novel is *Manon Lescaut*, the laſt volume of *Mémoires d'un homme de qualité* (1728–31).
2 The "exception" is probably Margerie's moderate success with *The Shapes That Creep*.

81 : *From* LOWRY *to* AIKEN

TS H 2532

Dollarton, B.C.
Canada,

Sept. 28, 1950.

Dear old Conrad:

Have juſt received short stories[1] with much thanks and great pleasure in rereading, where not often reread — Though I have not had time to reread all, let me say many have for me mellowed with age, if affection and noſtalgias evoked have not made me uncritical. This is true of some stories such as Spider Spider, and Your Obit, which I was not so fond of at the time when I firſt read them in Coſtumes,[2] but I guess I did not fully underſtand them. They now seem excellent. Strange Moonlight is better than ever, if possible, and of relatively new ones Hullo Tib seems to me a marvellous little story. Jesus that poor cat. And for all one's perception! – And did I say little? Morally her fate has considerably more meaning than that of Anna Karenina under similar circumſtances, and her continuance in heaven seems to me far more assured than that of that dame.[3] May endless dances with moths undying in the Elysian Fields be her lot! I remember Smith and Jones once meeting with your severe disapproval so have not reread but it looks as if you have cut it. I somewhat miss Pure as the Driven Snow and the Moment,[4] but you can't have everything: too bad, too bad. (That is not criticism but friendly quote) Of the merits of Secret Snow and Circularis[5] you muſt have heard more than enough. What is now the status of the play? I am now scaring myself with The Disciple – I guess it is an excellent volume, I hope you are

---

1 *The Short Stories of Conrad Aiken* (New York: Duell, Sloan and Pearce, 1950). Lowry's copy of this book is in the UBC Lowry Collection.

2 *Coſtumes by Eros*; "Spider, Spider" and "Your Obituary, Well Written" were originally published in this volume. In his 2 January 1946 letter to Jonathan Cape, Lowry says that it was Cape's edition of *Coſtumes by Eros*, which he read in 1928 or 1929, that "led to [his] laſting and valuable friendship" with Aiken (Breit 88).

3 At the conclusion of "Hello, Tib," the cat, like Anna Karenina, is killed under a train.

4 "Pure as the Driven Snow" is printed in *Among the Loſt People* (New York: Scribner's, 1934); "The Moment" appears in *Coſtumes by Eros*.

5 i.e., "Silent Snow, Secret Snow" and "Arcularis."

satisfied with the selection and that it has much success!

For ourselves, am a great hit in France, and am in the equivalent of the Modern Library thingmetight there[1] and in Norway.[2] We are frighteningly poor at the moment, but life in the old – or rather new – shack is better than ever. We are working hugely so finances may improve, with a rush, in which case hope to see you, in fact will, if humanly possible. Hope you and Mary are keeping very well, we are, myself never better. We had some fan mail from a gent in Minnesota named Z.L. Begin, a lawyer. Where? or why bother? Or maybe a symbol. For example, I broke my back with the result that I am no longer constipated and have even started to grow again. (Though you can forgive me for feeling I was a bit "knocked oop" at the time.)

Send us your news, God bless and best love to you both from us both

Affectionately,

Malc

---

1 See letter 80, n. 1, p. 215.
2 *Under vulkanen*, trans. Peter Magnus, foreword Sigurd Hoel (Oslo: Gyldendal Norsk Forlag, 1949).

82 : *From* MARY AIKEN *to* LOWRY

MS UBC 1–2

[323–2nd St. S.Eaſt]
[Washington, D.C.]

[16 Dec 1950]

323–2*nd* St. S. Eaſt   332 – Eaſt 33*rd* St.[1]
Washington 3–D.C.   New York City
Li–7–6342   Mu–4–6699
                                       once–in–a–while.

Believe it or not!

until Sept 15 '51   This is our cold-water flat
where Conrad has
the Chair of Poetry
at the Library of Congress.[2]
We're nearly always in Wash. but will be in N.Y.C. for Xmas

MERRY XMAS
&
lots of love
from
Mary & Conrad

---

1 The Aikens had a flat in New York which they stayed in whenever they were in the city (cf. letter 83); according to David Markson, Lowry visited Aiken at this address in 1954 before attending the party at which they were to see each other for the laſt time ("Malcolm Lowry: A Reminiscence" 224).
2 In 1947 Aiken had been eleĉted a Fellow in American Letters of the Library of Congress, and from 1950–52 held the Chair of Poetry there with the title of Poetry Consultant.

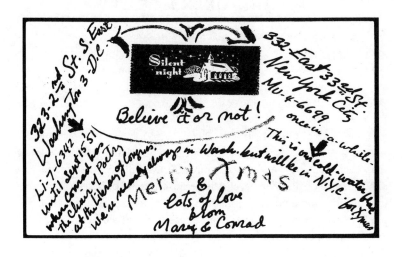

Facsimile reproduction of letter 82

83 : *From* AIKEN *to* LOWRY

TS UBC 1–2; KILLORIN 296

5
poetry room
Library of Congress

jan 22 52

Dear Old Malc:

10   Your card chided us.[1] We sank lower than ever this year, under an accumulation of dull necessities, and sent almost nary a card anywhere, chiefly because a friend of Mary's chose that unpropitious moment to commission her for a design of a tiled mantelpiece, heaven help us all, and so our Xmas Artist was otherwise, though *15* gainfully, employed. Anyway, it was good to hear from you, even if with the accustomed Chorus behind you, and over your shoulder, of the whuling Elements, which god knows do seem to be active in your niche of the world. How do you survive? and do you never tire? or long, as we do passionately, for something else? Washington gets us down like billy-o, *20* despite pleasant interludes. We had fun last May, when a very good local theatre-group, who do plays "in the round" in an adapted cinema — and with astonishing skill — put on our Arcularis. Panned by the local press, who are a lot of movie hacks (the reviewers, I mean) but a huge success with the actors and audiences, and, what's best, very satisfactory to me *25* — we'll get it to New York or bust. I've just been revising it for the fortieth time, and adding (out of Osiris Jones!) a prologue and epilogue, after which, as soon as typed, it's going to Burgess Meredith, who had heard of it from Hume Cronyn,[2] who almost put it on with Jessica Tandy last year — you see how it is, almost almost almost, always almost. Just as it *30* almost got put on at the Cherry Lane in New York two years ago, and almost by Experimental Theatre the year before that. And is this very moment again almosting, or trying to, with a *new* group at the Cherry Lane (Oscar Williams[3] and WmCarlos Williams among them) who aim to specialize in Poetic Drayma. It was damned interesting seeing the thing

---

1   This Christmas card from Lowry is missing.
2   Burgess Meredith (1909–), American actor, director, producer, and writer. Hume Blake Cronyn (1911–), Canadian-born actor and director who married the actress Jessica Tandy (1909–) in 1942.
3   Oscar Williams (1900–64), American poet and editor; author of *The Golden Darkness* (1921), *In Gossamer Grey* (1921), *The Man Coming Toward You* (1940), and *Selected Poems* (1947); editor of *New Poems* (1940).

done sans sets, and to see how effective, how *more* effective, language became when put out there all nakedly by self: interesting, too, to find with how extremely little change the play cou[l]d be made to fit this sort of performance. To revise a passage, and see it immediately put to to the
5   test in action is one of the most instructive experiences in re the written and spoken word I've ever known. You really learn something. . . But Washington, no. And the Library, no. I'm this minute deep in an imbroglio with the top brass of the bureaucracy, who, in the toils of a millionaire nonogenarian female, who has given them money, and from
10   whom they hope to filch more, have pretty effectively manacled and gagged the Consultant in Poetry; but he has at last, after many sleepless nights of sweating conscience, decided to speak his mind. I did this in the form of a letter to the Fellows in Am. Letters of the Lib. of Cong.,[1] whose annual meeting is held here next month: but as the letter, being
15   official, has to clear the hierarchies of Control downstairs before it's allowed to go forth, I'm now awaiting the sound of a muffled explosion and the dread summons. All very sickening. None of them know *anything* about literature, none of them have the least notion of a sensitive regard for it or pride in it, they rewrite (or try to) my letters into their gobble-
20   degook choctaw (and I rewrite 'em back again), they expect me to draft letters for the Librarian's signature about matters which don't concern me, and about which I know nothing, and then return them to me with a memo to the effect that I mustn't address the recipient by his Christian name, which not even his best friends would dare to do, but by something
25   else: this last, an actual instance, was what finally took the sanguinary bun, and I'm proposing, at the meeting, that *this* custom at least be abolished. But you see what I mean, you see why *we* yearn for other scenes, other climes. New Zealand: we toy with the idea of settling in New Zealand. It sounds all right. It's very cheap. It's very Far. It has fern trees,
30   and sea, and mountains, and the beginnings of a poetry movement. It has a year-round climate — you can swim or ski on the same day, and you can hunt down your venison, if that is what you w[a]nt to do, any day in the year. So why not New Zealand? The unanswered question is, how is the gin supply: we shall look into that. Next time we visit our $14 a month
35   slumlet in NYC (did you know? ground floor, with a garden and nine trees, eight of them ailanthus, and at the back of the building, in east 33d Street, so that it is very quiet — and only round the corner from your Bellevue Hospital)[2] — next time we go up there, as we do for long

---

1 Aiken was himself a Fellow from 1947–54.
2 Lowry was admitted to New York's Bellevue Hospital in 1935 or 1936 for treatment

weekends, in our swift little Austin, we shall go to the N Zealnd Consul
and bombard him with q uestions. . . Meanwhile, we sweat it out, taking
such relief as we can in going the rounds of three or four good restaurants
and the movies, which are many and pretty good. . . But chiefly what I
write to tell you, dear old Malc, in addition to thanking you for contributing to that suicidal issue of WAKE,[1] which of course I haven't read yet
— your contribution, that is — is, that USHANT has miraculously, and all
by itself, as in a sort of dreamlike parthenogenesis, got itself written at
last — ain't it incredible? I now look back on the curious process with
pure astonishment: I read a page or two without in the least recalling what
it felt like to write them: it wasn't me, at all, in fact, that wrote it, but an
invisible company of tiny visiting firemen. It will come out next fall, Duell
Sloan & Pearce — Little, Brown & Co., — and for once, as Cap Pearce
seems to be reduced to a kind of speechlessness of enthusiasm, I dare to
hope we may make a few much needed dollars, just when, this job over,
we shall most want them. Frankly, I don't know what to think of it. It
grew, all by itself, into a New Shape, its own, a spiral unwinding of
memory into a spiral projection of analysis: it has a design, and yet it
would be hard to say what it is. It seems to me, if I may be presumptuous,
to achieve a *kind* of livingness, as of a living presence right beside you,
that is perhaps new: or maybe it's a new "order". I dunno — I dunno.
It's pretty orful explicit about many things. Yourself included, for you are
a fellow named Hambo,[2] and one of the Heros. I pray you won't be
offended by any of it: I pray when you read it you will continually say to
yourself, this guy loves me, or he wouldn't be so bloody candid about me.[3]
But actually, ectually, I venture to hope that you will not only *like* the
book, but find the treatment of yourself basically and deeply affectionate.
What Tom Eliot is going to think is another tassie of tea. I call him the
Tsetse, and have already so informed him (no comment from him.) And
his Retreat to the Church gets what I think it deserves. Will he be a
forgiving Christian, a benevolent Martyr, and bless me from the Cross?

---

for alcoholism; his novella *Lunar Caustic* is based upon this experience.

1 The 11th issue of *Wake*, published in 1952, was entirely devoted to Conrad Aiken;
there, too, Aiken calls the issue "suicidal" ("A Note" 1). Lowry's contribution (80–89)
is a letter to Seymour Lawrence (the editor of *Wake*) dated 28 November 1951 in which
he discusses his relationship with Aiken. An excerpt from *Ushant* appears in *Wake* 11:
3–9.

2 Lowry also appears as "Hambo" in Aiken's *A Heart for the Gods of Mexico*.

3 According to both Clarissa Lorenz and John Aiken, Lowry was deeply hurt by
Aiken's portrayal of him in *Ushant*, and the publication of the book caused a lasting
break between the two (*Lorelei Two* 219; "Malcolm Lowry: Some Reminiscences" 39);
the evidence of their correspondence, however, would seem to suggest otherwise.

— As for poor dear Martin Armstrong, whose homosexuality (along with that of the English scene at large) gets a thorough going over, well, I hope he never reads it, that's all, and have warned the kids, in England, that they had better conspire to keep it out of his and Jessie's hands[1]. . . And my own erotic career, dear god, dear jesus, what are people going to think of that — ? New Zealand, New Zealand, come autumn — under a fern tree, far from the very very madding crowd. . . . Of course you know all about the Noxon bust-up[2] — a sad bad business, very naughty, we feel, of Betty, to go and do such and such, and they so near, as it were, to port. But god knows I've myself done exactly that, and more than once; and I can only say I'm sorry for them all, and not too sanguine, I regret to say, about G's new tie-up with Olga, whose slightly infantile coyness, along with so buxom a frame, tends to get us down. Well, the dear Bassett thought well of her, and I hope he was right. Did you know incidentally of *that* tragedy — ? For the dear Bassett came down with Gerald for our very first weekend at Brewster last June, and died in his sleep — I found him so when I went to call him in the morning. As he would have wished it — five miles from his family lot in the churchyard at South Dennis, and after a Surfeit of Lobsters, and a life completely without illness. A marvelous fellow, and as one of his teachers wrote me, an irreperable loss. I can't face Boston or Cambridge or the Harvard Club without him: even Brewster now looks a little gray. Alas.   heave us a line —

                                        our loves
                                        Conrad

                              pertry room
                              L of C
                              Feb 2 52

        P S — I thought, beloved Malc, that you wou would want to know of the death, which we learned of yesterday, of Mrs. Neeves — Tom's wife — at Rye.[3] I'm sure the old boy would love it if you were to drop him a line or two. Devonshire House, Winchelsea Road, Rye, is the address. Apparently she hadn't been ill long, but with some rare disease,

---

1 Jessie (McDonald) Armstrong (1889–1969), Aiken's first wife and mother of their three children; she and Martin Donisthorpe Armstrong (1882–1974), British poet and novelist, had married in 1930 after her divorce from Aiken.
2 Gerald and Betty (Lane) Noxon were divorced in 1951.
3 Tom Neeves was the owner of the The Ship Inn, Rye. In his letter to Seymour Lawrence in *Wake* 11, Lowry tells of Mrs. Neeves's fondness for Aiken (86).

and luckily (so the neighbor who writes reports) pretty much without pain. Poor old Tom — I wonder how he'll make out. She looked after him with her whole life — but then, he did the same for her, a complete symbiosis, one of the moſt perfeĉt. Jeeſt. Gives one to think. Rye, September 5, 1924, and I am going into the Ship to celebrate the birth of my daughter Joan, in Jeake's House, the house which had been bought four months before, what time the hawthorn was in bloom, for that very purpose. And there, of course, were old Tom and the missus, newly moved from the Ypres, on the steps, where they used to roll the empty barrels up that bloody little railway track, remember? And there, only a few bright seconds later, you and I were to appear with an eye out for sausage rolls.
well well well and well

Conrad

84 : *From* LOWRY *to* AIKEN

MS H 2533; MSPC UBC 3–3

[Dollarton]

Vernal Equinox.
/Eaſter Monday.
[21 March/ 31 March 1952]

Address is now
Dollarton again, &
perhaps almoſt
Ascension day by now.

My beloved old Conrad:
    Your old Hammbo ain't been feeling well, in faĉt has been going through a hell of a passage, but is back on deck, in faĉt, come to think of it, never left the deck: Margie is fine, work goes well, publishing relations

not quite so fine, what with the old firm of Reynal & Hitchcock split up,[1] so that one is divided in one's loyalties & legalities — all this bedside reading to you.

Poor old Dollarton was nearly washed away in a hurricane: but our old self-built second house still stands, to the 'grave delight' of the few remaining fishermen; however we had to seek refuge here[2] finally & don't return till April Fool's day, when the skunk cabbages will be found singing among the Love's lies bleeding & Evening star, as you might say, not to mention Death Camas & the contorted lousewort.

You were wrong to say I had no way with cats though, as I have a sort of feeling you did on our passage from Gilbraltar,[3] in a friendly fashion, or perhaps you were right, & I merely inherited your way: at all events our cat that we could not bring with us would not stay with the fisherman (though his first owner) with whom we had left him, & instead has gone wild in the bush & the forest, haunts our house, will speak to noone but ourselves by proxy, & is even terrorizing the neighbourhood — perhaps he is ¼ lynx — so that not liking to think of that among other things, we shall be glad to get back and bail him out of his rowan tree.

Meantime I have contrived a letter to poor old Tom Neeves, reminding him of rabbits & bacon & things that will be forever unforgotten, not forgetting the Dutch ship like a haystack, & which perhaps will help to assuage his bereavement: how truly compassionate & good of you to think of this, though it is of course but what one would have expected of you.

I congratulate you from the bottom of my heart on getting Ushant done under such circumstances, i.e the Library etc,[4] am looking forward enormously to reading it, certain it will be great (& also hoping that you will have spared me some of my obscenest failings to use myself — no matter, I would probably plagiarise them anyway etc.) I am very proud to be there though, believe me, however foul.

I hope you can read my article in Wake,[5] if it appears, written when

---

1 While Eugene Reynal had left the firm of Reynal & Hitchcock for Harcourt, Brace, taking the Lowry account with him, Lowry's old editor at Reynal & Hitchcock, Albert Erskine, had moved to Random House. Lowry's "loyalties" were divided because his agent had sent his recent work to Robert Giroux at Harcourt, Brace, while Lowry wanted to keep Erskine as his editor (Day 427).

2 The Lowrys had rented an apartment in Vancouver for the winter (see my first textual note for this letter at the end of this volume); however, by the time of *mailing* this letter, they had returned to Dollarton.

3 On their way to Spain in the summer of 1933, and on their return, the Aikens and Lowry had stopped in Gilbraltar (Lorenz, *Lorelei Two* 149, 158).

4 i.e., The Library of Congress where Aiken was working from 1950–52.

5 "A Letter," *Wake* II (1952): 80–89.

the foundations were rising under us, without vomiting: all I wanted to say really was that I considered you not only one of the ten or so greateſt writers who ever lived, but one of the greateſt sportsmen. So, if I don't get it over, I am telling you that that was what I wanted to say.

5   I send you a piƈture of a cat up a telegraph pole.[1]

I'm a pynter & gilder, I am, & by Jesus now I LIVE in Vancouver![2] Or don't I? (At leaſt I did when I wrote the firſt draft of this) Nevermind, we will all meet in New Zealand.

Alas, that bloody little mowing machine. . .[3]

10   But in spite of that old small grass be assured of my love & undying respeƈt from ourselves to yourself & Mary from your ever devoted old friend —

Hambo-hambone!

15   P.S I am juſt grieved, period, about Gerald & Betty, who were so damned good to us, & such truly good friends, albeit Betty did not like me, she did her beſt to try, was swell to us, & Margie loved her; I loved them both in my way, & while I wish them every luck in their apparent change of heart, I can't help wishing them together again. My feeling is they were 20 & are both genuine artiſts, genuinely courageous, the beſt of people, but as for that good old Betty she read too much of that good old Tchechov, & when you do that on the shores of Lake Ontario, or even of the Bass River, with so many seagulls around, anything may happen . . .[4] But I loathe like hell to think what it may have done to poor old Gerald. 25 Fortunately he has plenty of guts. But what are guts, as Pontius Pilate might have said? . . Especially when you have to use them as bootſtraps.

P.P.S. Let the almoſting of Arcularis become, in New York, a positiveing — or rather the only kind of Positive that gives relief to man. (There is 30 a swell small — & in faƈt not so small — beginnings of a theatre here — that is paying its way — No Exit, The Flies, & the Ascent of F6[5] (not to

---

1 See Lowry's letter in *Wake* in which he tells of Aiken rescuing a cat from a telegraph pole (85–86), and *Blue Voyage* (147). In a 3 March 1901 letter to Harold Tillinghaſt, Aiken tells of climbing a telegraph pole to rescue their cat from a roofſtop (Killorin 6). This photograph is missing.

2 See *Blue Voyage*: " 'A pynter an' gilder, I am, an' I've been to Vancouver' " (36).

3 Cf. *Blue Voyage* (4, 36, 67), and *Under the Volcano* (67, 173).

4 The allusion here is to Chekhov's play, *The Seagull* (originally produced in Russian in 1897); the story is set beside a lake, and depiƈts the romantic complications and infidelities among a small group of people.

5 "The Ascent of F6": play by W.H. Auden and Chriſtopher Isherwood firſt published as *The Ascent of F6: A Tragedy in Two Aƈts* (London: Faber, 1936; New York:

mention Much ado About Nothing), all playing at different theatres, &
to crowded houses, & also some marvellously bizarre dramatists, including perhaps even me; no writers to hold a candle to yourself or anything,
or within a million miles, but at least one (who is poeticising something
5   of my own) potentially a hell of a lot better than Christopher Fry,[1] which
is not saying much maybe; name of Newton,[2] & the son of a Holy roller,
& not above rolling himself, from time to time — so you might, though
not for this reason, bear our town in mind with the finished Arcularis?
not for free either, for you might make some cash, & they would be
10   honoured. Technical standard of production is extremely high, acting not
so hot, or erratic, though there are some fine actresses: by & large though,
there is an extraordinary feeling for *language*, which would be good for
Mr A.[3] As also, enthusiasm.)

15   P.P.S. Have just received the news, after many months of Carlsening upon
a flying enterprise with breaking tow-ropes[4] (as a consequence of which
I didn't want to post this letter in case it depressed you) that Random
House & the Modern library people are taking me in tow with a large
advance & contract upon the wing.[5] (of course one still keeps one's fingers
20   crossed. In the army they call it chest. 'What about a game of chequers?'
'Sure, I don't mind.')[6]
God bless you. Malc
P.S. But alack we have not found the cat.

Random House, 1937). "No Exit" ("Huis clos" 1945) and "The Flies" ("Les mouches"
1943): plays by Jean-Paul Sartre, translated by Stuart Gilbert and published together
in one volume by Knopf in 1947.
1 Christopher Fry (1907–), British playwright, actor, and director.
2 Norman Newton (1929–), Canadian writer, actor, and composer whom Lowry
met in 1949. In the early 1950s, he and Lowry worked together on a stage version of
Nordahl Grieg's *The Ship Sails On* which was never completed. Cf. Newton's letter to
Lowry in the UBC Library [1–52] and letter 18, n. 4, p. 66. Newton's memoir of Lowry
appears in Sheryl Salloum's *Malcolm Lowry: Vancouver Days* (84–91).
3 i.e., "Arcularis."
4 Hendrik Kurt Carlsen was the American captain of the cargo ship *The Flying
Enterprise*. On 28 December 1951 the ship went adrift in the North Atlantic and
Carlsen himself stayed alone on the ship for 13 days trying to save it. The tow-lines
between *The Flying Enterprise* and the *Turmoil* (a tug boat) broke as they tried to pull
it to shore. Finally, on 10 January 1952, *The Flying Enterprise* sank. See the numerous
articles in the London *Times* from 29 December 1951 to 11 January 1952 about this event.
When Carlsen arrived in Falmouth on January 11th, he received a hero's welcome.
5 In April 1952 Random House offered Lowry a contract which called for two novels
and a book of short stories within the next two-and-a-half years. Lowry was unable
to fulfill the contract, and in January 1954 Random House cut him off.
6 Cf. *Blue Voyage* (93–94).

P.P.P.S. I enclose you carbon of letter airmailed to old Tom. I wrote it twice in my own handwriting: finally decided he couldn't read it, so typed it, but was so moved couldn't get the grammar straight even then.[1]

Excuse this messy letter: it was the bloody pen, not to mention the bloody paper, combined perhaps with a slightly bloody mind at the time.

85 : *From* LOWRY *to* AIKEN

TS H 2534

Dollarton, B.C.,
Canada,

Sept. 14, 1952.

Dear old Conrad:

Ushant is a knock-out – ow, how it hurts![2] A great book, in many ways, technically, a marvel, in plain words a maſterwork. That much I can glean though naturally so far I've tended to read it a bit in the manner of the wind turning the pages of the book in the garden, save that the wind, for all the skirts it has blown up, is perhaps not reading the book like me with the objeċt of finding its own pants taken down on the next page. This plus pressure of one's own work and the usual elemental difficulties of keeping alive in the wilderness have made it hard to form a dispassionate judgement as yet. In other words I ain't really had time, and when I make time, I don't read it dispassionately. Meantime there are wonders of prose, profound perceptions and apperceptions and complexities expressed in miraculous limpidity. The form is a triumph, and

---

1 This letter is contained in the Huntington Aiken Colleċtion (TS 2539). Permission to reproduce the letter was not forthcoming from the Lowry eſtate.
2 Lowry's copy of *Ushant* in the UBC Library bears the following inscription by Aiken:
For our beloved
   Malc-Hambo-Blackſtone
  with all devotion
    from Conrad
Auguſt 23–1952

the end, as hot musicians say, is out of this world. No criticisms (though
I might – and certainly with it more enlightened praise – have some later)
save that now and then I felt a slight failure of tone, e.g., round about the
section of uncles' ashes.[1] And he, though it would certainly have given
him "an unaccustomed wetness in the trousers,"[2] might have complained,
as once before, of an occasional unnecessary coarseness. What the hell.
But I thought you unfair to B.V. at one point. In those days, young fellow,
dealing with those complicated issues of prose, you were content sometimes not to 'write', but to 'decorate the page', as Tchechov somewhere
advises[3] (Sounds like bad advice too, but you get what I mean — if
anything; as a matter of fact I simply wanted to reassert my pristine loyalty
to B.V, but became involved in a tangential & largely unfounded speculation I couldn't develop without getting into a fine muddle) one to do.
Perhaps you have forgotten the technical problems that seem solved at
every moment in that book, on every page, in every word, and by the
placing of words. All maybe largely unconscious, [—] Jeez Conrad I don't
mean that though I mean the rest [—] but I've never read a book that
appealed to so many senses at once as that, including some not in the
roster. Ushant possesses a similar genius in the art of communications;
never too much fed into the channel, though you've involved yourself with
all the temptations of complete freedom. But I'm not writing an appraisal
of Ushant here so much – there are tremendous things almost wherever
you open it – as a note to set your mind at rest about Hammbo, in case
you were worrying, lest I be hurt. H'm. Our sweating self, but better. And
considerably more intelligent. Still:

> What a fearful account *he* will have to give
> of himself at the judgement day!
> OW, HOW IT HURTS!

the reference being to the sinister inscription upon the glass case containing a bepoxed Liverpudlian waxwork in the old Museum of Anatomy in
Paradise outside which it also said: Man know thyself![4]

---

1 See *Ushant* (283–87); see letter 55 from Aiken in which he tells the story of his Uncle
Alfred's ashes upon which the episode in *Ushant* is based.
2 Cf. letter 70, p. 192, from Lowry.
3 See Chekhov's 15 February 1895 letter to L.A. Avilov in *Letters on the Short Story,
the Drama, and Other Literary Topics*, sel. and ed. Louis S. Friedland (New York:
Minton, Balch, 1924): ". . . a writer should not write, but should 'ornament' the paper,
so that his work will be careful and slow" (98). In "The Art of Poetry" in 1968, Aiken
tells how Lowry "chided me for not taking more pains to 'decorate the page'" (110).
4 Cf. Day's *Malcolm Lowry: A Biography* in which he tells of the five-year-old Lowry
being taken to the "Syphilis Museum in Paradise Street" by his brother Stuart (67),

This, to make you laugh. Seriously, so far as I'm concerned, it seems to me you've been very sporting and charitable though naturally one wishes one had acquitted oneself differently in real life. Also it is a bit hijeous (as our old cook used to say) from the exiſtential point of view, to
5 think that at those few moments one aĉtually did imagine one was being truly helpful – however intolerable – or sharing in some mutually sacred or secret — don't take this too seriously, old man, my hypocrisy is exposed overleaf [—] drama that one was in faĉt (one forgets only in part, it is true) being eyed (as Strindberg might say) as a rabbit for viviseĉtion. And
10 worse still, eyeing one's fellow Conrad, for I'm juſt as bad, no doubt, in faĉt worse. And when I think what gobbets of Hammbo you might have chosen for display I can only affirm that in the matter of forbearance Clive of India has nothing on you.[1] And of course one is also honored. Hope it is all Ushantih with the Tse-Tse.[2] — And I hope the real Hammbo
15 may prove a credit: the work – and God how much of it there is – is going well. And so is our life. Another book should be finished soon,[3] and there are thousands of pages of drafts of future ones (in the vault of a bank, this time).[4] We've had a pretty rough tough time the laſt years, what with moſt of our assets frozen in Europe.[5] And on occasion, the typewriter
20 frozen too. But baſta![6] Congratulations upon, and the beſt of luck with Ushant. With devotion and all the very beſt love to Mary and yourself from us both – in faĉt from all 9 of us, Mr. and Mrs. Blackſtone, Mr. and Mrs. Hammbo, Mr. and Mrs. Lowry, not forget not forgetting Mr. and Mrs. Demareſt,[7] and from the old Malc himself.
25   As ever

                                Malc

---

and Michael Mercer's *Goodnight Disgrace* (52–55). In *Ultramarine* Lowry writes of a similar visit to a Syphilis Museum: "'. . . what a fearful account he will have to give of himself at the JUDGEMENT day . . .'" (148). Aiken mentions a "Paradise Street" in *Ushant* (43), but gives no account of the visit to the museum.

1 Cf. George Alfred Henty's *With Clive in India, or the Beginnings of an Empire* (London: Blackie, 1884); these tales of British adventurers in India were read in the British school syſtem for generations.

2 "Tsetse": the charaĉter in *Ushant* based upon T.S. Eliot. "Ushantih": cf. letter 13, n. 3, p. 42.

3 *Hear Us O Lord from Heaven Thy Dwelling Place*.

4 Probably *Dark as the Grave Wherein My Friend Is Laid*; cf. Day (431).

5 After the death of his mother, Evelyn (Boden) Lowry, on 6 December 1950, Lowry had begun to receive sporadic payments from the family eſtate.

6 "baſta": Spanish, "enough."

7 William Blackſtone is the central figure of Aiken's *The Kid*; Demareſt is the protagoniſt of *Blue Voyage*.

P.S. I was delighted and moved to get a reply from old Tom (after you'd put the deeply good suggeſtion in my head he'd be glad to get a letter after the misses' death)

T.W.Neeves   52 New Winchelsea

5 Dear Mr. Lowry very pleased to hear
from you we hear from Mr. Aiken at times
and from Mr. Rice and Mrs. Rice[1] they stade
we with us two year age we hear from them
at Times now the Old Ship was good place! –
10 to live we Left their 17 years age laſt
March Mr. Aiken was shocking [—] he wrote speaking of course, it
only looked like shocking [—] to us of you
He was a nice kind of gentleman –

15 I myself have juſt come out Hospital
had bad operation came home 4 weeks ago
Felling better now, Blader Troble now
for about 6 Monnths I had a bad times Doꝸor
tell me your man 80 year to be alive
20

hope for little better time coming
feel more like old time on way
wis hing beſt very Pleased to hear from you
Sincerely Your Old Thomas Neeves Cheero!
25

---

1 The American writer Jennings Rice (1900-?) and his wife Maria Gandia were friends of Aiken and Edward Burra; they eventually settled in Florence.

86 : *From* LOWRY *to* AIKEN

TS H 2535

Dollarton, B.C.,
Canada,

July 16, 1954.
*(See below)

My beloved old Conrad:

All too hard the letter it would seem I *should* write, especially as to the question – the question also raised by you p. 329 – 330 in and of Ushant (and therein, by you, triumphantly solved!) as to where, in God's name, to begin, or "step on;"[1] — especially now, after far too long a silence, a silence for which I have felt increasingly of late to blame, and this for having left you with the ungenerous and niggling impression – and what was worse, about the only impression – that I was "hurt", more even than anything else, more even than honoured, by Ushant itself: all this is so far from being the case as to be almost funny, or would be, save that, by leaving you that impression – if indeed I did – and venturing nothing more articulate later, I feel I may have inadvertently wounded you by my apparent ingratitude, or angered and disappointed you by my bloody imperceptiveness, not to say stupidity: not to say meanness; you could rightly have thought me guilty of an injustice too, for the book is a great one, and I should have said so – would have said so in extensive detail but for certain "auxiliary circumstances" that were responsible for my not being able to give it my full objecive attention till recently.   There turns

* I had left this letter to gather a little dust before sending it, feeling it still unworthy: purposing then to send it in time for your birthday[2] (of which, old man, very many happy returns): then, coming across some of *your* old letters, all of them so kind, so understanding, & so generous to another (even in the midst of your own troubles) I felt deeply ashamed & that I could not leave you longer without a line.

---

1   See *Ushant*: ". . . the primary question as to where, in god's name, in all that welter of material . . . one was to make one's first entry; or at exactly what point of the nebular spiral . . . dare to step on" (329–30).
2   5 August 1889.

out to be another reason for this too which I hope I'll convey as I go along, since it is a splendidly Ushantesque one. — Meantime, and for the rest, I feel that I'm largely not guilty of anything save that sort of narcissism – and I submit that if narcissism it is at least of the most unselfish kind,
5   in intention, if not in effect – that keeps one from writing at all rather than say anything not masterly about a masterpiece. — Well, I've conquered this inhibiting factor, — this letter must still be largely inarticulate, and still say little that I want to say, but yet is going to go, as better than none. I note that it seems I haven't taken into account that your silence
10 might likewise have been occasioned by "certain auxiliary circumstances": I hope in that case not as painful as mine which range all the way from false angina and dog bite on Margie's side to myself getting caught in a trap (the trap: a half uprooted root [—] symbolical perhaps?) set by boys playing cowboys and Indians of all things!: — and smashing my right leg
15 and ankle and likewise dislocating the latter – this over a year ago, largely spent in a cast, and I've only been able to walk properly again the last month.[1] (What! dead silence in the stalls, you are supposed to laugh; and indeed the whole thing was incredibly funny in one way, looking back on it, since Margie was bitten by the dog on the way to phone the ambulance
20 for me, so that we both arrived in hospital together, where a good time was had by all.) The worst has been the slowly tightening net – or noose – of eviction around us as British Columbia's industrial boom (perhaps one should say derrick, further to complicate the image) has lowered upon the Loweries.[2] With the oil-refineries daily gaining ground down the
25 banks of the inlet – at the base of the biggest one a huge illuminated cerise HELL appears nightly – they having, in the interests of truth, no doubt, omitted aphaeretically the prefatory S[3] – on the mountainside where the aspens all, all – or nearly all – are fallen, and the simultaneous polution to a great extent, it often seems, of everything, air, sky, water, people. Our
30 oasis still stands, we still even add to it, our well gives forth pure mountain water still, the sea between oil-slicks is still marvellous to swim in, out of the window, of from a pier, near which lies our boat, — the mountains

1   According to Douglas Day, Lowry's account of this accident was overly drama- tized, as was his suggestion that the "trap" had been deliberately set by children. In Day's version, Lowry "had broken his leg while stumbling about in the woods, drunk" (434).
2   The "squatters" in Dollarton had been periodically threatened with notices of eviction over the years, and in 1954 the District of North Vancouver was preparing to develop Cates Park in that area; in 1958 the last shacks in the area were demolished (Salloum 123).
3   Cf. Lowry's "The Forest Path to the Spring," *Hear Us O Lord from Heaven Thy Dwelling Place* (Philadelphia: Lippincott, 1961) 256.

are there, so is the dogwood bursting into bloom ten years after it was burned with our first house, and another shack we acquired in addition to the one we rebuilt with our own hands, [—] though in them days ones own hands really *were* one's own hands — of the Better Life as represented by the "Shoulder Parade" etc, as a kind of prepioneer we remain slightly sceptical, or perhaps feel a bit wryly jealous. [—] inhabited by a mink and family who use old drafts of the Volcano as a toilet, and the view at night with the two towering burning oil wastes – which from time to time emit in concert a single great subterranean growling belch, so that one has become almost fond of them – spouting 500 feet into the sky – "really beautiful creatures, Malc," I can almost hear you saying – with the other refinery noises of a thousand Jew's harps is something to see and hear and smell, by Crikey, if it is not: but a truce to this drooling about the mountain scenery: the point was – but I imagine you done got it already. To abandon the place, the house in its peril seemed, seems, traitorous but to stay simply inviting madness: how both to abandon it without treason and remain without going cuckoo but at the same time go – and by the way where? – whole yet leaving the door open to come back, and supposing there not to be a door, how to keep one in the heart – how to do all this with a sense of adventure while staying, so to say, where you are, or one was, advancing with dignified gait toward some extramundane yet (with a motion as natural as a transhumance) eminently practical haven elsewhere that though several thousand miles away still in a mysterious way was the same place, though as yet unknown – j'y suis, me voici, je reste là, me voilà![1] – how to do all this sort of thing with no money yet having at the same time more than enough – all this has been of the essence of the problem: in brief, brother, had I not suddenly found myself taking good old Ushant from its hiding place again – between Shakespeare and Brownstone Eclogues but still a kind of hiding place, — I don't know what I would have done. All this, which has been brutally aggravated for the last years by the fact that I've been trying to write about this very thing – I mean specifically here, the life, the wonderful wonderful life, the approaching eviction, the horrible horrible eviction[2] – not fiddling while Rome burns, more like making a tape recording of one's own execution – was somewhat too dramatically borne in upon me the other night when I found myself while swimming being swept two miles downstream and out of course by a fifteen foot rip tide (to combat such

---

1   French, "I am here, here I am, I am staying here, here I've come"; cf. "J'y suis, j'y reste," words of Maréchal Mac-Mahon (1808–92).
2   Lowry is probably referring to his novel, *October Ferry to Gabriola*.

has been, of late, a chief amusement) to be deposited upon a far shore, like Byron, with the palsy (but without having swum the Hellesponte) in the pitch dark on the edge of the wilderness where, upon espying a friendly, as I thought, fisherman (also, as it turned out, a benevolent character of mine, though he didn't know *that*) and having asked shiveringly for the loan of a lantern to find my way home and a towel, not to say some warmth from somewhere to stay *this* little potter's trembling hand,[1] instead of offering any such thing, some dark Hambogtrottery suspecting, he smote me wickedly upon the snoot. . . There's Natty Bumpo[2] for you – brings you up with a bump. He also hacked me viciously on the shins. His name was Clarence, and I think I'm buried under a lilac tree, the way I've felt since.[3] He was an ex-sea cook too: I forgot to say my first name was Clarence. . .[4] But a truce to this.

What I'm trying to say is that (though I admit that the previous paragraph doesn't seem any too logically to lead up to it) it has been a case, both within and without, with the work and with one's life, of being almost completely lost in the dark, involved with a suffering I felt to be unique, and with which I didn't know what to do: lost, and then suddenly, as if round a point in chaos, and at precisely the critical moment, suddenly to observe the beneficent light of Ushant itself, no less, *your* Ushant, swinging its transfluent crossbeams ahead, to guide *me*. (And therein – in the book this time, I mean, and don't try to unmix these metaphors – not to be socked on the snoot, not to receive a stone, but an Egg, in fact perhaps the Cosmic Egg itself, but without the bad smell I attribute to this celestial fruit in the Volcano.). .[5]

What it comes down to anyway, it has enabled me to make a series of wise and swift decisions that would have been otherwise, I think, nearly impossible for me. Among the most important of these is that enables me to say now that we are retreating, but – like the regiment who buried the bodies after Custer's Last Stand, – in good order: retreating but – the financial problem also having been solved quite triumphantly – likewise

---

1 Cf. *Ushant*: "'the hand of the potter shakes'" (286), and the *Rubáiyát of Omar Khayyám*, stanza 86; "Potter" was the maiden name of Aiken's mother and also Aiken's middle name.

2 Natty Bumppo (Lowry has misspelled it) is a character who figures under various pseudonymns in the "Leatherstocking" series of novels by the American writer James Fenimore Cooper (1789–1851).

3 In *Ushant* the narrator, D., tells of planting lilac bushes with someone named Clarence (333–34); there is a similar scene in Aiken's *Conversation*.

4 Lowry was christened "Clarence Malcolm Lowry." The name "Boden," which he often quoted as his middle name, was actually his mother's maiden name.

5 See *Under the Volcano* (66).

advancing: – (just to keep the Ushantesque records straight, I should have mentioned that the other person I have to consider in our little saga of withdrawal and return,[1] namely Margerie, is descended on one side of the family from the Crafts, and on the other from the Winthrops – her
5   great-great-I don't know how many great grandfathers — on her mother's side being the founder of Roxbury, Mass, no less, and another one the Priscilla Winthrop of Miles Standish fame (Margerie's sister is named Priscilla) etc. etc. she is, through Betsy Patterson of Baltimore, also related to Napoleon Bonaparte (Betsy married his young brother Jerome) as I
10   sometimes like to remind her – i[t] would be extraordinary, or perhaps not so extraordinary if she turned out to be a collateral relative of your own, anyway I like to think she is): – we are advancing upon Greece (first to Syracuse) there to live for a few years: meantime we are leaving the house in good hands that will give and take from it the most good (and
15   won't I hope, fill the stove full of bones) and with the understanding that if we want to come back anytime it's still ours, if it's still there: and who knows, it may be, and the oil refineries gone. . .

But for Ushant I feel all this would have been a rout though. It is the identity less with Hammbo (though there's plenty salutary there, includ-
20   ing that which "hurts") but with your good self – in your multiple and passionate relation to houses[2] – that has saved my bacon: you have suffered through this, for *me*, it is as if I can tell myself, and this not only takes away half of the otherwise unbearable pain, but acts as a wholesome release. What psychological abyss I might have been heading for other-
25   wise with so much libido invested in this spot of earth I shudder to think. I would have fetched up like one of the characters in Desire Under the Elms or something. My current work would have been a rout too, maybe abandoned. But more of this later. I know better what to do now. Meantimes, thanks largely to yourself, the present is exciting, the future
30   full of adventure, and the bleeding is almost exhilarating. We are sailing, D.V.[3] sometime in September by an Italian freighter bound for Naples or Genoa.[4] Because I shall have only a transit visa and we can't be leaving

---

1 Images of "withdrawal and return" abound in *Ushant*.
2 Aiken was very attached, not only to Jeake's House, but also to the house in Savannah in which he'd been born, and in 1960 he and Mary moved to Savannah and into the house next door to this house. According to John Aiken, Jeake's House bore a remarkable resemblance to Aiken's childhood Savannah home on Oglethorpe Avenue (*Conrad Aiken Remembered* 28).
3 "Deo Volente": Latin, "God willing."
4 The Lowrys left Dollarton for the last time on 11 August 1954, travelling to New York via Los Angeles, and then, in September, aboard the ss *Giacomo* to Italy.

here till the end of August at earliest, and we're stopping off to see Margie's
mama in Los Angeles, I shall have only a few days in New York, if that,
and can hope only that some miracle may occur whereby it coincides with
one of your visits there if you're not in New Zealand by this time:[1] for of
5 course I can't say how much I'd love to see you: but if we can't see one
another I'll send you a telegram anyway – at the moment plans are still a
bit uncertain; I have to hear further from the shipping company.
—— For the rest, after the foregoing chaos, it seems a bit redundant
– and the paragraph after that is probably going to be, I see, redundant
10 too – to go on to say that I have experienced here in B.C. for the first
time, the revelation – v. top of 332[2] – not to mention, if so to speak in
reverse, and for a slightly different reason, the revelation on bottom of
333[3] – no no no, they're all too near the knuckle, these pages: – I can't do
any of it justice: which is to repeat that I have found the whole magnificent
15 book of enormous help: just at the time I needed Ushant, here was Ushant
to help me: what has been worst for me has been to approach to "this
other domain of love" bottom of 332, but without any ritual poem to be
the celebration of it.[4] But maybe even that will come. (I've done an
enormous lot of work – some of it good – in this place, I mean Dollarton
20 – much of it, you will one day see, quite terrifying in the light of Ushant
itself, much of it having been written while you must have been writing
the other, but a lot of this work has become very unbalanced – again
Ushant supplies the redress.) And the passage on 336: beginning "That
little love: the truth was, that the poem had been D's unexpected confes-
25 sion etc " – Jeeze how I understand *that* now.
Finally I ought to say that Ushant is obviously one of the best books
ever written – if not necessarily, in so many words, *your* "best" book: but
it is an ADVANCE not only on your account, but it does move literature
forward surely, with an almost imperceptible jolt, every bit as much as
30 Finnegan's Wake, though for almost precisely opposite reasons: one; its
marvellous generosity, as of a uranium mine, with your stake planted there
but as if it were left open for other people to work it —— (as a librarian

---

1 Cf. letter 83 from Aiken.
2 See *Ushant*: ". . . what nevertheless became unavoidably conspicuous in it was the
basic importance in it of love. Love! Good heavens, how blind he had been" (332).
3 See *Ushant*: "But the real truth was that to touch that earth [i.e., the earth of a
foreign country] was treason" (333).
4 *Ushant*: ". . . one was beginning to approach that other domain of love which had
had its way with him . . . and the writing of the ritual poem which was his unforesee-
able celebration of it" (332); essentially, Aiken is here writing about spiritual love
transcending sex.

here said to me 'You have to have a high class intellect — like to write a book like that, mr Lowry'.) it is also a purely *intellectual* triumph of the first water. And the thesis: collosal. — But you have had enough of my incomprehensible stuff. "And the waves of wildflowers, asking now to be
5 remembered. . ." I won't say anything about that either, which I feel myself to have misquoted – I can't find the page (bad light) if I've buggered it up I'm sorry: it's near the end of a marvellous passage, about 298.[1]

Well god bless you, my dear fellow: I've read practically nothing else for nearly the whole past month and always with increasing devotion.
10 May grace descend on you and Mary whatever your direction. Best love from us both. And to old Gerald too, should you be in touch (Also the bridge, tripartite, once crossed tripartight. And a house in South Yarmouth. Yes, I remember it *all*.) And talking of telegrams, as perhaps might not another character have wired: Ushantih. . . Ushantih. . .
15 Ushantih. . .[2]

God bless you.   the old Malc.

P.S. D didn't say "He thinks I'm a bird in a tree," but "he thinks I'm a tree with a bird in it." Hambo was empathasing more than you remembered.[3]
20 P.P.S.   For what it is worth, Po' H. in fact wasn't pursued by a Chinese coolie in Kowloon[4] but, as I remember, by an Arab hawker who remained on board the ship after he should have got off at Pord Said, for his nefarious purpose (together also, if I remember aright, with a sowsow woman whose blind eye socket could be procured for a mere song) bribing
25 the pure young sailor with a whole tray of "real gold rings stolen off the mail boat," and even went so far as Dar es Salaam with the ship down the Suez Canal before he was rid of.
P.P.P.S.   But just to show you I haven't entirely lost my articulacy, perhaps I could venture to cap – unless this be discourteous or a thought too
30 pleonastic – the Beloved Uncle's witticism, already capping D's (top 287: and what a damn fine scene this is, especially in the cemetery) "And" – said the Uncle instantly – "did she take it in?" by "Or, having taking it in, *did she get the point properly?*"
PPPPS (Or was this perhaps just another case of "withdrawal and
35 return"?)

---

1 This passage is, as Lowry says, on page 298.
2 Cf. letter 85, n. 2, p. 230, and letter 13, n. 3, p. 42.
3 See *Ushant* (357) and *Under the Volcano* (134); in *Ushant* Aiken (D.) insinuates that Lowry (Hambo) stole this anecdote from him for use in *Under the Volcano*.
4 See *Ushant* (116).

87 : *From* LOWRY *to* AIKEN

TS H 2536

5

[WESTERN UNION]
[NEW YORK NY]

[Saturday; 8:43 AM]
[4 Sept. 1954]

10

CONRAD AIKEN –

41 DOORS –

BREWSTER MASS –

15   MALCOLM NEEDS TALCUM BE WALCOM CARE OF DAVID MARKSON[1]
610 WEST 113 STREET BEFORE TUESDAY IF POSSIBLE WHEN ALL
KRAKENS[2] GET TOGETHER

LOVE

HAMBO —

20

---

1 David Markson (1927–   ), American novelist who in 1951 wrote a Master's thesis on *Under the Volcano* at Columbia University which was later revised and published as *Malcolm Lowry's Volcano: Myth Symbol Meaning* (New York: Times, 1978). He and Lowry corresponded for a year until they finally met in the summer of 1952, when Markson visited the Lowrys in Dollarton, and remained good friends until Lowry's death in 1957. The Lowrys stayed with Markson in his New York apartment in 1954 before leaving aboard the ss *Giacomo* for Italy. A reminiscence of Lowry by Markson appears in Markson's *Malcolm Lowry's Volcano* (219–31) and in *Malcolm Lowry: Psalms and Songs* (120–27).
2 "Kraken": cf. letter 70, n. 3, p. 193.

239

88 : *From* AIKEN *to* LOWRY

TS H 4785

5   [WESTERN UNION]
                                             [DENNIS MASS]

[4 Sept. 1954]

10   MALCOLM LOWRY, CARE DAVID MARKSON =
                    610 WEST 113 ST =

HALLILEUH CAN YOU COME UP DIFFICULT FOR US TO COME DOWN
BUT WILL IF NECESSARY PLEASE TELEPHONE DENNIS 385 AFTER 5
15   TONITE LOVE =
                    CONRAD =

20

89 : *From* LOWRY *to* AIKEN[1]

MS UBC; TS H 2541

5

[WESTERN UNION]
[NEW YORK NY]

[8:15 AM]
[12 Sept. 1954]

10

CONRAD AIKEN

FONE 41 DOORS

BREWSTER MASS

15   WAS ON DECK AT 7AM TO SEE YOU OFF WEDNESDAY BUT WAS OFFSET
BY HURRICANE[2] IF NOT OFF CAPE HATEROUS[3] AM GOING TO ENCOUN-
TER MONDAY AFTERNOON YOUR POST CARD RECEIVED[4] GOD BLESS
YOU AND LOADS OF LOVE TO YOU AND MARY

20   MALCOLM AND MARJORIE

---

1 See Appendix 1 for an earlier handwritten draft of this letter contained in box 1–8
of the David Markson Papers at UBC. Presumably Margerie Lowry altered Lowry's
handwritten version when phoning the text in to the telegraph office. The
"misspellings" of "Haterous" and "Marjorie" are probably transcriptional errors on the
part of the telegraph office.
2 "Hurricane Edna"; cf. Peter Churchill's memoir in Day's *Malcolm Lowry: A
Biography* (8) where he mentions this hurricane and Lowry's odd reaction to it.
3 Cf. Aiken's poem "Hatteras," *Atlantic Monthly* Mar. 1942: 334; reprinted in revised
form as "Hatteras Calling" in *Brownstone Eclogues*.
4 This postcard from Aiken is missing.

Appendix I

Letter 70: From LOWRY to AIKEN
(Aiken's variant transcription)

Letter 89: From LOWRY to AIKEN
(Lowry's handwritten draft)

70 : *From* LOWRY *to* AIKEN

(*Aiken's variant transcription*)

TS H 2525

(Dollarton)

(Oct. 24 1945)

Dear old Conrad:

Thanks awfully for yours, and have been meaning to write a really fat
and informative and diverting letter – in fact, made all the notes for same,
but I want to get this letter off now so it will be in time to wish you bon
voyage, therefore I must make a sacrifice of the other for the time being.

Yes, the phoenix clapped its wings all right all right, in fact gave such
a bloody great resounding clap that the poor bird nearly broke its neck
and had to be immolated all over again. As you know we went east after
the fire. The grave preceded us however. The interminable golden bittersweet awful beautiful eastern autumn (which I'd never experienced)
restored Margie, whose childhood was in Michigan, to *some* extent, but
me it almost slew. It had a worse effect upon me than on Henry Adams,
though the Noxons Niagara-on-the-Lake is something to see: really I
was in shocking bad form, and worse company so all in all, though I was
very disappointed not to see you – albeit I *heard* you – it was perhaps just
as well I didn't. How the Noxons put up with me – if they really did – I
don't know. Actually the business of the fire seemed to drive us both
slightly cuckoo. Its traumatic result alone was shattering. We had to live
through the fire all over again every night. I would wake to find Margie
screaming or she would wake to find me yelling and gnashing my teeth.
Apart from these diversions (fortunately the Noxons are sound sleepers
but when we moved to a house of our own it grew much worse) fire itself
seemed to follow us around in a fashion nothing short of diabolical.

Betty had painted a picture of a house in Oakville, that Margie and
I had thought of renting, because it vaguely resembled our old one, for
the winter, and one day when everyone was out I sat in the attic studying
the picture which I liked very much. My concentration on the picture was
somewhat marred by the fact that in my imagination the house kept
bursting into flame and sure enough, about a week later, that's precisely
what the house did; they couldn't get the fire engines through the woods,

nothing of the kind had happened for fifty years in that rural route, and there was a terrific to-do, through all of which Margie and I, for once, calmly slept.

Then when we went to Niagara-on-the-Lake the house next door to ours, one night while we were over at the Noxons, went up in a blaze. We heard the shouts and bells and saw the awful sun (E.D. again – I don't know why so much Emily Dickenson today) and of course thought it was *our* house and ran over in a panic, so much so that Margie was not even convinced it was *not* ou[r] house by the time we got there and took all our manuscripts out into the street. And to cap everything, when we returned here, it turned out that the house where someone had been good enough to let us store our bedding and some few things we had left after *our* fire, had in our absence itself been burned down, totally demolished, and our bedding and stuff with it, the house mysteriously bursting into flame for no reason at all apparently one calm mild evening when the owners weren't even there. Margie and I had invented, in a horror story, a murderer, a black magician one of whose specialties was the starting of fires by means of incomprehensible talismans. This fictional gent's name was Pell, and the mss concerning him I had happened to rescue from ou[r] fire. S'Welp me bob if the owners of this house didn't turn out to be called Pell too, though there had been no connection at all originally. And so forth. Altogether about fifty odd senseless sad terrifying and curiously related things that make me sometimes think (taking it all in all!) that maybe I am the chap chosen of God or the devil to elucidate the Law of Series. Unfortunately it would seem to involve one in such rotten bad art. At all events, I have been reading Kant's Critique of Pure Reason to see if that would help.

Well, we returned and began to rebuild our little shack, ourselves, I mean, with our own hands and the help of two fishermen. Margie ran a four inch spike through her foot the first day we got the lumber in – cellulitis set in, bloodpoisoning, shortage of doctors, finally hospital, and probings and she nearly died, and a horrible anxious time that was. Meanwhile she received the first part of her proofs for her novel but we are still waiting for the promised copy of the second part, Scribner's having held her first novel now for four years without publishing it and although they signed a contract for a second novel with a time limit set for publication date this fall it is already this fall and still Margie hasn't had so much as a smell of the proofs of her second novel, which was supposed to be at the printers last Christmas, so it looks as though a breach of contract looms with what small comfort that is for the poor author. Scribners have proved the world's most undependeble and unscrupulous people to deal with and you are certainly well rid of their new outfit. Granted they dared not behave like that with someone like you, but what the hell.

I then proceeded to cut off the end of my thumb while doing some ripsawing with an ordinary saw, which set us back with the building, what with Margie still hobbling with a cane, and for the laſt two months I have been in bed praĉtically unable to move with a toxaemia caused by oſteomyelitis due, they say, to an abscessed tooth that became abscessed and had to be removed owing to malpraĉtice. There is a shortage of dentiſts – they will not take new patients, even if you are hopping with agony as I was, and on V.J. day too, with the drugſtores all shut. But on the other hand there is apparently a surplus of dentiſts: they are threatening to open offices on the ſtreet, because of the housing shortage. But I myself have not been able to find a trace of these dentiſts. Meantime there has been an average of two murders a week here, moſt of them by or of children: a pet slayer likewise is at large who has disembowelled thirteen goats, several sailor's monkeys, twelve pet rabbits, and is doubtless also somewise responsible for the apparition of half a cocker spaniel in a lane near Weſt Vancouver. Juſt the same we have built our house and paradise has been regained. I forgot to say that no sooner had paradise been regained than we received the notice that a new law had gone through and that all our lovely foreſt was to be torn down and ourselves with it within a year and turned into "Autocamps of the Better Class." This placed our new house – which, by the way, has the diſtinĉtion of being the laſt example of such pioneer aĉtivity on the Vancouver waterfront property – under a sentence of death that was finally too much for our sense of humour and my temperature went up within a quarter of an hour to 104. A sad story, you say, almoſt as poignant as The Triumph of the Egg? Not a bit of it. Reprieve has come. There will be no autocamps of the better class, and no neighbours either, of the worſt class. We may live here for three years at leaſt as we are doing without moleſtation, and may even have a chance to buy the land, that is the part we want, at a reasonable price. Thus does your old Malc, if still a conservative-Chriſt ian-anarchiſt, at heart, at laſt join the ranks of the petty bourgeoisie. I feel somewhat like a Prometheus who became intereſted in real eſtate and decided to buy up his Caucasian ravine.

At the moment we are living in the house, without any inside walls, it's pouring with rain, and it doesn't leak. What triumph. Herewith our handiwork – also the pier we built ourselves, all that was left of our old house.

My novel, Under the Volcano, seems to have gone smack into the void

– no intelligent comments so far, or encouragement. I think it is really good, though the Loſt Week End may have deprived it of some of its impaƐ – alack – prosaic juſtice? – if not to be confused with The *Laſt Week End*, by J. Summerfield, in which it aƐually is old Malc who goes all too recognizably down the drain, and pretty feeble too. I was planning to send you the Volcano with some trepidation but with some pride too but I don't like to saddle you with the only copy in my possession at present and I don't see how I can get back the only available other one before you sail. So please take the will for the deed for the time being. I'll learn 'em eventually, as Mr. Wolfe once said, I feel.

The only difference in my present status since I wrote the above is that while we are living in the house without inside walls the roof is leaking in six different places. But now your letter about the ColleƐted Poems has arrived and I haſten to make some reply in time, though please forgive me if what I say seems haſtily digeſted. In brief, these are the ideas which immediately occur to me and I hope they are not merely confusing. I think the idea of reversing the chronological order is a very good one, in faƐ as good as can be – though I think perhaps The Soldier might profit by being dislocated out of the new order and being placed, if not aƐually among the symphonies, somewhere near them in the second volume. What I mean is, if it doesn't belong to the symphonies, The Soldier does to the notion of the Divine Pilgrim. Houſton Peterson or somebody once put the possibly erroneous idea in my head that you had once thought of including Teteleſtai also under the Divine Pilgrim heading and even if this is erroneous and Teleleſtai not a symphony this is worth thinking of if you haven't already rejeƐted it. As for the early poems I would certainly put in every thing that can possibly be of use to the fellow-poet and student of your work, "Discordants with Youth that's now so bravely spending" and as many of the aƐual Cats and Rats turns and movies as you have space for. The latterly certainly stay with me as unique and powerful work, whatever you may think of them. I would also take the opportunity of exhuming from undeserved limbo such pieces as Red petals in the duſt under a tree, Asphalt "tossing our tortured hands to no escape" (though not very early, 1925 model?) but very fine, and even the "succubus you kissed" lampoon you wrote agin the Imagiſts which has a hiſtorical intereſt, and giving the dates of all these. I don't know about a seleƐtion from Earth Triumphant, but I would be inclined to make a short one: possibly you are right to disown it, but I myself cannot forget the "unaccuſtomed wetness in my trousers" with which I read it at your Uncle Potters. The only other departure that comes to me would be to start the whole colleƐted poems with The Morning Song of Senlin and end them with The Coming Forth by Day of Osiris Jones. I muſt say I like this notion per se exceedingly, if it would not play too much hob with your reversed chronology. Whatever you do, I am very glad a Colleĉted Poems is coming out and the very beſt of luck with them.

If by the way you have any old Harper's Bazaars, Vice Versas, Southern Reviews or what not you are thinking of throwing away – no old Dials, alack? – we would be immensely beholden if you would wrap a paper around them and shoot them in this direĉtion C.O.D. or something for we are absolutely stuck here for such reading matter, all intelligent American magazines having been unprocurable for donkey's years: on the other hand it occurs to me it is probably a poor time to ask with you packing and all: so if it's too much trouble, juſt forget it.

Well, bon voyage, old fellow, and our very beſt love to you both and beſt wishes for Mary's success and our very beſt again to her and you and also to Jeakes

Malc.

89 : *From* LOWRY *to* AIKEN

(*handwritten draft*)

MS UBC MARKSON I–8

[New York]

[September 1954]

——Was on deck at 7:am to see you off Wedenday but was offset by hurricane am going to encounter Monday afternoon if not off Cape Hatteras loads of love to you & Mary & gratitude from us both

Malcolm
& Margerie

Appendix II

Letter from MARGERIE
BONNER to MARY AIKEN
(12 January 1940)

Letter from MARGERIE
BONNER to MARY AIKEN
(29 January 1940)

From MARGERIE BONNER *to* MARY AIKEN

(*12 January 1940*)

TS H 2547

595 W. 19th Ave.,
Vancouver, B.C.,
Canada,

January 12, 1940

Dear Mary:

First of all I want to add my thanks and deepest gratitude to Malcolm's. I wanted to write and tell you how much I appreciate all you've done and offered to do before this. Perhaps I can realize even more keenly than Malcolm does just how much your kindness means to us now, for I assure you, were I in your position, I should be dubious indeed about taking some strange woman into my home – particularly one who has apparently deliberately put herself in a position that for all you know is invidious. Please, Mary, believe me, I shall do everything I can to see that you never regret it should things work out as we hope they will.

I feel that more explanation is due you as to why we are situated as we are, for surely, to an unbiased observer, it must seem insane, unwise and unnecessary, but I almost despair of trying to make clear, by letter, a complexity such as this – I can only trust to your generosity and tolerance until we can really sit down and talk it out. Under ordinary circumstances we should, of course, never be here as we are, but these were, and are, not ordinary circumstances and there was no other way out if Malclom and I were to ever see each other again. It seems to boil down to this: it was a fight for our very existence. Presuming that you know the whole story in more or less detail, I should add that I thought long and hard before I gave up my position in Hollywood, thereby cutting off my only source of income at the moment, means of retreat, etc., but I considered all this of less importance than Malcolm. Well, all this is as maybe, but it does mean that I have no sheet anchor else where, no "home". I lived by myself there, had a job with Penny Singleton – of course I have friends, but none sufficiently immobilized for me to return on them for any length of time.

It was a time of crisis, a matter of burning bridges. I was quite aware of the latter, but I don't know if Malcolm has managed to convey to you just how much of a time of crisis it was for him. Anyhow, he desperately needed me, his work, if any of it was to survive, needed me, I came and that was that. I could have gone back within a fortnight and held my job, but, seeing the circumstances, stayed and am glad I did. I am only deeply thankful, finally, that I was able to get here and to stay with him – under any conditions.

You may think, from what you have gathered, that he had no right to let me stay – to take on the responsibility of my support with his affairs so apparently hopelessly tangled. In a certain sense you may be right, but it is not entirely his fault that he cannot support me by his own efforts at present. He was dumped by his trustees in a place where he couldn't get work, a trap if I ever saw one, and it was a case of now or never, too vitally important to bicker over the normal conventionalities. Of course, since I have supported myself for many years, I am quite able and willing to continue to do so but cannot take a job in Canada for the same reason that Malcolm cannot. If we can get back to the States I'm sure I can find something to do where ever we are. Also, I do help Malcolm with his work and save the expense of a typist – which his trustees do not see fit to allow him. With the war hanging over our heads it may be that we will only have these few months together and if we have to remain here in Vancouver it may be only a few more weeks. If the war continues on into the spring, and I can see no hope at present that it will not, there is a very large chance that Malcolm will be forced into it. That is a fear that I must live with 24 hours a day. How he feels I'm not sure as we seldom discuss it by mutual consent.

I know that many of our descriptions of how we are living must have sounded like some intermediate stage in a record breaking bender but so help me, we have been living in the greatest state of sobriety I have experienced for many years. Of course we have had literally no money to get tight on even if we wished to (which I'll admit from time to time has seemed like a good idea) but Maurice Carey has been on a bender which if it didn't break any records certainly made a few. We have had bottles waved under our noses pretty consistently and have lain shivering in our room many an icy day and night listening to cheery sounds downstairs around the fire place, so it was not for lack of opportunity that we stayed cold and sober and wondered whether we were being hypocritical. There are occasions on which it is good to get tight, but the only way to meet the severity of these conditions, we decided, was with an equal severity of mind.

And right here I want to say that I can imagine what was in whatever reports Conrad has had from Parks. There is sometimes, when it suits him, something genuinely well-meaning about the man, but I am sure that at least half of them are that kind of lying which is all the purer for having its basis in remote truth, and a good deal of the rest colored by cynical indifference, under whatever guise of watchfulness and anxiety. *I know* because I was *there* exactly what the situation *was* in Hollywood – I was with Malcolm pretty constantly the last months before he left and I know how unfairly he was treated, even from an impartial standpoint at first, and with what truly masterly misunderstanding and misapplication his affairs were handled. From a psychological standpoint everything that was supposed to be for his good was having the opposite effect and there was nobody who gave a damn what happened to him. And as for that cheerful hypocrite Parks – I suppose he is about an average sort of chap but certainly he was not the one to cope with Malcolm's problems even if he had sincerely tried – which he did not. As an instance of this, when Parks brought Malcolm to Vancouver and left him here, he said that Colonel McLean was a man whom he had known a long time and had had many business dealings with. McLean, not having been primed, or, possibly, just being honest, said later that he had never seen Parks before in his life and knew nothing of it until Parks arrived with a letter from some business acquaintance. McLean, in turn, passed Malcolm on to a mere acquaintance of his, this Oxford Grouper, who is a nasty old man and a homosexual in the bargain, with all the endearing traits and tolerance usual to a reformed roué. With much obvious enjoyment and smacking of lips he recounted his own juicy past and then talked glibly of reforming Malcolm for the "sin" of being in love with me, while being divorced from his wife, who in the first place deserted him. Between them they made it neatly impossible for Malcolm to have a normal life and spent their time either praying over his soul or blocking every attempt on his part to work, thus driving him to the very thing they piously protested they were trying to stop. Then the Oxford Grouper had the temerity to say they'd let him spend a few days i[n] the dirtiest flophouse in town without a cent and maybe that would teach him a lesson!

That all this sounds impossible among civilized people, or at least among the civilized people one associates with oneself, Malcolm well knows and I know also that he feels that Conrad, who is aware of Malcolm's more or less 'ex'-wildness, may have said "me-thinks he doth protest too much." But all this is a *fact*. And a definite fact also is it that everything has been done to discourage him and deter him from his work, because Carey has evidently been given to understand that it is too obsessed with sex and drink and that 'his father doesn't want that.' That his father merely wants him to be successful in the prosecution of his work seems to me to be demonstrated by the fact that as soon as some 'personal' contact was established with him by Conrad he suddenly began to do everything in his power to bring about the state of affairs which would allow him to finish it. Meantime, however, I have my own eyes and ears as absolute witnesses of the fact that the only encouragement he got with it was to "be finished with all that stuff" – and in this regard and also in the regard of the personal responsibility for his existance it ought to be said right here and now that the only person who has done anything to save it, before he managed to contact you both again, was himself. I am glad to think that I too have helped. But, to be absolutely honest about the whole matter, by an ironic twist, everything that Parks has done seems to have run counter to what I presume was the object of the arrangement – distasteful and ruinous to his initiative as it was – in the first place.

In all this you may think it queer that there is little to be said on the other side. There is little, save perhaps this: Parks, of course, was not a friend of Malcolm's, it was a purely business arrangement to him, so, basically, what did he care what happened to Malcolm so long as he himself was apparently doing his best? And, at the beginning, Parks was disposed to treat him more fairly, but he was never trusted and the very hotel clerks were told to report on his movements and watch him and all the saloon keepers told not to serve him. He was continually 'watched' and reported on, which nearly drove him out of his mind. While at the same time Parks was establishing contact with his wife which he was unable to establish himself. He therefore deceived Parks to begin with simply because he regarded him as an enemy: he found his own way of rebribing servants, saloon keepers, etc., and when I met him was drinking very heavily indeed on apparently less than nothing. On the other hand, he seems to have made no secret of the fact that he would continue to do what he pleased, so long as he was treated in the way he was by Parks, his argument being that, anyhow, there was nothing to live for. All this gradually changed after we met, but the damage had been done, not only to his own integrity so far as Parks was concerned, but to the integrity of any relationship he formed. Parks insisted that Malcolm should have no freedom, that he should legislate even on his friends. Small wonder that when I met him his acquaintanceship was composed of crooks and people of every description from the nether regions and small wonder that I too might be considered to belong in the same category as the Doſtievsky-like harpies with whom he associated, – and I don't blame him! There was virtually no hope, all this being considered, of his putting over our own relationship on an accepted basis, so long as he lived as he did. This was roughly my argument, and although I never subjeѐted him to exhortations on his way of living, it seems that he muſt have agreed with me, judging by the way he changed and ordered his life, only to find that so far as any freedom was concerned it was all to no avail. The more conſtruĉtively he lived the tougher things were made for him and when I came up here he was virtually on the point of suicide. For the paſt six months even these Oxford Groupers have had to acknowledge that they had nothing to criticize (outside of his effort to get back to me in Hollywood laſt September) and have even written Parks that he was leading an exemplary life. But ſtill he is reſtriĉted to the point of having to give receipts for toothpaſte and shoeshines. What kind of exiſtance do they think he is leading in this barren and dreary town? The answer is, of course, that they don't care. It makes me ill to think of what he'd be doing if I weren't here to give him some companionship. I asked him if I could mention what he calls this "silliness" and he says he sees no reason why not. I think it should be cited juſt to show what all these people have done for him.

It is because of all these things, and I have only mentioned a few of the many, that Malcolm felt no disloyalty to anyone in suggeſting that we go to Montreal where we could live by ourselves with some dignity and privacy. I feel that even Malcolm's father, if the true faĉts were sympathetically presented, would realize how essential it is that Malcolm be given some freedom now if he is to preserve his self respeĉt and pride and what will happen to him if his application to reenter the States is turned down and we are left here in the hands of these people I don't know. The kind of fight he has been putting up for the laſt few months may be a good thing for him up to a point, but if he is utterly fruſtrated and defeated at every turn for *too long* when he is trying so hard, the result may be a bitter one.

I'm not going into the kind of life we're living here now, Mary, but let me tell you as woman to woman, it's a nightmare. It's not juſt boredom – though of course there is certainly no mental ſtimulation here and we can't even go to a movie – it's really horrible. We have no heat in our room and there is usually such pandemonium going on downſtairs that even slowly freezing seems the better alternative. Of course it doesn't help Malcolm in his work to have to stamp up and down the floor bundled up like an Eskimo, or to type wrapped up in our one blanket with his fingers blue and stiff. But he does it. All this may sound like piling on the agony, but very well, it *is* agony. He's been writing articles for the local paper in an effort to earn my fare back east but they don't pay much and we had to get his overcoat out (which Maurice had pawned) and we have to rent a typewriter (Maurice pawned or sold Malcolm's ty[pe]writer too) so we haven't saved much – only $8.00 – but it's a start and we hope to have more before permission arrives for Malcolm to go to the States. I think it might be well for Malcolm to go to you first and we have arranged for me to remain here for two weeks if necessary after he leaves. It would cost too much for me to go back to Hollywood and doesn't seem practical.

But now we come to the serious stumbling block: Malcolm thinks there's only a fifty-fifty chance that he will be allowed to reenter America. When he first wrote Conrad he thought it was only a matter of cash but it now seems that due to the war and his divorce that it is not quite so simple. In that event, what are we to do? I know it is of paramount importance to Malcolm that he see Conrad. He talks of it constantly and I know how much it is on his mind. He feels that he has wronged Conrad in some way in the past, or that he has not sufficiently acknowledged how right Conrad was in certain matters important to him, that his first wife poisoned something between them from the outset, that there are many things he wishes to straighten out between them and the thought that he may have to go to war without seeing him is preying on his mind. Their friendship, of which he takes a more or less Lawrentian view, is one of the most important things in his life.

Well, I suppose there is now nothing to do but wait for news from Washington and pray that it will be good. I cannot tell you with what hope and longing we are looking forward to seeing you and Conrad. Malcolm has talked so much about you both and I am so anxious to meet you myself. Malcolm has told me of your work which he admires, which I know of, so circumscribed is life, only by repute, and I am particularly interested since I wanted to study painting and never was able to. I daub about whenever I have a few spare hours and ruin a lot of good clean canvas and nice white paper and have a wonderful time. My young cousin, Alexander Clayton, is making a name for himself in Washington, D.C., doing postoffice murals and an occasional portrait. One of his murals was reproduced in *Life* the other week. He had his first exhibition this year and it was quite a success I hear, though I could not go east to see it.

I wanted to write you all this before since I felt that there were so many things Malcolm would not, or could not, say for himself and that I was the only one who knew all the facts or who would tell them. So now I feel better anyhow and I hope this will help a little towards straightening out a few of the doubts and questions you must have. I would be so happy to hear from you – we lay in wait for the postman and eagerly pounce upon him twice a day – as all our thoughts and hopes and plans are now Eastward Ho!

We both send our love, and once more, our sincerest thanks.

Margerie Bonner

From MARGERIE BONNER *to* MARY AIKEN

(*29 January 1940*)

TS H 2548

595 W. 19th Ave.,
Vancouver, B.C.,

January 29, 1940.

Dear Mary:

I can't tell you how happy I was to get your sweet friendly letter and how much I am looking forward to meeting you and Conrad. I know how difficult it is to find time for corespondence when one is as busy as you are; perhaps I can repay some of your kindness to us by taking the household work from your shoulders while we are with you.

Isn't it the queerest coincidence that you should know Alex and Penny! Truly life seems at times to have a curious pattern.

And now to answer your questions. In a situation as complicated as our[s] is at present it is difficult to get everything explained by letters – no matter how hard you try to be sure you've covered the ground thoroughly something always seems to get left out. By this time Conrad will have received Malcolm's last letter, which explains pretty fully, I think, why we feel it impracticable to tell his father about me at this time. Of course we wish and intend to do so as soon as possible, but we feel it would be a mistake to do it now. If Malcolm could deal directly with his father, or deal with him through Conrad, we think it would be all right. But so long as he is still in the clutches of Parks, A.B.Carey and Co., everything will be sifted through them and their opinions and we have good reasons to know that we cannot trust them to be fair to Malcolm or to me. Of course, to be perfectly frank, Conrad may not like me but we know that in any event he will be fair to Malcolm.

As to my room and board here, the situation is briefly this: Maurice and Phyllis Carey receive $15 a week for boarding Malcolm, which, were he here alone, would afford him ample, if not luxurious, lodging. They agreed to include me as well and provided us with a sort of attic room, furnished with a bed and nothing else, no stove or heat in it, one meal a day, and I help Phyllis with the work. (Out of this $15 a week they feed the whole family, us, three children and nurse). Any clothing Malcolm needs is provided for him (after a struggle and much argument,) and his incidental bills such as cleaning, I do all our laundry, toiletries, etc., are paid for (after much struggle and argument) by Carey and Co., and he receives $3.50 a week for himself with which to buy cigarettes, carfare or whatever. Maurice having pawned Malcolm's typewriter we now must pay a dollar a week out of our $3.50 to rent this one, since we can't get much work done without one. What happens to the rest of his money we don't know for sure but have been told that it was sent back to Parks. In short, we are both living on a little more than half of what Malcolm was supposed to have for himself. We are not squawking about these conditions and are quite prepared to put up with anything so long as we can be together. It is not the physical harrassments so much that we are trying so hard to escape, although these are vexing, it is the unjustified humiliation to Malcolm of being treated like a mental incompetent, the general web of lies and interference and chicanery, the essential dirt and sordidness and squalor of our present surroundings and the almost unsurmountable difficulties of trying to build a decent, intelligent and lasting future together in such surroundings. Well, so much for that.

I'm sure I shall like Boston, I haven't been there since I was a child but I have some cousins there, pretty stiffnecked as I recall them, who rather cast us off when my sister and myself became ACTRESSES in the MOVIES. I left Hollywood in such a hurry and flurry that I brought no references with me, besides, I really left on a two weeks leave of absence and expected to go back to my job, but I'm sure I'll have no trouble in writing back for any I need. It is more than kind of you to offer to help me get a job there as I appreciate the difficulties involved in hunting for any kind of a position in a strange city, but that is a problem that can be solved when we get there. South Dennis sounds heavenly to me but I'm sure wherever we are I shall be happy with you.

Now about Malcolm's trouble over his application: When Parks brought him to Canada it was, supposedly, only for the business of obtaining a visa. This done he was to return to Los Angeles. As soon as he had the visa he wrote Parks, saying that he was ready to return. I won't go into their altercations in detail, but Parks flatly told him he was to stay here with that damned Oxford Grouper and said it was too expensive for him to come back. This was silly because he needn't have gone in the first place, he could have gotten an extension on his visa right there in Los Angeles. Anyhow, after many pros and cons Malcolm asked me for the money to return, which I sent him. Hoping to make the trip as cheaply as possible, he started back on the bus and was stopped at the border. He had his visa which he believed was all that was necessary, but had no papers to prove that he had an income, and the authorities at the border, thinking I suppose, that he wouldn't be traveling on a bus if he had any money, and he couldn't prove that he had, turned him down. They kept him there for hours while they went through all his baggage, letters, etc., cross questioned him minutely and I gather gave him a pretty bad time. The American immigration laws say that if you are refused at the border for any reason at all that you cannot even make application for readmission for one year, so what he has had to do was to apply to have his case reopened on the grounds that they were mistaken in saying that he would become a public charge since he is now in a position to prove that he will not. It is a question whether they will see fit to reopen the case or not and the whole thing had to be referred to our Secretary of Labor, Madam Perkins, at Washington. Who will actually pass on the case we don't know. Malcolm feels that the fact of his having been divorced in the meantime and the fact that they may hav[e] read some of my letters at the border may be held against him and perhaps it will, I suppose it all depends on who has the final decision to make and the sort of mood they happen to be in that day. The letters for his reapplication were all made out for him by Parks, all in his very best legal form, and sent here for Malcolm to sign and forward.

And finally we come to the last problem – how am I to get to you. I will of course come the cheapest way possible, which is by bus and will cost $45. When I arrived here I had sufficient funds to get me back to Hollywood but Maurice got that almost immediately on one pretext and another and there was nothing to do about it since we were and are completely at his mercy. Part of it was to pay some bills for Malcolm, which we found out later Maurice hadn't paid at all, and the rest he simply held me up for. I cannot borrow any more money from Penny, since I sent Malcolm all I had to get back to Los Angeles and had to borrow the money from Penny for my trip here, which needless to say has not been repaid but will be. There are a limited number of people from whom I can borrow money and I am trying to locate them and see how much I can get. Malcolm is also trying everybody he can think of or locate so perhaps between us we'll dig it up. We were trying to write articles for the local newspaper and earn my fare that way but the pay is very small, the subjects are very limited, Malcolm is not a journalist and he had a titanic struggle to produce the ones he did. Malcolm feels that if he could get a job reviewing that would be a swifter compromise but that is impossible in Canada. There is apparently no literature. He also thought he might be able to sell what he calls "some of the less bloody poems" to Poetry Magazine or some such. Some of them have already rung quite loud bells in England "among them wot are a little less stern than Conrad and think him still the Young Idea." He also thought The Last Address, if the dialogue chapter Conrad spoke of were rewritten, could be sold, Whit Burnett having already virtually accepted it. We are now up to our ears in the Volcano and working like mad to get it done. We wake up in the morning talking about it and go to sleep still sitting up in bed writing. We are right in the mood and swing of it, Malcolm is writing with flying pen and a gleam in his eye and turning out work that anybody would be proud of and I think it would be criminal for him to have to stop in the middle of the book to write some articles which would take weeks of struggle. Not that he minds writing them or anything but it took him four solid weeks to produce two of them, one on Hollywood and the war, the other on Mr. Chips, more time than it has taken to accomplish 30,000 words of ebb and flood of stark narrative, as different as chalk from cheese to anything Malcolm has done and I think far better. He might never re-achieve the feeling and enthusiasm and flow that he has now were he to be interrupted and I *can't* let that happen since I feel that his work is the most important thing in his life. Especially do I feel that to be true now, when he may only have a few more months and there is so much he wants to accomplish. I help all I can, which he is nice enough to say is a lot, but which is really very little of course. He is trying to arrange a contract with the editor of the paper here for a series of articles to be written later, when the book is finished, but to be paid for in a[d]vance and which would cover my fare. If all else fails we thought perhaps Conrad could come to the rescue in this manner: we understand that Parks has a lump sum which is drawn against as needed and which will be turned over to Conrad on Malcolm's arrival. We thought that from this he might advance us just enough money for my fare, to be paid back later, but *definitely* paid back, says Malcolm, not, as in days of yore, just chalked on the wall and later confused with the ping-pong score. If he doesn't feel that he can do that we'll just have to stay here until we can raise or earn the money somehow else.

Maurice, in a burst of generosity, or conscience, said that I could stay here for two weeks after Malcolm left without paying so that gives us that much leeway, which isn't very much but every little helps. In a reaction from his gleam of sublimity the other day Maurice has gone on one of his recurrent rampages and is threatening to throw us both out of the house and bring down all sorts of dire dooms on our heads. We think he is about half crazy due to injuries received in the last war and he is an almost unbelievable character who is capable of doing very nearly anything. Phyllis is wonderful, she has been so good to us that we almost welcome these rampages because when he takes it out on us he stops beating her – she hasn't had a black eye now for a week. Well, if he's in a good mood when Malcolm leaves he'll probably let me stay for a couple of weeks and we'll just have to hope for that.

I do hope I've answered all your questions, and if I've made everything clear to you that's more than it is to us, since we are having to lay our course through a fog, surrounded by icebergs and sharks and with a storm threatening to break over our heads at any minute. But just now and then we catch a glimpse of you and Conrad, with halos round your heads and a heavenly choir in a sort of valance effect singing peace on earth good will to men, and we exist in the hope that this vision is drawing nearer in fact and not only in our fevered minds.

And once more, our love and deepest gratitude to you both.

Margerie

Textual Notes

LETTER 1

7.3–4 The crowd of faces wavered \ The crowd {of faces} wavered

7.10–11 My letter may not even interest you; \ <It> <—this> {My} letter <of mine> may not even interest you; <possibly it may strike you as [illeg.]> [the words "<—this> {My} letter <of mine>" originally appeared at the end of the clause before the semicolon; the transfer was indicated by Lowry with an arrow]

7.14 impossibility in getting \ impossibility <to get> {in getting}

7.16–17 write to tell me so. \ write <and> {to} tell me so.

7.17–18 tell me whether, if you are coming to London any time, you would \ tell me {whether,} if you are coming to London <soon> {any time}, <if> you would

7.19 away from here. \ away from <me> here.

LETTER 2

date [the envelope is postmarked 13 March 1929]

8.11–12 once general Editor \ once {general} Editor

8.18 (respectfully again) \ (respectfully {again})

8.25–26 window set between two mysterious green curtains, to the right of the head of my bed \ [the words "set between two mysterious green curtains," originally appeared after the word "bed"; the transfer was indicated by Lowry with an arrow]

8.29–30 mirror, I saw a long and never ending procession \ mirror, {I saw} a long {and never ending} procession

8.30 labouring \ labour<ed>{ing}

8.31–32 great pile for other people was \ great pile {for other people} was

9.5–6 of writing me. [—]can't express myself properly here sorry[—]\ of writing me. <You didn't like the way I asked if you would have time ever to see me in London when you might have *time* but hardly time enough to trouble about having a lunch on someone you'd never seen. I perhaps didn't make it clear enough that I'd go anywhere within my reach from Pimlico to the Isle of Dogs if only there was half a chance of seeing *you*. And then it is possible I should have sent a poſtal order in anticipation for Nocturne of Remembered Spring because even if you hadn't got it I take it even though you would have found it a nuiseance (spelling mine) you would have sent the poſtal order back which would have meant at leaſt a cautious letter of some sort on it.> {[—]can't express myself properly here sorry[—]}

9.6 But \ <Sorry> {But}

9.10 I shall say \ I <will> {shall} say

9.18 Let me \ Let <[illeg.]> me

10.10 (Remember too that \ (Remember {too} that

10.11 I know you are \ I know <that> you are

10.15 preserve this absurd idea \ preserve this <childish absur> absurd idea

10.16 for having done so.) \ for <having done> <{doing}> {having done} so.)

10.18 to be \ <is> {to be}

10.20 before you reply—if you do reply—that you are \ before you reply{—if you do reply—}that you are

11.7–8 writing anything serious they \ writing anything {serious} they

LETTER 3

[Handwritten note at top of page reads: "Original from Malc apropos material sent to C.A. at Cambridge MASS"]

12.36 Please excuse *poor* typing. \ [handwritten by Lowry at bottom of page]

enclosure [4 poems; TS H]

address [Lowry has used a St. Catharine's letterhead card; I have quoted the letterhead as the heading for the letter]

15.24 *marktplatz?.* \ <market> *marktplatz?.*

16.2 I played *hockey* \ <I have a ga> I played *hockey*

16.4 I was \ <myself> {I} was

16.17–18 in my blood; in the very plasm \ in my blood; <into> in the very plasm

16.24–25 of quilted cotton, \ of <cotton> quilted cotton,

18.11 you \ <[illeg.]> you

18.11–13 you don't mind [. . . .] Gods acre. \ [written at top of first page]

LETTER 5

19.17 run out of semen \ run out of <shot> {semen}

19.17 *la* \ <the> {*la*}

19.18 anybody \ <anything> anybody

19.19 polished; \ polished <like an apple>;

19.20 wept; so I didn't \ wept; <my good god> so I didn't

19.24 if one \ if <you> {one}

19.28 with Charlotte Haldane last night \ with Charlotte Haldane <who is> last night

20.1 reviewed it favourably in an Oxford paper *Revolt.* \ reviewed it {favourably in an Oxford paper *Revolt*}.

20.7 It is sort \ It is <a> sort

20.9 in Trinity \ in <Ca> Trinity

20.16 your having a radio: \ your having <gone> a radio:

20.17–18 & occasionaly \ & <some> occasionaly

20.18–19   who makes \ who <lets> makes

20.22   we all \ <I> we all

21.2   I have been elected the Editor \ I have been <offered> {elected} the Editor<ship>

21.4   Not only my poetic faculty \ <[illeg.]> Not <even m> only my poetic faculty

21.6   I had left up here. \ I had {left} up here.

21.10   a book \ <on> {a} book

21.12–13   as you remarked 'the most \ as you remarked <of> 'the most

21.15   aroun' \ <about> {aroun'}

21.19   Selected poems \ <s>{S}elected poems

LETTER 6

22.13   jingle, which is informing \ jingle, {which} is informing

22.19   rooted in an honest enough transmission. \ rooted in {an} honest {enough} transmission.

22.21–22   of objectifying \ of <a> objectifying [above this line is written "Wednesday."]

23.20   get directly as I can to Rye. \ get <me <<as best I may to Rye>> > directly as I can to Rye.

24.9   we shall see— \ we shall see<. . .>{—}

24.10   The preludes (which\ <The preludes (which I did not acknowledge) — & after all why should I? <<(>> is this mr demarest? not william demarest? not william demarest of Yonkers, & anyway whats' his address <<?)>> {?}> The preludes (which

24.11   jeer at me for \ jeer at me <for> for

24.18   otherwise the book would be a book of preludes \ otherwise <there would be just> {the book would be} a book of preludes

25.1   and in the latter case being without any poetry separable \ and {in the latter case being} without any poetry <which was> separable

25.7 increasingly \ <more and more> {increasingly}

25.15 & sleeps \ & sleeps<.>

LETTER 7

[On the verso of the first two pages are typed passages, one with handwritten alterations, from *Ultramarine*; the third page is written on the verso of a March 1931 cover of *St. Catharine's College Magazine*]

26.14 turn over on me \ turn over {on} me

26.16 and any other sort \ and {any} other sort

26.18 But to be specific \ {But} <T>{t}o be specific

26.19 (I) The subject \ (I) The<re are> subject

26.20 although this is \ although {this} is

26.21–22 one *Examination* but spread out \ one *Examination* {but} spread out

26.26 that period—you answer \ that period—<and> you answer

26.27 the Elizabethans—Ben Jonson & his circle \ the Elizabethans—<Shakespeare> <{Heywood}> {Ben Jonson} & his circle

26.28 Life & Thought of that period; \ Life & Thought {of that period};

27.6 the Victorians (and the Orig. Contribution). . . \ the Victorians {(and the Orig. Contribution)}. . . [the insertion is written at the bottom of the page]

27.10 What about: \ What about<?>{:}

27.10–11 like this with modifications?. \ like this {with modifications?}.

27.17 As far as I \ <From what> As far as I

27.21 moreover the time \ moreover <they> the time

27.21–22 that for answering them one has to \ that {for answering them} one has to

27.22 a mind like a sort of machine gun, \ a mind like a <machine gun to answer them> sort of machine gun,

27.30 correct this for his exam but \ correct this {for his exam} but

27.30–31 one of those things I have found \ one of those things <which <<cannot be corrected>> not> I have found

27.31 cannot be corrected but ought not to be— \ cannot be corrected but <which> ought not to be—

27.32 make him—*tee-hee!*— \ make him <as>—*tee-hee!*—

27.34 forgetting \ <failing> forgetting

28.1–2 unreasoning panics—say over the Preraphaelites—he certainly will— \ unreasoning panics <he certainly will>—say over the Preraphaelites—he certainly will—

28.5 all one can expect \ all <you> one <could> {can} expect

28.6 And even a pass \ And {even a} pass

28.8 another subject next year,—only after that does he \ another subject next year, <&>—only<—then> {after that} does he

28.13 English—thats me—& a fragment \ English{—thats me —}& a fragment

28.22 biographers \ <writers> {biographers}

29.4–5 —I wonder why she knocked at my door the last night all the same— — \ —{I} wonder wh<at>{y} she knocked at {my} door <for> the last night <though> all the same— —

29.9 pieeyed \ <pissed> pieeyed

29.10 just sat \ just <[illeg.]> sat

29.24 people once wore tights. \ people {once} wore tights.

LETTER 8

[Note written by Aiken in left-hand margin of first page: "No date: written from St Cath. College to me, at Rye— the 8 Plympton street is of course M's joke — it was *my* address in the *other* Cambridge. C.A."]

30.18 & on the whole \ {&} on the whole

30.30 experience etc. \ experience<.> {etc.}

30.31 becoming with me a desire \ becoming {with me} a desire

31.15 damn all to me now, \ damn all to me {now},

31.21–22 a week or two back side by side with \ a week or two back
<next to> side by side with

31.25 —of my own contribution \ —of my <[illeg.]> {own} contribution

31.27–28 —I can't remember it in detail but \ —I can't remember {it
in detail} <anyway> {but}

31.29 wrongly done & I \ wrongly done & <[illeg.]> I

32.1 to look at: \ to look at <it>:

32.1 this is a rather selfish \ this is {a} rather selfish

32.2–3 the rest of the paper in my opinion is well worth reading \
the rest of the paper {in my opinion} is well worth reading
<in my opinion>

32.12 I could do well without it, but as I write \ I could do {well}
without it, but <as it happ> as I write

32.16–17 to pay the debt means \ to pay the debt <or write about i>
means

32.22 a farthing, and not a halfpenny \ a farthing, and <a> not a
halfpenny

32.23–24 walking outside a Fullers café, \ walking outside <the Fu> a
Fullers café,

32.25–26 all over London or Cambridge \ all over London {or Cam-
bridge}

34.2–3 So I replied \ So I <said> replied

34.7 I am King Elephant Bag \ I am King Elephant <b>{B}ag

34.12 Moreover his letter \ <However> {Moreover} <the> {his}
letter

34.13–14 —I sent him hopefully my biography \ —I sent him {hope-
fully} my biography

34.16 If you have any notion \ <Have> {If} you {have} any notion

34.19 from Experiment \ from <mine> Experiment

35.1–2 publish the thing in the 1931 volume, American & have already \ publish the thing in <Best short> the 1931 volume, American<. But will I get forced out for being English?> & have already

35.4 O'Brien \ <[illeg.]>{O}'Brien

enclosure ["Bone Dream"; MSPC UBC. Note written by Aiken on verso: "A fragment of Great Circle (or B. Voyage? I can't find it) which Malc proposed to incorporate in Ultramarine—I said No! The interpolation at left is Malc's I think. C.A."]

35.25 no sauce, \ no <sour> sauce,

35.27–30 the ribs—'
'—like the story [. . .] heard it—'
'—and the spine [. . .] mouth, \ the ribs<,>{—'} <and the> <{And the} spine tasting like the dead sea, like ashes> {'—like the story of the <fell> <chap> {{feller}} <I dreamt about once> who dreamt he saw the results of—stop me if you've heard it—'} [this paragraph is written in the left-hand margin of the page and is the "interpolation" mentioned by Aiken above] {'—and the spine tasting like the dead sea, like ashes} in the mouth,

35.32 charcoal, \ <ashes> {charcoal},

35.36 like a woman—' \ like a woman—'
<'I knew a chap once who dreamt he saw>
(P.T.O.) [the "P.T.O." may have been added later by Aiken to direct the reader to his note on the verso]

LETTER 9

36.10 I thought Socrates \ <471>
I thought Socrates

36.10–11 sending you this. See page 471 of six plays. Its' not bad, \ sending you this. {See page 471 of six plays.} Its' not bad, [the insertion is written at the top right-hand side of the page]

LETTER 10

39.4   Gibson. \ <Wilfrid> Gibson.

39.4   I noticed \ I <[illeg.]> noticed

39.9–10   they were talking all this while about Henrik Ibsen — \
they were talking {all this while} about Henrik Ibsen—

LETTER 12

[This letter was probably not sent in this form but is
perhaps a draft for a telegram. It is written at the bottom
of a 14 February 1933 letter to Lowry from his father]

LETTER 13

[Note written by Aiken at top of first page: "3 pages
missing—C.A." On the verso of the two extant pages are
typed passages from *Ultramarine*]

41.30   who admittedly lives \ who {admittedly} lives

41.31–32   a vicariousness beyond a statement of vicariousness \ a
vicariousness beyond <vicari> a statement of vicariousness

41.33   he quite genuinely is "cuckoo" \ he quite genuinely <does
think in other peoples terms> is "cuckoo"

41.33   he *is* a poet \ he<'s> {*is*} a poet

42.1   I find it in Ultramarine however much a cento being written
\ I find it in <the book> {Ultramarine} {however much a
cento} being written

42.2   Blue Voyage \ <it> {Blue Voyage}

42.3   the other 14999? \ the other <1,49> 14999?

42.3–4   under the reign \ <with> {under} the reign

42.5   these are being absorbed \ these <have> {are} being absorbed

42.5–6   apart from its being the best \ apart from {its} being the best

42.11   (but I couldn't \ (but I <like> couldn't

42.13-14 The Waste Land. Philosophers [. . .] yourself. (Shantih \
The Waste Land. {Philosophers & tinkle tonkle etc could
be hooked out if you want them yourself.} (Shantih

42.15-16 I have sat & read \ I {have} sat & read

LETTER 14

[Letterhead reads: "VAUGHN-AIKEN, Publishers' Representative, Apartado 7162, Mexico City," MEXICO." On each
of the three pages Lowry has inserted an "a" into the
"VAUGH{a}N," and beside "AIKEN" a pun on an English
author's name as follows: "—it's a Marvell!"; "—*aherrick!*
[pardon, just a little onamatopoei<[illeg.]>{c!}]"; "—all
Donneations please to Lowry/Charlies." Note written by
Aiken at top of first page: "Sent to me by hand from
Charlie's Bar in Cuernavaca, 1937. C.A."]

44.1 But these \ But th<o>{e}se

44.2 concern for us \ concern for <you> {us}

44.13 [Oh yeah.] \ [the square brackets throughout this letter are
Lowry's, not the editor's]

44.16 death to you too; \ death to you {too};

44.24 though I can't \ though I can<no>{'}t

44.29 battle \ <battle> battle

44.34-36 what this is, [though we [. . .] pentametre,] so suppose \ what
this is, {[]though we are coming back to the iambic pentametre,[]} so suppose

45.4-10 [daughter; especially when the announcer pronounces his r's
like w's.]. \ [in the original this phrase appears in the
right-hand margin of the second page]

45.11 Some hint of something more than this is here. \ [this line
is enclosed by square brackets with "omit?" written beside it.
As this may be Aiken's annotation, I have not included this
in the text of the letter.]

45.19 I myself seeing \ <While> I myself see{ing}

45.22–24 delirium of God.
Here we are, \ delirium of God.
<(4)>
Here we are,

46.1 —(Livers at laſt [. . .] hankered!)— \ {—}(Livers at laſt of lives for which they hankered{!})){—}

46.9 my hoſt \ my <friend> {hoſt}

46.10 trying—for him, too, I guess,— \ trying{—for him, too, I guess,—}

46.16 somethink \ <[illeg.]> somethink

LETTER 15

[Note written by Margerie Lowry at top of page reads: "to Conrad Aiken 1937"]

address [Lowry has used the Hotel Francia letterhead which I have quoted as the address for the letter]

47.26 Where it does arrive it is \ Where is does {arrive} it is

LETTER 16

[This letter may never have been sent to Aiken]

48.11 end of \ end <of> {of}

48.13–20 not so churlish (churchish not richard)
        ref. Richard Church.
        ref. Landscapes Etc.
        ref. memory.
way or as it ochurls to me \ not so churlish {(churchish not richard)}
        {ref. Richard Church.
        ref. Landscapes Etc.
        ref. memory.}
way or as it ochurls to me [these indented lines are written at the top right-hand side of the page]

48.22–23 mignotorio of grief & an excu(ruci)sado of hate,— \ mignotorio {of grief} & an excu{(ruci)}sado {of hate,—}

48.23-24 Rewritten: 'excrucifiado of hate.'—Joke over. \ [written in left-hand margin]

48.24 Joke over. [Note: Excusado [. . .] lavatory.] & you \ Joke over. {[Note: Excusado is Mexican for lavatory.]} & you [the insertion is written at the bottom left-hand side of the page; the square brackets are Lowry's, not the editor's]

50.5-14 Was shot[. . . .] crack at dad? \ [written at left-hand side of bottom half of page]

50.20 And all love to her. \ And {all} love to her.

50.22 & John & Joan \ [written in bottom right-hand corner of page]

LETTER 17

[No original is available for this letter; I have therefore had to rely on Joseph Killorin's transcription in *Selected Letters of Conrad Aiken* (234)]

LETTER 18

[It is unlikely that the manuscript version of this letter in the UBC Library is the one actually received by Aiken. The beginning of this letter, from the salutation to "& Parks had guessed all that— " (59.4), has been crossed out by Lowry; however, because no revision of these passages is available, I have chosen to include them in my text. Note by Margerie Lowry in top right-hand corner of first page reads: "<autumn> March 1939"; this date is not correct]

57.4-5 the railroad being \ the railroad <was> {being}

57.6 went the most roundabout way, \ went the most <circular> {roundabout} way,

57.15 blame her,—better off \ blame her,—<I was> better off

57.15-16 but no matter. \ but <to continue> {no matter}.

57.20-22 I suffered horribly but was [. . .] Parks to Canada \ I suffered<, quite> <{mildly}> {<mildly> {{horribly}}} but was taken out of the Brown Derby & despair by a grand gal

named Margerie Bonner but no sooner had this to happen
than I was taken suddenly by Parks to Canada} [this second
insertion is written in the right-hand margin]

57.22–23   I was taken suddenly to Canada, by Parks \ I was taken
{suddenly} to Canada, {by <him> Parks}

57.23–24   this jaunt here was \ this jaunt {here} was

57.27   secret service, was & is \ secret service, {was &} is

58.2   in his feet, but also the moſt \ in his feet, {but also} the moſt

58.3   of Vancouver, \ of <the town> Vancouver,

58.7–8   All might have been well [. . .] Oxford Grouper discovered
\ <For him> All might have been well had not this <blood.>
Oxford Grouper <heel> discovered

58.8   in love with Margerie whom I hope \ in love with <one
Margerie> <a <<girl>> {swell gal} named Margerie Bonner>
<a. grand gal named> Margerie <Bonner> whom I <had left
behi> hope [although the two "a" 's above have not been
individually deleted, it would seem that they were forgotten
amongſt the other deletions, so I have chosen to represent
them as such]

58.9   stuck by me through thick & thin moſtly thin, \ stuck by me
through <all my complications> {thick & thin} {moſtly
thin},

58.10   which make \ which <made> make

58.11   comedy. When A.B. Carey \ comedy. <She is a film star,
<<late twenties,>> {of} the early thirties, had to quit because
of heart trouble; <<but>> had, <<a>> when I met her, a
secretarial job in Hollywood.> When A.B. Carey

58.11–12   discovered that I was married, as a matter of faſt \ discovered
that I was < in love with another woman & proposed to
return to her> married, as <m> {a} matter of faſt

58.13   return to another girl, \ return to <her> {another girl},

58.15   read my letters, & aſtually \ read my letters, {&} aſtually

58.17   I had the visa, to get back but A.B. Carey \ I had the visa,
{to get back} but <Carey w> A.B. <Care> Carey

58.17–18   no money. So I wired \ no money. < <<So I>> or damned
little & no accounting of what he> So I wired

58.18   the trip back to \ the trip {back} to

58.19   border \ <ord> border

58.21   the other side. \ the other side<,which>{.}

58.22–23   these baſtardos by which [. . .] as well by any means \
these baſtardos { by which I mean also the entire Oxford
Group as well} by any means

59.3   this part is very complicated, \ this {part} is very complicated
<this part>, [this deletion and insertion has been done in
pencil by Margerie]

59.4–5   later—A.B. Carey [. . .] all that— \ later—{A.B. Carey &
Parks had guessed all that—}

59.5   I now found myself then \ I {now} found myself {then}

59.6–7   we (I shall explain later) are \ we<,> {(I shall explain later)}
are

59.7–8   state more clearly that \ state {more clearly} that

59.9   a series of other circumſtances I won't \ a series of {other}
circumſtances <which> I won't

59.13   the faḴt that Jan & she \ the faḴt that <I> <{they}> {Jan &
she}

59.14   on one side, A.B. Carey on the other, and the family solicitors \ on one side, <and> A.B. Carey on the other, and <on
both sides by> the family solicitors

59.15–16   the kind with caſt iron whiſtles whiskers \ the kind with {caſt
iron whiſtles} whiskers

59.17   in one part port or another. \ in one part {port} or <noth>
another.

59.18   finish all the work, \ finish {all} the work,

59.19–20   appoint you, if you were to be found, a literary executor, and
I *had* accomplished much. \ appoint {you}, {if you were to be
found,} a literary executor, and I *had* accomplished much
<work>.

59.20–21   wash with the family, \ wash {with the family},

59.22–23   return ticket via the Berengaria, which although long since broken up as a firetrap \ return ticket <there, on> {via} the Berengaria, which although <since> long since broken up as a <f> <condemned> firetrap

59.24–25   in Mexico & turned in at Cooks in the Avenida de Madera. \ in Mexico<.> {& turned in at Cooks in the Avenida de Madera.} [this insertion is written in the right-hand margin; directly above it is written "P.T.O for 3"]

59.25–26   So, Conrad, to make a short story longer, \ So, Conrad, {to make a <long> {{short}} story longer,}

59.26–27   at the dock's dark's edge, knowing how cold the water was, I wired Margerie \ at the {dock's} dark's edge, {knowing how cold the water was,} I wired Margerie

59.28–60.1   to Vancouver, a distance rather farther than that from London to Warsaw, as I needed her, which she did. \ to Vancouver, {a distance rather farther than that from London to Warsaw,} as I needed her<.> {,} {which she did.}

60.6–7   if we're lucky. And secrecy, [. . .] Maclean. There is \ if we're lucky. {And secrecy, fom A.B. Carey & Maclean.} There is

60.7–8   including a loud speaker, a howling wind [. . .] all day, twins \ including a loud speaker, {a howling wind which rages through the house all day,} twins

60.10   Nor would you, think so, \ Nor <do we, th> would you, think so,

60.10–11   I forgot the dog, the canary, & a Hindoo timber merchant, \ I forgot the <{hound}> dog, the <{bloated}> canary, & a Hindoo <credit> timber merchant,

60.12   Corpus Christi, Oxford—you can't get away from Oxford— \ Corpus Christi, Oxford{—you can't get away from Oxford—}

60.13   hoping, with his fine Oriental calm, \ hoping, <in his> with his fine Oriental calm,

60.14   paid for the wood. \ paid for the wood. <Richly as I deserve hell fire, & like it, this Kafka <<like>> set up is really getting me down.> [crossed out in lower left-hand margin]

60.15 therefore, as you might guess, more or less \ therefore, {as you might guess,} more or less

60.16 we have stoutish hearts \ we <muſt> have stout{ish} hearts

60.18–19 because once it is known by A.B. Carey— \ because <if> {once} it is known <that> by <Car> A.B. <{Oxford Group}> Carey—

60.20–21 deported, since she is by now in Canada illegally, to parts unknown, \ deported, {since she is {{by now}} in Canada illegally,} to parts unknown, [this insertion is written in the right-hand margin]

60.22 lineaments of laſt weeks love \ lineaments of <love> laſt weeks love

60.22–23 week before, not *that* that one day \ week before, <it is> not *that* <we> that one day

60.24 found—there was \ found{—} <drowned.> there was

60.25 tenderly out of the toilet—myſteriously drowned, \ tenderly <out of the> <{from}> <toilet, it is not the radio> {out of} <the bottom of> the toilet— myſteriously drowned,

60.25–27 —not that the oversexed Hindoo has an axe downſtairs & that [. . .] the sound of \ —<it is> not that the {oversexed} Hindoo has an axe downſtairs {& that we know he intends to use it} <or> {nor} that the sound of

60.28 Maurice Carey, who is \ Maurice Carey, <{wh}> who is

60.29 a disability, and how, has \ a disability, {and how,} has

60.31–32 several thousand times,—not misery, oh Demareſt—and is \ several thousand times,{—not <the> misery, <[illeg.]> oh Demareſt—}and is

60.32–33 of the loſt, not all the bells and clashes of the night, which appal us: \ of the loſt, {not all the bells and clashes of the night, <not this not that,>} which appal<s> us:

60.33–34 the thought rather of the \ the thought {rather} of <{rather}> the

60.35–61.2 communication, and the thought also that a sentence which is beginning [. . .] our lives out. \ communication <{(Even with you)}>, and the thought {also} that {a sentence which} is beginning (with of course the above reservations) to be fair, may at <one> {any} moment be finished with a blot: that will <wreck> {ſtamp} our lives out<,>{.}

61.2-3 But from brass bedſteads to brass tacks. \ But<, my dear> from brass bedſteads to brass tacks. [it is unclear whether the two "brass" 's were meant to be deleted or not, so I have chosen to leave them in the text]

61.3 For by now you can see by now \ For {by now} you can see by now [this sentence was originally written in pencil by Margerie and then traced over in pen by Malcolm; the "by now" insertion was done by Malcolm]

61.10-11 I agreed to this as at the time \ I agreed to this <[illeg.]> {as} at the time

61.13 certain methods to solve them \ certain methods <not> <not som> to <assuage> {solve} them

61.16 like, this one is borrowed, \ like, {this one is borrowed,}

61.17 control of the money, we \ control of <it> {the money}, we

61.20-21 help us (& try [. . .] to you), & we are \ help us {(& try & realise that <is> {{your help}} is not juſt help, only, I muſt see *you* & also owe a duty to you)}, & we are [this insertion is written in the right-hand margin]

61.23 without money, & were she [. . .], she would \ without money, & <if s> were she deported <to Los Angeles, whi> {it would be to} Hollywood, she would [although Lowry neglected to delete the firſt "to" above, it is clear from the layout and sense of the sentence that he meant to do so]

61.26-28 nervous collapse, though [. . .] & I \ nervous collapse, {though cheerfulness is always breaking in} & I know that if Margie {(whom you & Mary would adore)} & I

61.29 friend of yours, or somewhere \ friend of yours, <or> {or} somewhere

61.30 seeing me again, or near \ seeing me again, {or} near

61.31 loss, which she \ loss, <she> which she

61.31–32 break up because—but why go on? We would both break. \
          break up <{& so would I}> because <I know she would>
          {—{{but}}} why go on?} <not {now} have initiave left
          <<{to}>> even to try for a job: in fact, we would both <<go
          under>> > {We would both} break{.}<on a psychological reef
          of continual anxiety.>

61.32–34 I would take any [. . .] recruits. \ I would take {any} <now,
          could you write my father & say> one, but I cannot {because
          of my status here}: nor are they taking any more recruits.

61.34   recruits. I have frequently \ recruits. <I have frequently
          wanted to go to New York or Boston, but have been foiled
          by Parks, who would {not} let me get hold <<where I would
          be touch with friends of yours & get a job:>> enough where
          I would be in touch with friends of yours, & get a job, but
          have been foiled always by Parks, who would not trust me
          with the money, {& never seemed to able to earn any at the
          right moment} & the family idea was I would be free lancing
          around & "not under proper supervision." {(Yes, it has come
          to that.)} It is queer, when all I wish is to be independent,
          that I should be placed now in a position where it is impossi-
          ble.> I have frequently

61.35   with friends of yours \ with <friends> {friends} of yours

62.6   goings on, that I \ goings on, <would be> that I

62.11–12 by cable, (a little long perhaps) which \ by cable, {(a little
          long perhaps)} which

62.12–13 among other things which may occur to you, \ among other
          things <that may> {which may} occur to you,

62.16   your position would be to \ your position {would be} to

62.20–21 my income, if any, for \ my income, {if any,} for

62.26–27 being rendered unable to finish all my work, but unable \
          being <rendered unable to finish my work> <{rendered}>
          {rendered} unable to finish all my work, but <if I we> unable

62.28–29 or that the definite understanding \ or <(4) [illeg.]> that the
          definite understanding

62.31   my going East on my own hook before to see \ my going
          {East} on my own hook before <to I> to see

62.35 people who are interested in my work. \ people who are
<{(5)}> interested in my work.

62.38 because of health or status, \ because of <health of> {health
or} status,

62.40 your own home is only \ your own home is <near> only

63.1 again taking recruits, \ again taking <more> recruits,

63.3-4 army but it probably would not be tactful \ army but it <is
[illeg.]> probably would <{(6)}> not be tactful

63.7 to my father that \ to my father <w>{t}hat

63.12 situation, which is intolerable & hopeless, but \ situation,
{which is intolerable & hopeless,} but [this insertion is
written in the right-hand margin]

63.13-14 to make any statement of my own side \ to make any
<explan> statement of my own <si> side

63.18 done to me, that my \ done to me, that <I> my

63.26-27 understand me, & if I am to go to the war, you would like
me at least \ understand me, <or can> & if I am to <the> go
to the war, you would like me <to> at least

63.30-31 in England, as I stated to them when war broke out, but \ in
England, {as I stated to them when war broke out,} but [this
insertion is in the right-hand margin]

63.32 Boston is be the \ Boston <would> {is} be the

63.35-36 *drink*, that if there is \ *drink*, that {if} there is

63.36-37 from what you \ from what <he> {you}

64.4 the family as you probably have gathered, are not \ the family
{as you probably have gathered,} are not

64.7 —so \ —<So>{so}

64.8 secret for the time being \ secret for the <moment and you>
time being

64.10 I would be at least thousands \ I would be <thousands> at
least thousands

64.13 sprung up between us \ sprung {up} between us

64.14–15 you knew I was fundamentally unhappy \ you knew <, first that I would be [illeg.] unhappy fundamentally with her, then which> <that> I was fundamentally unhappy

64.16–17 upon you practically to the point of betraying our friendship, for my self-conceit, \ upon you <almost> {practically} to the point of <betrayal> betraying <*my*> {our} <own> friendship, for <you [illeg.]> my <own> self-conceit,

64.18 I know now that all \ I know now <thatl> that all

64.21 life & sanity. We are \ life & sanity<;>{.} <I do sincerely> <I am perfectly adj> We are

64.22 happy: And she is \ happy: <the only thing wrong is [illeg.]> <she helps me {marvellously} with my work & I want to work as I> And she is

64.23 you always wanted me \ you always <wan> wanted me

64.24 the right gal: & I do have \ the right gal: & I <have the ri> do have

64.25 just waking from a nightmare; \ just waking <from a> <{out}> from a nightmare;

64.25–26 this God awful environment of rain and fear, for although we fear \ this <god> God awful environment <of abysmal nothingness, if we could only be near you> of rain and fear, <though> {for although} we fear

[written upside-down in bottom left-hand corner of page and deleted:

c/o Sgt. Major Carey. [illeg.]
don't forget the Mauri.
595 W 19th Avenue.
Vancouver. B.C.
Canada.]

64.27 dead truth, its \ dead truth, <the> its

64.4–28 [An earlier draft of this paragraph reads as follows: "The family are not likely to take kindly to the idea of my marrying again so soon after one marital disaster, {but in this connection it should be mentioned that I can't anyhow, having only {{as I said}} an interlocutory decree I can't be married for a

year} the more especially since Park's & Jan's <law> Jewish
lawyer obviously collused about the whole matter <inl> <&>
railroad<ing>{ed} my Father behind my back into paying
<for the dam> a large cash settlement to Jan—there had been
a verbal agreement between Jan & myself <that it could have
been> {to} settle<d> {the thing} out of court <&> {with}
merely <the lawyers fees payed> a small sum pay<ed>{able}
<a> {to a lawyer by myself which of course Parks wouldn't
truſt me with} it was subsequent to this that Parks got *me*
out of the states, <—> devilish clever of him too{) [inserted
in pencil]}—So besides everything else we muſt keep Margie a secret for the moment & you muſt not mention her in
<my> {your [inserted in pencil by Margerie]} letter. (It would
also be as well to say that with you I would be thousand of
miles away from Jan, of whom you thoroughly disapproved
& againſt whom you had warned me <I> {again & again—
that she had been the source of a sort of antagonism that
sprang up between us at one time {{that would have}}
conſtituted <praſtically> {{almoſt}} a betrayal of
<one>{{your}}self by me had you not known my motives so
well—} so that there would be no possible chance of my
seeing her again.) . . . {([inserted in pencil]} Finally, I want
to say this, that my plans for the future *muſt* include Margie
{whom Parks vaguely knows & disapproves of}: not only
<does [crossed out in pencil]> our devotion to each other is
the only thing holding me to life and sanity {) [inserted in
pencil]} <& of course [crossed out in pencil]> it is partially
because of the things she did which I may say were
monſtrosities that I am in my present condition financially
& physically. Moreover, I do want to say this, that my work,
if I can get hold of it is in good shape: that I do sincerely want
to make myself utterly independent of the old man but that
he has put me in an impossible position to do it{— [inserted
in pencil]}: <that> {but [inserted in pencil by Margerie]}
since I can't be married for a year it is absurd to suppose that
I should remain entirely away from Margerie for that time:
{& [inserted in pencil by Margerie]} that, if I have to enliſt,
I want to marry before I go, so that she can draw my pay.
But this is {all} for your private ear: & as for the war,
considering the way England has treated me, I am now in a
far worse position than anyone under a Nazi regime—I have

to account & double account, even for toothpaste—"] [This paragraph is written in ink; the pencilled insertions are probably Margerie's]

64.29-65.5 Of course [. . . .]last time. \ [these paragraphs are written in pencil by Margerie. A note written by Malcolm in pen at the bottom of the page reads: "— <Bit.> Clarify this"]

64.29 Of course \ <I hate to mention the war to you> Of course

64.29 join up to fight \ join up <and> {to} fight

64.33 we can & definitely be \ we can & <certainly> {definitely} be

65.4 quick before \ quick <f> before

[portion of a letter from Maurice Carey to Arthur O. Lowry (Malcolm's father) typed and crossed out at top of page: "a bottle of very cheap hair oil as it did to plan and launch the battle of the Somme area. Since I have obtained Mr. Carey's full approval as to my capabilities in certain matters, I must insist that I am given equal credit as to my capabilities to determine the extent and nature of his needs without the embarrassment of such petty scenes. It is unfortunate that your appointee, Colonel Victor McLean is now occupied in military duties and therefore unable to collaborate with me, but I can assure you that it is definitely my intention to aid Malcolm in his expressed desire to serve his country at this critical period, giving him the advantage of my own experience in the last war in order that he may be better equipped to take care of himself proficiently in this one."]

65.6 I have some other ideas about \ I have some <other> other ideas <of> about

65.7 by cable, a one, which would suggest \ by cable, a <cable> {one}, which <,[illeg.]> would suggest

65.9 that you had seen my publishers \ that <my publishers> you had seen my publishers

65.11 I could then stay with you: \ I could {then} stay with you:

65.11-12 or perhaps put a publisher, [. . .] up to sending \ or <the>

perhaps <get> {put} a publisher, or Bernice, or Linscott, or someone wholly imaginary, <simply> up to sending

65.14   Any of these things \ Any of these <ruses> things

65.16   far more my father \ far more <f> my father

65.17–18   engineered from there financially; it has been done before: \ engineered <by y> from there {financially}<:>{;} <You could> {it has been done before} <to both our <<adv>> advantage>:

65.19   the perfect reconciliation, \ the perfect <adjustment> {reconciliation},

65.20   or to a new life: \ or {to} a <happy life.> <per> new life:

65.21   this would be, in reality, \ this would <really> be, <another> in reality,

65.24–25   that time, & I do want for her sake [. . .] marry her, & if \ that time, & <I do> I <do want to stay out of the army now that> do want {for her sake} to stay out of the army long enough to marry her, <now that> & if

65.27–28   volunteered in both England & Canada & been refused \ volunteered <& been tur> in both England & Canada & <I can't do more tha> been refused

65.30   to avoid the possibility of the deportation angle, would it \ to avoid the <deportation angle> possibility of the deportation angle, <would it not, if I could get hold <<[illeg.]>> of a hundred dollars or so> would it

65.31–32   that if can lay my hands \ that if <I could lay> can lay my hands

65.34–35   like hell on the old man. \ like hell on the <ol> old man.

65.36   if I tragically cannot, \ if I {tragically} cannot,

65.36–40   I could by that time [. . .] point of vantage, \ I could <get as> by that time possibly have amassed enough money to get <far East in Canada> sufficiently far East in Canada, to be <near Margie; but she at any rate> not more than a nights journey from Margie{,}<—and yourself,> Mary & yourself, {—I am presuming of course you could find somewhere for Margie to stay in the meanwhile,—} & from that point of <view> vantage,

65.41–66.1 over again? If this [. . .] yourself. \ over again? {If this isn't too much of a <terrible> presumption on Mary & yourself.} [this insertion in right-hand margin]

66.2–3 by the way, quite bluntly, that you feel definitely from my letter, that now it has turned impossible \ by the way, <that <<I have stated>> you feel <<to you>> > quite bluntly, <that I am> <if I am thwarted in my wish now to see you & com> that you feel definitely {from my letter}, that <now the army> {now it} has turned <out> impossible

[typewritten at top of this page and carbon-copied upside-down at bottom of following page: "I am sent to save my father, t find my son, to heal the eternal horror of three, to resolve the immedicable horror of three, to resolve the"]

66.9 Under the Volcano & a play: \ Under the Volcano {& <the> {{a}} play}:

66.11–12 Bernice. As this is, among other things, [. . .] Melville, \ Bernice. <So by> {As this} <next week sometime I should be> is, <about a man's> among other things, about a man's hysterical identification with Melville, <I would be grateful if you would pass it on to Harry Murray, if you think it would be of interest.>

66.13 Harry Murry, & would \ Harry Murry <too>, & would

66.15 So, Conrad, \ <Well> {So}, Conrad,

66.15 please help. So deeply \ please help. < <<I know deeply>> {So deeply} <<in my heart <<<that>>> {do I know that} yours is the only>> {do I feel that yours is the *only*} help <<I can turn to>> in this crisis, <<I feel almost as though>> {I sense that} my heart had made provision for so turning to you in the end by its first journey to the Cape.> So deeply

66.16 we can guide our bark on \ <I> {we} can guide <my> {our} bark on

66.16 now I sense that \ now <without foundering> <I feel almost as though, by {so} turning to you <<in>> {at} the end, that <<my>> my heart had made provision fo> I sense that

66.18–19 & lives worth saving, & lives \ & <ones> {lives} worth saving, <if you make your appeal desperate enough to the old man.> & lives

66.19–20   thank you from the bottom of my heart for \ thank you <for> {from the bottom of my heart} {for}

66.20–21   already made:
My very beſt \ already made: <All>
My very beſt

66.21   to Mary, I have \ to Mary, <[illeg.]> I have

66.22–67.1   do you send \ do you <both> send

67.5   'Reading a book'? \ 'Reading a book<?>'?

67.9   hazard. \ <*mazard*> {hazard.}

67.11   The thing \ <[illeg.]> The thing

67.18–19   A   , for better or worse
B   A thousand lines \ <B>{A}   , for better or <for> worse
            <A>{B}   A thousand lines

67.22   Numbers \ <n>{N}umbers

68.1–36   P.S. Since [. . . .] despair. \ [this paragraph is typewritten with all alterations done by Lowry in green ink]

68.1   letter laſt \ letterlaſt [typo.]

68.3   like the poſtulated end \ like the {poſtulated} end

68.3–6   in which K. was dying, [. . .] write. he was too worn out to write. \ in which {K. was dying, surrounded by the villagers, worn out with the struggle, <but> which Kafka himself was too worn out to write.} he was too worn out to write.

68.6   we are staying in \ <To tell the brutal truth,> we are ſtaying in

68.12   which is \ whichis [typo.]

68.14–15   a strange & [. . .] ugly country \ a strange {& believe me damned hoſtile & ugly} country

68.17–18   and if I tell the truth about him, \ and {if} I tell the truth about him{,}

68.18   should have \ shouldhave [typo.]

68.20   no choice \ nochoice [typo.]

68.20   in this matter, \ in th<e>{is} matter,

68.22   it has turned as you see. \ it has turned <out for the worse> {as you see}.

68.22–23   I actually fear as for, different reasons, I feared A.B. Carey— trusting to trusting him \ I actually fear {as for, different reasons, I feared A.B. Carey— trusting} to trust{ing} him

68.25   staying but where shall \ staying but {where} shall

68.25–26   receive mail, and better send another \ receive mail <{there}>, and <perhaps> {better send} another

68.27–28   help. We had an understanding about this. Or \ help. {We had an understanding about this.} Or

68.29   all of us, \ allof us, [typo.]

68.30–34   Sea? Or can you [. . .] most of it. But \ Sea? {Or can you [. . .] most of it.} But

68.35–36   for the last time into this more than sea, this Sargasso sea of despair. \ for the last time<.> into this <{[illeg.]}> <Sargasso s> more <{more}> <than> {than} <Sargasso> sea{,} <of despair> this Sargasso sea of despair.

68.37–69.6   We huddle [. . . .] on us— \ [written in green ink in lower half of page]

68.38–39   icy rain which hasn't stopped for days doesn't even bring melancholy any longer: \ icy <and continuous> rain {which hasn't stopped for days} doesn't even bring melancholy any <longer.> <more> {longer}:

69.1   damp, muscles contract \ damp, <our> muscles contract

69.3–5   (because of a "war" injury caused by falling off a streetcar) is having one of his 'crazy fits', \ (because of a "war" injury<)> {caused <probably> by falling off a streetcar {()}} <when plastered)>} is having one of his <mad> {'crazy} fits',

69.5   "fictitious people," etc. Now \ "fictitious people," etc. <Useless,> Now

69.6–7   So you see, as well as snow there is fog. \ [written in lower left-hand margin]

LETTER 19

[No original is available for this letter; I have therefore had to rely on Joseph Killorin's transcription in *Selected Letters of Conrad Aiken* (236)]

LETTER 20

71.8   T[h]e \ Tne [typo.]

71.24   opinion, \ opini<l>{o}n,

71.34   adolesc[e]nt \ adolescdnt [typo.]

72.3   let's let in \ <:>{l}et's let in

72.3   high time \ high<t> time

LETTER 21

72.36   that it would be advisable for me *anyhow* \ that <anyhow> it would be advisable for me {*anyhow*}

73.1   Eye? \ Eye<.>{?}

73.4   meantime, \ meantime{,}

73.20   b[r]ings \ beings [typo.]

73.28   the copy \ the cop<u>{y}

73.34   the version you have, \ the version you have{,}

74.2   Shitehouse, \ Shitehouse{,}

74.25   anyhow,- \ anyhow,{-}

74.32   more moral, \ more moral{,}

74.34   f[or]m \ from [typo.]

74.41   Vancouver! \ Vancouver<.>{!}

75.25–36 As ever [. . . .] Dicktasters! \ [handwritten in ink at end of letter]

LETTER 22

[No original is available for this letter; I have therefore had to rely on Joseph Killorin's transcription in *Selected Letters of Conrad Aiken* (240)]

LETTER 23

78.8   it is a genuine \ it {is} a genuine

79.29   Surely, this being so, it will \ Surely{, this being so,} it will

80.8–9   your letter, — and I have to thank you also, for this,—since
\ your letter, { — and I have to thank you also, for this, — }
since

80.10–11   with Margie, (behind which [. . .] kindness.) were Margie \
with Margie, {(behind which thought do not think I do not
also detect the hand of loving kindness.)} were Margie [this
insertion written in left-hand margin]

80.12   you don't *know* after all! \ you don't *know* {after all}!

80.12–13   trouble, gave me a neat \ trouble, {gave me} a neat

80.13–14   relationship I might subconsciously \ relationship I {might}
subconsciously

80.14   Margie's reaction as it should be was \ Margie's reaction {as
it should be} was

LETTER 25

85.26–27   cuties — strange typographical error! — remain to me, \
cuties { — strange typographical error! — } remain to me,

85.35   is now in \ is no<t>{w} in

87.30   [s]hould \ whould [typo.]

87.32–33   the Parks that Be then that, \ the P<owers>{arks} that Be
{then} that,

88.12–13   glad, finally, that you were good enough to make the agreement with him. \ glad, finally, that <[illeg.]> {you were good
enough to make} the agreement with <[illeg.]>{him}.

LETTER 26

[No original is available for this letter; I have therefore had
to rely on Joseph Killorin's transcription in *Selected Letters
of Conrad Aiken* (241)]

LETTER 27

90.31 My dear Conrad ———\ My dear Conrad{ ——— }

91.17 Parks is trusted \ <Now> Parks is trusted

91.21 pr[o]ving \ priving [typo.]

91.27 contempt (and pity), \ contempt {()and pity()},

92.24–25 the truth to A.B.Carey \ the truth <of> {to} A.B.Carey

92.26 sentimentalist \ sent<a>{i}mentalist

93.5–8 surprising, (a manner [. . .] characters) which seemed to us almost sublime! \ surprising, {()a manner [. . .] characters()} which seemed to us almost sublime<.>{!}

93.11 heard some queer excerpts \ heard some <almost equally {"}sublime{"}> {queer} excerpts

93.13 such complicated verbs as to be, \ such complicated <predicates as the> verb{s} {as} to be,

93.14–16 spell blackguard [. . .] posted it. \ spell <the repr[illeg.]> blackguard, was actually <[illeg.]> {improving it}, and by now may well have <done> {posted it}.

93.40 as best I may, \ as best I may{,}

93.41 painful story, \ painful story{,}

94.28–29 cracked rib [. . .] but I was \ cracked rib <which> {()her husband had cracked {this} for her three months previously, {though}()} <and> {but} I was

94.29–30 for the female some days \ for the female <for the female> some days

94.32–33 Fortunately it was [. . .] and Parks, \ {Fortunately it was only a localized row, no police, or anything like that, and} Parks,

95.4 New York, — I had [. . .]time, — \ New York,{ — }I had [. . .] time,{ — }

95.7–8 criminal offence. \ criminal offence <1>.

95.8 could I do?) \ could I do?{()}

95.12 at this, \ at this{,}

95.13–15   something [. . .] it did not alter \ something{,} <{()>which {however} might have happened to anybody<{)}>}{,} <but it did> {upon the aunts and proſtitutes at home, it did} not alter

95.18–19   needed in the sense you suggeſt, the only \ needed {in the sense you suggeſt,} the only

95.19   any rescue \ <the> {any} rescue

95.24   dislike to *beg*, \ dislike to *beg*{,}

95.27–28   did not write me[—]I mean you, personally, didn't: not Mary.[—]after \ did not write me[—]{I mean you, personally, didn't: not Mary.}[—]after [this insertion written in left-hand margin]

95.39   exploited, \ ex<[illeg.]>{ploi}ted,

96.5   alas, \ alas{,}

96.11   deceives \ dec<ie>{ei}ves

96.13   intercourse. \ intercourse{.}

96.18   exhortations \ ex{hor}t<or>{a}tions

96.31   yet to meet the teetotaler \ yet to meet <a> {the} teetotaler

96.32   truſt. However. So much then, \ truſt. {However.} So much then,

96.34   'obliquity' \ {'}obliquity{'}

96.38   rheumatic bosom, \ rheumatic bosom{,}

97.3   blame you in \ blame you <for> in [this deletion is made on the typewriter]

97.6–7   (non-infeðious) sort of *atrophy* [. . .] in them parts. \ {(}non-infeðious{)} <f>{s}or<m>{t} of *atrophy*{,} approaching infantile paralysis{,} which sometimes is the accompaniment of rheumatic fever in th<ose>{em} parts.

97.12   precipice \ precip<a>{i}ce

97.22   ridiculous \ r<e>{i}diculous

97.23–24   I muſt add \ I <need scarcely> {muſt} add

97.28 expense, \ expen<c>{s}e,

97.30 their words, \ their words{,}

97.31 truth, \ truth{,}

97.39 myself \ <M>{m}yself

97.39–98.3 to come. (Another thing [. . . .] be proved.) \ to come. {(Another thing I have heard about myself. That I had got into trouble with the <[illeg.]> Police, due to drink. I never have. {{Except once, years ago, at college.}} It is a bloody lie. And {{it}} can be proved.)} [the insertion, "Except once, years ago, at college.", is written in the top right-hand corner of the page]

98.10 If it so be that some money \ If <so be> it {so be} that some mo<[illeg.]>{ne}y

98.13 willing and even eager to support *me*, until \ willing and {even} eager to support *me*{,} until

98.20 and do freely \ and {do freely}

98.26 natural generosities \ natur<e>{a}l genero<u>sities

98.31 proteſt about it. \ proteſt <for harboring her> {about it}.

98.33 knows \ {k}nows

99.1 waive \ <wave> {waive}

99.3–4 these self-same extenuating circumſtances. \ the{se} {self-same} extenuating circumſtances{.} <of the war>

99.11 digeſted \ digeſte{d}

99.19 tha[t] \ thas [typo.]

99.35 'disease of integrity.' \ {'}disease of integrity.{'}

100.3 that war, once more, \ that war{,} once more{,}

100.9 work in which Margie \ work<.> {in which} Margie

100.15 peace that we waſted our time with \ peace that <[illeg.]> <one> {we} waſted <one's> {our} time with

100.16 of which we are bitterly \ of which <one is> {we are} bitterly

100.30–31 to queer Stuart's marriage, which turned out well, \ to <bitch> {queer} Stuart's marriage, which turned out well{,}

100.32   (He was \ <'>{(}He was

101.11   my own) \ my o<[illeg.]>{wn})

101.15   dispense \ dispen<c>{s}e

101.16   you would probably suggeſt, \ you would <be forced to>
{probably} suggeſt{,}

101.20   your own hands and I \ your own hands <as> {and} I

101.23   cope with, \ cope with{,}

101.25   approval \ approv<l>{al}

101.27   saying, At night \ saying, <a>{A}t night

101.28   while a passing relationship \ while <my> {a passing} relationship

101.34   I feel you have come to hold \ I feel you <[illeg.]> {have come
to} hold

102.5   reiterated thanks \ reiterated than<[illeg.]>{ks}

102.11   prophesied \ proph<[illeg.]>{e}sied

102.12   litel book, \ litel book{,}

102.17–22   with Both our Loves [. . . .] p.c. \ [handwritten in ink at end
of letter]

LETTER 28

[No original is available for this letter; I have therefore had
to rely on Joseph Killorin's transcription in *Selected Letters
of Conrad Aiken* (242)]

LETTER 29

104.22   Dick Eberhart \ Dick Eberhar<d>{t}

104.26   another f[or]m \ another from [typo.]

104.29   Richards, \ Richards<on>{,}

104.29   thumb," \ thum<g>{b},"

LETTER 30

105.32 of snow \ o<r>{f} snow

106.3 unit, \ unit<e>,

106.5 go over \ go {o}ver

106.9 your talents \ you{r} talents

106.10 useful \ usefu{l}

106.22 I was ill \ I was <both> ill

106.23 some reason \ so{m}e reason

107.10 So, \ So{,}

107.11 meanwhi[l]e \ meanwhioe [typo.]

107.14 A[n]d much \ Abd much [typo.]

LETTER 31

110.26–27 help us. That is, all save the genius stuff; but the new book *is* going well. We are \ help us. {That is, all save the genius stuff; but the new book *is* going well.} We are [this insertion is handwritten at bottom right of page]

110.30 expenditures \ <[illeg.]> {expenditures}

LETTER 32

111.10–12 Dear Conrad and Mary: (Apologies [. . .] *both*) \ Dear Conrad and Mary: {(Apologies in advance, Mary, for this self-conscious 'Waile of a letter' which contains TOmch I have no right to bore you with — only I wanted it to be to you *both*)}

112.20 'immorality' \ {'}immorality{'}

112.22 somewhere \ <a place> {somewhere}

112.25 not enough action, \ not enough action{,}

113.16 taking with me \ taking <we> {with} me

113.18 saleable; \ sal{e}able;

113.23–25   your own unities [. . .] painful, etc., \ your own unit{ies & health} such as the Summer School, {your book, the impending dental misery which we hope will not turn out too <[illeg.]> painful,} etc.,

113.26–28   Lady of the Snows, (in [. . .] in Summer. \ <l>{L}ady of the <s>{S}nows{,} {()in the not remote Montreal regions which I underſtand are very beautiful,()} might have held some possibility of attraction for yourselves<.> {in Summer.}

114.9   beſt for me? \ beſt for me<.>{?}

114.41   Doſtoievskish M., Carey, \ Doſtoievskish M.{,} Carey{,}

115.12   If you only knew \ <My [illeg.]> <i>{I}f you only knew

116.8   Yours very weſt of Eden \ [handwritten at end of letter]

LETTER 33

[No original is available for this letter; I have therefore had to rely on Joseph Killorin's transcription in *Selected Letters of Conrad Aiken* (244)]

LETTER 34

117.23–25   Athenia [. . .] in In Ballaſt! \ Athenia leaves {The} same port, sinks in {the} same place with Norse boat to the rescue{,} as Arcturian in In Ballaſt<.>{!}

117.31   Pyrrhus \ Pyrr{h}us

117.32   Pyrrhus \ Pyrr{h}us

118.5   One mentioned, \ One mentioned{,}

118.6   Pyrrhus \ Pyrr{h}us

118.19–20   "That when Venus \ {"}That when Venus

119.10–11   Or thought it not worth expressing. \ [this sentence is handwritten in ink]

119.13   I gather from *Life* that \ I gather {from *Life*} that

119.18   in Time this week, \ in Time <with> {this} week,

119.32   The Volcano is rapidly reaching its laſt belch. \ [this sentence is handwritten in ink]

LETTER 35

120.13 heard from Parks, \ heard <word> from Parks, [this deletion is done on the typewriter]

120.26 someone. \ som{e}one.

120.27 jeopardize \ jeopardi<n>ze

120.32 return \ ret<i>{u}rn

120.39 whatsumever, \ whatsume<e>ver,

LETTER 36

122.12 melancholy \ mel<[illeg.]>{a}ncholy

122.31 Paris change, mais rien de ma mélancholie, s'a bougé. . . \ Paris change{,} mais r<ei>{ie}n de ma mélancolie, s'a{/}bougé. {. .} [Lowry has added a slash mark by hand to separate "s'a" and "bougé"]

122.34 Love zu haus zu haus. \ Love<,> <Z>{z}u haus <z>{z}u haus.

LETTER 37

123.11 *"The Conversation* \ {"}<t>{T}*he Conversation*

123.16–18 unnoticed (and of course in being unfinished. This Queen Elizabeth analogy is getting us into trouble but it means well!) and may it \ unnoticed {(and of course in being unfinished. This Queen Elizabeth analogy is getting us into trouble but it means well!)} and may it [this insertion is handwritten in the top left-hand corner of page]

123.23–27 (Here:
     Ott flies to Dimaggio,
     Rippla pops to Dimaggio,
     Mcmathy flies to Dimaggio, —
     No runs, no hits, no errors.) \ [these lines are handwritten at the end of the letter before the signature]

LETTER 38

[postcard of the "Ruinas de Mitla" in Mexico; addressed to:

Mary Hoover Aiken
c/o G. Wilbur.
South Dennis
Massachusetts.
U.S.A.]

date [poſtmarked 23 March 1940]

124.10 Or some new patterns \ {Or some new} patterns

LETTER 39

124.31 I've \ I'<b>{v}e

124.33 am still \ am<d> still

124.34 find that \ find t<j>{h}at

124.35 operation \ operati{o}n

124.35 fibroids \ fibr<p>{o}ids

LETTER 40

125.28 & a funny pome \ {&} a funny pome

126.1 damn it, to the purse, \ damn it, <though> to the purse,

126.16–17 maliciousness \ <[illeg.]>{m}aliciousness

126.21–23 (This time [. . . .] Poor Malc.) \ {(}This time it is parasitic however on some of your wisecracks in Mexico, {&} upon your political opinions! Poor Malc.{)}}

126.31–32 in connećtion with this for the day after I'd written that scene \ in connećtion with this {for the} <D>{d}ay after I'd written th<is>{at} scene

127.1 by name, \ <in> {by} name,

127.12–13 dramatic reason) \ dramatic reason <[illeg.]>) [this deletion is made on the typewriter]

127.17 similarities or NUANCES \ similarities {or NUANCES}

129.3–4 to Mary, to whom a letter goes on same poſt and \ to Mary, {to whom a letter goes on same poſt} and

129.8   Both our loves \ [this is handwritten in ink]

129.12–13   You Said you were [. . . .] S. Dennis. \ You Said you were ſtaying at Commonwealth Av. till 8th. This {is} 9th, so {we} send it to S. Dennis. [these sentences are handwritten in ink at end of letter]

enclosure   [poem; TS H]

LETTER 41

130.18   application \ appl{i}cation

130.21   Canada, \ Canada{,}

130.25–26   through Blaine, – near Vancouver [. . .] here \ through Blaine, <here,> – near <Vn> Vancouver – that he has manipulated all this so that I would be kept here<,>

130.27   said \ sai<s>{d}

130.28   informed! \ informed<.>{!}

130.29   done, however, \ done{,} however{,}

130.33   sake of preserving \ sake of <the> preserving

130.34   something like \ something <as> {like}

130.35   Thoma's story. . (. Both \ Thoma's story. {. (.} Both

131.4   said the boy. \ said t<[illeg.]>{he} boy.

131.6   right.'. \ right{.}'{.}

131.7   said: 'Only \ said{: '}<o>{O}nly

131.9   maſter were \ maſte{r} were

131.17   position. . .) \ position. . .{)}

132.4   from my work that I can't \ from my work<,> {that} I can't

LETTER 42

133.2   so there[']s \ so there(s [typo.]

133.15   ope[r]ation \ ope ation [typo.]

LETTER 43

134.19 a prophet. \ a p<h>{r}ophet.

135.4 from that quarter. \ from <any> {that} quarter.

135.4–5 may give the O M some \ may give <him> {the O M} some

135.17–19 Venuti swings,
           yours,
                Malc. \ Venuti swings,{/}yours,
                        Malc.
    [Lowry has inserted a slash between "swings," and "yours,"
    to indicate a movement of the second phrase to a lower line]

LETTER 44

136.9 mattress \ m<e>{a}ttress

136.11 E.C. \ [This is not a typo. for "W.C.," but is the abbreviation
    for "earth-closet," meaning outhouse]

136.16 cranberrey bog, \ cranberrey bog{,}

136.16 below, \ below{,}

137.4 rheumatically \ rheumat{i}cally

LETTER 45

138.5–6 Blue Voyage. — (I am trying [. . .] Conversation.) \ Blue
    Voyage.{ — (I am trying to get the Province to let me review
    Conversation.)}

138.17 somehow myself, \ somehow.myself, [typo.]

138.18–19 one bright spot on \ one bright spot <i>{o}n

138.31 on the way up. Up where? \ on the way up. {Up where?}

139.8–10 what you heard from Parks[—]And do not, worse, think
    that I've turned into a pious teetotaler.[—]which at one
    time \ what you heard from Parks[—]{And do not, worse,
    think that I've turned into a pious teetotaler.}[—]which at
    one time [this insertion handwritten in ink at end of letter
    before the postscript]

139.14 to and fro, \ to and f<or>{ro},

139.34-36 P.S. I see [. . .] forgive you.' \ [handwritten in ink at end of letter]

LETTER 46

[on verso is a handwritten note from Malcolm to Margerie]

140.30 possible/ possib<o>{l}e

LETTER 48

143.30-32 conscription.) If you have [. . . .] anyhow??.) \ conscription.)<.> If you have any suggestions for either, *do* please send the<.>{m.} {<[illeg.] In Ballast> {{(The}} <I suppose> same thing applies perhaps to In Ballast as to the Volc, for the present anyhow{{??}} <perhaps>.)}

LETTER 49

144.16 by [i]t. \ by kt. [typo.]

144.16 ask for the[m]. \ ask for the . [typo.]

144.19 refugees \ refugee{-}s [Aiken has inserted a line to close up the word]

144.22 bargain.) \ bargain.{)}

144.24 though no takers \ though no<r> takers

144.29 liste[n] \ listeh [typo.]

144.34 aff. \ [handwritten in ink]

   [Note handwritten by Lowry at bottom of page reads: "Is Bob Morss Robert Ely Morss who wrote This Swan upon the icy waters of my hearts glides ever on?"]

LETTER 51

146.35 monad, \ monad{,}

147.1-2 adolescence, still stuck in my throat I wonder \ adolescence{,} still stuck <there> {in my throat} I wonder

147.17 homes for two, \ homes <'f> for two,

147.32 surgeons' & could \ surgeons' {&} could

148.1–2 deficiency of having none & now I see another: 'muted.'
B.V?) \ deficiency<.> {of having none & now I see another:
'muted.' B.V?)}

148.20 all, but great \ all{,} but great

148.23 come to investigate, \ <s>{c}ome to investigate,

148.31 blessed by \ blessed b{y}

LETTER 52

149.33 this letter \ this let{t}er

150.7 sent \ s{-}ent [Lowry has inserted a line to close up the word]

150.13 more than ever, \ <n>{m}ore than ever,

150.27 you, & Mary, \ you, {&} Mary,

150.31–32 And, of course, Gawd with a capital H. And good god, why
not? \ [handwritten at end of postscript]

LETTER 54

152.29 Love from both to both \ Love from both<,> {to both}

152.33 P.S. My explanation [. . .] no attention. \ [handwritten in ink
at end of letter]

LETTER 55

153.10 I[']ve \ I(ve [typo.]

153.21 about \ a<n>{b}out

[Notes handwritten in ink by Lowry in top left-hand
corner of letter:
Startling, as {like} a dog that takes a false step.
<Men have silence>
Death hath this silence in common with us
Home runs, {perhaps} but who may find the ball?]

LETTER 56

155.17 'Deserter' \ 'Desert<ion>{er}'

LETTER 58

157.15 occasionally wit[h] \ occasionally witn [typo.]

157.19 poet-critics[,] by Cowley \ poet-critics. by Cowley [typo.]

157.20 r[e]sucitate \ r sucitate [typo.]

157.27 adapte[d] \ adapte [typo.]

157.27 celebration of joy-in-love, \ cel{e}bration of joy{-}in{-}love,

157.30 gemütlichkeit \ gemütlich{k}eit

157.31 portrait \ <[illeg.]>portrait

158.2 straightened \ straightene{d}

158.6 love to you both \ [handwritten]

LETTER 59

158.32 h[a]ve \ h ve [typo.]

158.33 where \ whe{-}re [Lowry has inserted a line to close up the word]

159.32 what a Godsent \ what {a} Godsent

LETTER 61

163.11 Marvellous \ Marve llous [typo.]

163.16 [b]rilliantly. \ nrilliantly. [typo.]

LETTER 62

170.14 combined \ combine<e>{d}

170.19 anything \ any{t}hing

170.23 clamped down on me \ clampe{d} down on <[illeg.]> me

170.26 nimbly \ nimbl<e>{y}

170.34   son \ son<e>

170.37   spleen \ <sp>{sp}<ele>{lee}n

171.2   husband at Saskatoon, \ husband at <at> Saskatoon,

171.12   society \ soci{e}ty

171.13   what with that there \ what with<at> {that} the<ir>{re}

171.21   characters, \ charac<j>{t}ers,

171.31   mostly \ most<o>{l}y

171.34   attempting \ attemp{t}in<t>{g}

171.35   new title: \ new title{:}

172.4   shery, in fact; \ she<e>ry, in fact<,>{;}

172.11–14 Do you ever hear [. . . .] Floor! \ [handwritten at end of letter]

LETTER 63

address [Aiken has used a letterhead postcard with the address as quoted]

date   [the postcard is postmarked Oct 21 1942]

172.32   brief \ br<ei>{ie}f

173.2–3 leaves us \ leave{s} us

173.4   relief \ reli{e}f

173.5   has had \ ha<d>{s} had

173.6   plaster \ pla<ts>{ste}r

LETTER 64

173.34   L[a]urence \ Lsurence [typo.]

174.4–5 I didn't know about it \ I didn't {know} about it

174.29   partly sold \ partly {sold}

175.20   prostate \ pros{t}ate

LETTER 65

176.25 put in, however, \ put in{,} however{,}

176.28 the Squire one put out \ the Squire <and> one put out

[handwritten in margin of first page: "1+

1

2+

2+

1+

2

1"]

177.6–7 finish a Poem \ finish a <[illeg.]>{Poe}m

177.10 progression, or parabola, \ progression{,} or parabola{,}

177.11–12 imperfectly, or something \ imperfectly, {or} something

177.13 and end, \ and end{,}

177.17 would n't \ would n<o>{'}t

177.22 simple note, like \ simple note{,} like

177.27–28 sound of breaking \ <[illeg.]>{s}ound of <B>{b}reaking

178.1 never liked it — er — as well \ never liked it{ — er — }as well

178.5–7 on the down. My parabola [. . .] mind[.] I have \ on the down. {My parabola should perhaps have been the other way up; but never mind}[.] <[illeg.]> I have [the insertion is written in the left-hand margin]

178.8 Borborigmi, \ Borbori<[illeg.]>{gm}i,

178.10 — one would \ { — o}ne would

178.15 unfair); \ unfair){;}

LETTER 66

179.16 spontaneous \ spon{t}aneous

179.31 see. . . \ see. . {.}

180.13 firemen, \ fir{e}men,

180.20–21 I fear \ Ifear [typo.]

181.8 end-of-summer \ end{-}of{-}summer

181.9 portrait \ portr{-}ait [Aiken has inserted a line to close up the word]

LETTER 67
[Christmas card]

182.3 outlaw or dissenter \ outlaw {or dissenter}

182.12 thank you, again Conrad — \ thank you, {again} Conrad —

182.15–23 — Afraid that [. . . .] Love Malc. \ [written on inside left-hand page of card]

182.25 *from Malc & Margie.* \ [written on inside right-hand page of card]

LETTER 68
183.19 perform \ pe{r}form

184.13 verses, \ verse<e>{s},

184.22 And do you \ A<b>{n}d do you

LETTER 69
185.12 to my other \ t<l>{o} my other

185.14 for a few \ <g>{f}or a few

185.17 under \ und<w>{e}r

185.26 any other, and \ any other <about this>, and

LETTER 70
[It is unlikely that the holograph of this letter in the UBC Library is actually the one received by Aiken; see Appendix I for Aiken's incomplete and variant transcription of this letter]

date [someone has written "[Fall] 1945" at top of letter]

186.11   Dear old Conrad: \ <[illeg.] how do you do.>
                     <Dear C>
                  Dear old Conrad:

186.13–14   fat informative & diverting letter — \ fat <and good>
            {informative & diverting} letter —

186.14–15   but I want to get this letter off now so it will be in time \ but
            <where are they now, I know where they are but> I want to
            get this letter off <in a hurry> {now} so it will <wish you bon
            voyage> be in time

186.16   sacrifice of the other for \ sacrifice of <my letter> {the other}
          for

186.17–18   the phoenix clapped its wings all right all right, [. . .] broke
            its neck \ the phoenix <has> clapped its wings<, in fact gave
            such a resounding clap> all right {all right}, in fact gave such
            a <resounding> <{[illeg.]}> {bloody} great {resounding} clap
            that the <bloody> {poor} bird <nearly> {nearly} broke its
            neck

186.20   The interminable golden \ The <long> {interminable}
          golden

186.20–21   bittersweet awful beautiful Eastern autumn \ bittersweet
            {awful beautiful Eastern} autumn

186.21   I'd never experienced) \ I'd never <seen> {experienced})

186.22   Margie, [(]whose childhood \ Margie,<to some extent>
          [(]whose childhood

186.22–23   me it almost slew. \ me it {almost} slew.

186.23   upon me, in fact, than \ upon me, {in fact,} than

186.24   though the Noxon's \ though <Nox> the Noxon's

186.24–25   really beautiful. I was in shocking bad form, \
            really beautiful <, & really {quite} unique>. I was in
            <Sadness is so much part of me that I
            May not, encumbered <<without>> as [illeg.] dare hope
            Sadness is so the [illeg.] part of me
            That I am may dare add a little hope
            My grief is like a<<n old iron cookstove
            which — >> {battered old cookstove}

<<As I remembered that>> >
shocking bad form, [the above unfinished poem appears to
have been written on the page before Lowry began the letter]

186.26   though I was very disappointed \ though I was {very} disappointed

186.26–27   see you, — albeit I *heard* you — it was perhaps juſt \ see
you,{ — albeit I *heard* you — } it was {perhaps} juſt

186.28–29   seemed to drive \ seemed <to have> to drive

186.29   traumatic result alone was shattering. \ traumatic {result}
<effeſt> <{consequences}> <alone w<<as>>{ere}> {alone
was} shattering <{enough — if very intereſting}>.

186.30   the bloody fire \ the {bloody} fire

186.31   find Margie screaming \ find <her> {Margie} screaming

186.31–32   find me yelling and gnashing my teeth; \ find <her> {me}
yelling <or [illeg.]> and gnashing <my> my teeth;

186.32   teeth I have left \ teeth I <have> {have} left

186.33   these diversions \ these <little domeſtic> diversions

186.34   our own, \ our <[illeg.]> own,

186.35   in a fashion nothing short of diabolical. \ in a <diabolical
fashion> {fashion nothing short of diabolical}.

187.1   a neighbouring house \ a {neighbouring} house

187.2–3   for the winter [. . .] old one and \ for the winter {because it
<rather> {{vaguely}} resembled our old one} and

187.6   sure enough, about a week \ sure enough, {about} a week

187.7   house did; \ house did <do>;

187.10   when we went down to Niagara \ when we <got back> {went
<ov> down} to Niagara

187.10–11   to ours, one night while \ to ours, {one night} while

187.11   went up in a blaze: \ went up in <smoke> {a blaze}:

187.12–13   saw the awful sun, [. . .] to-day — \ saw the <">awful sun<">,
{(E.d. again) — I don't know why so much Emily Dickenson
to-day — }

187.15–16 took all our manuscripts \ took all <the> {our} manuscripts

187.16 And to cap \ <But to cap> And to cap

187.16–17 returned here, it turned out that \ returned here, <the house where we'd> {it turned out that}

187.17–18 where someone [. . .] few things \ where <we'd> {someone had been good enough to let us} store<d> our bedding <[illeg.]> & <[illeg.]> some few things

187.19 had in our abscence itself been burned down, \ had {in our abscence itself} been <itself [illeg.]> <consumed by fire> {burned down},

187.20 bedding & stuff with it, \ bedding {& stuff} with it,

187.20–21 into flame [. . .] evening \ into flame <one> for no <valid> reason at all {apparently,} one calm {mild} evening

187.22 weren't even there. \ weren't even <inside> there.

187.22 Margie & I \ Margie <had invented> & I

187.25 the m.ss [. . .] rescue \ the m.ss<,> {concerning him} I had <rescued> {happened to} <from our fire> rescue

187.28 fifty other odd senseless sad terrifying & curiously related \ fifty other odd <things> {senseless sad} <things> {terrifying &} curiously related

[handwritten by Lowry at top of page: "Mem — who gave me my first drink etc"]

187.29–30 make me sometimes think [. . .] chosen of God \ make me {sometimes} think {(taking it all in all!)} that maybe I am the <person> <{chosen}> {chap} chosen of God

188.1–2 would help. Or perhaps [. . .] tie up. \ would help. {Or perhaps Bergson's[.] Osbert Sitwell — & some of James Joyces experiences seem to tie up.}

188.3–4 someone, strangers & vultures, had \ someone, {<city> strangers & vultures,} had

188.4 our burned stakes & notices and \ our {burned} stakes & {notices <a>} and

188.4–6 smack on half [. . .] full \ smack on {half} our {old} site, {blocking our southerly view,} a great tall ugly <thi> Erection {to be} full

188.6–7 children & hysterical fat women, who \ children {& hysterical fat women}, who

188.7–8 pulled down the flags [. . .] flying \ pulled down the <{American & Canadian & English}> flags we had left— {perhaps too dramatically — } flying

188.10 the local folkways, \ the {local} folkways,

188.11 legal toehold \ legal <standing> {toehold}

188.11–12 — one incidentally of the prime causes of jungle warfare — \ [this sentence is written at the top of the page]

188.12–13 been abolished: our few fishermen friends — with \ been <{almost}> abolished: <[illeg.]> {our few} fishermen friends <hadn't> — with

188.14 prevent it & our \ prevent it <happening> & our

188.16–17 tried to put [. . . .] their house down \ tried to <prevent it.> {put a stop to it. They had no excuse, <&> knew we were coming back.} We <had> could have knocked <it> {their house} down

188.18 but like a fool or not I \ but <for some reason> {like a fool or not} I

188.20 on what space \ on what <was left> space

188.20–21 new neighbours even [. . .] that, \ new neighbours <having the nerve to call> {even calling} us greedy because {we made} the most <even> of that,

188.22 one day the owner came over and asked \ one day the <fat female> owner came over <in hyst> <nearly> <{almost}> <in hysterics> and asked

188.23 accused me of \ accused {me} of

188.24–25 they'd couldn't [. . .], and \ they'd <never> {couldn't} be<en> happy {there}, that <her> {the} youngest child, {for instance,} had almost drowned the day before, {& so on,} and

188.26 another, [. . .] to which \ another, <and so on,> {ever since they'd <been> {{built}} there,} to which

188.29   a guy's soul, \ a <person's> guy's soul, <you had or worse {still}
          the soul of two people,>

188.29   couldn't be sure \ couldn't be <precisely> sure

188.29   if something \ if <you> something

188.30   no use coming \ no use <compla> <{[illeg.]}> coming

188.31   as if they'd swallowed Paddy Murphy's Goat \ as if <they'd>
          {<[illeg.]> they'd} swallowed <a live> {Paddy Murphy's}
          Goat <hole>

188.32   out of their \ out of <his> their

189.1   To be frank, \ <However,> To be frank,

189.1   have had a share of \ have had <most> {a share} of

189.3   set in — \ set <[illeg.]> in —

189.4   hospital and probings, and \ hospital {and probings}, and

189.6–7   second part, Scribners having held \ second part, <they>
          {Scribners} having h<ad>{eld}

189.7–8   for over four years (it is getting into the fifth year) \ for
          <nearly f> over four years ({it is} getting into the fifth<)>
          year)

189.8   they signed \ they <were not forced into> <in the n> signed

189.9   with a time limit set for publication date at \ with <the> a
          time limit<ation> {set} for publication date <they have al>
          <it is already past that date> at

189.10   still Margie \ still <they have> Margie

189.12   looms with what \ looms with <what [illeg.]> what

189.14   undependable and unscrupulous people to deal with \ unde-
          pendable<,> and unscrupulous <people — their behavior>
          <to deal with> people to <[illeg.]> deal with

189.16   with someone like you, \ with {someone like} you,

189.17   while doing some ripsawing \ while doing some <hacksaw-
          ing wi> ripsawing

189.18   which set us back \ which set <me> {us} back

189.19–20 caused by an osteomyelitis \ caused by an <abcessed t> osteomyelitis

189.21 owing to malpractice. \ owing to <a shortage of dentists and finally> malpractice.

189.22 not take new patients, \ not take {new} patients,

189.22 hopping with agony \ hopping <in> {with} agony

189.23 drugstores all shut. \ drugstores {all} shut.

189.25 street, because \ street, <They The> <being usuall> <other accomodat> because

189.28–31 thirteen goats [. . .] West Vancouver. \ thirteen goats, <twelve> several {sailors' monkeys, twelve} pet rabbits, and is doubtless also {somewise} responsible for the apparition of half a cocker spaniel in a lane <by> <in> {near} West Vancouver.

189.31– 190.1 On the other hand [. . .] omen. \ {<And> {{On the other hand}} a murderer — no relative but embarrasingly also of the name Trumbaugh — {{has shot a policeman}} that was several months ago, but was reminded of it for at time of writing he has just received a reprieve & wondered if that were a good omen.} [this sentence is written in the left-hand margin]

190.3 received the notice \ received <a report> the notice

190.5 'autocamps \ '<b>autocamps

190.6–8 This placed [. . .] waterfront \ This <this> placed our new house <under a> — which, <built with our own hands> {by the way} <it> has the <merit of> distinction of being the last <bit> {example} of such pioneer activity on <waterfront> Vancouver waterfront

190.8–9 that was finally too much \ that was <at last> {finally} too much

190.10–11 almost as poignant as \ almost as <sad> {poignant} as

190.11–12 Reprieve for Mr Trumbaugh also has come. \ Reprieve {for Mr Trumbaugh also} has come.

190.13 neighbours either, of the \ neighbours either, <at least of the present calibre> of the

190.14   molestation or paying \ molestation <and then> or paying

190.15   land too, that is the \ land too, <what pa> {that is} the

190.16   price. Thus does \ price. <At the moment> Thus does

[handwritten by Lowry on the verso of eleventh page:

      Nocturne of Remembered Spring
          <Punch>   House of Dust
        Charnel Rose
    Forslin
    Festus   Punch]

190.18–19   I feel [. . .] ravine. \ I feel <some> <sometimes> somewhat like [. . .] Caucasian ravine. [this sentence is handwritten at top of page]

190.19–20   At the moment we are \ {At the moment} we are

190.23–24   beyond, hoping \ beyond, <the pier> hoping

190.25   My novel — the Volcano — , seems \ My novel{ — the Volcano — }, seems

190.27   good, though \ good <in its bizarre way>, though

190.28   — alack — prosaic justice? — if not \ — alack — <poetic> {prosaic} justice? — <though> if not

190.29   in which it actually is old Malc who goes \ in which <old> <po old Malc> <{old}> <plays a rather more recognizable> <goes rather more recognizably down the drain> it actually is old Malc {who} goes

190.30–31   too. I was planning to send you the Volcano in \ too. <In spite of> I was planning to send you the <book> {Volcano} in

190.32– 191.1   with the only copy in my possession at present and I don't see \ with <[illeg.]> {the} only copy <& I can't> in my possession {at present} and I don't <the only available other> see

191.1–2   other one before you sail. So please [. . .] being. \ other one <in time> {before you sail}. <But> {So} please take the will for the deed {for the time being}.

317

191.6   But now your letter \ But <meantime> {now} your letter

191.7   make some reply \ make {some} reply

191.7–8   though please forgive me \ though <forgive me if> <you must> {please} forgive me

191.10   order is a very good one, \ order is a <good> very good one,

191.11   as good as can be, — \ as good as <[illeg.]> can be, —

191.11   The Soldier might \ The Soldier <would profi> might

191.14–15   volume. What I mean [. . .] Pilgrim. \ volume. {What I mean is, if <it> {{the poem}} does not belong to the symphonies, The Soldier does to the notion of The Divine Pilgrim.}

191.18–19   Teteleſtai not a symphony this is \ Teteleſtai <not> not a symphony <it is nonetheless> this is

191.20   every thing \ every <bloody> thing

191.20–21   possibly be of use to the fellow-poet \ possibly <of> be {of} use to the <ſtudent> fellow-poet

191.21   Discordants with Youth \ Discordants <and> with <'Youth> <Disenchantment and> Youth

191.22   the aĉtual Cats & Rats Turns \ the aĉtual {Cats & Rats} Turns

191.23   The latterly \ Th<ey>{e} latterly

191.24   you may think \ you may <have come to> think

191.27–28   even the "succubus \ even the <lampoon> "succubus

191.29   hiſtorical intereſt, [. . .] these. \ hiſtorical intereſt<.>{, & giving the dates of all these.}

191.30   Triumphant, but I \ Triumphant, <read at your Uncle Potters [illeg.]> but I

192.3   departure that comes \ departure <I can suggeſt> that comes

192.4   start the whole \ start the <whole> whole

192.7   your reversed chronology. \ your <reversed and> reversed chronology.

192.9   If by the way \ If <as you prepare to depart> <you> by <should> the way

192.11   alack? — we \ alack? — <I>{we}

192.12–13   and shoot them in this direction C.O.D or something for \ and <send> {shoot} them in this direction {C.O.D or something} for

192.14   magazines having been unprocurable for \ magazines <are under a ban here> {having been unprocurable} for

192.15–16   it is probably a poor time to ask what with \ it is {probably} <probably> a poor time to ask <so if it's> {what} <too much trouble> with

[handwritten by Aiken at top of sixteenth page: "No date: but mention of Brownstone Eclogues makes it 1942 or later. C.A." This and the next page make up the postscript of this letter; MS H; MSPC UBC]

192.26   When I suggested starting \ When I <said> suggest{ed} starting

192.31   running throughout your work. \ running through{out} <all> your work.

192.33–193.1   as irritating — perhaps you say — as when \ as irritating{ — perhaps you say — }as when

193.12   [? mouthesills] \ [doubtful reading]

193.13–14   Silberstein, the engineer [. . .] of course \ Silberstein, {the engineer with long-beaked oilcan, the shipboys,} & of course

193.16   & don't forget the sea. \ & {don't forget} the sea.

LETTER 71

194.14   blithely \ blith{e}ly

194.16   navel \ nav<a>{e}l

194.17–18   more side-walls, \ more <in> side{-}walls,

195.6   'career' \ {'}career{'}

195.13   the Ship. \ the <s>{S}hip.

195.17   rereading \ {re}rereading

LETTER 72

196.32 by a fire \ bya fire [typo.]

197.7 above it, and the afrit-black \ above it, {and the} afrit-black

197.13 queſtion \ qu<r>{e}ſtion

197.13–14 where, more or less permanently, \ where{,} more or less permanently{,}

197.16 th[e] cash. \ thr cash. [typo.]

197.17 every inch \ every inc<e>{h}

197.26 Melville \ Melvill{e}

197.26 Willard \ Willar<s>{d}

197.27 Henry)) \ Henry){)}

197.27–28 Dickinson?)?? \ Dickinson?<?>{)}??

197.28 "Kid" \ {"}Kid{"}

198.3 Pearce \ Peacre [Aiken has indicated by hand a reversal of the "c" and "r"]

198.6 mr eliot, \ m<t>{r} eliot,

198.13 Seems \ <Semme{s}s> {Seems}

198.17 to make \ to{/}make [Aiken has inserted a slash mark to separate the two words]

198.18 made of it. \ ma<o>{d}e of it.

198.22 at the \ at th{e}

198.26 it had done \ it had don{e}

LETTER 73

[Chriſtmas card; Lowry has written on the inside of the card only]

199.14 We sail day after to-morrow, the 23rd, \ We sail <Monday> {day after to-morrow}, the 23rd,

199.24–25 your old — & new — pupil. \ your old{ — & new — }pupil.

LETTER 74

[No original is available for this letter; I have therefore had to rely on Joseph Killorin's transcription in *Selected Letters of Conrad Aiken* (277)]

LETTER 75

203.4 Enclosed [. . .] pilgrimage \ [handwritten before signature at end of letter]

LETTER 76

205.5 Nervenkranken. \ Ne<[illeg.]>{r}venkranken.

205.6 'catacombs to live,' \ {'}catacombs to live,{'}

205.8 and wherefore, \ an{d} wherefore,

205.10 if true. — The penis \ if true.{ — }The penis

205.12 getting somewhat panned, \ getting {somewhat} panned,

205.13 Heironymus \ Heironym<o>{u}s

205.16–17 (Just the same, [. . .] 10 days.) \ [handwritten at top of page]

206.2 especially \ espe<[illeg.]>{cia}lly

206.8 perhaps, too, like \ perhaps{,} too{,} like

206.14 seventy-five) — We \ seventy-five)<.>{ — }<[illeg.]>{W}e

206.15 grander \ <d>{g}rander

LETTER 78

208.15 unction) \ unction<,>{)}}

208.18 nights & we hit \ nights & {we} hit

208.23 from all I can \ from <what> {all} I can

208.25 doesn't belong \ <i>doesn't belong

208.29–209.1 — over its certain ironic implications \ — over its <various> <{their}> {certain} ironic implications

209.1–2 here goes the rave review \ here goes the {rave} review

[When quoting from the review, Lowry has used slash marks to indicate line breaks and indentation symbols to indicate new paragraphs. My lay-out of the text accords with these notations.]

210.11–12 in this civilisation. \ in this <generation> {civilisation.}

210.14 [How's that, old feller me lad?] \ [these square brackets are Lowry's, not the editor's]

210.15–16 (at laſt) [this 'at laſt' is what gets me too] inspiration \ (at laſt) {[this 'at laſt' is what gets me too]} inspiration [these square brackets are Lowry's]

210.17 if he had remained \ if he had <not> remained

210.30 in Canada too, I may \ in Canada {too}, I may

210.33 a sympathetic article \ a<n> {sympathetic} article

211.10–11 aeſthetic.
Mr Mitchell \ aeſthetic./ Mr Mitchell [Lowry has used a slash mark to indicate a new paragraph]

211.21 Beethoven's \ Be{e}thoven's

["P.T.O" is written by Lowry at the bottom of the 7th page]

211.23 This is signed — \ <(>This is signed —

LETTER 79
[Chriſtmas poſtcard]

LETTER 80

213.33 feſtive (& beautiful) card. \ feſtive {(& beautiful)} card.

214.1–2 your card — ha ha — what \ your card — {ha ha — }what

214.7 Mr Arcularis \ <m>{M}r Arcularis

214.10 beautifully done here otherwise & \ beautifully done here {otherwise} &

214.16–17 memory of which, applied to other happenings, I muſt have \ memory of which, <one muſt> {applied to other happenings,} I <would> {muſt} have

215.6 by me (among others) apparently \ by me {(among others)} apparently

215.9 current one. (or *are carried along*.) \ current one. {(or *are carried along*.)}

215.11 God bless you & you both — \ God bless {you &} you both —

215.11 With love from us both \ With love from {us both}

215.14–15 P.S. There [. . .] this?\ {P.S. There is snow this morning falling <out> quite heavily, in [. . .] this?} [handwritten in left-hand margin of first page]

LETTER 81

216.13–14 rereading, [. . .] let me say many \ rereading{,} where not often reread<,>{ — }<t>{T}hough {I} have not had time to reread all{,} let me say<,> many

216.16 Your Obit, \ <y>{Y}our <o>{O}bit,

216.17–18 Costumes, [. . . .] Strange Moonlight \ Costumes{,} but I guess I did not {fully} understand them. {They now seem excellent.} Strange Moonlight

216.25 her lot! \ her lot<.>{!}

216.28–29 quote) Of the merits \ quote) <Secret Snow and the merits> Of the merits [this deletion is done on the typewriter]

217.9 symbol. For example, I broke \ symbol. {For example,} I broke

217.12 at the time.) \ at the time{.})

LETTER 82

[Christmas postcard]

date [postmarked 16 Dec 1950]

218.15 *Believe it or not!* \ [sticker above this reads: "Silent night"]

LETTER 83

220.12   friend of Mary's \ friend of Mar<g>y's

220.18   never tire? \ never tire<d>?

220.26–27   after which, \ after{/}which, [Aiken has inserted a slash mark by hand to indicate a separation of the two words]

220.29   it is, almost \ it is{,/}almost [Aiken has inserted a slash mark to indicate a separation]

221.2   interesting, \ inter{e}sting,

221.3   the play cou[l]d \ the play coukd [typo.]

221.4   put to to \ put{/}to to [Aiken has inserted a slash mark to indicate a separation]

221.11   but he has \ but <who> {he} has

221.23   address the recipient by \ address the recipient <as> by

221.26   proposing, \ p<t>{r}oposing,

221.32   what you w[a]nt \ what you wqnt [typo.]

221.38   — next time we \ — next {time} we

222.26   But actually, \ But act<u>{ua}lly,

222.26   not only *like* \ not {only} *like*

222.31   Christian, \ Chri<i>stian,

223.8   a sad bad business, \ a s<a>{a}d bad business,

223.24   our loves \ [handwritten at end of letter]

224.7   hawthorn \ ha wthorn [typo.]

224.11   appear with \ appear<,> with

LETTER 84

address   [deleted at top of letter:
<Apt 33
1075 Gilford Street
Vancouver
British Columbia.>]

225.7 will be found singing \ will be {found} singing

225.10–12 cats though, [. . .] or perhaps \ cats though, {as I have a sort of feeling you once did on our passage from Gibraltar, in a friendly fashion,} or perhaps

225.19 contrived a letter to poor \ contrived {a letter} to poor

225.20 of rabbits & bacon \ of <th>{r}abbits & bacon

225.24 I congratulate you [. . .] getting \ I congratulate {you from the bottom of my heart} on getting

225.25 circumſtances, i.e the Library etc, \ circumſtances, <am looking> i.e the <l>{L}ibrary etc,

225.28 plagiarise them anyway \ plagiarise <it> {them} anyway

225.28–29 to be there though, \ to be there <,> though,

226.1 without vomiting: \ without <vomiting> {vomiting}:

226.1–2 to say really was \ to say {really} was

226.19–20 they were & are \ they {were &} are

226.21 that good old Betty \ that {good} old Betty

226.25 Fortunately \ [“P.T.O” is written beneath this at bottom of third page]

226.30 a swell small [. . .] beginnings \ a swell {small — & in faſt not so small — }beginnings

226.31–227.1 F6 [. . .], all playing \ F6 {(not to mention Much ado About Nothing)}, all playing

227.7–8 — so you might, [. . .] bear \ — so you might, {though not for this reason,} bear

227.18 Modern library people are \ Modern library {people} are

227.19 one still keeps \ one {ſtill} keeps

228.1–3 *P.P.P.S.* I enclose [. . . .] even then. \ [written in top left-hand corner of firſt page]

228.5–6 Excuse this [. . .] at the time. \ [written in left-hand margin of firſt page]

LETTER 85

229.4   And he, though \ And he{,} though

229.5   "an unaccuſtomed wetness in the trousers," \ {"}an unaccuſtomed wetness in the trousers,{"}

229.5–6   complained, as once before, \ complained{,} as once before{,}

229.9   to 'write', \ to {'}write{'},

229.9   'decorate the page', \ {'}decorate the page{'},

229.10–13   advises (Sounds like [. . .] muddle) one to do.\ advises {(Sounds like bad advice too, but you get what I mean — if anything; as a matter {{of faĉt}} I simply wanted [. . .] muddle)} one to do. [this insertion is handwritten in the left-hand margin]

229.16–17   unconscious, [—] Jeez Conrad I don't mean that though I mean the reſt [—] \ unconscious,[—]{Jeez Conrad I don't mean that though I mean the reſt}[—] [this insertion is handwritten in the right-hand margin]

229.23   Hammbo, \ Ham{m}bo,

229.32   Man know thyself! \ Man know thyself{!}

230.4   used to say) from\ used to say) <to think that those> from [this deletion is made on the typewriter]

230.6–8   sacred or secret — don't take this [. . .] overleaf [—]drama\ sacred or secret{—don't take this too seriously, old man, my hypocrisy is exposed overleaf}[—]drama [this insertion is handwritten at the bottom of the page]

230.11   Hammbo \ Ham{m}bo

230.14   the real Hammbo \ the real Ham{m}bo

230.18   rough tough time \ rough <thou> tough time [this deletion is made on the typewriter]

230.22–23   Mr. and Mrs. Hammbo, \ Mr. and Mrs. Ham{m}bo,

230.23–24   Lowry, not forget not forgetting Mr. and Mrs. Demareſt, \ Lowry, <and> {not forget not forgetting} Mr. and Mrs. <[illeg.]> {Demareſt},

230.25 As ever \ [handwritten before signature]

231.11–12 Mr. Aiken was shocking[—]he wrote [. . .] shocking
[—]to us \ Mr. Aiken was shocking[—]{he wrote speaking of course, it only looked like shocking} [—]to us
[insertion handwritten in right-hand margin]

LETTER 86

date July 16, 1954. *(See below) \ July 16, 1954. {*(See below)}

232.14 solved!) \ solved{!})

232.15 "step on;" — \ "step on;"{ — }

232.24 meanness; \ meanness{;}

232.27 "auxiliary circumſtances" \ {"}auxil<l>iary circumſtances"

232.31–36 *I had leſt this [. . .] without a line. \ [handwritten at bottom
of firſt page and keyed to date above]

233.2 Ushantesque one. — Meantime, \ Ushant<i>{e}sque one.
{ — }Meantime,

233.5 that keeps one \ that keep{s} one

233.6 maſterpiece. — Well, \ maſterpiece.{ — }Well,

233.7 faƈtor, — this letter \ faƈtor,{ — }this letter

233.10 auxiliary \ auxil<l>iary

233.13 root[—]symbolical perhaps?) \ root[—]{symbolical perhaps?}) [insertion written in leſt-hand margin]

233.14 of all things!: — and \ of all things{!}:{ — }and

233.23 derrick, \ derrick{,}

233.27 omitted aphaeretically the prefatory S – on the \ omitted
{aphaeretically} the prefatory S – <om> {on} the

233.32 our boat, — the mountains \ our boat,{ — }the mountains

234.3–6 hands,[—]though in [. . .] wryly jealous.[—] inhabited \
hands,[—]{though in them days ones {{own}} hands really
were one's own hands — of the Better Life as represented by
the "Shoulder Parade" {{etc,}} as a kind of prepioneer <I> we

remain slightly sceptical, or perhaps feel a bit {{wryly}} jealous.}[—]inhabited. [this insertion written in left-hand margin]

234.13   by Crikey, \ by <c>{C}ri<c>key,

234.14   To abandon \ <">{T}o abandon

234.20–21   or one was, \ or <won> one was, [this deletion is made on the typewriter]

234.25   me voilà! - \ me voilà{!} –

234.25   this sort of thing with \ this {sort of thing} with

234.29   hiding place, — I \ hiding place,{ — }I

235.9   snoot. . . \ snoot.{. .}

235.21   (And therein \ {(}And therein

235.23   an Egg, \ an <e>{E}gg,

235.25   Volcano.). . \ Volcano.{)}. .

235.28   for me. \ [passage originally meant to be inserted at this point is deleted and illegible in the left-hand margin]

235.30   retreating \ ret{ — }reating [Lowry has drawn a line to close up the word]

236.2   saga of \ sag<[illeg.]>{a} of

236.4   Crafts, \ [passage originally meant to be inserted at this point is deleted and illegible in the left-hand margin]

236.6   founder of Roxbury, \ founder of <Du>{Ro}xbury <{Great [illeg.] it is Roxbury. (I had said Duxbury.)}>, [this insertion is crossed out in the left-hand margin]

236.10   i[t] would be \ if [typo.] would be

236.19   Hammbo \ Ham{m}bo

236.23   acts as a wholesome \ acts {as} a wholesome

236.30   exhilarating. \ exhil<[illeg.]>{a}rating

237.6   I'll send \ <I8ll> {I'll} send

237.8   —— For the rest, \ { —— }For the rest,

237.9   after that \ after that<t>

237.16 has been to \ h<ar>{as} been to

237.20 you will one day see, \ you will {one day} see,

237.26–27 beſt books ever written \ beſt books {ever written}

237.27 necessarily, in so many words, \ necessarily{,} in so many words{,}

237.30–238.2 reasons: one; its [. . .] mr Lowry'.) it is \ reasons: {one; its marvellous generosity, as of a uranium mine, with your stake planted {{there but}} as if {{it}} were leſt open for <an> other people {{to work it}} — (as a librarian here said to me 'You have to have a high class intellect — like to write a book like that, <[illeg.]> mr Lowry'.)} it is [the insertion is written in the left-hand margin]

238.3 collossal. — But \ collossal.{ — }But

238.11 should you \ s<g>{h}ould you

238.11–12 (Also the bridge, \ (Also t<i>{he} bridge,

238.16 God bless you. \ [handwritten before signature]

238.29–30 too pleonaſtic - \ to{o} pleonaſtic -

238.30 witticism, \ witticism{,}

238.30–31 (top 287: and \ (top 287 <!>{:} and

238.32 in?" by "Or, \ in?" {by} "Or,

238.34–35 *PPPPS* (Or [. . .] return?) \ {*PPPPS* (Or was this {{perhaps}} juſt another case of "withdrawal and return"?)} [handwritten at end of letter]

LETTER 87

[telegram]

LETTER 88

[telegram]

LETTER 89

[telegram; see Appendix I for transcription of Lowry's slightly different handwritten draft of this letter]

Selected Bibliography

Aiken, Conrad. *Among the Lost People.* New York: Scribner's, 1934.

——— . *And in the Human Heart.* New York: Duell, Sloan and Pearce, 1940.

——— . "The Art of Poetry IX." With Robert Hunter Wilbur. *Paris Review* 42 (1968): 97–124.

——— . "Asphalt." *Dial* June 1920: 733.

——— . "Back to Poetry." *Atlantic Monthly* Aug. 1940: 217–23.

——— . *Blue Voyage.* London: Gerald Howe, 1927.

——— . *Bring! Bring! And Other Stories.* New York: Boni & Liveright, 1925.

——— . *Brownstone Eclogues and Other Poems.* New York: Duell, Sloan and Pearce, 1942.

——— . "Cabaret." *Coterie* 3 (1919): 51–52.

——— . *The Charnel Rose; Senlin: A Biography; and Other Poems.* Boston: Four Seas, 1918.

——— . *Collected Poems.* New York: Oxford UP, 1953.

——— . *The Coming Forth by Day of Osiris Jones.* New York: Scribner's, 1931.

——— . *Conversation: or Pilgrims' Progress.* New York: Duell, Sloan and Pearce, 1940.

——— . *Costumes by Eros.* New York: Scribner's, 1928.

——— . *The Divine Pilgrim.* Athens: U of Georgia P, 1949.

——— . *Earth Triumphant and Other Tales in Verse.* Boston: Four Seas, 1914.

——— . "The Father Surrogate and Literary Mentor." *Malcolm Lowry Remembered.* Ed. Gordon Bowker. London: Ariel, 1985. 38–40.

——— . "Gigantic Dreams." *New Republic* 27 June 1928: 146–47.

——— . *Great Circle.* London: Wishart, 1933.

——— . *A Heart for the Gods of Mexico.* London: Secker, 1939.

——— . *The House of Dust: A Symphony.* Boston: Four Seas, 1920.

——— . Interview. *Remembrance of Lowry.* Writ. George Woodcock. Prod. and dir. George Robertson. CBC Explorations Series. Vancouver. 22 & 29 Nov. 1961.

——— . *The Jig of Forslin: A Symphony.* Boston: Four Seas, 1916.

——— . *John Deth: A Metaphysical Legend, and Other Poems.* New York: Scribner's, 1930.

——— . *The Kid.* New York: Duell, Sloan and Pearce, 1947.

——— . *King Coffin.* London: Dent, 1935.

——— . *Landscape West of Eden.* London: Dent, 1934.

——— . Letter. "Reply to letter of 26 Jan. 1967." *Times Literary Supplement* 16 Feb. 1967: 127.

——— . *A Little Who's Zoo of Mild Animals.* Illus. John Vernon Lord. New York: Atheneum, 1977.

———. "Malcolm Lowry: A Note." *Malcolm Lowry: The Man and His Work.* Ed. George Woodcock. Canadian Literature Series 3. Vancouver: U of British Columbia P, 1971. 101–02.

———, sel. *Modern American Poets.* New York: Modern Library, 1927.

———. *The Morning Song of Lord Zero: Poems Old and New.* New York: Oxford UP, 1963.

———. "Movements From a Symphony: Sudden Death." *Coterie* 3 (1919): 55–57.

———. "Movements From a Symphony: 'Overtones.'" *Coterie* 3 (1919): 53–55.

———. *Mr. Arcularis: A Play.* Cambridge: Harvard UP, 1957.

———. *Nocturne of Remembered Spring and Other Poems.* Boston: Four Seas, 1917.

———. "Not Too Lost." *Time* 16 June 1961: 7–8.

———. "Palimpsest: A Deceitful Portrait." *Coterie* 5 (1920): 7–16.

———. *The Pilgrimage of Festus.* New York: Knopf, 1923.

———. *Preludes for Memnon.* New York: Scribner's, 1931.

———. *Priapus and the Pool and Other Poems.* New York: Boni & Liveright, 1925.

———. *Punch: The Immortal Liar, Documents in his History.* New York: Knopf, 1921.

———. *Selected Poems.* New York: Scribner's, 1929.

———. *Senlin: A Biography.* London: Hogarth, 1925.

———. *The Short Stories of Conrad Aiken.* New York: Duell, Sloan and Pearce, 1950.

———. *Skylight One: Fifteen Poems by Conrad Aiken.* London: Lehmann, 1951.

———. *The Soldier: A Poem.* The Poets of the Year Series 39. Norfolk: New Directions, 1944.

———, and Malcolm Lowry. "those cokes to newcastle blues." *The Festival Theatre Review* 4.68 (14 Feb. 1931): 8–9.

———. "Three Preludes." *Experiment* 6 (1930): 33–36.

———. *Time in the Rock: Preludes to Definition.* New York: Scribner's, 1936.

———. *Turns and Movies and Other Tales in Verse.* Boston: Houghton, 1916.

———, ed. and pref. *Twentieth-Century American Poetry.* New York: Modern Library, 1944.

———. *Ushant: An Essay.* New York: Duell, Sloan and Pearce, 1952.

WORKS BY MALCOLM LOWRY

Lowry, Malcolm. *The Collected Poetry of Malcolm Lowry.* Ed. and introd. Kathleen Scherf. Explan. annotations Chris Ackerley. Vancouver: U of British Columbia P, 1992.

——— . *Dark as the Grave Wherein My Friend Is Laid.* Ed. Douglas Day and Margerie Lowry. New York: NAL, 1968.

——— . "For Nordahl Grieg Ship's Fireman." *Cambridge Poetry, 1930.* Ed. John Davenport, Hugh Sykes and Michael Redgrave. Hogarth Living Poets 13. London: Hogarth, 1930. 47–49.

——— . "Garden of Etla." *United Nations World* 4 (1950): 45–47.

——— . "Goya the Obscure." *The Venture* 6 (1930): 270–78.

——— . *Hear Us O Lord from Heaven Thy Dwelling Place.* Philadelphia: Lippincott, 1961.

——— . "Hotel Room in Chartres." *Story* 5.26 (1934): 53–58.

——— . "In Cape Cod with Conrad Aitken [sic]." *The Festival Theatre Programme* 1.16 (8 Mar. 1930): 10.

——— . "In Le Havre." *Life and Letters* 10 (1934): 462–66.

——— . "In Memoriam: Ingvald Bjørndal." *Atlantic Monthly* Oct. 1941: 501.

——— . "A Letter." *Wake* 11 (1952): 80–89.

——— . *Lunar Caustic.* London: Cape, 1968.

——— , and Margerie Bonner Lowry. *Notes on a Screenplay for F. Scott Fitzgerald's* Tender is the Night. Introd. Paul Tiessen. Bloomfield Hills, Michigan: Bruccoli Clark, 1976.

——— . *October Ferry to Gabriola.* Ed. Margerie Lowry. New York: World, 1970.

——— . "On Board the *West Hardaway.*" *Story* 3.15 (1933): 12–22.

——— . "Port Swettenham." *Experiment* 5 (1930): 22–26.

——— . "Punctum Indifferens Skibet Gaar Videre." *Experiment* 7 (1931): 62–75.

——— . "The Real Mr. Chips." *Vancouver Daily Province* 13 Dec. 1939: 4.

——— . "Seductio Ad Absurdum." *The Best British Short Stories of 1931.* Ed. Edward O'Brien. New York: Dodd, 1931. 89–107.

——— . *Selected Poems of Malcolm Lowry.* Ed. Earle Birney and Margerie Lowry. San Francisco: City Lights, 1962.

——— . *Ultramarine: A Novel.* London: Cape, 1933.

——— . *Under the Volcano.* New York: Reynal and Hitchcock, 1947.

——— . "Where did that One go to 'Erbert?" *Vancouver Daily Province* 29 Dec. 1939: 4.

SELECTED BIBLIOGRAPHY OF SECONDARY WORKS

Ackerley, Chris, and Lawrence J. Clipper. *A Companion to* Under the Volcano. Vancouver: U of British Columbia P, 1984.

Aiken, John. "Conrad Aiken, My Father." *Conrad Aiken Remembered*. Ed. Anthony Neville. Rye: Anthony Neville, 1989. 9–38.

——— . "Malcolm Lowry: Some Reminiscences." *Encounter* 69.3 (1987): 38–9.

——— . "A Memoir." *Edward Burra: A Painter Remembered by his Friends*. Ed. William Chappell. London: Andre Deutsch, 1982. 50–53.

Aiken, Mary Augusta. "The Best Painter of the American Scene." *Edward Burra: A Painter Remembered by his Friends*. Ed. William Chappell. London: Andre Deutsch, 1982. 84–99.

Bax, Clifford. "Socrates." *Six Plays*. London: Gollancz, 1930. 461–578.

Binns, Ronald. "Douglas Day's Biography." *Malcolm Lowry Newsletter* 4 (1979): 12.

——— . "5 Woodville Road." *Malcolm Lowry Newsletter* 4 (1979): 13.

——— . "5 Woodville Road." *Malcolm Lowry Newsletter* 5 (1979): 29.

Bonnell, Florence W., and Fraser C. Bonnell, comps. and eds. *Conrad Aiken: A Bibliography (1902–1978)*. San Marino, CA: Huntington Library, 1982.

Bonner, Margerie. *Horse in the Sky*. New York: Scribner's, 1947.

——— . *The Last Twist of the Knife*. New York: Scribner's, 1946.

——— . *The Shapes That Creep*. New York: Scribner's, 1946.

Bowker, Gordon. "The Biographical Lowry: A Case of Inconsistent Ambiguity." *Malcolm Lowry: Eighty Years On*. Ed. Sue Vice. New York: St. Martin's, 1989. 147–58.

——— , ed. *Malcolm Lowry Remembered*. London: Ariel, 1985.

——— . "Two Notes: The Taropatch." *Malcolm Lowry Review* 19/20 (1986/1987): 149–50.

Bradbrook, Muriel C. "Lowry and Some Cambridge Literary Friends." *Proc. of the London Conference on Malcolm Lowry, 1984*. Ed. Gordon Bowker and Paul Tiessen. London: Goldsmiths' College, 1985. 4–20.

——— . "Lowry's Cambridge." *Malcolm Lowry: Eighty Years On*. Ed. Sue Vice. New York: St. Martin's, 1989. 125–46.

——— . *Malcolm Lowry: His Art and Early Life; A Study in Transformation*. Cambridge: Cambridge UP, 1974.

Bragg, Melvyn, and Tristram Powell, prods. *Rough Passage*. BBC-2 New Release programme. 2 Feb. 1967.

Breit, Harvey. "Talk With Conrad Aiken." *New York Times Book Review* 24 Dec. 1950, sec. 7: 10.

Breit, Harvey, and Margerie Bonner Lowry, eds. *Selected Letters of Malcolm Lowry*. Philadelphia: Lippincott, 1965.

Brittain, Donald and John Kramer, writs. and dirs. *Volcano: An Inquiry into the Life and Death of Malcolm Lowry*. NFB, 1976.

Bruccoli, Matthew J. *James Gould Cozzens: A Life Apart*. San Diego: Harcourt, 1983.

Burgess, Anthony. "Europe's Day of the Dead." *Spectator* 20 Jan. 1967: 74.

Butscher, Edward. *Conrad Aiken: Poet of White Horse Vale*. Athens: U of Georgia P, 1988.

Calder-Marshall, Arthur. "John Davenport's 'Tame Genius.'" Bowker, *Malcolm Lowry Remembered* 73–80.

Carey, Maurice J. "Life with Malcolm Lowry." Ed. Anthony Kilgallin. *Malcolm Lowry: The Man and His Work*. Ed. George Woodcock. Vancouver: U of British Columbia P, 1971. 163–70.

Chittick, V.L.O. "*Ushant*'s Malcolm Lowry." *Queen's Quarterly* 71.1 (1964): 67–75.

Constable, John, ed. *Selected Letters of I.A. Richards*. Introd. Richard Luckett. Oxford: Clarendon, 1990.

Costa, Richard Hauer. "Conrad Aiken (1889–1973): The Wages of Neglect." *Fiction International* 2/3 (1974): 76–80.

——. "The Lowry/Aiken Symbiosis." *The Nation* 26 June 1967: 823–26.

——. "*Ulysses*, Lowry's *Volcano*, and the *Voyage* Between: A Study of Unacknowledged Literary Kinship." *University of Toronto Quarterly* 36 (1967): 335–52.

Cowley, Malcolm. "Biography With Letters." *Wake* 11 (1952): 26–31.

Dahlie, Hallvard. "Lowry's Debt to Nordahl Grieg." *Canadian Literature* 64 (1975): 41–51.

Davies, Hugh Sykes. "He Was Different from the Rest of Us." Bowker, *Malcolm Lowry Remembered* 40–45.

Day, Douglas. *Malcolm Lowry: A Biography*. New York: Oxford UP, 1973.

Denney, Reuel. *Conrad Aiken*. Pamphlets on American Writers 38. Minneapolis: U of Minnesota P, 1964.

Dodsworth, Martin. "Empson at Cambridge." *The Review* 6/7 (1963): 3–13.

Doyen, Victor. "Fighting the Albatross of Self: A Genetic Study of the Literary Work of Malcolm Lowry." Diss. Katholieke Universiteit te Leuven, 1973.

Durrant, Geoffrey. "Aiken and Lowry." *Canadian Literature* 64 (1975): 24–40.

Edmonds, Dale. "Malcolm Lowry and Conrad Aiken." Paper read at the South Central Modern Languages Assn. 11 Nov. 1966.

——. "*Under the Volcano*: A Reading of the 'Immediate Level.'" *Tulane Studies in English* 16 (1968): 63–105.

Ellmann, Richard. *James Joyce*. Rev. ed. Oxford: Oxford UP, 1982.

Gabrial, Jan. "Marriage Beneath the Volcano." Bowker, *Malcolm Lowry Remembered* 113–27.

Grace, Sherrill E., ed. *Swinging the Maelstrom: New Perspectives on Malcolm Lowry*. Montreal: McGill-Queen's P, 1992.

———. "Thoughts Towards the Archeology of Editing: 'Caravan of Silence.'" *Malcolm Lowry Review* 29/30 (1991/1992): 64–77.

———. *The Voyage That Never Ends: Malcolm Lowry's Fiction*. Vancouver: U of British Columbia P, 1982.

Grieg, Nordahl. *The Ship Sails On*. Trans. A.G. Chater. New York: Knopf, 1927.

Gunn, Drewey Wayne. *American and British Writers in Mexico: 1556–1973*. Austin: U of Texas P, 1974.

Haldane, Charlotte. *Brother to Bert*. London: Chatto & Windus, 1930.

———. "The Flash of These Beautiful Blue Eyes." Bowker, *Malcolm Lowry Remembered* 55–6.

———. *I Bring Not Peace*. London: Chatto & Windus, 1932.

———. *Truth Will Out*. London: Weidenfeld & Nicolson, 1949.

Harris, Catherine Kirk, comp. *Conrad Aiken: Critical Recognition, 1914–1981: A Bibliographic Guide*. New York: Garland, 1983.

Hepburn, James. "Visits to 'La Tour Bourgeoise.'" Bowker, *Malcolm Lowry Remembered* 59–63.

Hoffman, Frederick J. *Conrad Aiken*. Twayne's United States Authors Ser. New Haven: College and University P, 1962.

Jackson, Charles. *The Lost Weekend*. New York: Farrar, 1944.

Joost, Nicholas. *Years of Transition: The Dial 1912–1920*. Barre, Mass.: Barre, 1967.

Kilgallin, Tony. *Lowry*. Erin, Ont.: Press Porcepic, 1973.

Killorin, Joseph. "Conrad Aiken's Use of Autobiography." *Studies in the Literary Imagination* 13.2 (1980): 27–49.

———, ed. *Selected Letters of Conrad Aiken*. New Haven: Yale UP, 1978.

Kirk, Downie. "More Than Music: The Critic as Correspondent." *Malcolm Lowry: The Man and His Work*. Ed. George Woodcock. Vancouver: U of British Columbia P, 1971. 117–24.

Knickerbocker, Conrad. "Swinging the Paradise Street Blues: Malcolm Lowry in England." *Paris Review* 38 (1966): 13–38.

———. "The Voyages of Malcolm Lowry." *Prairie Schooner* 37 (1963/1964): 301–14.

Lawrence, Seymour, ed. *Wake* 11. Conrad Aiken Number. New York: Wake Editions, 1952.

Lorenz, Clarissa M. "Call it Misadventure." *Malcolm Lowry: Psalms and Songs*. Ed. Margerie Lowry. New York: NAL, 1975. 59–71.

———. *Lorelei Two: My Life With Conrad Aiken*. Athens: U of Georgia P, 1983.

Lowry, Margerie Bonner. "His Mind Was Just Like a Fireworks Factory." Bowker, *Malcolm Lowry Remembered* 130–43.

———. "An Interview With Mrs. Malcolm Lowry." With Laura M. Deck. *Malcolm Lowry Newsletter* 3 (1978): 11–18; 4 (1979): 22–26; 5 (1979): 30–40.

Lowry, Russell. "Malcolm — A Closer Look." *The Art of Malcolm Lowry.* Ed. Anne Smith. London: Vision, 1978. 9–27.

———. "The Songwriter Goes to Sea." Bowker, *Malcolm Lowry Remembered* 34–38.

"Malcolm Lowry." *Times Literary Supplement* 26 Jan. 1967: 57–59.

Markson, David. "Appendix: Malcolm Lowry: A Reminiscence." *Malcolm Lowry's* Volcano: *Myth Symbol Meaning.* New York: Times, 1978. 218–31.

Martin, Jay. *Conrad Aiken: A Life of His Art.* Princeton: Princeton UP, 1962.

Mercer, Michael. "Author's Comment." *Shakespeare Plus Souvenir Program* 1.1 (July/Aug. 1984): 6.

———. *Goodnight Disgrace.* Vancouver: Talonbooks, 1986.

Mota, Miguel, and Paul Tiessen, eds. *The Cinema of Malcolm Lowry: A Scholarly Edition of Lowry's "Tender is the Night."* Vancouver: U of British Columbia P, 1990.

New, William H. *Malcolm Lowry.* Canadian Writers Series 11. Toronto: McClelland, 1971.

———, comp. *Malcolm Lowry: A Reference Guide.* Boston: Hall, 1978.

Noxon, Gerald. "Malcolm Lowry: 1930." *Malcolm Lowry: Psalms and Songs.* Ed. Margerie Lowry. New York: Plume-NAL, 1975. 106–11.

———. *"On Malcolm Lowry" and Other Writings by Gerald Noxon.* Ed. and introd. Miguel Mota and Paul Tiessen. Waterloo: Malcolm Lowry Review, 1987.

Peterson, Houston. *The Melody of Chaos.* New York: Longmans, 1931.

Redgrave, Michael. *In My Mind's Eye: An Autobiography.* London: Weidenfeld & Nicolson, 1983.

Robertson, George, prod. and dir. *Remembrance of Malcolm Lowry.* Writ. George Woodcock. CBC Explorations Series. Vancouver. 22 & 29 Nov. 1961.

Robillard, Douglas. "Conrad Aiken and Herman Melville." *Studies in the Literary Imagination* 13.2 (1980): 87–97.

Salloum, Sheryl. *Malcolm Lowry: Vancouver Days.* Madeira Park, B.C.: Harbour, 1987.

Sawyer, Thomas M. "Experiment." *The Modern Age: 1914–1984.* Vol. 4 of *British Literary Magazines.* Ed. Alvin Sullivan. New York: Greenwood, 1986. 4 vols. 177–79.

Scherf, Kathleen, ed. and introd. *The Collected Poetry of Malcolm Lowry.* Explan. annotations Chris Ackerley. Vancouver: U of British Columbia P, 1992.

Slide, Anthony. "The Film Career of Margerie Bonner Lowry." *Malcolm Lowry Review* 29/30 (1991/1992): 20–26.

The Student's Handbook to the University and Colleges of Cambridge. 28th ed.
Cambridge: Cambridge UP, 1929.

——— . 29th ed. Cambridge: Cambridge UP, 1930.

——— . 30th ed. Cambridge: Cambridge UP, 1931.

Sugars, Cynthia. "Lowry's Keepers: Victor MacLean and A.B. Carey." *Malcolm Lowry Review* 28 (1991): 34–39.

"Terrible Tragedy This Morning." *Savannah Evening Press* 27 Feb. 1901: 1.

Thomas, Hilda. "Lowry's Letters." *Malcolm Lowry: The Man and His Work.* Ed. George Woodcock. Vancouver: U of British Columbia P, 1971. 103–09.

Tiessen, Paul, ed. *Apparently Incongruous Parts: The Worlds of Malcolm Lowry.* Assisted by Gordon Bowker. Metuchen, N.J.: Scarecrow, 1990.

——— , ed. *The Letters of Malcolm Lowry and Gerald Noxon: 1940–1952.* Vancouver: U of British Columbia P, 1988.

——— , ed. *Malcolm Lowry and Conrad Aiken Adapted: Three Radio Dramas and a Film Proposal.* Waterloo: Malcolm Lowry Review, 1992.

Tollers, Vincent L. "Coterie." *The Modern Age: 1914–1984.* Vol. 4 of *British Literary Magazines.* Ed. Alvin Sullivan. New York: Greenwood, 1986. 4 vols. 110–13.

Vice, Sue, ed. *Malcolm Lowry: Eighty Years On.* New York: St. Martin's, 1989.

"Wife, Then Himself." *Savannah Morning News* 28 Feb. 1901: 6, 10.

Willis, J.H. Jr. *William Empson.* New York: Columbia UP, 1969.

Woolmer, J. Howard, comp. *Malcolm Lowry: A Bibliography.* Revere, PA: Woolmer–Brotherson, 1983.

Index

75–78, 80–82, 84, 88–90, 95–97,
105–08, 110, 111, 113, 116, 117, 117n,
119, 119n, 120, 122, 124, 125, 129–31,
133–36, 139, 143, 146, 147, 150, 151,
153, 156n, 158, 159, 161, 171, 174,
181–84, 192–94, 194n, 195–97, 197n,
198, 199, 201n, 203, 203n, 206,
211–13, 214n, 215, 217, 218–20, 226,
230, 236n, 238, 241, 249, 250,
253–59, 260–64, 283, 289, 290, 291,
296, 299, 302, 306, 324
Allan, Andrew 214n
Anabasis (Xenophon) 192n
Anderson, Sherwood 190n, 247
Anna Karenina 113, 216, 216n. *See
also* Tolstoy, Leo
Antigone (Sophocles) 36
Appleseed, Johnny 197
Aristophanes 36
Aristotle 27
Armstrong, Jessie. *See* McDonald,
Jessie
Armstrong, Martin 31, 31n, 136,
136n, 223, 223n
Arnold, Matthew 27
Ascent of F6, The (Auden and
Isherwood) 226, 226n, 325
Auden, W.H. 71, 106, 143, 226n

Bank Holiday (film) 20, 20–21n
Bassett, Gordon 133, 133n, 223
Baudelaire, Charles 122n
Baumgarten, Bernice 55, 55n, 65, 66,
70, 71, 184, 289, 290
Bax, Clifford 36, 36n, 274
Beethoven, Ludwig van 211, 322
Begin, Z.L. 217
Bellevue Hospital (New York) 4,
221, 221–222n
Bergson, Henri xxv, 188, 188n, 313
*Best British Short Stories of 1931, The.
See* O'Brien, Edward
Billy the Kid 197
Birney, Earle 204, 204n

Black, Joan 168, 208, 208n
Black Prince, the 16, 16n
Blackstone, William xxvii, 197,
197n, 201, 203n, 209–10, 228n,
230, 230n. *See also* Aiken, Conrad;
works by: *The Kid*
Bonaparte, Napoleon 236
Bonner, Margerie. *See* Lowry,
Margerie
Bonner, Priscilla. *See* Woolfan,
Priscilla
Boone, Daniel 197
Bosch, Heironymus 205, 205n, 321
Boswell's Life of Johnson 61n, 65
Bradstreet, Anne 197
Brandt & Brandt. *See* Baumgarten,
Bernice
Bravery of Earth, A (Eberhart) 104,
104n
Breit, Harvey. *See Selected Letters of
Malcolm Lowry*
"Bridge, The." *See* Crane, Hart
Bronowski, Jacob 15n
Brother to Bert 19–20, 20n, 23n. *See
also* Haldane, Charlotte
Brown, Libby 174
Brown, Ronald 180
Browne, Sir Thomas 15
Browning, Robert 32, 32n
Buchan, John 142, 142n
Bumppo, Natty 235, 235n
Burnett, Whitney 66, 66n, 73, 128,
135, 136, 139, 142, 145, 149, 263
Burra, Edward xxi, 4, 28, 28n, 55, 72,
75, 75n, 106n, 137, 141, 149, 162,
163, 170–71, 174, 180, 183, 193, 195,
196–97, 197n, 198
Byron, Lord 235

Cambridge Poetry, 1930 20n, 21, 21n,
24, 24n, 29n
Cambridge Review 104, 105n
Cambridge, University of xviii, xix,
xx, xxiii, 3, 4, 9, 9n, 16, 19, 20n,

Printed in Canada
Imprimerie Gagné Ltée